AGE OF REVOLUTIONS

AGE OF REVOLUTIONS

*Progress and Backlash
from 1600 to the Present*

FAREED ZAKARIA

W. W. NORTON & COMPANY

Independent Publishers Since 1923

For information about permission to reproduce selections from this book, write to
Permissions, W. W. Norton & Company, Inc., 500 Fifth Avenue, New York, NY 10110

For information about special discounts for bulk purchases, please contact
W. W. Norton Special Sales at specialsales@wwnorton.com or 800-233-4830

Manufacturing by Lakeside Book Company
Production manager: Anna Oler

ISBN 978-0-393-23923-2

W. W. Norton & Company, Inc., 500 Fifth Avenue, New York, N.Y. 10110
www.wwnorton.com

W. W. Norton & Company Ltd., 15 Carlisle Street, London W1D 3BS

1 2 3 4 5 6 7 8 9 0

*One of the sages of Mishnah is quoted as saying,
"May you be covered in the dust of your Rabbi."*

*To my teachers and mentors, who have helped me on my journey
and whose dust I bear with gratitude.*

*Khushwant Singh, Girilal Jain, Robin W. Winks,
Paul M. Kennedy, Samuel P. Huntington,
Stanley Hoffmann, Robert O. Keohane, Joseph S. Nye Jr.,
James F. Hoge Jr., Leslie H. Gelb, Richard M. Smith,
Mark Whitaker, Jonathan Klein, Richard Plepler, Jeff Zucker.*

Constant revolutionising of production, uninterrupted disturbance of all social conditions, everlasting uncertainty and agitation distinguish the bourgeois epoch from all earlier ones. All fixed, fast-frozen relations, with their train of ancient and venerable prejudices and opinions, are swept away, all new-formed ones become antiquated before they can ossify. All that is solid melts into air, all that is holy is profaned, and man is at last compelled to face with sober senses his real conditions of life, and his relations with his kind.

—Karl Marx and Friedrich Engels,
The Communist Manifesto

CONTENTS

AGE OF REVOLUTIONS

INTRODUCTION

A MULTITUDE OF REVOLUTIONS

THE COMEDIAN ROBIN WILLIAMS SOMETIMES TALKED about politics in his stand-up routines. He would begin by reminding people of the origins of the word. "Politics," he would explain, comes from " 'Poli,' a Latin word meaning many, and 'tics' meaning bloodsucking creatures." He always got a big laugh. In fact, alas, the word derives from ancient Greek, from *polites*, which means citizen and itself comes from *polis*, meaning city or community. Aristotle's *Politics*, written in the fourth century BC, is a book about the ways to govern communities, and it discusses all the elements of politics that we would find familiar today—the nature of power, types of political systems, causes of revolutions, and so on. Politics is one of those rare human enterprises that hasn't changed that much over the millennia. Its outward forms have shifted, but its core concern remains the same: the struggle for power and what to do with it. In 64 BC, Rome's greatest orator, Cicero, ran for the office of consul. His younger brother decided to write for him a guide of sorts to winning elections, a set of practical lessons for his sometimes too idealistic sibling. Among his suggestions: promise everything to everyone, always be seen in public surrounded by your most passionate supporters, and remind voters of your opponents' sex scandals. More than two thousand years later, political consultants charge hefty fees to dispense the same advice.

Despite these constants, in recent centuries, politics has taken on a particular ideological shape that would have been alien to those living in the ancient or medieval world. Modern politics around the world has been characterized as a contest between the Left and the Right. The simple demarcation of Left and Right has traditionally said a lot about where someone stands, whether in Brazil, the United States, Germany, or India: on the left, a stronger state with more economic regulation and redistribution; on the right, a freer market with less governmental intervention. This left-right divide had long dominated the political landscape of the world, defining elections, public debates, and policies, even provoking violence and revolution. But these days, this fundamental ideological division has broken down.

Consider Donald Trump and his run for the presidency in 2016. Trump was a departure from the past in so many ways—his bizarre personality, his ignorance of public policy, and his flouting of democratic norms. But perhaps the most significant sense in which Trump was different was ideological. For decades, the Republican Party had espoused a set of ideas that could be described as the Reagan formula. Ronald Reagan became an extraordinarily popular Republican by advocating limited government, low taxes, cuts to government spending, a muscular military, and the promotion of democracy abroad. He also ran on a platform that was socially conservative—in favor of banning abortion, for instance—but he often downplayed these parts of the program, particularly once in office. To his many fans, Reagan was a sunny, optimistic figure who celebrated America's free markets, openness to trade, and generous immigration policies and wanted to spread its democratic model to the rest of the world.

Trump argued against most elements of the Reagan formula. While he did advocate some of the same policies—low taxes and limits on abortions—he devoted the vast majority of his time and energy to a very different agenda. Trump's hour-long campaign speeches could be boiled down to four lines: *The Chinese are taking away your factories. The Mexicans are taking away your jobs. The Muslims are trying to kill you. I will beat them all up and make America great again.* It was a message of nationalism, chauvinism, protectionism, and isolationism. Trump broke with many core elements of Republican economic orthodoxy, promising never to cut entitlements like Social Security and Medicare, which reversed decades of Republican fiscal conservatism. He denounced George W. Bush's military interventions in Afghanistan and Iraq and condemned his geopolitical project of spreading democracy. In fact, Trump savaged nearly every Republican standard-bearer in recent memory, and all the party's living presidents and almost all the living nominees rejected him. And while genuflecting before the Reagan myth, Trump could not have been more different—an angry, pessimistic figure who warned that America was doomed and promised a return to a mythic past.

Trump is not alone as a man of the right in breaking with traditional right-wing ideology. In fact, he's part of a global trend. In Britain, the Conservative Party under Boris Johnson openly embraced a policy of big spending. He and other advocates of Brexit ignored conservative economists who insisted the United Kingdom would suffer from losing free trade with the European Union. Hungary's populist leader, Viktor Orbán, freely mixes big government programs with attacks on immigrants and minorities. Italy's right-wing leader, Giorgia Meloni, denounces consumerism and market capitalism while building a new nationalist movement based on identity—ethnic, religious, and cultural. Outside Europe, Narendra Modi in India has promoted economic growth and reform, but he and his party have also zealously pursued an agenda of Hindu nationalism, at the expense of Muslims, Christians, and other minorities. In Brazil, Jair Bolsonaro's right-wing party described its project as returning the country to its Christian past, from which it had been led astray by cosmopolitans, leftists, and minorities. Left-wing movements have also cropped up that share with their right-wing counterparts a scorn for the establishment and a desire to take down the existing order. Figures like Bernie Sanders in the US and Jeremy Corbyn in the UK have failed to gain power, but left-wing populists have won control of Latin American countries with long-dominant conservative parties such as Chile, Colombia, and Mexico.

Platforms vary from country to country, between right-wing populists and left-wing populists, but they share a dismissive attitude toward norms and practices like free speech, parliamentary procedures, and independent institutions. Liberal democracy is about rules, not outcomes. We uphold freedom of speech, rather than favoring specific speech. We want elections to be free and fair, rather than favoring one candidate. We make law by consensus and compromise, not by decree. But increasingly there are those—frustrated by the process, sure of their virtue, loathing the other side—who want to ban what they regard as "bad" speech, make policy by fiat, or even manipulate the democratic process. The ends justify the means. This dangerous illiberalism is more prevalent on the right, but there are examples on both sides of the aisle—Andrés Manuel López Obrador in Mexico is a classic illiberal populist from the left.

British prime minister Tony Blair presciently observed in 2006 that the twenty-first century was seeing the fading of "traditional left-right lines." Instead, the great divide was becoming "open versus closed." Those who celebrate markets, trade, immigration, diversity, and open and free-wheeling technology are on one side of this divide, while those who view all these forces with some suspicion and want to close, slow, or shut them down are on the other. This divide does not map easily onto the old left-right one. One sign of a revolutionary age is that politics get scrambled along new lines.

ORIGINS OF REVOLUTIONS

I was standing with Steve Bannon in the Campo de' Fiori, one of the oldest squares in Rome, when he pointed excitedly to the statue standing in the center of the square. It was June 2018, and Bannon was in town to encourage a coalition of two very different populist parties that had collectively won half the vote in the recent Italian elections. His message was that these two groups, though perhaps appearing far apart on the traditional political spectrum, were allies on the new political landscape. They both embraced "closed" policies toward trade, immigration, and the European Union and were opposed to the established left- and right-wing parties that had dominated Italy for decades and had, with slight variations, all supported free-market reforms, open trade, European integration, and multiculturalism. Bannon is a colorful, controversial, and volatile personality who lasted only a few months as Donald Trump's chief strategist in the White House. His star has long faded, and though he never had much direct impact on policy (nor much of a moral compass), he did have insights into the populism that is coursing through the world. Ignoring the dozens of vendors selling everything from olive oil to T-shirts, Bannon began praising the dark, brooding figure in flowing robes with a hood almost completely covering his face. It was a monument to Giordano Bruno, a philosopher-monk who was put to death at that very spot in 1600 AD. Bannon was so interested in Bruno that years earlier, he'd filmed a documentary about him that was never completed.

Bannon reveres Bruno because he was a defiant radical who openly challenged the establishment of the day, the Catholic Church. Bruno dissented from the church's most important dogmas, insisting that the Earth was not at the center of the world and that the universe was in fact infinite. "Galileo, who is the hero to us today, actually recanted," Bannon said, speaking of the famous Italian astronomer who also insisted that the stars did not revolve around the Earth. "It was Bruno here that actually was burned at the stake, five hundred years ago," because he refused to recant. (The offices of the Papal Inquisition, set up to suppress free thinking and heresy, stood overlooking the Campo.)

I pointed out to Bannon that there was one important difference between his Italian hero and his American patron. Bruno was a progressive. He was taking on the conservatives and traditionalists, arguing for ideas that would later become a foundational part of the Enlightenment. That didn't seem to bother Bannon. To him, Bruno was a bold free-thinker who defied the existing power structure. At his core, Bannon is a revolutionary who wants to take down the establishment, attacking it from any side he can. He admires Lenin for his revolutionary tactics. He admitted that he was drawn to Bruno because Bannon believed that in times of turmoil, take-no-prisoners radicalism is the only option. "George Soros said the other day about the Italian elections, we live in revolutionary times," Bannon said. "I believe that. I think you're seeing a fundamental restructuring."

It is strange that we use the word "revolution" to describe radical, abrupt, sometimes violent change in society. In science, where the word was first used, it means something else entirely. Revolution, in its original definition, is the steady movement of a body around a fixed axis, often the regular orbit of a planet or star. That suggests order, stability, a set pattern—movement that always returns the object back to its original position. The Earth revolves around the Sun in an established, predictable manner. The second meaning of revolution, which began to be used soon after the first and is now the most common, is a "sudden, radical, or complete change," a "fundamental change" or "overthrow"—movement that takes people far from where they were. The French Revolution is the archetypal use of the word in this sense.

Why does a single word have two almost opposite definitions? The English word comes from the Latin word *revolvere*, meaning "to roll back." That spawned not only "revolve" but also "revolt," which grows out of the idea of "rolling back" one's allegiance to a king or institution. Perhaps there is some strange affinity between these two meanings. We see that dualism right from the start, in the most famous initial use of the word in science, by the astronomer Nicolaus Copernicus. In 1543, Copernicus published his treatise *On the Revolutions of Heavenly Spheres*, which used the word in its first, scientific meaning. But while Copernicus was using "revolution" in its regular sense, he was proposing a thesis that radically reordered our understanding of the cosmos, moving the Earth from the center of the universe to the periphery. For the way it overturned both astronomy and theology, the shift he set in motion came to be known as the Copernican Revolution. His was a "revolutionary" theory in both senses of the word.

Our times are revolutionary in the commonly used sense of the word. Wherever you look, you see dramatic, radical change. An international system that had seemed stable and familiar is now changing fast, with challenges from a rising China and a revanchist Russia. Within nations, we see the total upending of the old political order, as new movements that transcend the traditional left-right divide gain ground. In economics, the consensus that emerged after the collapse of communism around free markets and free trade has been overturned, and there is deep uncertainty about how societies and economies should navigate these uncharted waters. In the background of all of this is the full flowering of the digital revolution and the coming of artificial intelligence—with new and disruptive consequences.

In fact, our seemingly unprecedented moment also constitutes a revolution in the other sense of the word, a nostalgic desire to roll back to where we began. Radical advance is followed by backlash and a yearning for a past golden age imagined as simple, ordered, and pure. This is a pattern we see throughout history: aristocrats pined for knightly chivalry even as the gunpowder age dawned; Luddites smashed machines to try to hold back the industrializing future; and now politicians are touting family values and promising to turn back the clock, to make their countries great *again*.

Modern history has seen several broad, fundamental breaks with the past. Some of these were intellectual, like the Enlightenment, while others were technological and economic. Indeed, the world has gone through so many industrial revolutions that we have to number them—the First, Second, Third, and now Fourth. There have been even more political and social revolutions, and they too are happening today.

For decades now, we have watched a world in overdrive, with accelerating technological and economic change, fluctuating conceptions of identity, and rapidly shifting geopolitics. The Cold War yielded to a new order that began to crack just a few decades after it formed. Many have celebrated the pace and nature of these changes; others have decried them. But above all we need to understand just how disruptive they have been, physically and psychologically, because this age of acceleration has provoked a variety of backlashes. We must understand and respond to them.

Consider the epigraph to this book: "All that is solid melts into air, all that is holy is profaned, and man is at last compelled to face with sober senses his real conditions of life, and his relations with his kind." Those lines sound like they could have been written today, perhaps by a right-wing intellectual who laments the breakdown of traditional society and yearns for a return to simpler times. But they were in fact published in 1848, in a similarly revolutionary age, when the old agricultural world was rapidly being replaced by a new industrial one, when politics, culture, identity, and geopolitics were all being upended by gale-force winds of structural change. And they were written not by conservatives, but by Karl Marx and Friedrich Engels, in *The Communist Manifesto*. Marx brilliantly understood the enormously disruptive effects of capitalism and technology, and the many problems they caused, even though his solutions to those problems proved disastrous wherever and whenever they were tried. That this statement could have come from the right today shows vividly that we are moving into a new era of politics, one that upends the divisions of the past.

A REVOLUTION AMONG NATIONS

These revolutions *within* nations are happening at the same time as a revolution *among* nations—a fundamental reordering of global politics. From 1945 onward, for over three-quarters of a century, the world has been remarkably stable. First, for the almost half century of the Cold

War, the two nuclear-armed superpowers deterred each other. Their intense competition often transmuted into bloody conflicts in places like Korea and Vietnam, but among the most powerful states—the ones that could start a third world war—there was a deadlock. Then, after 1991, when the Soviet Union collapsed, we entered something extraordinarily rare in history, at least since the fall of Rome: an era in which there was just one superpower.

The closest analogue was the British Empire in its heyday, yet in the most important geopolitical arena, Europe, nineteenth-century Britain always remained one great power among many, all constantly jockeying for advantage. But America after 1991 towered above all other nations everywhere, and this produced something as unprecedented as a unipolar world: the absence of great-power competition itself. For most of history, political and military struggles among the richest and most powerful nations had defined international life and made it inherently tense and unstable. But suddenly, after 1991, there was a calm borne of the lack of competition. How could there be rivals? China was still an impoverished developing nation, making up less than 2 percent of global GDP. Russia was reeling from the communist collapse. Its GDP declined by 50 percent during the 1990s, even more than it had during the Second World War. Even economic competitors like Japan and Germany were not really in the game. Japan had entered a long period of stagnation, and Germany was consumed with integrating its eastern half into the newly reunified country.

Washington in its unipolar phase was determined to shape the world in its own image. It made mistakes, sometimes by being overly cautious, other times by greatly overreaching. But there were two crucial effects. First, unipolarity created an era of global stability—no major geopolitical struggles, no arms races, and no great-power wars. Second, American ideas became global ideas. The United States encouraged the rest of the world to globalize, liberalize, and democratize. Markets, societies, and political systems all opened up, while technology connected people across the planet on vast open platforms.

All of this seemed natural and inevitable, the expression of innate human desires. Americans certainly thought so.

There was a sense that politics mattered less than in the past. Economics had triumphed. I recall a senior Indian official telling me in the 1990s that even if his party lost, the opposition would come in and enact very similar policies because the other side also recognized that it needed to find ways to attract investment, improve efficiency, and grow. As Margaret Thatcher said when justifying her laissez-faire policies in Britain a decade earlier, "There is no alternative." And the 1990s and early 2000s—a time of stability, low inflation, global cooperation, and technological progress—really seemed to embody the idea that economic liberalization was inevitable. But that wasn't quite right. These forces were in fact undergirded by America's overwhelming military and economic power as the global, unipolar anchor. So was the proliferation of liberal democracies around the world.

One important note: when I use "liberal" throughout this book, I generally do not mean its modern American connotation, where it is used interchangeably with "left wing." Rather, I refer to classical liberalism, the ideology that came out of the Enlightenment in opposition to monarchical and religious authority. While a contested term that today's right and left squabble over, it is typically understood to mean individual rights and liberties at home, freedom of religion, open trade and market economics, and international cooperation within a rules-based order. Ronald Reagan and Bill Clinton were both, in this sense, classical liberals, with Reagan emphasizing economic liberty and Clinton equality of opportunity (in order to be able to exercise one's liberty). The new populists, from the right and left, attack the entire liberal project. They are suspicious of neutral procedures like freedom of speech, believing it vital to punish the speech they abhor. The Republican Speaker of the House of Representatives, Mike Johnson, has been openly critical of one of the pillars of America's founding, the separation of church and state. In the extreme, these illiberal populists are willing to discard the rules of electoral democracy to achieve a higher goal, the election of

a candidate or passage of a policy they support. In fact, Mike Johnson was one of the architects of the strategy to invalidate Joe Biden's
election as president in 2020.

An international system dominated by a liberal hegemon—like
Britain in earlier times and now the United States—encourages the
spread of liberal values. But the linkage can work in reverse as well.
As American dominance started to erode, openness and liberalism
came under pressure. America remains extraordinarily strong, but it
is not quite the colossus it was during the unipolar moment. The first
challenge to American hegemony was the first major backlash—9/11,
a vicious attack from a part of the world where liberalism had yet to
take hold and where Islamic fundamentalism stood in violent opposition to Enlightenment values. But the bulk of the damage came
not from the attackers themselves—a band of terrorists who lacked
the power to change the world—but from the United States' massive
overreaction. Above all, America sapped its strength by deciding to
occupy Afghanistan and then invade Iraq. The failure of those interventions broke the mystique of America's military might. Worse, the
invasion showed the US violating the rules-based order it had long
championed. Next came the global financial crisis of 2008, which
dispelled the aura of America's economic might. In the 1990s, the
United States' economy seemed to be a model for the world, especially
its dynamic and efficient financial system. Developing countries used
to enviously copy aspects of the American system, hoping to replicate
its success. But when the crash hit, it revealed a financial system that
was studded with hidden, catastrophic risks, convincing many that
there was little worth emulating. As one of China's top leaders, Wang
Qishan, told Treasury Secretary Hank Paulson in the midst of the
crisis, "You were my teacher, but . . . look at your system, Hank. We
aren't sure we should be learning from you anymore."

This was all happening as American political stability was also
cracking. Congress had lost the ability to perform some of its most
basic functions, like passing a budget. Threats of government shutdown
became routine. Long-standing norms and practices in Washington

were eroded, even destroyed. Filibustering of bills became routine, and nominations that were once waved through quickly were slow-walked, throwing sand into the government's gears. Raising the debt ceiling became an existential partisan battle risking national default. Political polarization reached a peak not seen since the aftermath of the Civil War.

This is not a case of a pox on both sides. One of America's two great parties, the GOP, has fallen prey to a populist takeover that cares less for the norms of liberal democracy and more for maintaining a revolutionary radicalism. President Trump questioned or reversed time-honored policies at home and abroad, leaving many allies worried about America's reliability. And then, in a protracted effort that culminated in the Capitol riot of January 6, 2021, Trump tried to overturn his election defeat and stay in power, something no American president had ever done in the country's history. Following his lead, in another unprecedented move, the majority of House Republicans voted against the certification of Joe Biden's election as president, even though dozens of court rulings had dismissed all allegations of fraud. The shining city on a hill was not glittering anymore.

The erosion of America's standing would mean much less if the country were not facing new challengers. Over the last three decades, the rising tide of growth across the world has resulted in a phenomenon I have called "the rise of the rest," with countries like China, India, Brazil, and Turkey all gaining strength and confidence. Of course, the two most disruptive forces by far have been the rise of China and the return of Russia, bringing new and profound tensions to the international realm. After a thirty-year "holiday from history," we once again live in a world that is shaped by great-power competition and conflict. This animosity has sabotaged the forces that seemed to be binding us all together—trade, travel, and technology—as new barriers spring up every day. Covid-19 accelerated the tendency toward protectionism and nationalism as countries searched for ways to be more self-reliant. Then there is the war in Ukraine, which has returned us to an age of geopolitical conflict of the oldest kind, over territory. We have witnessed the kind of warfare that many of us believed had been relegated to history books and black-and-white documentaries of World War II: European cities crumbling under merciless bombardment, civilians fleeing their homes by the millions, tanks rolling into the smoldering ruins. As American power has receded in the Middle East, regional powers have tried to fill the power vacuum, with tensions rising, and many intense local conflicts—from Syria to Yemen to Gaza. Asia has seen the return of classic balance-of-power politics, as China searches for greater influence and many of its neighbors court America's assistance to balance against the rising Asian hegemon. The language of cooperation has given way to talk of nationalism, competition, and conflict.

Even where the danger of war doesn't loom, a new atmosphere has descended. After three decades of liberalization, democratization, and openness, we are seeing a backlash. Ever since the financial crisis, market economics has been losing its halo. Today, everywhere you look, politics trumps economics. With Brexit, the United Kingdom chose to sever its preferential trade ties with its largest market, the European Union, for reasons that can only be described as political. Xi Jinping in China abandoned the market-driven approach that had catapulted his country into the top tier of nations, instead doubling down on state control. Donald Trump did not succeed in building his border wall, but he did impose higher duties on foreign goods than any American president had levied since Herbert Hoover signed the Smoot-Hawley Tariff Act in 1930. Trump's successor, Joe Biden, has insisted that many of his spending plans be anchored with "Buy America" provisions. Other countries have tried to follow suit. Across the globe, countries are privileging resilience, self-sufficiency, and national security over growth and efficiency. Immigration, once celebrated and encouraged, has become a dirty word, and countries view immigrants with a jaundiced eye. Cultural shifts that seemed impossible to reverse—like the right for a woman to get an abortion— have been reversed.

"Do we embrace the challenge of more open societies or build defenses against it?" asked Tony Blair in 2006. More and more leaders have chosen the "closed" path. Once again, they believe that this time there is no alternative.

CHANGE AND ITS DISCONTENTS

What makes a period revolutionary? Are there other predictable consequences of a revolutionary era? And how does it all end? These are some of the questions I try to answer in this book. I do so by going back in time to try to understand previous ages of revolution—their origins and their aftermaths—and then examine our present age.

I begin with the dawn of the modern era, the first liberal revolution, which—in defiance of centuries of monarchy—created the republican form of government that now dominates the world. It took place in the Netherlands in the late sixteenth and early seventeenth century but might not have changed the world if elements of it had not spread to Britain in 1688. That latter episode was described in 1689 as the "Glorious Revolution" by one of its supporters, and resulted in the supremacy of Parliament. In the long run, it put Britain on the path to become the world's leading industrial power, spreading its liberal ideals and practices far and wide—ideas that have outlasted the British Empire. I then look at two revolutions, one that failed spectacularly, the French Revolution, and one that succeeded beyond belief, the Industrial Revolution. They have both, in very different ways, shaped the world we live in now. And finally, I spend the second half of the book trying to understand our present age, which, like many earlier eras, is a period when revolutionary change has torn through multiple realms at once—economics, technology, identity, and geopolitics. I devote a chapter to each of these current-day revolutions.

While the examples I study have many variations, a basic pattern persists. First we see broad structural changes—tremendous advances in technology and accelerations of economic activity and globalization. These disruptions trigger another significant shift—in identity. As people begin to face new opportunities and challenges, they start defining themselves differently. You might think that I am describing our current era of identity politics, but consider the late sixteenth century: the Netherlands' economic rise and new technologies like the printing press gave birth to a new sense of identity among its people. They now saw themselves as Protestants, as Dutch, and, most important, as separate from the Habsburg Empire, their Catholic overlords.

A similar transformation took place when Europe and the United States industrialized, changing the roles of the landed gentry and creating a new category of people: the "working class." To be conservative once meant to be a landed aristocrat, deeply suspicious of markets, merchants, and manufacturers—whose interests were in those days promoted by liberals. But those identities soon changed as industrialization created a whole new elite in the West, one based on money rather than bloodlines. Conservatism became a defense of the new commercial elite, and liberals moved toward solidarity with the working class. More recently, the post-industrial age—marked by technological leaps and globalization put into overdrive—has produced its own revolution in identity, moving culture to center stage and shifting workers who were once left wing to the right. Sometimes this identity revolution is about positive affirmation, instilling a sense of pride in one's own background. Other times it is negative, stoking grievances and hostility toward others. Either way, it is powerful and consequential.

These three forces—technology, economics, identity—together almost always generate backlash that produces a new politics. Human beings can absorb only so much change so fast. The old politics, inherited from a prior era, often cannot keep pace. Politicians scramble to adjust, modifying their views and finding new coalitions. The result is reform and modernization or crackdown and revolt, and often some combustible combination of both.

Today, transformations within nations have also produced a geopolitical revolution, with several countries challenging the US-led liberal order—especially an ambitious China and an aggressive Russia. China owes its rise to economic and technological revolutions that have catapulted the country into the ranks of major powers, while Russia under Vladimir Putin has harnessed identity politics and jingoism as a response to his nation's structural decline.

When you consider the multitude of dramatic changes in the world today, we are living through one of the most revolutionary ages in history. These changes do not always take place simultaneously, and not all the revolutions play out the same way. I have described a series of forces that often coincide, but it would be impossible to cleanly separate out cause and effect in every case. Each revolution is somewhat different. But all of these changes do seem to interact and reinforce one another. They tend to give rise to backlashes of some sort. Past examples show how managing changes well leads to stable and successful outcomes, while mismanaged changes careen toward dismal failure. In the sweep of history, there has been real movement forward—toward greater collective prosperity and more individual autonomy and dignity. There have been forceful reactions, too, as those left behind cling desperately to the past and fight back with dogged determination. But in the long run, as King Arthur tells Sir Bedivere, the last of the Knights of the Round Table, in Tennyson's poem: "The old order changeth, yielding place to new."

I cannot and do not cover *all* revolutions. Readers in the US will perhaps be surprised that the American Revolution plays only a minor role in this book—for all its political audacity, it did not immediately transform society's deeper structures. (It is better thought of as a war of independence; many colonists were initially trying to preserve their rights as Englishmen that they believed the British government had "usurped.") You will find little discussion here of many other revolutions that shaped our world. Undoubtedly, communist takeovers and Islamist uprisings have had profound consequences. They have often resulted from economic and technological upheaval, and the formation of new identities, and are in that sense related to earlier revolutions in the West. Consider the way rapid modernization destabilized Iran, drove people toward fundamentalist Islam, and ended in the ouster of the shah in the Iranian Revolution. Some revolutions were directly inspired by the revolutions I discuss; Lenin's Russian Revolution consciously borrowed from the French Revolution, as did Mao's Chinese Revolution, with devastating effects. But rather than dwell on each revolution from around the world, I have chosen to stay with the main Western plot line, which is a kind of master narrative that has cast a long shadow on politics everywhere.

The story I'm telling is deeper and more fundamental than a debate over whether markets work better than the state. It is about the push and pull between the past and the future. Since the sixteenth century, technological and economic change have produced enormous advances but also massive disruption. The disruption and the unequal distribution of its benefits stoke huge anxiety. Change and anxiety, in turn, leads to an identity revolution, with people searching for new meaning and community. And all these forces then produce a political revolution. Throughout this story, we will see two competing plotlines: liberalism, meaning progress, growth, disruption, *revolution in the sense of radical advance,* and illiberalism, standing for regression, restriction, nostalgia, *revolution in the sense of returning to the past.* That dual meaning of revolution endures to this day. Donald Trump sees himself as a revolutionary, but one who wants to bring back the world of the 1950s.

I am not an unbiased observer of these trends. I believe that economic growth, technological innovation, and cultural openness have helped the vast majority of people live better lives, with greater control over their own destinies. I respect and understand the many concerns that people over the ages have raised about rapid change and the growing freedom and autonomy of individuals, but I have no desire to return to the comforts of an imagined past. For many people, the dimly remembered "golden age" was not so golden after all, with vast swaths of society largely excluded from power and prosperity. I grew up in an India where "community" often went hand in hand with social conformism, repression, and patriarchy. I do believe that sometimes the pace of change needs to slow down, that elites should be careful not to impose radical and abstract notions of progress on a society, and that those left behind deserve more help than they are getting. It is important to appreciate the organic nature of society, which can absorb only so much disruption without being torn apart. But at the end of the day, there is only one plausible path in the long run: forward.

We cannot predict with certainty what shape our revolutionary age will take—whether progress or backlash will dominate the years ahead. The future is not some settled fact out there for us to divine. It will depend on human actions and interactions over the years and decades to come. Backlash sometimes sounds like a temporary setback, a phase along the road of progress. But societies can spend decades under a reactionary regime, as in Iran. We also face new and in some cases unprecedented challenges, like climate change, itself an environmental reaction unleashed by human agency. If unaddressed, it could be the revolution that overwhelms all others—and that will surely transform politics along with much else. There are many possible futures out there; we have to work toward the one we desire.

THE ORIGINS OF LEFT VERSUS RIGHT

Before we get to the new politics and culture, with its open-closed divide, let's first understand the old order being replaced—the traditional left-right division. Where did that split come from in the first place? How did we end up thinking of people as left wing and right wing? The terminology begins in a revolutionary era: France in the late eighteenth century. And it arguably is the work of one man: an architect named Pierre-Adrien Pâris.

Pâris was not considered a talent of the highest order. He was competent at execution, though, and was often tasked with additions or renovations, especially courtyards and gardens. He worked on such projects as the Paris Opera and even the Élysée Palace. Pâris was eventually invited to design a large room at Versailles, the seat of the French monarchy, where the Estates General, the parliament of sorts that advised the king, would meet in 1789. No one knew it at the time, but this period in French politics was about to be filled with drama and world-historical change: the French Revolution. That atmosphere of upheaval produced the division of Left and Right.

When the Estates first met, their seating chart reflected the power structure of the French state since medieval times. The king or his representative was at the center, to his right sat the clergy, to his left sat the nobility, and at the back of the room, looking straight at the king, sat the people. But the commoners quickly compelled the three medieval estates to merge into a single unified body with true law-making power—the National Assembly.

The new legislature moved from dealing with minor fiscal issues to tackling much larger questions about the church's power and the monarchy's future. As discussions grew more intense, seating division by class and region gave way to a more spontaneous arrangement, with people sitting next to those with whom they agreed—ideological clusters. On August 29, 1789, the conservative Baron de Gauville noted in his diary, "We began to recognize each other; those who were loyal to their religion and the king took up positions to the right of the chair so as to avoid the shouts, speeches, and indecencies that enjoyed free rein in the opposite camp." Thus began the division in France between those on the right, who wanted to conserve the existing order, and those on the left who wanted to push forward the power of the people. That divide, forged in the fires of the French Revolution, is why, more than two centuries later, we still speak of the Left and the Right.

As the left wing gained momentum, getting Louis XVI to share power with the people, the seat of government was moved from Versailles to Paris. For Louis, this was easy, as he had a pied-à-terre in the city—the Louvre. The National Assembly, however, needed an urban home, and Pierre-Adrien Pâris was engaged once again, this time to transform the indoor riding ring of the Tuileries Palace into a legislative chamber.

It does not appear to have been a resounding success. The new space was a long, narrow hall with poor ventilation. More important, because of the room's shape, the prior oval arrangement gave way to a strictly rectangular one—a chair for the presiding officer flanked by long rows on his right and left. This new geometry exacerbated the tendencies that had already developed in the old chamber. As historian Timothy Tackett writes, "The structure of the hall compelled everyone to sit either on the left or on the right: a physical reality that invariably contributed to the polarization of the Assembly."

A few years later, the left–right division was deeply entrenched in French politics and viewed by all as deleterious to cooperation and sensible politics. So the Assembly decided to reconstruct its chambers with a semicircular seating arrangement that had no aisle separating left from right, so some people sat in the middle. But the deeper divide, in political orientation, had already set in.

In fact, this division soon spread well beyond France. In Britain, whose government was deeply hostile to the French Revolution, groups supporting the French Revolution and related causes sprouted up and were crushed. But the demands of later nineteenth-century British reformers sounded familiar to French ears. A group called the Chartists, for instance, called for universal male suffrage, the removal of property qualifications for members of Parliament, and annual general elections featuring the secret ballot. In the House of Commons, the Chartists' supporters were sometimes described as the "parliamentary left." In Italy, liberals also echoed the themes of elections, limits on monarchical powers, and individual rights, under the banner of "the left" (*la sinistra*). The German debate came later and was slightly different—with a stronger respect for state power and less attention to individual rights—but there were "leftists" who were democrats there as well.

Decades after the French Revolution, in 1848, most of Europe was convulsed by a movement to destroy the old order and usher in a new, more democratic one, led by people often described as leftists or left-wing radicals. In the short run, the Revolutions of 1848 failed. But in the ensuing years, many of the revolutionaries' ideas were quietly adopted in country after country. Naturally, these pressures from the

Left produced a response from the Right, a conservative movement dedicated to opposing left-wing disruption and preserving the existing order. Conservatives often idealized the staunch monarchies of Russia and Austria-Hungary, just as liberals denounced them. The divisions between liberals and monarchists were reflected in international politics, where absolutist monarchies banded together to crush democratic uprisings and defeat freedom fighters, allied in a shared desire to suppress political change. And so the left-versus-right debate became an all-encompassing one, with the old monarchical and aristocratic order squaring off against the new, more democratic forces pressing for change. In the twentieth century, the divide was reinterpreted to be centrally about economics. It continued through the world wars and the Cold War. But it has run its course, and today we are seeing a new set of divisions.

Although the French Revolution was a fiery struggle between the old order and the new, France itself was not actually the inventor of modern politics. The failure of the French Revolution makes this plain. The first constitution enacted during the revolution was quickly contested and gave way to others. Since that original document was signed, France has adopted fifteen more constitutions and been governed by three monarchies, two empires, five republics, a socialist commune, and a quasi-fascist regime.

The successful establishment of modern politics began somewhere else, through a less tumultuous revolution, in a place that has had functioning constitutional government and a thriving economy ever since—a small, water-logged country in the north of Europe, which blazed a trail for the great powers of the future.

PART I

REVOLUTIONS PAST

1

THE FIRST LIBERAL REVOLUTION

The Netherlands

S OME YEARS AGO, THERE WAS A BOOMLET OF BOOKS about how the Greeks or the Jews or the Scots "saved" or "invented" the world. In that spirit, one could argue that the Dutch invented modern politics and economics. By the seventeenth century, the tiny United Provinces of the Netherlands had become the wealthiest nation on the continent, boasting the highest per capita income. With the establishment of the Dutch Republic (as the confederation was also known) in 1588, the Dutch created a successful social, economic, and political order that would last some two hundred years and catapult them to the top of the ranks of nations. Their Golden Age produced some of the world's most gifted artists. Those painters—Rembrandt and Vermeer, among others—presented images from the world's first merchant society, portraits of manufacturers and traders. When Dutch artists depicted the interiors of homes, even modest ones, they showed landscapes and portraits hanging on the wall, paintings within paintings that revealed how access to beauty had become the norm not just for elites but for the middle class and workers, too. Politically, the Dutch system stood out for rejecting absolute monarchy, which was standard in the rest of Europe at the time, and embracing republican forms of representation. As scholars like Simon Schama and Jonathan Israel have pointed out, in its celebration of individual rights, its embrace of markets and trade, and its toleration of religious minorities, the Netherlands saw the earliest flourishing of classical liberalism anywhere in the West.

The Dutch also set the trend that has defined power in the modern world: that the dominant country is not the one with the largest population or the strongest army but the one with the most prosperous economy and innovative technology. The great economic historian Angus Maddison argued that "in the past four centuries there have been only three lead countries," defined as the global frontrunner in technology and labor productivity. Since around 1890, that leader has been the United States. For most of the nineteenth century, it was the United Kingdom. And before that, Maddison contended, the "Netherlands was the top performer." Even today, almost five centuries after their Golden Age, the Dutch boast one of the highest average incomes on the planet and routinely rank in the top ten on the United Nations Human Development Index (which measures quality of life: wealth, life expectancy, and education). Not bad for a tiny place with just seventeen million people.

Back in 1566, when a smattering of Dutch principalities revolted against their Habsburg rulers in Spain, few could have foreseen the world-historic impact this rebellion would have, let alone imagined that the small, soggy Netherlands, then a collection of mostly little towns along a chilly, flood-prone coast, would create the modern nation-state. So why the Dutch, and not the great landed empires like France, Spain, or even Ottoman Turkey? The answer lies in the three great waves of change that were sweeping through Europe at the time: newfound *globalization* as the West, no longer a backwater, launched the Age of Exploration; *innovations* in technology and finance, spurred by incessant war-making and the drive for economic expansion; and a radical *identity revolution*, sparked by the Protestant Reformation.

Many established empires feared and resisted these structural changes. But for reasons of geography, politics, and culture, the Dutch Republic was the only country in sixteenth-century Europe that capitalized on all three revolutions. In so doing, it became the most prosperous nation in Europe and probably the world. Today, as we undergo our own great waves of globalization, technological innovation, and identity revolution, the Dutch story has much to tell us. The story of their rise, Golden Age, and downfall shows the power of trade, openness, and free thinking—as well as the grave risks that arise when economic growth and ideological change leave many behind.

FALSE START IN VENICE

There was one important precursor to the Dutch Republic, a state that was just as small, low-lying, and entrepreneurial as the Netherlands but ultimately failed to become a model for the modern world: Venice. By the fifteenth century, it and other Renaissance republics in Italy were dazzling the rest of Europe with their wealth and scientific achievements. In Venice, the oldest and most powerful of these city-states, traders were the leading economic and political force, importing textiles, spices, and other exotic goods from Asia via the Middle East. Venice's technologically advanced navy dominated the Eastern Mediterranean and established an empire of ports and territories stretching from Croatia to Greece to Cyprus. The Venetians were not just powerful but creative, too. They perfected the accounting method of double-entry bookkeeping to keep track of complex commercial transactions. They innovated politically, regularizing the transfer of power through elections following the death of the city-state's leader as opposed to automatically passing the throne to an heir. In a Europe dominated by kings and emperors, Venice stood apart. Asserting its sovereignty in a world of much larger rivals, it claimed the impressive superlative "the Most Serene Republic."

But the Venetians' efforts to create a modern state ultimately failed. Over time, their political institutions ossified. Venice's executive, the doge, had seen his power steadily decline. Cliques of nobles ruled the city-state. These oligarchs descended from ambitious merchants who had risen through risky ventures and merit to attain noble titles. But these rich elites pulled up the ladder after themselves, denying nobility to newcomers and monopolizing political power. Starting with a 1297 law known as the *Serrata*, or Lockout, Venice's Great Council declared itself hereditary rather than elective. Closed off to new blood, the scrappy merchant republic became a corrupt, self-dealing aristocracy. The power brokers' imperious attitude extended to Venice's territories in mainland Italy and around the Mediterranean. More than ninety percent of Venetian subjects lived in the broader Venetian Empire, a collection of territorial possessions that functioned as an extractive enterprise to funnel tax money and raw materials to serve the elite 10 percent of citizens who lived in Venice proper. It was a centralized and parasitic system, with adversarial relations between the metropole and the periphery.

Venetian innovation also weakened as the society turned inward. One of the technological and aesthetic marvels of Venice's heyday was glass from the island of Murano, considered finer than any other. But Venice's strategy for maintaining its lead in this industry was to concentrate all glassmakers on Murano and imprison any who tried to leave the Republic, or even execute those who leaked their secret techniques to foreigners. (Suffice to say, such "rewards" did not encourage new inventions.) Militarily, Venice faced threats from all sides: Italian rivals, France, the Habsburgs, and the rising Ottoman Empire. Venice the city could be defended by the Venetian navy, but its wider empire lay vulnerable to overland attack. Proximity to the continent had an intellectual downside, too. Venice remained tethered to the European intellectual orthodoxy, namely the rigid and hierarchical tendencies of the Roman Catholic Church. The city-state could not shield itself from the heretic hunters of the Inquisition and the censorship of the Counter-Reformation. Venice's Jews suffered, while dissent and heterodoxy of all kinds were snuffed out.

Above all, Venice became a victim of its own success. Its stranglehold on Eastern trade spurred Western European powers to seek alternative routes to Asia through the Atlantic Ocean. These powers desperately coveted Asian goods but resented the markups that accrued over the course of a supply chain that stretched from China

to Venice, so they sought to cut out all the middlemen. They succeeded by sailing down the Atlantic Ocean and around Africa—and
in so doing, heralded the rise of western Europe and the decline of
the once-vaunted Venetian Republic.

GLOBALIZATION GETS GOING

The country that led this disruption was another small state, this one
nestled in Europe's southwest corner on the Atlantic coast: Portugal.
It had ambitions to tap into trade routes in nearby North Africa, and
in 1415, its king, John I, conquered the Moroccan city of Ceuta. He
appointed his son Prince Henry to govern the city, and soon the
ambitious prince was sponsoring expeditions to nearby islands and
down the coast of West Africa, earning him the nickname Henry
the Navigator. Portugal colonized the islands, established trading
posts across the west coast of Africa, laying the foundations for the
plantation system and the Atlantic slave trade. Portuguese mariners
kept pushing farther south, and in 1488 Bartolomeu Dias rounded
the Cape of Good Hope on Africa's southern coast. A decade later,
Vasco da Gama took that route all the way to India—a new path to
the East had been opened.

In 1492, another explorer rocked the world with his own daring
voyage. Christopher Columbus had been born in Genoa, Venice's
rival, but as a young man had moved to Portugal, training among the
greatest sailors of the day. In the 1480s, after years spent traveling on
merchant voyages around the known Atlantic, he presented an audacious plan to the Portuguese Crown. He would sail west across the
Atlantic in order to reach the East. Portugal passed on the proposal, so
Columbus took it to Portugal's neighbor and nemesis, Spain, which
agreed to fund the expedition. Columbus, of course, never reached
Asia. But his gamble opened the Americas to state-backed European
projects of exploration and exploitation.

Columbus's expedition also set off a race between the two maritime
kingdoms. In 1494, Spain and Portugal came to an agreement (later

ratified by the pope) to divide the newly discovered territory in the Treaty of Tordesillas, which granted Spain rights to the land west of an agreed-on meridian and Portugal rights to the land east of that line. Spain got the better end of the deal. It turned out most of the unclaimed territory lay on its side of the line, and with great gusto, the Spanish went about conquering the inhabitants and extracting vast wealth from the Americas. Portugal got Brazil but focused more on making commercial inroads in Asia. Sometimes peacefully and sometimes through conquest, Portugal set up a sprawling network of trading centers reaching as far as India, Indonesia, China, and Japan. Spain would also get involved in trade in the Far East, conquering the Philippines and turning Manila into a major entrepôt.

The age of globalization had begun. Admittedly, the Silk Road had long carried travelers and commerce across far-flung dominions. But now, for the first time, all major economies became interlinked— often violently—by a worldwide network of mariners and traders.

Like its successors, this first globalization revolution was closely tied to a technological revolution. Spanish and Portuguese conquistadors boasted naval and military technology far superior to anything indigenous people had. They invented the carrack, for example, a three- or four-masted ship with a capacity of five hundred tons or more, along with the caravel, a smaller ship that could be easily maneuvered. The Spanish and Portuguese coupled this technology with accurate methods of celestial navigation, allowing for long-distance voyages. Whereas China had developed advanced naval technology centuries earlier, by the early 1500s the Chinese destroyed their entire ocean-going fleet as part of their inward turn. On the high seas, Europeans were unmatched.

As they sailed farther and farther, the Spanish and Portuguese brought with them new weapons. By the sixteenth century, much of Western Europe was undergoing what historians call the Military Revolution. Thanks to near-constant feuding—a consequence of plentiful mountains and thick forests, which facilitated division and made principalities easier to defend than conquer—Europe had become the planet's greatest innovator in war. The continent's armies had made dramatic improvements in firepower and tactics—more accurate crossbows, deadlier guns, longer-range cannons, stronger fortifications, and more tactical troop formations. Its navies, meanwhile, transformed fighting at sea, creatively mounting cannons onto ships to turn them into efficient war-making machines. The ships themselves grew larger and more sophisticated. As a result, when Europeans ventured out into the wider world, their forces were usually far more lethal than those of indigenous groups. (Of course, this was nothing compared to the lethal impact of European pathogens, which wiped out up to 90 percent of the indigenous populations in the Western Hemisphere.) Even compared to the mighty landed Chinese and Ottoman empires, both of which endured despite the Western onslaught, Europeans were pulling ahead on every dimension.

THE DUTCH CREATED THE NETHERLANDS

In the sixteenth century, few would have seen the Dutch as the next great empire or a model for the future. Their decentralized political system was regarded as old-fashioned, even backward. The modern form of government at the time, gaining ground everywhere, was absolute monarchy. The Middle Ages had been a period of muddled authority, when local chieftains jostled for power with one another and monarchs had to strike alliances with them to achieve tenuous rule. But as the Middle Ages waned, so did the authority of these local barons, with power increasingly being usurped by the king. By the sixteenth century, European monarchs were gaining both financial and military primacy, centralizing their power, challenging the reach of the Catholic Church, and administering large kingdoms from ever-growing capital cities. It was the beginning of an era dominated by great modernizing rulers like France's Louis XIV and Spain's Philip II. The messy medieval world, with its competing centers of power, was giving way to an efficient, neatly organized one, centered in the capital city and better able to accomplish the two chief tasks of the state in those days—raising taxes and waging war.

The Netherlands was different. One would have searched in vain for a single ruler or head of state. Power lay in a patchwork of city and provincial governments, with elected princes and rowdy assemblies, merchant associations, and guilds. It was a place where each small city and community exercised authority within its own territory. People had to work together to get anything done. Authority was diffuse.

Why did this area resist the centralizing trend? Probably because of its geography. In much of the rest of Europe, vast swathes of fertile land had been controlled by a chieftain of some sort, who ruled over the peasants working the fields. As the historian Marc Bloch showed, the "manorial" system, as this feudal arrangement was known, ordered every aspect of medieval communities. The chieftain ruled over his peasants, economically, politically, and socially. Over time, however, the lord of the manor increasingly had to bow, in turn, to the king. The story of the end of feudalism and the triumph of modernization in Europe is in part a story of the weakening of the aristocracy and the rise of strong monarchs. These royals cemented their power by breaking up old feudal estates and granting property rights to elites for parcels of land that had previously been held as public commons, a process known as enclosure. This exercise in appropriation dispossessed many, but it had an important flattening effect: it turned the most significant economic asset of the day—land—into a tradable commercial asset, thus creating the beginnings of a market economy.

In the Netherlands, by contrast, land was never the property of a few nobles, tilled by peasants. For starters, there was hardly any of it. Most of what is now the Netherlands was created during the Ice Age, when rivers flowing from continental Europe deposited silt in the estuaries, creating a few spits of land. Humans managed to settle there, but the marshy soil at first made it hard for them to farm the land. Early inhabitants faced the problem of both too much and too little water, living on land that was prone to flooding with seawater but lacking steady access to fresh water. Constant water management was critical for survival. At first, inhabitants built "terps," artificial hills to which the population retreated whenever the floods came. Around the eleventh century, they built dikes to control the inflows of water. And in the late Middle Ages, the Dutch began doing for themselves what nature had left unfinished, depositing silt and other materials to reclaim land and add to their territory. Hence the phrase that became a founding mantra of the nation: "God created the Earth, but the Dutch created the Netherlands."

The process of managing water and reclaiming territory meant that even before the Dutch Revolution, land in the Netherlands was regarded not as the property of an earl or duke; rather, it belonged to the people who had worked to salvage it from the sea. The great seventeenth-century philosopher of liberalism, John Locke, famously formulated the idea that when human beings mixed their own labor with land, they created private property. Locke's theory found its truest expression in the Netherlands.

Thus the Dutch never fully developed a manorial system. Instead, in the words of historian Jan de Vries, there were "free peasants,

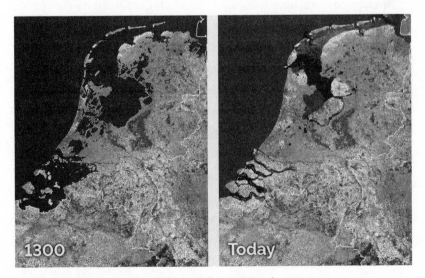

Map depicting land mass of the Netherlands from 1300 to the present.

enclosed fields, and private control over land." Whereas its European neighbors featured vast agricultural lands ruled by a central capital city, the Netherlands was a collection of towns. The Dutch were an urban people in an age when most of Europe was rural. Land elsewhere was farmed by peasants and owned by the king, aristocrats, and the church. Dutch towns boasted a broader set of industries. By 1514, less than a quarter of workers in the province of Holland were in agriculture, while over half were involved in trade, transport, and manufacturing.

The difference between the Dutch model and the typical European economy can be seen in architecture. By the eighteenth century, the Dutch Republic was richer than its monarchical neighbor, France, with Amsterdam's per capita income four times that of Paris. Yet there are few Dutch equivalents to Vaux-le-Vicomte, country mansions on vast estates that ruled over thousands of surrounding acres. Instead, one finds elegant townhouses densely clustered along Amsterdam's bustling canals. The wealth of the Dutch accrued to the merchants in towns and cities. Het Loo, which could be seen as the Dutch version of Versailles, is a far more modest hunting lodge with little of the ornate extravagance of the French palace.

In order to build and maintain their land, the Dutch had to invent impressive new technologies, from sophisticated dikes and sluice gates to water pumps powered by windmills. But they also had to innovate politically in order to foster cooperation among the scattered towns and raise revenue. For these purposes, they set up water or drainage boards (*heemraadschappen*) and levied broad-based taxes such as excise taxes. All of this meant that power was shared, and that the population had a stake in their own rule. Government worked by bringing groups of citizens together for collective decision-making, with the costs and benefits of the resulting actions also shared collectively.

At the time, this was a peculiar form of politics in Europe, or anywhere else for that matter. It made the country fertile territory for a movement that would challenge central authority and convulse all of

Europe—an identity revolution that would usher the continent into the modern age.

THE FIRST IDENTITY REVOLUTION

"Every man must do two things alone. He must do his own believing and his own dying." That was the credo attributed to a thirty-three-year-old Augustinian priest, Martin Luther, and it led him to launch an attack on Europe's most powerful institution, the Catholic Church. Through his Ninety-Five Theses that he is said to have nailed to the door of the All Saints' Church in Wittenberg in 1517, Luther sparked a series of theological battles and religious wars against the church hierarchy that would become known as the Protestant Reformation. Although Luther's specific grievances concerned Catholic corruption and the issuance of the notorious "indulgences"—bribes that allowed the sinner's soul to cut the line into Heaven—he unleashed a much broader process of critical thinking about religion that would endure well past his lifetime. By undermining the top-down authority of the Catholic Church, Luther cracked the door open for individual reasoning.

It was the printing press that made Luther's revolution possible. The invention transformed the written word from rare texts intended for an elite audience—say, an illustrated medieval Bible meticulously copied by hand in a monastery—to cheap books and pamphlets for a mass readership. The Reformation showed the power of this new information technology to "disintermediate," or cut out the middlemen when it came to spreading ideas. No longer did distant bishops interpret the Latin Bible for the obedient, illiterate masses. Instead, Luther produced his own German translation so that the individual believer could decide what was true—for good or ill. In this "priesthood of all believers," as the new intellectual atmosphere was known, no one man's idea could enjoy a monopoly of wisdom. Not even Luther—who soon came to feud with many of his fellow reformers, whose beliefs went well beyond Lutheranism.

The Protestant explosion formed part of an even grander crescendo: the rise of reason, individualism, and science. Did it cause those other processes? Many different forces were at work in those times, but the Reformation certainly helped the cause. The sociologist Max Weber would later credit northern Europe's success to "the Protestant work ethic." That claim is debatable, but what is not is that by the sixteenth century, the dogmas and superstitions of the Middle Ages had begun to yield to critical thought, humanistic inquiry, and empirical experimentation. These intellectual trends had wide-ranging political effects all over Europe, plunging the continent into long and bloody conflicts over religion.

THE DUTCH BREAK FREE

In northern Europe, the trend toward a more individualistic faith drove the Dutch to seek their liberation. By the early sixteenth century, the inhabitants of the Netherlands were already chafing at increased taxation by the distant Habsburg monarchy in Spain. But when they reached a breaking point, it was over religion, not riches. Because the Netherlands was a haven for independent minds and religious dissenters, the Protestant Reformation spread quickly across the Dutch provinces, with much of their population converting to Calvinism, a strand of Protestantism named after the French theologian John Calvin. When the Habsburg rulers, staunch Catholics, tried to stamp out this heresy, a group of Dutch nobles came together in 1566 to petition the Habsburg governor in protest against the persecution.

Later that year, Calvinist mobs in the Low Countries erupted against the continuing presence of Catholic imagery they saw as idolatrous. They smashed stained glass, tore down saints' statues, and defaced religious paintings. In Antwerp, zealots stormed the Church of Our Lady, one of the city's most prominent Catholic churches, and sacked it so ferociously that one observer wrote the scene "looked like a hell." One shocked Catholic chronicler reported that rioters trampled the sacramental bread and "shed their stinking piss upon it . . . as though, if it were not Christ's own body." This outbreak of iconoclasm, which spread throughout what is now Belgium and the Netherlands, was known as the *Beeldenstorm*, the "attack on the images." (Today an iconoclast is someone who figuratively attacks cherished beliefs.) Ironically, this spasm of violence was part of an uprising that created the world's first liberal revolution.

The crackdown came swiftly. From his imperial seat in Castile, Philip II, the Habsburg king, dismissed local rulers and appointed new governors, but the unrest only deepened. With clashes spreading over the course of 1566 and 1567, the Habsburg court sent in troops to enforce imperial rule and church dogma. The commander of these forces, the Duke of Alba, brought a new level of butchery when he established the Council of Troubles, an infamous tribunal that tried those suspected of heresy or rebellion. Even local leaders could not escape punishment; the mayor of Antwerp was tortured and beheaded. This tribunal, called the "Council of Blood" by the resentful Dutch, meted out over a thousand death sentences.

The Southern Netherlands submitted under this pressure. Always more faithful to Catholicism, the region remained within the Spanish empire (and would eventually become modern-day Belgium). But in the north, the Habsburgs' brutal campaign failed. Those provinces fought ferociously for their autonomy and Calvinist faith. Over the course of 1579 and 1580, they signed the Union of Utrecht, forming a confederation, the United Provinces of the Netherlands. Their independence struggle would drag on—it goes down in history as the Eighty Years' War, and the Dutch were ultimately victorious—but the creation of this union marks the moment when the Dutch effectively became independent from the Spanish crown.

The new political order created by the Union of Utrecht presaged two great trends of modernity. First, it emphasized decentralization over centralization, leaving local authorities with considerable power and ceding only a few select functions to the central government. That idea is an essential underpinning of today's European Union, with its principle of "subsidiarity," whereby national governments retain as much power as possible. (One can also hear the echoes of the Union of Utrecht in the system of decentralized federalism established by America's founders.) Second, the Union of Utrecht formally established the freedom of religion and religious thought, which marked a break from centuries of ideological monopoly exercised by Rome.

Globalization had fueled Spain's rise to become the most powerful country in Europe. But the Dutch succeeded in casting off the yoke of Spanish domination and quickly came to exceed their erstwhile masters. Spain, the early trailblazer of globalization, did not turn out to be the most successful state in the early modern age. This is an important lesson: Those who enter a new era with size and strength often do not master it. Those who *adapt* best to that new age thrive. The Spanish model was based on top-down governance and a heavy dose of repression. It was focused on territorial expansion and wealth extraction more than trade. The victorious Dutch Revolution inaugurated an era when the old logic of power gave way to economic and technological sophistication. Those latter qualities flourished more in a society that distributed power beyond the court to the citizenry at large.

CORPORATIONS AND CONVOYS

The famous windmills of the Netherlands exemplify how the country's innovations built on one another to generate sustained economic growth. After first being used to grind grain and pump out water to create arable land, windmills powered all kinds of industrial processes, including, perhaps most importantly, sawmills—providing lumber that helped the Dutch produce superior ships. With better ships came Dutch advances in cartography and navigation, including the refinement of the magnetic compass. These advantages created the Pax Hollandica—Holland was the dominant province in the union, and often served as shorthand for the entire confederation—a maritime peace that Dutch traders and merchants used to generate even more wealth and influence.

Geography had spurred earlier Dutch ingenuity. Now geopolitics sparked a new wave of Dutch innovation. As the Dutch waged war against Spain, they found themselves barred from the network of Spanish and Portuguese ports that they had always used. They were frozen out of familiar markets and forced to find new ones. So they built an entirely new trade network from New Amsterdam in North America to Cape Town in southern Africa to Batavia in the Indonesian archipelago.

The most important tools at their disposal were their commercial ships, which were by now the envy of the world. The country's signature vessel, the *fluyt*, was a nautical marvel, a wide-bodied cargo ship that could be manned by a small crew. The fluyt's carrying capacity, up to twelve tons per sailor, easily surpassed the largest English ships, which at best could carry five tons per sailor. As a result, the Dutch enjoyed extraordinarily efficient shipping, with costs that were sometimes half those of their competitors. Like the standardized shipping container some four hundred years later, the fluyt turbocharged global trade.

The key to the fluyt's success was not purely technological. The vessel functioned so well for trade because it made no provisions for combat. It wasn't rigged for speed, and, crucially, it had small crews and little military hardware, with most fluyts carrying no cannons at all. This meant that alone, these ships were utterly defenseless. But they were not alone—they were protected by the Dutch navy. The Netherlands had a large, fearsome fleet whose objective was not to go out and conquer foreign lands—though it did some of that—but chiefly to enforce the Pax Hollandica, making the seas safe for private Dutch traders. This was the most visible of many public-private partnerships that allowed free trade to prosper under the protective eye of the state.

And prosper it did. From the 1590s to the 1740s, this tiny republic dominated global shipping, and with it, the flow of goods, money, and ideas. At its peak, the Netherlands had a merchant fleet of 568,000 tons, "more than that of France, England, Scotland, the Holy Roman

Empire, Spain and Portugal *combined*," by one historian's calculation. The Dutch were regarded as the most prodigious technological innovators across Europe and beyond. When Peter the Great wanted to modernize Russia in the late seventeenth century, he went looking for the latest techniques in everything from ship building to watch making to street lighting. He found them all in Amsterdam. When he visited in 1697, the technology-obsessed tsar even briefly apprenticed as a ship carpenter at the city's dockyards.

The Dutch complemented their technological advantages with innovations in finance. One of their main natural resources was the ocean's bounty, specifically the herring. Some might balk at this intensely flavored fish, but that smelly seafood formed the basis of a huge new type of economic activity, one that was dominated by the Netherlands. The traditional model for investment in fishing was to put up money for a single boat's expedition. But this was risky, since many boats sank before they became profitable. So the Dutch pooled their capital, investing in multiple voyages or boats to spread the risk. The government helped by providing a legal framework to settle disputes, but its most crucial intervention was extending naval protection to Dutch fishermen to ensure that rival ships (usually English) did not interfere. In the Netherlands, the government saw itself as a partner in the activities of merchants that could make them, and the country, rich. That was how the Dutch invented the profit-seeking business as we know it.

The rise of global trade circulated many products that had once remained beyond the reach of most Europeans, from porcelain to textiles to spices. Thanks to trade, commoners got used to a steady supply of stimulants like sugar, tobacco, and coffee, while those with more money indulged in ivory, sandalwood, and silk. Meanwhile, the economy was democratizing in other ways, too, most crucially through the Amsterdam Stock Exchange. There anyone could raise money on the general market, without the benefit of connections to wealthy investors.

The stock exchange actually began with the Dutch East India

Company, formed in 1602 through the merger of several smaller companies. The firm is believed to be the first in history to sell shares to the public, which could be bought and sold on the open market. That helped it raise capital. But it also enjoyed a monopoly granted by the Dutch government over trade from the East, as well as official permission to conquer territories in distant lands and levy taxes there. The company would become one of the first multinational corporations and the largest commercial enterprise the world had ever known, with 40 warships, 150 trading ships, ten thousand soldiers, twenty thousand sailors, and nearly fifty thousand civilian employees. Its revenues were immense. The historian T. C. W. Blanning dubbed it "the richest corporation in the world."

Facilitating all this trade was the Bank of Amsterdam, which was created in 1609 and allowed merchants to exchange currencies, make deposits, obtain credit, and settle debts by transferring money from one account to another. While it was an initiative of the City of Amsterdam and backed by the government, it functioned as an independent, self-governing entity. It was not technically a central bank, but it did serve to maintain the stability of the financial system. Visiting Amsterdam in the 1660s, the English statesman William Temple called it "the greatest Treasure either real or imaginary, that is known any where in the world." The economist Adam Smith was equally fascinated by the bank, describing its workings in detail in *The Wealth of Nations*. It was telling that the Netherlands gained fame not for its castles or cannons but for its banks and merchants. Compared to the vast imperial treasuries built on plunder, this little republic excelled at creating value out of ingenuity and hard work.

RIDING THE DISRUPTIVE WAVE

As a cosmopolitan trading hub with a particularly cooperative form of government, the Netherlands had long enjoyed a reputation for tolerating differences. Across Europe, people who had been marked as enemies or heretics in their homelands sought refuge among the

Dutch. When the Jews were expelled from Spain in 1492, for instance, many of them settled in the Netherlands. But it was only after the Dutch Revolution, when the Netherlands broke with the Catholic Church, that the country truly became an open marketplace of ideas. The general distaste for Inquisitors and censors allowed philosophical strains that would have been repressed elsewhere to flourish. As a deadening blanket of repression and censorship known as the Counter-Reformation fell across Catholic Europe, Protestant societies began producing significantly more scientists than their Catholic counterparts.

Amsterdam in particular was a haven for Protestants from all over Europe fleeing persecution. It was even a refuge for Protestants from other parts of the Netherlands. In 1576, when Spanish troops brutally sacked Antwerp, then the chief trading entrepôt, tens of thousands of expelled Protestants found safe harbor in Amsterdam. In Antwerp and beyond, heavy-handed tactics by the Netherlands' former overlords led to a brain drain that benefited the tolerant Dutch. From 1580 to 1630, one-third of Amsterdam's merchant community were either Protestant refugees or the children of refugees. Most of these immigrants arrived penniless, but what they lacked in funds they more than made up for in perseverance and drive.

No one illustrates the Netherlands' penchant for tolerating difference and celebrating talent better than the philosopher Baruch Spinoza. Born in Amsterdam to Portuguese Jewish refugees who had fled the Inquisition, Spinoza was an optical lens grinder by day, fashioning microscopes and telescopes for leading Dutch scientists. But he earned far more renown for the spirited critiques of religious dogma and celebration of individual liberty he produced in his free time. One of the earliest and most radical figures of the Enlightenment, Spinoza was excommunicated by the Jewish community in Amsterdam for his skepticism toward religion, but he had no trouble continuing to live and write in the city. Nor did his fellow Enlightenment titan René Descartes, who lived in the Dutch Republic for most of his life rather than in the repressive atmosphere of his native

France. With intellectuals like these, Amsterdam acquired a reputation as a haven for free thinkers—becoming *The World's Most Liberal City*, as the historian Russell Shorto subtitled his book on the subject.

In fact, the very idea of cities as centers for innovation and entrepreneurship perhaps originated in the Netherlands. The country was the most densely populated in Europe. The Netherlands had an extremely high level of urbanization for the era—as early as 1622, up to 56 percent of the population lived in medium-sized cities and towns. (By contrast, the figure for France even a century later stood at only 8 percent.) Amsterdam benefited most of all, with commercial wealth from trade and investment transforming it into the first modern city, complete with not only a stock exchange but also public transportation on canal boats, relatively clean water, and the world's first-ever system of public street lamps to deter criminals.

In the Netherlands, for the first time, the wealthy and educated saw city living as desirable. Since the fall of the Western Roman Empire in the fifth century, European elites tended to decamp to country estates or gather at a monarch's court. Cities were squalid and disease-infested, filled with laborers. The educated clergy cloistered themselves far from the ignorant masses. Yes, kingdoms had capital cities, but these were more often showcases for palaces and other royal vanity projects, rather than economic hubs in their own right. But the Netherlands had a network of urban centers, each of which competed with the others, all without a monarch's patronage.

Now, Dutch professionals—merchants, bankers, lawyers, craftsmen, artisans, engineers—clustered in cities. In doing so, they reaped material benefits from the network effects of proximity. A merchant looking for better telescopes for his shipping fleet had easy access to an expert lens grinder like Spinoza. A writer exiled from France could find like-minded dissidents clustered around Descartes's intellectual circle, and plenty of presses eager to print seditious literature. Markets operated on a grander scale than ever before, making commodities cheaper and more attainable for the middle class, while higher tax revenue allowed for government investment in infrastructure that made Dutch cities pleasant and livable. For the Dutch of this era, profit-seeking wasn't reserved for super-rich businessmen. In 1620, an eighth of Amsterdam's working population consisted of entrepreneurs of some shape or form—from upstart dairy farmers expanding into commercialized cheese production to wealthy shipping magnates investing in the Indonesian spice trade. Such a business-friendly culture was nearly unique in Europe at the time. As the historian Karel Davids has argued, unlike elsewhere in Europe, "the pursuit of private gain was in the Dutch Republic commonly not considered an unlawful or immoral act."

Today we would recognize well the culture of hustling, consumer fads, and the speculative cycle of boom and bust that defined the Dutch Golden Age. There was plenty of irrational exuberance, as seen in the notorious tulip bubble of the 1630s, when what began as mere flower collecting and trading turned into a veritable craze. At the peak of "tulip mania," a single bulb sold for more than the average Dutch yearly salary. But such occasional excesses were the inevitable price of inventing modern consumerism. Dutch prosperity was built by a mass consumer revolution that fueled (and was fueled by) an *industrious* revolution, to use the historian Jan de Vries's term. At least when one's tulip investments weren't crashing, life for the average Dutch consumer was more enjoyable than ever. Thanks to global trade, expanding markets, and the iniquity of African slave labor, goods like sugar and tobacco became available to everyday Dutch. Laborers were thus incentivized to work a little harder, for a little more money.

THE FIRST MODERN REPUBLIC

The Dutch were not just rich and innovative—their politics were exceptionally audacious. For most of human history, politics was essentially court politics, centered on the ruler (king, queen, emperor, priest, or chieftain) and consisting of the machinations of advisors and relatives jockeying for influence. What mattered most was one's ties to the ruler and the ability to marshal military forces on his behalf. Local landowners and lords were allies who provided fealty, troops, and money.

There had been exceptions, of course. The government of ancient Rome started as a republic but morphed into a monarchy as the city transformed from minor player to mighty empire. For millennia afterward, the only republics had been small city-states. As late as the Enlightenment era, many political philosophers believed that representative institutions could only operate on a local level—even the radical democrat Jean-Jacques Rousseau believed that his native Geneva showed the proper scale for a republic was the city. But when the Netherlands grew into a great power, it stayed true to its decentralized, republican roots. Or more accurately, it became a great power in part *because* it kept its decentralized political structure.

The Dutch Republic's governing structures divided up governing authority—somewhat like the United States under the Articles of Confederation. There was a Dutch executive, the Stadtholder, but he was more figurehead than king. Even when princes from the House of Orange held that office, they were only semiofficial rulers, beholden to each provincial legislature. In fact, it would be more accurate to characterize the Oranges as a popular *political* dynasty rather than a *royal* dynasty. Like the Roosevelts and Kennedys, the family had to manage a diverse constellation of political players, from the national legislature to provincial legislatures and city councils.

In this decentralized system, it was local authorities who held the most power. Any province could veto national legislation. Even Holland, home to Amsterdam, was only first among equals despite being the most populous and richest of the seven provinces (providing 58 percent of all tax revenues). Dutch towns and provinces had to continually find ways to cooperate, especially when facing external threats. Whether on land or at sea, whether seizing economic opportunities or managing security threats, spontaneous, bottom-up mechanisms of self-government remained at the heart of the Dutch model. They stood in sharp contrast to the top-down, statist, and centralized systems of the great continental empires.

What kind of society did this novel political order create? In its treatment of regular people, Dutch society was an outlier. As the historian Jonathan Israel notes, "Many a foreign gentleman traveling on the Dutch passenger barges—a routine conveyance found nowhere else in seventeenth-century Europe—was disconcerted to find the most ordinary folk casually engaging him in conversation as if he were just anyone, without the least regard for his rank." This was the seventeenth-century version of the New York City subway car in its diversity, equality, and rambunctious energy. You never knew what might happen or whom you might meet. Israel notes that the Dutch Republic was "widely perceived in Europe as a seedbed of theological, intellectual, and social promiscuity which subverted the usual, and proper, relations between men and women . . . masters and servants, nobles and non-nobles, soldiers and civilians."

These egalitarian forces fueled (and were fueled by) the relentless rise of the Dutch Republic. But they were not universally popular. The main divide in Dutch politics is one that will sound familiar to our ears today. That republic was deeply split between those who viewed openness, tolerance, diversity, and freedom as unalloyed virtues—and those who did not.

THE BACKLASH

So far, I have painted the history of the Dutch Republic in broad strokes. Looked at more closely, however, it was hardly a paradise of harmony and prosperity. No country, however successful, has ever been that. There was much disagreement and discontent in the Netherlands' messy state.

Politics in the Dutch Republic was a tug-of-war between those who believed, in Shorto's words, that "the idea of liberalism contained promise for a better world" and those "for whom the idea of liberalism contained the seeds of destruction for everything they knew." (They did not use the word "liberalism" at the time, but Shorto and several other historians persuasively argue that the Dutch embraced ideas and practices—non-monarchical politics, free markets, free trade, and religious pluralism—that would later be so described.) On each side of the broad division were familiar camps. Religious conservatives believed in a strict adherence to Calvinist doctrine, while liberals took a more relaxed and tolerant approach to Protestant dogma. Although Dutch merchants embraced free trade and globalization, many other economic players tried to place obstacles in the way of the market. Traditional artisans, for example, enforced guilds' monopolies on specific crafts and lobbied for tariffs and other protectionist regulations. These ideological differences could be mapped geographically, with the coastal cities being more tolerant, technocratic, and supportive of free markets while the rural areas were more traditional, hierarchical, and autarkic. As the Dutch economy ballooned, liberal ideas and practices powered the nation forward but destabilized it internally. The pace of change was so fast that many people simply wanted a return to normalcy.

Conservatives followed the lead of the Dutch nobility, especially the House of Orange. The Oranges had provided a backbone of patriotic nationalism during the struggle for independence. William the Silent, assassinated by a Catholic loyal to the Habsburgs, became a martyr, cementing his legacy as "Father of the Fatherland" and the Orange family's near-mythical status. But soon there emerged a divide between these Orangists and the States Party, a group of wealthy, urban merchants who could be described as liberals. Members of the States Party were not really democrats but they were liberals. They believed in elite technocracy, which in practice meant rule by smart and well-read merchants like themselves. They advocated greater openness and embraced the dynamism of their modern country, harboring no nostalgia for the past.

These two groups were not formal political parties, more like factions within the governing class. In the first decade of the 1600s, as the war for independence continued, Spain offered the Dutch a truce but not a permanent settlement. The States Party wanted to accept the offer, while the Orangists clamored for more war. The States Party espoused a more liberal form of Calvinism, while the Orangists believed in religious purity. The States Party also embraced such novel concepts as freedom of the seas and international arbitration, pioneered by one of its intellectual supporters, Hugo Grotius, often described as the "father of international law." For a brief moment, this clique presided over the most liberal government that history had yet seen anywhere on the planet.

For Dutch coastal cities, this government racked up triumph after triumph, with the manufacturing and shipping sectors creating ever-better-paying jobs. Immigrants flocked to Dutch ports seeking opportunity. But all the while, inland and rural areas suffered. Many rural regions had depended on military spending on fortresses and garrisons. The cessation of hostilities with Spain hollowed out their economies and shrunk their populations, causing, in Israel's words, a "drastic widening of the gap in vitality between most of Holland" and inland regions, which produced "a mounting spiral of rural deprivation and poverty."

Culturally, guilds tended to be bastions of Calvinist social conservatism that the States Party considered backward; economically, they sought protectionist regulations that the liberal States Party considered inefficient. These tensions flared in the province of Utrecht in 1610, when dissatisfied guilds seized control of the city government and demanded a monopoly on brewing and other urban industries. The local legislature, dominated by merchants, appealed to the liberal leadership in the Hague, which sent an army to defeat the guildsmen.

This geographic resentment, of impoverished smaller towns and villages against the major cities, was augmented by nostalgia. Once the war for independence was over, peace eroded the social cohesion and unity of purpose that patriotic nationalism had provided. Conservative Calvinists harked back to the good old days, when the Dutch Republic waged a righteous war against Spanish Catholic heretics.

Now the cities were teeming with non-Dutch migrants. Everyone seemed to be concerned only with getting rich, striking deals with anybody, be he Protestant, Catholic, or Jew. As fate would have it, the Dutch conservatives would get their wish. A new war was coming.

LIBERALISM'S NEAR-DEATH EXPERIENCE

As Dutch liberalism rose, it triggered a backlash not just among Dutch conservatives but also in the most powerful court in Europe: France. At the time, the absolutist centralization practiced by France had its own claim to being a forward-looking political model. "Enlightened" despots like Louis XIV could cut through the messy, irrational layers of feudal privileges to forge a modern state with a national bureaucracy. The Sun King sat at the center of all orbits, an unquestioned but rational ruler, with all his subjects revolving around him.

The Dutch were republican, tolerant, and commercial. Louis hated them for all three qualities. He saw the Dutch as arrogant rebels and heretics, and their Republic as an open sore on the body politic of Europe. While the Dutch harnessed the expertise of exiles fleeing the Inquisition, Louis created a humanitarian catastrophe by cracking down on his own religious minorities. His repression of French Protestants—Huguenots—grew increasingly harsh over the course of his seven-decade rule, eventually driving at least 150,000 to flee France. (This exodus so shocked the conscience of Europe that it gave us the word "refugee," from *réfugié*.)

Not just Descartes, but also French freethinkers and dissidents of all stripes had long found safe haven in Amsterdam. So long as the Dutch sheltered Louis's religious and ideological enemies, the supremacy of the French royalist model remained in jeopardy. Louis decided to solve his Dutch problem the way any absolutist monarch of the era would: through war. In invading the Netherlands, he wanted to force the Dutch to humble themselves and pay him homage—and to surrender much of their land to France. He would try to crush the Dutch Republic's bold experiment.

In May 1672, a massive French army poured into the Netherlands. City after city fell, and Louis XIV rode triumphantly through Utrecht. These early French victories utterly discredited the liberal government's policy of seeking peace and harmonious free trade with France. The republic's States Party leaders were lynched by street mobs, creating a leadership vacuum filled by the latest William of Orange, great-grandson of war hero William the Silent.

The Dutch Republic survived, but only at a terrible price. The Dutch intentionally broke their dikes, forming a vast moat to stop the invasion but flooding the land they had so doggedly created over centuries. The almost-suicidal gambit succeeded in saving the Netherlands, but at the cost of ruining large swathes of its territory.

1672 would be remembered by the Dutch as the *Rampjaar*: the disaster year. In many ways, it marked the end of the Dutch Golden Age. Ever after, they would live under the shadow of invasion. Amsterdam would no longer occupy the same dominant position in Europe's trade and financial networks, nor would it serve as the premier safe haven for minorities.

It is possible that liberalism could have died here, under the boots of Louis's soldiers. But by trying to demonstrate the strength of absolutism, Louis made one crucial error: he let the twenty-two-year-old William of Orange claim power after the fall of the liberal leadership, thinking the Dutch prince would be an obedient puppet monarch. But Louis misjudged the young nobleman. While William's preference for monarchy made him a conservative relative to the republican States Party, his tolerant attitudes and deference to legislatures marked him as liberal compared to other rulers on Europe's political scene. Eventually, the ambitious Dutchman would be crowned king of England, planting the seeds of the liberal Dutch Revolution across the Channel. That "Glorious Revolution" ensured that the Dutch experiment in politics would take root in another powerful European state, one that would soon become the first global superpower of the modern age.

THE GLORIOUS REVOLUTION

England

T HE BRITISH LIKE TO CLAIM THAT THEIR ISLAND HAS never been successfully invaded since William the Conqueror came in 1066. That's not quite right. England was successfully invaded in 1688, and by another William at that—William of Orange. The country has never been the same since that Dutch invasion almost 350 years ago. Although that event and its consequences came to be known as the Glorious Revolution, many today remember it as bloodless and moderate, even unrevolutionary, merely restoring the traditional English status quo. The English historian Thomas Macaulay characterized it as "a revolution strictly defensive." In fact, although 1688 was marked by its moderation in means—there was little fighting or bloodshed—it was truly revolutionary in its effects. It created an Anglo-Dutch fusion, as the Dutch Republic's modern political institutions and embrace of pluralism were adopted by the larger English kingdom. Liberalism found a new, bigger, and more permanent home across the North Sea.

The Glorious Revolution was really the culmination of several revolutions. First, beginning around 1500, came several centuries of economic and identity revolutions across northern Europe. These shaped politics in the seventeenth century, as England lurched back and forth between competing visions of modernity. After 1688,

England reached a final settlement, adopting a Goldilocks form of government, neither too rigid nor too chaotic, that catapulted the nation into its position of global dominance and remade the world.

ENGLISH EXCEPTIONALISM

So how did a Dutchman, head of the first modern republic, become the king of England? England's distinctive historical development provided fertile soil for Dutch institutions and ideas. As with the Netherlands, England's story begins with geography.

Separated from continental Europe by the English Channel, the Roman province of Britannia had been one of the farthest from the imperial core in Italy and always experienced a looser kind of rule. When the Roman Empire's western provinces fell in the fifth century AD, "the Roman order collapsed more spectacularly in Britain than it did anywhere else." Nothing resembling the strictly hierarchical Roman system took its place. Instead, England became a messy patchwork of feuding fiefdoms. This lack of imperial structure made England the perfect incubator for the same quality underpinning Dutch success: competing centers of power. Political power was wielded by many different groups and institutions, including, crucially, Parliament.

The institution of Parliament developed gradually over time. Medieval England had strong local governments, organized into small self-administering units: shires and boroughs. Once these little fiefs consolidated into larger kingdoms, the king gathered *witan* (Old English for wise men) together in *witenagemots* (assemblies of the wise) to get advice and build consensus. That practice continued in modified form after the Norman conquest of 1066. Then in 1215, rebellious barons forced the tyrannical King John to accept some formal limitations on royal authority, codified in Magna Carta. Subsequent kings periodically summoned notables and clergy to assist with raising taxes or legal matters. The first relatively representative parliament was held in 1295.

The word parliament comes from the Old French word *parler,* meaning to speak, but unlike many courts, councils, and estates throughout continental Europe, medieval England's parliamentary gatherings were more than talk shops. Members were not just advisors to the king but often lawmakers in their own right. A representative parliament did more than merely constrain royal power; in some ways, it strengthened it. A formal apparatus for getting buy-in from the country's elites enabled stronger nationwide governance. As in the Netherlands, greater legitimacy translated into greater powers of taxation: the Golden Age Dutch had some of the highest taxes in Europe, and the English arguably set up the world's first effective welfare state, passing the Elizabethan Poor Law, which provided relief, not punishment, to paupers. Throughout the late medieval and early modern eras (roughly from the 1300s to 1600s), parliamentary institutions were neutered or died out in France, Spain, Germany, and elsewhere in continental Europe. As the historian Walter Scheidel has noted, England, with its comparatively strong parliament, operated not as a monarch's personal property but as a "community of taxpayers."

Bolstering the more egalitarian structure in England was the peculiar effect there of the Black Death, which hit in the middle of the fourteenth century. By killing some 30 to 50 percent of Europe's population, the plague immediately made labor more precious and land and capital less so, boosting average incomes. In continental Europe, most countries saw their post-plague bounce fade as populations recovered. But in England—for reasons scholars still hotly debate—the Black Death led to enduring higher living standards for the average farmer and worker. It also accelerated the adoption of the "European marriage pattern," whereby women chose to marry later and have fewer children in order to avoid falling back into subsistence living. (In the present day, this pattern is simply called the "demographic transition" and has been observed in modernizing societies from Peru to China.) The overall effect of the plague—fewer workers, with higher productivity and more bargaining power—was to empower English commoners vis-à-vis the aristocracy and landed gentry. Though the masses didn't yet hold formal power, they exerted influence on those who did.

SHEPHERDING ENGLAND INTO MODERNITY

England had the right political ingredients for a liberalizing, modernizing revolution. In the centuries before 1688, it also gained an economic structure that would make the Glorious Revolution possible.

Let's start with wool. Unglamorous and scratchy, wool had for centuries allowed shepherds to make profits well beyond what subsistence-level agriculture offered. It was wool that had driven the enclosure movement (beginning in earnest in the fifteenth century), by which public lands were parceled out, privatized, and largely turned into pastureland for grazing sheep. Enclosure drove a wider shift from subsistence-oriented peasantry to market-oriented farming. Meanwhile, innovations in fertilization and cultivation techniques helped maximize output, producing more food from less land.

As large-scale commercial wool production replaced farming on individual plots, higher wages in manufacturing attracted the displaced farmers to the cities. Pastures expanded and agricultural production rose, but for these farmers the greater efficiency was traumatic, reminding us that social disruption has long been the price of economic modernization. Through enclosures, England transformed a medieval, tight-knit village world of stability and security into a modern society that was wealthier but marked by insecurity, flux, and inequality. In the new capitalist world, money making was essential, not shameful. The bourgeois virtues of Prudence (to buy low and sell high) and Temperance (to save and accumulate) were paramount. Landowners, meanwhile, ceased to be distant, uninvolved nobles who ruled by lordly right, paying little attention to management so long as the grubby peasants paid their feudal dues. The gentry came to resemble profit-hungry businessmen. In this respect, the English gentry increasingly aligned itself with the rising bourgeois class of entrepreneurial merchants and craftsmen.

Thus two potentially resentful "losers" of the new modern economy—lords who disdained money and peasants suspicious of the market—gradually vanished from the scene. Remarking upon the magnitude of change, the sociologist Barrington Moore Jr. wrote that unlike elsewhere, "modernization could proceed in England" without being constrained by a "huge reservoir of conservative and reactionary forces." Although the English gentry may still have been wary of newfangled industrial ventures, they didn't actively oppose them. Indeed, they often indirectly helped industrialization proceed by providing capital for infrastructure like canals, docks, and mines.

Another structural factor helping England modernize was that English urbanization was more widespread than anywhere else in Europe. The country had many distinct and thriving cities with their own economic niches, not a single dominant metropole based in its capital city. Norwich, Colchester, and Manchester all produced textiles. Gloucester made pins, Birmingham forged metal tools, and Newcastle mined coal. Despite its status as the influential capital, London didn't lord over the English counties the way Paris did over its provinces (or the way twenty-first century London dominates a hollowed-out, post-industrial Britain).

Nor was English economic dynamism limited to urban areas. Even the countryside thrived and modernized, getting in on the proto-industrial boom. Mills, mines, and factories sprouted up across rural England. By the early eighteenth-century, some 40 percent of rural English workers were engaged in trades other than farming—mining and manufacturing were especially popular. All these economic advances created a springboard from which England could leap into the future, with a middle class that could participate in parliamentary governance and an economy that was ready to industrialize.

FROM REFORMATION TO REVOLUTION

Favorable as the structural conditions may have been, England's path toward the Dutch model proved incredibly bumpy. English political history, like Dutch political history, was dramatically shaped by the Protestant Reformation. In 1534, Henry VIII broke with the pope because he needed a divorce. The new Church of England no longer answered to Rome. That decision would reverberate far beyond Henry's love life. In the short term, the monarchy became more powerful by absorbing church property and nationalizing control of the religious hierarchy. In the long term, the English Reformation encouraged parishioners to question authority, which would work against the monarchy.

By the seventeenth century, England was split between those who wanted it to become more like Catholic France, an absolute monarchy, and those who wanted it to be more like the Protestant Netherlands, a decentralized republic. There were reasonable arguments to be made for both models. As an aspiring absolutist, King Charles I understandably preferred the French style. He was also married to a Catholic Frenchwoman who just so happened to be the sister of King Louis XIII.

Compounding these suspicions, Charles made religious reforms that seemed to favor Catholic-style hierarchy. Meanwhile, he displayed an imperious flair by undertaking various schemes throughout the 1630s to raise taxes without Parliament's say-so—similar gambits had sparked revolts in centuries past. Constant feuding between Charles and Parliament ultimately erupted in bloodshed in 1642. The English Civil War, which involved one in eight English men and killed some 150,000 total, ended in victory for the parliamentary army. In 1649, Charles I was beheaded, the monarchy was abolished, and a republic was proclaimed (for the first and only time in British history).

England's republican era has gone down in history not for its humanism and democracy but for its repression. The regicide of Charles I set off a cycle of escalating radicalization and political infighting. This violent mess unleashed many *illiberal* forces—for example, empowering Puritan hardliners who aimed to impose a strict Calvinist theocracy on society. They banned theater (even Shakespeare!), seeing plays as "Spectacles of Pleasure" full of "lascivious

Mirth and Levity." Centuries before Fox News sounded the alarm, these killjoys really did declare a war on Christmas, denouncing the holiday as debauched, pagan, and frivolous. The Puritans' relentless culture war on acting, singing, dancing, partying—or any kind of fun—hurt the new regime's popularity. The disdain for this endless censorship and drive for cultural control paved the way for a much more moderate, liberal sort of revolution in 1688.

Puritan rule sparked a backlash. Aristocratic and religious conservatives supported the Crown against Parliament, taking up arms for the king and spiriting his heirs away to exile when Charles lost his head. The Puritans dismissed these royalists as "Cavaliers," an epithet that shares the same root as "chivalry," and indeed, the group harked back to an England of knights and ladies fair, a world of feasts and heraldry. The Cavaliers liked Christian hierarchy, rituals, and spectacle, formally Anglican but close to Catholicism in practice. They enjoyed wine, women, and song, and they wore their hair long, as opposed to the Puritans, who had dour bowl cuts and were nicknamed Roundheads. (Today, we might call them squares.)

The rule of the Roundheads was strict and austere not only on day-to-day matters but also in its broader methods of governance. Their republic quickly devolved into a military dictatorship under Oliver Cromwell. Frustrated by legislators he saw as too selfish and sluggish to govern, Cromwell dissolved Parliament at gunpoint and took the title Lord Protector. Cromwell's death in 1658 finally opened the door to counterrevolution. His hapless son took his place but was quickly forced out.

Hard-core royalists joined forces with moderate parliamentarians to put an end to this English experiment; they restored the monarchy under Charles I's son Charles II. The new king, backed by a parliament so conservative it was known as the Cavalier Parliament, set about undoing much of what had been done during the Interregnum. The new rulers were mostly magnanimous, issuing a general amnesty for those who had fought against Charles I or participated in the subsequent regime, but they did punish the men who had been involved in the execution of Charles I. A small number were hanged, drawn, and quartered—and Cromwell's body was exhumed, hanged, and decapitated.

Charles II feuded more with Parliament as time went on, but on the whole, he reestablished stability in the nation and reasserted the power of the monarchy. He ruled for twenty-five years and had such fun doing so that he was nicknamed the Merry Monarch. When he died in 1685, it was a natural death. His neck was fully intact.

ABSOLUTISM REDUX

Unfortunately, that meant his brother James II inherited the throne. Though Charles II shared their father's name, it was James who really took after Charles I. James, too, pined for the absolute monarchy of the French style. Charles I was suspected of being a closet Catholic; James was openly Catholic. The stage was set for a rematch between Parliament and the king.

James's religion had already generated opposition before he became king. One faction in Parliament, the less radical descendants of the Roundheads, wanted to exclude him from the line of succession due to his religion. This caused Charles II's biggest dispute with Parliament. The group that opposed James's eventual succession became known as the Whigs, while those who supported the succession plan, the same faction once called Cavaliers, became known as the Tories. Though the Tories triumphed, many of them would come to regret letting James take power.

After ascending the throne, James quickly triggered a backlash with his high-handed attempts to bend Parliament to his will and impose pro-Catholic policies by decree. Resistance to his rule came from lords, clergymen, merchants, and commoners alike. In 1688, several small uprisings erupted across the country. James's enemies smelled blood.

Here's where things began to play out differently instead of descending into another all-out civil war. A group of English nobles that included both Whigs and Tories invited William of Orange to invade and seize power. There was a certain logic to this scheme—William had married James's Protestant daughter Mary Stuart and was thus technically in the line of succession—but it was a surprising plot twist in a long story of Anglo-Dutch rivalry.

You might think that an Anglo-Dutch fusion would have been obvious. After all, the two nations were underdog Protestant powers with strong parliamentary traditions that fought Spanish armadas and felt threatened by Catholic tyranny. But instead of joining forces, the two naval powers of the North Sea had been fiercely competitive, even hostile, for decades. When William of Orange came to rule England, he at last ended the conflict. And he brought with him the revolutionary innovations of Dutch politics and commerce.

Before the Glorious Revolution, the English had long resented Dutch economic success. Why should England have to ship all its wool to the Netherlands to be spun and woven? And why should the high-and-mighty Dutch Republic be the hub of global trade, especially after all the havoc it had wreaked across the world? The Dutch East India Company acted as ruthlessly as any conglomerate today; its corporate raiders were literally cutthroat. On a small island in 1623, the company's local governor ordered the torture and execution of ten merchants who worked for the English East India Company and had tried to breach the Dutch monopoly on Indonesian trade. This atrocity, the Amboyna massacre, provoked outcries in England and inspired anti-Dutch songs, plays, and poems. A pamphlet printed in London in 1653 captured the depths of the vitriol: "The Dutchmen's PEDIGREE: or a Relation, Shewing how they were first Bred, and Descended from a *HORSE-TURD*."

One particularly humiliating moment for the English came during a Dutch raid in the summer of 1667, part of the Second Anglo-Dutch War. By the time the Dutch fleet withdrew from the River Medway, near London, their ships had blazed a path of destruction and struck terror into the heart of every Englishman. The English, having all but run out of money, had mounted a feeble defense of the Royal

Navy's main dockyard. A large number of English ships had been sunk. Some had been wrecked by the Dutch, but many had been intentionally sunk by the English themselves, in a desperate attempt to block the waterway and halt the attack. It was in vain. The Dutch carried off the English flagship *Royal Charles* as a prize, and with it the dignity of the reigning king, its namesake. Amid reports that the Dutch were now terrorizing other ports, one English naval officer burst out, "By God, I think the Devil shits Dutchmen." The diarist Samuel Pepys, himself a naval administrator, was more matter-of-fact about the situation: "Thus, in all things, in wisdom, courage, force, knowledge of our own streams, and success, the Dutch have the best of us, and do end the war with victory on their side."

Throughout the seventeenth century, England and the Netherlands would levy tariffs on each other's goods, prey on each other's merchants and fishermen, and go to war three times. In the last of these wars, New Amsterdam became New York. Several phrases that emerged during this period to deride the Dutch persist to this day, from "going Dutch" (to stingily split the bill) to "Dutch courage" (alcohol-fueled confidence).

Despite trade wars and shooting wars, many Dutch and English came to see reconciliation as indispensable—largely because they faced the same existential threat, Louis XIV's expansionist France. Both sides stood to benefit from peaceful trade, and the chance to develop their own economies and take on the common enemy. Recognizing the enduring value of an Anglo-Dutch alliance, English leaders seized upon James II's deep unpopularity and began to raise money and gather troops in port cities across the Dutch Republic. They planned a daring gambit. The Dutch fleet would ferry from the Netherlands an invasion force composed equally of Dutch troops and exiled soldiers from England and Scotland, led by disaffected nobles and merchants. Weather and luck cooperated, and once the Anglo-Dutch fleet made landfall, much of James's army mutinied. The would-be absolute king of England fled, spending his remaining years in a French palace living off a pension from Louis XIV.

William and Mary took London without a fight, and the Dutch Stadtholder and his wife were crowned king and queen. The Glorious Revolution had triumphed. For the first time in British history, the new royals were endowed with power by an Act of Parliament, making them limited, *constitutional* monarchs. This marked the turning point of England's political modernization. England was still far from a democracy, and 1688's bottom-up features should not obscure that it was largely driven by a group of elites. Nonetheless, politics had broadened significantly. From then on, England was governed by a class, not a court.

William himself embodied the Anglo-Dutch fusion, both in its liberalism and its contradictions. Long before he became king of England, he was in the more conservative faction of Dutch politics and was excluded from power by his liberal rivals. Opposing monarchy and strong executive power, the States Party had blocked William from becoming Stadtholder. A savvy and ruthless political operator, William eventually secured the post by revving up populist anger against these domestic opponents, casting them as traitors who had betrayed the country to France—even turning a blind eye when Orangist street mobs murdered his main rivals. In 1688, William again did not shrink from using darker, illiberal forces. He capitalized on anti-Catholic prejudice to build popular support in England, allowing his supporters to propagate conspiracy theories like the Irish Fright, which accused the wicked King James of shipping in thousands of Irish soldiers to massacre English Protestants. But once firmly in power, William's government accepted religious toleration and parliamentary rule, laying the foundations for the modern England we know.

IDENTITY POLITICS AND BIPARTISANSHIP

After decades of strife, the year 1688 brought a moderation of religious and political conflict in England. Stability allowed the country to solidify its national identity as a pragmatic country focused on profit. Ironically, the secret ingredient was the adoption of Dutch ideas and institutions, which would help forge English society into a stronger new alloy. A common telling of the story of 1688 is that as a Catholic ruler of a Protestant country, James II was doomed to fail. The historian Steven Pincus, however, dismisses the notion that the Glorious Revolution was wholly or even mostly motivated by sectarian bigotry. Religion surely played a role. But many English Catholics joined in overthrowing James. Despite their shared faith, they recoiled at James's French-style absolutism. "The English," concludes Pincus, "had begun to move beyond identity politics"—by which he means religious identity.

In the Glorious Revolution, conservative Tories and liberal Whigs found a consensus to reject the extremes of Catholic absolutism and radical republicanism that had wracked England. In 1689, they passed the Bill of Rights, whereby William and Mary recognized certain prerogatives of Parliament and the people. Given that a king and queen still reigned, the new regime was obviously not a full embrace of the Dutch Republic's political structure; it was something better, at least for that time and place. The English got the best of both worlds: the leadership and stability that came with having a monarch at the helm, plus the liberty and dynamism of having competing power centers checking that authority. This system, which empowered the profit-making bourgeoisie who were invested in England's success, could "crowdsource" the best policies from a wide swathe of society, and decide on a course of action through political give-and-take. The rising power of England's merchant class thus became ballast for the ship of state as modernization began in earnest.

The Glorious Revolution did not put one party in power permanently. Rather, it was a *bipartisan* escape from dangerous polarization. This is not to say that the Whigs and Tories no longer had disagreements. They certainly did, with Whigs attacking Tories as Catholic tyrants and Tories attacking Whigs as regicidal Puritans. But the two sides found some crucial areas of common ground. Perhaps most important, they both affirmed Parliament's central role in managing the kingdom's finances. With England's purse strings now firmly held by the legislature, creditors foreign and domestic could be confident that the English state would repay its debts. The Whigs and the Tories might have had different approaches to economic policy—the former promoted manufacturers while the latter championed the rural gentry—but both parties accepted that English prosperity defined the national interest, not dynastic glory or religious zeal.

On religion, the English also emulated the Dutch in embracing messy pluralism in lieu of coercive uniformity. The 1689 Act of Toleration extended Dutch-style religious tolerance to England (encompassing all Protestants, though not Catholics). As religion ceased to be the key political divide, domination by Catholics or by strict Puritans became unthinkable. Despite some remaining restrictions on holding public office and attending university, Nonconformist Protestant groups like the Baptists and Methodists were able to flourish alongside the Church of England without seeming like a threat to the political order. England was now a solidly Protestant country, but one that was no longer consumed with religious infighting. A positive side effect was that diversity of thought became more generally welcomed, helping England seize the Netherlands' mantle as the home for path-breaking new ideas. This was the England of Isaac Newton and John Locke. Indeed, only after the Glorious Revolution was it safe for Locke to leave exile in the Netherlands and return home.

Europe at large took notice that England was newly politically stable and culturally tolerant. Financiers from Amsterdam set up shop in London, and Dutch statesmen migrated with William to advise the new English monarch on foreign policy and economics. Immigration patterns after 1688 revealed the degree to which the English had surpassed the Dutch. French Protestant Huguenots, voting with their feet, increasingly picked England over the Netherlands as their refuge of choice. They stashed their savings in the brand-new Bank of England, an institution created by Parliament in 1694 to imitate the success of the Bank of Amsterdam. Some 15 percent of its starting capital came from French Protestants, and its founding charter was studded with Huguenot surnames.

The Glorious Revolution marked three crucial developments. First, it fused the Dutch and English empires' trade and naval interests, much like a modern-day corporate merger. Second, it moderated English politics to the point where both parties accepted a truce, rejecting royalist and republican extremes to forge a new consensus. Third, it led to adoption of liberal Dutch practices, especially in the economic realm, marking the definitive English embrace of Dutch commercial modernization over French absolutist centralization.

By the dawn of the eighteenth century, the English had surged past the Dutch. In the years to come, their lead would only widen as they raced to industrialize.

LITTLE DIVERGENCE, GREAT DIVERGENCE

Economic historians talk of two "divergences" from humanity's economic status quo. The Anglo-Dutch economic miracle of the 1600s is known as the Little Divergence, with the two North Sea economies breaking away from stagnation in the rest of Europe. Later, there was the Great Divergence, the exponential boost in economic, technological, and geopolitical power in the nineteenth century that pushed most Western countries ahead of all others and allowed them to subjugate powerful nations across the globe. This latter divergence was led by industrializing England, which became Britain when it united with Scotland in 1707. The Netherlands, once so precocious, stagnated.

Britain not only adopted the modernizing features that had let the Dutch Republic thrive but also surpassed its old tutor, leaving it behind in the dust. Why did Britain continue to succeed while the Netherlands fell back?

Fundamentally, the Dutch rested on their laurels. Despite all their ingenuity, the canals and corporations, and the civic spirit that made the Dutch so adept at commerce, they fell behind in the *industrial* economy. Dutch windmills and waterwheels were advanced for their time, but those power sources paled in comparison to coal and steam. The Dutch had long dominated textile manufacturing, but now Britain's coal-fueled mills overpowered them. Areas where the Dutch were conspicuously not technological leaders—mining and metalworking—were British strong suits, and would form the bedrock of the Industrial Revolution. Crucially, as an island set away from Europe, Britain was far more secure against continental military threats than the Netherlands. On this sturdy geographical foundation, the British took Dutch innovations—stock markets, multinational corporations, entrepreneurship, global trade—and supercharged them, applying them across a wider swathe of society and on a grander scale. At the time of the Glorious Revolution, the English labor force was more than double the size of the Dutch. This disparity would only grow with time as Scotland was absorbed, industrialization took off, and the population boomed.

By the mid-1700s, it was obvious that the Dutch had lost their technological and economic edge to Britain. At that point, they fell into what would become a common trap. Militarily menaced by France, and hammered by foreign tariffs, the Dutch Republic instituted protectionist measures of its own. A country that had once been the greatest champion of free trade was now restricting the flow of Dutch technology and shielding its domestic manufacturing from competition. It was Venice all over again.

Meanwhile, as the last vestiges of medieval guilds withered away across the North Sea, Dutch cities sought to strengthen their restrictive guild system and even set up new guilds. Incumbents, local elites, and special interests colluded to block the adoption of new industrial technology from outside the Netherlands that threatened their traditional livelihoods. None of this saved Dutch industries but instead merely handed the technological lead to Britain.

By then, the Netherlands was no longer the scrappy upstart it had once been, a place open to new ideas, industries, and technologies. It had become one that looked backward. The prevailing political mood was a pining for the bygone era of Dutch greatness. This would become a familiar story: rapid advancement, dislocation, and then a wave of conjured memories of a lost golden age.

HELLO GLOBAL CAPITALISM

The moment that Dutch commercialism was wedded to English power can be seen as the moment that the medieval world came to a close. Value began to be measured in pounds and shillings rather than noble rank and religious purity. Old medieval hierarchies faded, replaced by quantifiable measures of power, status, and wealth. You couldn't put a price on Christian virtue or chivalric honor, but you could measure the heft of your purse. The British historian Henry Maine called this the transformation from a world of "status" to a world of "contract" and identified it as the essential precondition for a modern society composed of autonomous individuals.

As the world of contract grew ever wider, so did the reach of the English language. English brought with it an inclusive nationalism and a shared identity to the British Isles. In today's world, liberals often see nationalism as a destructive force that breaks down international ties. But in the early modern era, nationalism was generally *constructive*, serving to consolidate larger and more functional polities out of a messy medieval patchwork. With Scotland joining England in the 1707 Act of Union, the new country knit itself together linguistically. Accompanying the growth of markets, English spread to the Welsh- and Scottish Gaelic–speaking regions of Britain. The peoples of Great Britain adopted English largely because it was commercially expedient, not because they were coerced to. Many of the troops and administrators who went overseas to rule the British Empire, derided by their subjects as arrogant "Englishmen," were in fact Scots. The English language and a common imperial project thus served as an engine to accelerate the creation of shared national identity, forging Great Britain out of Little England—and creating a lingua franca for globalization that has endured for centuries and only grown stronger in recent decades.

As the people of Britain came to share a common language and entrepreneurial identity, their social tastes expanded beyond the rocky shores of the British Isles. The change could be seen even in something as mundane as the evolution of breakfast: whereas medieval peasants and workers had neither the time nor the money for a morning beverage, now everyday Brits drank tea from China with sugar from the Caribbean. For the American anthropologist Sidney Mintz, the advent of English tea culture prefigured "the transformation of an entire society," the first drink of tea being akin to Adam's first bite of the apple—unleashing capitalism and globalization in one fell sip.

Unlike in other continental powers, consumerist impulses in Britain were not just for the elites. Increases in disposable income allowed even Britain's poor and working classes to enjoy the fruits of the free market. The average Englishman consumed some 2,450 calories a day by the end of the eighteenth century—his French counterpart a mere 1,850. British workers were making much more than their counterparts elsewhere in Europe, and far, far more than those who lived in Asia and Africa. Mass abundance was plain to see. The novelist and economist Daniel Defoe noted it in 1726:

> The working manufacturing people of England eat the fat, and drink the sweet, live better, and fare better, than the working poor of any other nation in Europe; they make better wages of their work, and spend more of the money upon their backs and bellies, than in any other country.

Contemporary historians concur. As they have calculated, some 60 to 80 percent of tax revenue raised by the increasingly powerful British state came from customs and excise duties levied on the new consumer goods: namely, treats and stimulants like sugar, tea, coffee, and tobacco that were in reach of the average person. As disposable income and consumer spending surged, so too did tax revenue. From 1500 to the 1780s, the average amount of tax collected per person grew by a factor of three in Spain and five in France; in England, it multiplied by ten. The British government knew that its long-term success depended on maintaining its war chest. So Britain did what any prudent commercial enterprise would do: reinvest. To keep the seas open for trade, the British built the world's strongest and most global navy.

Like the Dutch navy a century earlier, the Royal Navy innovated as its range grew. Britain's vast ship-building program spurred what was arguably the world's first military-industrial complex. Immense ironworks thrived on defense contracts to manufacture cannons. The blast furnaces burned coal, which encouraged the creation of the first steam engines to pump water from mines. Lacking anything close to the same technological and financial power, Britain's rivals simply could no longer compete, and British naval dominance became overwhelming. By the mid-nineteenth century, the Royal Navy counted almost as many ships as all other nations' fleets combined.

No wonder Pax Britannica was further-reaching and longer-lasting than Pax Hollandica. When it came to keeping the seas safe for trade, the British finished what the Dutch started. Although Britain did use the Royal Navy against foreign foes, its naval power was largely used to suppress piracy that preyed on peaceful commerce, including vessels not flying the Union Jack—in this sense Britain was notably less mercantilist than its contemporaries. Britain eventually embraced and encouraged free trade as its naval might expanded throughout the world (and blasted markets open at cannon-point, as during the Opium Wars against China). Thanks to the Royal Navy, British economic dynamism spread worldwide. The Anglo-Dutch miracle had gone global.

WHIG HISTORY?

Scholars who detail the way that material conditions and individual freedoms have improved over the centuries are often dismissed as peddlers of "Whig history." The term comes from the Whig Party, whose members later looked back at the Glorious Revolution as inaugurating an unstoppable stream of progress, glossing over setbacks and ignoring the people who were trampled amid history's onward march. But it has come to mean a school of optimists who believe that ever since modern politics and economics arrived on the scene around 1688, Britain (and by extension the world) had gotten better in just about every conceivable way: "physical, moral, and intellectual." In this telling, representative democracy and industrial capitalism are the most important developments in human history, and we should thank our lucky stars we were born in the modern age. Its present-day avatars include scholars like Steven Pinker and Matt Ridley.

Today, "Whig history" has fallen out of fashion in the academy. We are told that history is complex, that progress is difficult to measure, that life has been harsh for many groups, even in recent years. That's all true, but we have to bear in mind how unprecedented the notion of sustained progress was for early modern societies. The rise of science, technology, and industry starting in the sixteenth and seventeenth centuries truly marked a break from the past. Progress over time in modern history is a fact, not a theory. Where I differ from some "Whiggish" historians is that I find nothing inevitable or automatic about the Anglo-Dutch trajectory—it was a deviation from the prior trend line. Liberalism could easily have been snuffed out on the European mainland by Louis XIV or other absolutist tyrants. It could have died out among the Dutch or never been transplanted to England. Representative democracy and capitalism, classical liberalism, even modernity itself, could have been strangled in the cradle. After Rome fell, for centuries Europe entered the Dark Ages and lost knowledge of basic science and engineering, not to mention political organization. All this is much harder to imagine happening today. But liberal democracy could still decay in modern conditions, snuffed out by populism, demagoguery, and technology.

As history played out, however, the Dutch Revolution and the Glorious Revolution succeeded and lasted. In fact, these upheavals established the standard for successful revolutions—and set the stage for failed revolutions to come. The Dutch and English cases show political institutions being reformed bottom-up to match their modernizing societies. Elites played a leading role, but in driving political transformation they went with the grain of underlying economic changes and shifting identities. When American colonists demanded their "rights as Englishmen" in the years leading up to 1776, they were harkening back to the spirit of 1688 and the Bill of Rights it produced. Of course, dissent would turn into a fight for American independence—with a boost from Britain's rival, France.

But the costs of supporting the American Revolutionary War bankrupted the French monarchy and precipitated a crisis. In the final years of the eighteenth century, French leaders took inspiration from their American predecessors and overthrew their king. But they went far beyond reform and tried to create revolution from the top down, imposing modernization on a society unready for such dramatic change. It would prove to be a grisly failure, one that has echoed through the ages.

THE FAILED REVOLUTION

France

A FURIOUS MOB DESCENDED ON THE CAPITAL, MARCH-ing to the legislature. Resentment over the illegitimacy of their leaders had simmered for months, but now it burst forth into a violent rampage. The complex's guards, too few in number and unused to public rage on this scale, tried frantically to bar the doors against the intruders. The crowd's sheer size and relentlessness proved unstoppable. Scuffles at the doors turned deadly. In a chaotic melee, desperate guards fired on the intruders, while some enraged rioters beat guardsmen to death. The insurrectionists then burst in on the cowering politicians, left almost defenseless in their chambers. The terrified legislators fled in panic.

This was not Washington, DC, on January 6, 2021. It was Paris on August 10, 1792, and the seat of power being stormed was the Tuileries Palace, beginning a bloody and dark phase of the French Revolution. Two months earlier, King Louis XVI had actually been forced by another menacing crowd at the Tuileries to don a red cap—this one without "Make America Great Again" printed on it—a symbol of liberty used during the revolution. The king had wine thrust into his hand for him to toast the health of the nation. He sipped warily, letting out a grudging "*Vive la nation!*" to appease the mob.

Twenty-first century populism does not map cleanly onto the cha-otic factional politics of the French Revolution. But today, the shadow

Louis XVI has put on the red cap, he has cried "Long Live the Nation" . . .

The Populace Compelling Louis XVI to Adopt the "Red Cap."

of that revolution, with its polarization and extremism, extends across history. The modern Left and Right in many countries have each used the word "revolutionary" to describe themselves. But the French Revolution was not a rhetorical trope. It was an actual bloody reality, as radical ideologues forced rapid and drastic change onto an antiquated society. That effort failed in France—violently, dramatically, and with seismic consequences.

The broad contours of the French Revolution are familiar. In 1789, a bankrupt King Louis XVI needed tax revenue and called up the kingdom's long-defunct advisory parliament. But the commoners in that unrepresentative and powerless body declined to rubber-stamp fiscal reforms. Instead, they declared a new, more representative legislature and demanded a written constitution. Enraged citizens roamed the streets of Paris in solidarity, showing the power of street mobs as a revolutionary political force. The legislature abolished feudalism across France and curtailed the king's powers. A new age of democracy seemed to be dawning.

It was not to be. Looking on with alarm, Austria and Prussia invaded France. Panic and paranoia gripped Paris. The revolutionary leaders executed King Louis on the newly invented guillotine, kicking off the bloodletting known as the Reign of Terror. A radical faction led by Maximilien Robespierre seized power and denounced all their rivals as traitors. What had begun as a struggle for democracy and free speech had descended into an orgy of radicalism and repression.

Into this disorder stepped a charismatic young general, Napoleon Bonaparte. After he took power in 1799, France morphed into an empire and smashed coalition after coalition of rival nations. At one point, Napoleon's domain stretched from Spain to Poland. But his failed invasion of Russia in 1812 spelled his end. By 1815, another Louis was back on the throne, and the idealistic dreams of the French Revolution seemed dead.

What went wrong? Above all, the French Revolution shows the danger of revolution imposed by political leaders, rather than growing naturally out of broad social, economic, and technological changes. French leaders tried to impose modernity and enlightenment by top-down decree on a country that was largely unready for it. The core problem was this: modernization takes decades if not centuries to develop. In those countries where liberalism had taken deep root, it had developed by fits and starts, in the Netherlands' city halls and merchant associations or in England's parliamentary committees and joint-stock companies. It had grown through a bottom-up process of economic and technological transformation, coupled later with skillful leadership that navigated these new currents. When Dutch and English leaders tried explicitly to alter the political institutions of their countries, it was largely to implement, confirm, and codify the transformations that had *already* taken place in society, beneath the surface of politics. Unlike in the Netherlands and England, leaders of the revolution in France tried to reshape society in one fell swoop. They worked top-down, not bottom-up.

The French Revolution also shows how appeals to exclusive categories of identity can easily get out of control. When everyone is either a patriot or a traitor, heads will roll. The extremism, polarization, and identity politics of the French Revolution contrast strikingly with the moderation, pluralism, and liberalism of the Dutch and English revolutions. Change in society must take place organically; when forced too fast, the ensuing disruption, chaos, and backlash can often break civilization itself.

The fracturing of society into enemies and friends of the revolution (what we call Right and Left) was one inescapable legacy of the French Revolution. As the English historian Herbert Butterfield remarked, "Every man must have an attitude to the French Revolution—must make a decision about it somehow—as part of the stand that he generally takes in life." Even today, battles between liberals and conservatives are part of the political war that began in 1789.

REVOLUTION GONE WRONG

"What caused the French Revolution?" is one of history's million-dollar questions. As with asking, "Why did the Roman Empire fall?," the causes are so endlessly complex that even the most brilliant scholar will never tease out a single satisfying explanation. France could blame its upheaval on some combination of an ossified political structure, simmering class tension, trauma from losing the Anglo-French War, recurring budget crises, and ineffectual leadership.

For our purposes, the key question is not why the revolution happened—chaos and unrest are not unusual in history—but why it played out so violently and failed so spectacularly. The Dutch Revolution and its English sequel were relatively peaceful and incremental transformations. They succeeded in casting off tyranny and forging more effective political systems. The French Revolution, by contrast, conjures up a frightening series of images: mobs in the street, the plunge of the guillotine, Napoleon's dictatorship. Judged even by its own metrics, the French Revolution unquestionably went wrong.

In the beginning, the French Revolution seemed like a run-of-the-mill revolution pitting the people against their king. Its origins were principally financial. The French monarchy was famously profligate—the chamber pots at Versailles were made of silver—but the real back-breaking expenses were military. During the reign of the "Sun King" Louis XIV from 1643 to 1715, the army consumed 50 percent of royal revenue, and over 80 percent in wartime. In fact, those silver toilets all had to be melted to pay for Louis XIV's endless wars in Europe. Later came more global wars, including French intervention in the American colonists' revolt in 1776, which dealt a major blow to Britain's empire but eventually bankrupted France. In this financial sense, the American Revolution directly birthed its bloodier French counterpart.

In May of 1789, the cash-strapped Louis XVI convened the Estates General, the French kingdom's long-dormant legislature—closer to an advisory council than a true governing body like Britain's Parliament. Moreover, the Estates General hadn't met for 175 years! Hoping the Assembly would bless new taxes, Louis offered to undertake some minor fiscal reforms and rein in royal spending. Meeting in Versailles, the Estates General was divided into three assemblies representing the classes in France—the clergy (the First Estate), the nobility (the Second Estate), and everyone else (the Third Estate)—even though the last group comprised some 98 percent of the population. Soon, the Third Estate (represented mainly by well-to-do lawyers) refused the token reforms offered by the king. In concert with liberal nobles like the American Revolutionary War hero the Marquis de Lafayette and reformist clergymen like the Abbé Sieyès, they demanded fundamental political change. The commoners insisted on merging with the other two estates into one united National Assembly. In June, in a room at Versailles designed for royal leisure, they swore the famous Tennis Court Oath, vowing not to disperse until their demands had been met. Their vision was a new political order for France: a monarchy, but one with constitutional limits. Days later, Louis grudgingly accepted the legitimacy of the new National Assembly and its right to pen a new constitution. The absolute monarchy had cracked and then broken.

Beyond Versailles, events in the street pushed the revolution forward. On July 14, 1789, a Parisian mob, egged on by incendiary journalists and rabble-rousing orators, stormed the Bastille prison, which had become a symbol of royal tyranny—never mind that it held only seven prisoners by then. Although it was almost meaningless in practical terms, the Bastille's fall symbolized a new, violent phase to the revolution, with some of the guards killed by enraged Parisians. Legislators kept meeting in Versailles, in the ornate hall designed by Pierre-Adrien Pâris, where loose pro- and anti-monarchy groups coalesced into the Right and Left. But looming over all factions was a new reality: beyond the corridors of power, street uprisings could rewrite the political rules overnight.

With the Bastille broken, the "ancien régime" effectively collapsed.

In the provinces, a panic known as the Great Fear swept rural France. Conspiracy theories ran rampant, with commoners claiming that the bitter nobles, denied their old privileges and taxes, were plotting to starve the peasantry. (Robert Darnton argues that the proliferation of rumors, gossip, songs, and tracts over the prior decades had created a "revolutionary temper" in France.) Farmers plundered hundreds of chateaus, burned their old tax documents that showed their feudal obligations, and razed entire estates to the ground, all in the hopes of destroying the physical form of feudalism.

In a frantic, all-night session in August, the National Assembly voted to abolish all the legal structures of feudalism. Taking matters into their own hands, peasants in the countryside did not wait for official implementation but continued their rampage. Wary nobles began to eye the exits. A mass exodus of the French aristocracy was soon under way.

In these hopeful early days, many observers expected the French Revolution to produce what the Glorious Revolution had produced in England: a constitutional monarchy with parliamentary supremacy, stable finances, rule of law, and a measure of individual liberties and religious tolerance. That was the explicit aim of many liberal French revolutionaries. They notched some early victories: giving France a constitution, limiting the king's powers, issuing the Declaration of the Rights of Man and of the Citizen (co-authored by Lafayette and Thomas Jefferson, then the US envoy to France), and holding national elections. But the ground was shifting under their feet.

RADICALISM UNLEASHED

Events outside France combined with unrest within to undermine the liberal revolutionaries. European capitals had first greeted the French Revolution with a mix of monarchist anxiety and opportunistic glee. With France bogged down in chaos, its rivals had a free hand. Prussia, Russia, and Austria filled the power vacuum and collectively gobbled up Poland, which was wiped off the map for almost 125 years. But as the bright hopes of the revolution dimmed, France's neighbors grew nervous.

A royal prison break proved to be the turning point. In 1791, Louis XVI, his powers already curtailed by the new constitutional order, attempted to flee the country in disguise. He left behind a defiant letter denouncing the revolution, as well as incriminating correspondence showing that he was planning a counterrevolution with conservative forces in Austria. Had Louis escaped, the entire French Revolution might have traveled down a different historical fork. But Louis was caught, recognized on the road. An elderly magistrate who had lived at Versailles even instinctively knelt at his sire's feet. Escorted back to Paris surrounded by six thousand National Guards and armed revolutionaries, the king faced a grim sight. Crowds of people—once subjects, now citizens—greeted him with pure silence. He used to be hailed as the Father of the People, but now he was seen as a traitor on the run. The monarchy's legitimacy never recovered, and the royal family was put under armed guard in the heart of Paris.

With Louis XVI's life in danger, his fellow European monarchs decided the new revolutionary regime was too dangerous to be allowed to continue. A crucial alliance was formed between Austria, whose archconservative government wanted to snuff out the threat to royal absolutism, and Britain, whose more liberal government wanted peace and stability (and could afford to fund the war effort). The result was decades of war to try to undo the revolution. In July 1792, Austria and Prussia, declaring their aim to free the king and restore him to full power (and to protect Austrian-born Queen Marie Antoinette), invaded France.

The war decisively ended the revolution's liberal phase and ushered in a darker turn. Now nationalism, populism, and authoritarianism would be the order of the day. In its intolerance of dissent, and its violent enforcement of orthodoxy (which changed from month to month), the French Revolution broke decisively from the more tolerant Anglo-Dutch path.

Brimming with patriotic enthusiasm, the French public increasingly saw the stakes of the revolution as existential. With foreign armies marching on Paris, one of the Prussian generals, the Duke of Brunswick, issued a proclamation to the inhabitants of the capital, threatening the city with "ever-memorable vengeance . . . military execution and complete destruction" if any harm came to the royal couple.

Uncowed by this threat, Parisian street mobs grew ever bolder. Next came the insurrection at the Tuileries Palace in August 1792, à la January 6. Not content with terrorizing the royal family, the ascendant radicals moved quickly to abolish the monarchy entirely and proclaim the French Republic. The legislature voted to dethrone the king and put him on trial. In January 1793, after being found guilty of treason, the thirty-eight-year-old king was beheaded in front of a crowd at the Place de la Révolution. But the bloodletting had only begun.

LAFAYETTE THE DOOMED LIBERAL

The incremental Anglo-Dutch path to modernity was rejected in France in favor of a more radically egalitarian model. Why? We can tell the story through the lives of three key figures. At the beginning, Marquis de Lafayette, a committed liberal, tried and failed to lead France to moderate reform. Then came Maximilien Robespierre, the radical populist whose mass executions forever associated the French Revolution with the guillotine. Finally, amid the chaos of Robespierre's fall, the most successful revolutionary leader of all seized power: Napoleon Bonaparte. He channeled popular patriotism and modernized the state, but his military aggression doomed the revolution. In these three lives, we can see the revolution's failed liberalism, radical populism, and final transformation into authoritarian nationalism.

Lafayette embodied the French Revolution's early liberalism. A constitutional monarchist and reformer, he yearned for something like a Glorious Revolution or an American Revolution for his own country. He had in fact participated in the latter as an officer in the Continental Army, where he developed a close relationship with

George Washington, who became like a father to him. In the United States, Lafayette was celebrated as a hero for helping cast off the British Crown.

Lafayette returned to France a revolutionary swashbuckler, and in the early days of the French Revolution, he was in the vanguard. He didn't want a full republic like the United States, without a monarch at all—which he considered too radical and destabilizing for his own country. But he did push for the abolition of his own noble privileges, as well as more systematic and wide-ranging democratic reforms. These were heady days, with Lafayette and his fellow revolutionaries racking up some liberal successes of just the sort that transformed the Netherlands and Britain. The French people were given a larger voice in the National Assembly. Measures were put in place to finally deregulate the agricultural sector, eliminate internal barriers to trade, and rationalize the tax code so nobles (previously exempt) paid their fair share. But despite the establishment of near-universal manhood suffrage, voter turnout remained depressingly low; most citizens were too terrified by the mounting threat of political violence to make it to the polls. In the 1792 elections, turnout slumped to 15 percent nation-wide. In Paris, the epicenter of the revolution, it was even lower—an abysmal 8.7 percent, the worst in the country.

As the revolution took a turn toward extremism, Lafayette was left standing athwart history yelling, "Stop!" He wanted to safeguard the revolution from extremists on the right and left: to stop coun-terrevolutionary nobles from rolling back reforms, and to stop the bloodthirsty radicals from destroying the new constitutional system. As commander-in-chief of the new national guard, Lafayette led elite guard units drawn exclusively from the tax-paying middle class and charged with ensuring order. He earned the lasting hatred of the left by leading the national guard in dispersing a Parisian crowd that called for the king to be deposed, killing dozens. The Champs de Mars massacre, as it would become known, severely tarnished his reputation among contemporaries and later historians.

In the end, Lafayette could neither save the king nor the French constitutional experiment. His legitimacy in tatters, he lost control of his guardsmen, who defected in droves to the extremists. These radicals seized Paris, executed the king, and established a "republic" that was actually a dictatorship. Lafayette's attempt to carve out a middle path led him to ruin. He fled France and wound up in an Austrian prison for several years, despised at home as an aristocratic traitor to the revolution and abroad as a revolutionary traitor to his king. All of Lafayette's efforts to keep the French Revolution on a moderate, liberal road toward constitutionalism failed. France would not progress the way the Netherlands, Britain, or America had.

ROBESPIERRE THE POPULIST EXTREMIST

If Lafayette stood for the optimistic, early revolution of 1789, then Robespierre embodied its darker, bloodier phase, starting in 1792. Liberalism and human rights gave way to a vision of equality imposed by brute force. This second revolution, which lasted until 1795, saw the beheading of the king, the declaration of the Republic, and relentless radicalization. Not for nothing was this period called the Reign of Terror. None were safe from the guillotine.

This darker phase began with angry workers intimidating legislators they saw as too timid or even treasonous. The abolition of the monarchy wasn't enough. Rioting in the chambers of the National Convention, the new republic's legislature, the workers demanded radical economic measures that they hoped would feed the hungry masses, punish greedy merchants, and stabilize a teetering economy. Government regulation—such as setting maximum prices for grain and other goods (like baguettes)—were their proposed remedies. Those accused of price gouging or hoarding would be summarily executed as traitors to France.

Riding this tide were the Jacobins, a radical political club led by Maximilien Robespierre. Back in 1789, as a thirty-year-old lawyer, Robespierre had arrived as a member of the Estates General preaching idealistic measures: universal male suffrage, the abolition of slavery, respect for the rule of law, and even the end of the death penalty. It was he who had popularized the slogan, "Liberty, Equality, Fraternity." But the young dreamer proved to be a ruthlessly successful political infighter. In 1792, he had denounced Lafayette as a traitor and called for his ouster. By 1793, as a member of the euphemistically named Committee of Public Safety stacked with his supporters, Robespierre wielded effective control over the national government. With his unchecked power, he largely implemented the workers' economic demands. Many of these measures were retained by Napoleon and later French leaders to keep a lid on the populist powder keg. (Indeed, to avoid bread shortages, the government had the power to tell French bakers when they were allowed to take vacation—a law that remained in force until 2015!)

But Robespierre's philosophy was destructive. He saw shortages as caused not by natural disasters like drought or insects, nor by a mismatch between supply and demand, but simply by the greed of

An engraving of Robespierre guillotining the executioner after having guillotined everyone else in France.

"hoarders" and "speculators." So his policies fed the starving masses of Paris—but broke the French economy in the process. His interventions were in keeping with France's traditional attitude toward economics: bureaucratic, state-led, and top-heavy. In trying to cut the pie more equitably, the revolution did more to arrest rather than accelerate the process of market modernization. Farmers did not flood into cities to join the urban, industrializing workforce. The country retained a robust peasantry long after most farmers in the UK had been absorbed into modern industries. Industrial capitalism never quite took off as in the Netherlands or Britain.

Of course, Robespierre's name has entered the annals of history not for his counterproductive regulations but for his bloody purges, which would inspire future tyrants like Lenin, Stalin, and Mao. Robespierre is remembered best as the wielder of the guillotine. In practice, his targets were not merely the king and his supporters. We may have an image of angry workers decapitating the aristocrats, but most of the guillotine's seventeen thousand or so victims came from the working class—for instance, everyday grocers caught violating laws against hoarding food. Today, *terrorist* conjures up the image of a ragtag antigovernment insurgent, but the Reign of Terror (which gave us the word "terrorism") was a top-down program of state violence against ordinary people.

Meanwhile, the bounds of political acceptability contracted ever tighter. Once upon a time, it was considered a radical view to seek a republic. Now, even if you championed the French Republic but had not been sufficiently enthusiastic about the king's execution, you were under suspicion. In fact, even if you had called for the king's execution, but had not spoken up to denounce the legislators who had opposed the death sentence, your revolutionary credentials were questioned. The paranoia reached absurd levels: some legislators were accused of treason for merely having attended a dinner where some guests were later accused of treason. As one contemporary observed of the Terror, "The Revolution, like Saturn, devours its children."

The revolution devoured France's best and brightest. Prominent victims included Antoine Lavoisier, the "father of modern chemistry," and Marquis de Condorcet, a philosopher and mathematician. (Condorcet had run afoul of the Jacobins and attempted to disguise himself as a commoner to avoid arrest, but he blew his own cover when a suspicious innkeeper reported him for trying to order a twelve-egg omelet—a real example of the out-of-touch aristocracy, unlike Marie Antoinette's apocryphal remark, "Let them eat cake.")

As the body count rose, people started to see that Robespierre was out of control. His antireligious fervor also alienated much of the country. French peasants might have despised local lords and even some greedy priests, but in their hearts, they were God-fearing Christians. Robespierre wanted a new, "rational" religion, and styled himself as a kind of cult leader. He had an artificial mountain built at the Champ de Mars in the heart of Paris, for a ceremony he called the Festival of the Supreme Being. As a papier-mâché statue burst theatrically into flames, Robespierre donned a sash with plumes, and descended from the mountaintop. Appalled by the spectacle, one of Robespierre's opponents remarked, "[I]t's not enough for him to be master, he has to be God." This megalomaniac moment convinced many old allies that Robespierre had lost it.

The would-be Moses never made it to his promised land. The path was too bloody for his allies to stomach. In July 1794, a coalition of strange bedfellows from the left, center, and right sent Robespierre to the guillotine. But the fall of the radical Jacobins came too late to save the revolution. The worst of the guillotining was over, but the fragile alliance that had deposed Robespierre could not hold. A group of centrists seized power, whose only shared values were unscrupulousness and pragmatism. They attempted a deadly political balancing act, purging both the far right, which called for a return to the monarchy, and the far left, which wanted an even grander Reign of Terror.

The seemingly endless power grabs and instability that followed paved the way for the rise of a charismatic figure who promised to restore order. He was a war hero and populist icon: the general Napoleon Bonaparte.

NAPOLEON, L'EMPEREUR

Born Napoleone Buonaparte, he embodied French nationalism despite hailing from Italian-speaking Corsica. (He spoke French with a slight accent.) Napoleon first rose to prominence during the revolution as a brilliant artillery officer, using the latest military engineering to smash through enemy fortresses in the early wars of the French Republic. Promoted to general at age twenty-four, he soon became the most popular and famous man in the French army.

As the years of infighting after Robespierre's fall wore on, some statesmen saw enlightened dictatorship as the answer. Under a brief period of rule by emergency powers, the Abbé Sieyès, a clergyman and political theorist, masterminded a coup that he believed could salvage and reform the French Republic. Sieyès, a gifted politician, recognized that he needed muscle. Enter Napoleon. Backed by the young general's troops, the plotters seized power in November 1799. By November of that year Napoleon had been elevated to power and given the title First Consul. Initially thought of as a compliant puppet that could be used and then safely discarded, Napoleon proved a far savvier operator than his would-be handlers.

Throughout history, we see again and again conservative elites who underestimate a populist strongman, thinking they can use him as a mere figurehead without ceding power. They are almost always proven wrong. Indeed, after taking control of the government with Sieyès's help, Napoleon soon turned on his old ally, beginning fifteen years of dictatorial and later imperial rule that saw him conquering most of Europe. Napoleon was perhaps the most hyperactive, arrogant, and ambitious figure of the entire nineteenth century.

As dictator and emperor, Napoleon put an end to the chaos and instituted many reforms, some of them genuinely modernizing: emancipating Europe's Jews from second-class status, rationalizing the administration, establishing a meritocracy in the army and bureaucracy, and giving France a uniform, secular book of laws, the Napoleonic Code. But it wasn't modernization that gave Napoleonic

France its power. Napoleon managed to conquer much of Europe by harnessing France's traditional strengths: a vast (albeit poor) population that was mobilized for war, and a small (but technically skilled) elite that provided technocratic governance. Napoleon succeeded in firing up his Grande Armée with nationalist passion, supplementing superiority in numbers with high morale. It is unquestionable that Napoleon, as general and emperor, inspired mass popular enthusiasm.

Different as royal absolutism, Jacobin republicanism, and Napoleonic imperial rule were, they all reflected the desire to modernize France from the top down. In his famous historical study *The Ancien Régime and the Revolution*, Alexis de Tocqueville noted the surprising continuity between the state-led bureaucratic models of the French monarchy and the later revolutionary and imperial regimes. Whether in the name of God, the popular will, or national greatness, and each in their own way, Louis XIV, Robespierre, and Napoleon all opposed the Anglo-Dutch model of gradual reform toward representative democracy and the free market.

In the end, Napoleon was deposed and exiled. First he was forced into a comfortable retirement on the isle of Elba in the Mediterranean, but after plotting a failed comeback, he was sent into a harsher second exile. He was confined to Saint Helena, an island in the remote South Atlantic safely distant from any potential coconspirators, where his main companions were books and seabirds. In France, meanwhile, his era was followed not by the reassertion of parliamentary rule but by the restoration of the monarchy in the form of Louis XVIII, thus ending France's two kingless decades. By any metric, the French Revolution had failed.

For the historian Simon Schama, the French Revolution "was as much the interruption, as the catalyst, of modernity," an unnecessary, bloody detour from a steadier, reformist route to democracy and capitalism. Revolutionary chaos disrupted France's necessary process of societal change. To be sure, the French Revolution offered a corrective shock to an ossified old regime. But examining prerevolutionary France, one finds across the board a society far less structurally ready

for modernization. The forces that had been changing the Netherlands and Britain from the bottom up were much weaker in France.

NEW WINE IN OLD BOTTLES

Why was the French Revolution not able to create a stable, parliamentary regime whereas England's 1688 revolution was? Specific
political decisions and turning points mattered, but the main problem
was that French society under the ancien régime had not experienced
the structural economic and technological shifts that undergirded the
political trends toward liberty and democracy elsewhere.

France during the revolution can best be understood as new wine
in old bottles. It was a deeply traditional, rural, religious, and aristocratic society—into which the revolutionaries poured a more modern,
urban, secular, and republican spirit. Recall how the old system of
country lords with their manors had pervaded much of Europe but
not the Netherlands. For centuries France had embodied the manorial
system, whereby a local nobleman exercised political and economic
control, serving as both lord and landlord over his tenant farmers.
This deeply entrenched feudal structure was not at all conducive to
growth and market-based economics.

Faced with his kingdom's backward societal structure, Louis XIV
had tried to course-correct. Having pushed France into a series of
costly wars against Protestant rivals throughout the late 1600s and
early 1700s, he was forced to adopt some practices from the British
and Dutch in order to keep up, even sending agents to London and
Amsterdam to learn naval engineering techniques. But he could not
simply graft a few technological fixes atop France's rickety governing
apparatus and expect them to trickle down to the whole of society.

Ancien régime France may have been dazzled by the spectacle
of "Protestant capitalism," but it failed to absorb the deeper societal features of classical liberalism, pluralism, and competition that
had fueled Anglo-Dutch success. To make matters worse, the Sun
King's "enlightened absolutism," as some branded his rule, was not so

enlightened after all. Louis XIV's brutal persecution of the Huguenots led them to flee to Amsterdam and London. These French Protestant dissidents had been disproportionately educated and skilled, so their exodus created a brain drain, giving away business acumen and scientific expertise to France's enemies. (Centuries later, the Nazis would do the same to German Jews, and America would reap the benefits.)

Unlike in the Netherlands or England, the merchant class in France was politically weak. The origin of the term "laissez-faire" appears to have come from a legendary 1681 meeting between Louis XIV's finance minister, Jean-Baptiste Colbert, and French merchants. When Colbert asked how the state could promote business interests, the lead Parisian merchant replied, *"Laissez-nous faire"*: Let us do it. But the grand historical irony is that even though France coined the term, the Netherlands and Britain became by far the truer practitioners of this philosophy.

Maritime trade, rather than prized as a national strength, was often viewed by French kings with suspicion as a rival source of power. London long served as England's political capital *and* premier port, whereas France's maritime hub, Bordeaux, was politically neutered. After it revolted against Louis XIV in 1675, the disgraced city's local parliament was shut down. A poet of the era admonished the rebellious city: "People of Bordeaux, Louis reigns. Obey without protest." The French fleet, though large and powerful enough to give Britain headaches, never truly measured up, usually preferring decorative grandeur to technological innovation. If anything, higher naval spending served to further weigh down French finances, contributing to bankruptcy and revolution.

Another key defect was French urbanization—or rather the lack thereof. Around the time of the Glorious Revolution, some 40 percent of the English labor force worked in agriculture. At the time of the French Revolution—a century later—about 60 percent of the French did. Moreover, urbanization was more lopsided in France than it was in England. France was extremely centralized with Paris as its metropole. The capital region—Île-de-France, literally "the Island of

France"—was truly an urban island in a rural sea. We have seen how Britain developed bustling cities across the country. In eighteenth-century France, by contrast, Paris was the Sun, with the lowly provinces orbiting around it. The story was written in the roads, which mostly radiated out from Paris so the government could swiftly send troops to quell provincial revolts. The goal was never to stimulate travel and trade between provincial towns.

Technologically, ancien régime France was not entirely backward. Kings of France had long been patrons of the Scientific Revolution; in the sixteenth century, Francis I sponsored Leonardo da Vinci's work. Homegrown French scientists were leaders in many domains, too. Before he was claimed by the revolution, the chemist Antoine Lavoisier discovered oxygen's role in combustion. In a more exciting spectacle, the Montgolfier brothers launched the field of aviation by sending two passengers over Paris in a hot air balloon in 1783.

But much of French innovation was heavily state funded or dependent on aristocratic investors; it was willed into being rather than sprouting up organically. More importantly, while France respected scientists, it had less interest in the kinds of technicians and mechanics who dotted the British landscape. These engineers and tinkerers were no gentlemen. They got their hands dirty making inventions with concrete, practical, and marketable applications that eventually ushered in the Industrial Revolution (as we will see in the next chapter).

Napoleon supposedly dismissed Britain as "a nation of shopkeepers," which accurately captures French disdain for English values. French society was far less commercial than British or Dutch society and also much less consumerist, in large part because there simply weren't enough consumers. Although France boasted a far bigger population, a much smaller proportion of its people were members of the middle class with disposable income. Instead, a small class of wealthy aristocrats and merchants sat atop a pyramid primarily made of rural farmers, most of them working as subsistence-level peasants. By the late nineteenth century, British workers had already been wage laborers for generations, incentivized to produce more. Most

French, meanwhile, still patiently tilled the land, seeing their rewards as dependent on the grain harvest that year or the purchase of a new ox. Without the incentives to shift the peasantry from farms to factories, the engines of a parallel "industrious revolution" never started turning. The French middle class grew slowly and fitfully.

A SOLITUDE CALLED FREEDOM

Throughout history, there is often a pattern to great-power rivalry, in which an agrarian land power is pitted against a maritime trading power. Sparta fought Athens, and Rome battled Carthage. By the early eighteenth century, France was clearly Europe's predominant land power. Parisian elites had watched the plucky Dutch and English make gains in trade and technology, but measured on the hard factors that had determined state power for thousands of years—arable land, population, the size of the army—the Kingdom of France seemed to be on a different level.

By the time of the French Revolution, however, the rules of great-power competition were being rewritten across the English Channel. Britain was surging ahead industrially, able to finance its overseas expansion on a scale that no one could equal. Its parliamentary politics, too, had modernized, achieving a level of effective and stable governance matched by no other European power. Through its own revolution, France tried to reform its way to competitiveness. The English achievements of 1688—parliamentary supremacy, constitutional monarchy, a bill of rights, and rationalized administration—seemed like worthy goals for France in 1789. Indeed, in the first exhilarating months of the French Revolution, some moderates and liberals explicitly framed their goal as replicating England's Glorious Revolution. One revolutionary declared in a November 1789 speech:

> *Why should we be ashamed . . . to acknowledge that the Revolution which is now establishing itself in our country, is owing to the example given by England a century ago? . . . It was from*

*that day our hatred of despotism derived its energy. In securing
their own happiness, Englishmen have prepared the way for that
of the universe.*

But the goalposts moved rapidly. In the modern parlance of political science, the "Overton window"—the range of acceptable policy
positions—shifted so fast that many French liberals and moderates,
once seen as radical, were left flat-footed. Their more limited aims
were swept away by populist and nationalist currents after 1792.
France became ever more radical at home while plunging into decades
of war abroad. The chance for more gradual liberal reform was lost.

The chief goal of liberalism in the Age of Enlightenment, especially
in England and Scotland, was the dissolution of arbitrary restraints
on political and economic behavior. Viewed in the grand sweep of
history, these changes may appear as pure progress. But many French
citizens of the time, especially in the countryside, experienced it
differently. To the French peasant, modernity—liberalized agrarian
laws, for example—seemed corrosive and destabilizing. The French
Revolution is often viewed through the lens of its elite theorists and
leaders, the radical Enlightenment thinkers who demanded change.
But the revolutionary violence was fueled by the fears of everyday
Frenchmen who felt themselves to be the victims of change.

By 1789, workers had already grown acutely suspicious of the free
market. Their belief was not an abstract academic concept, but a bone-
deep conviction borne of decades of distrust. In seeking to recreate
in a few months the enclosure movement that had taken centuries in
Britain, the French revolutionaries were playing with fire. As the historian Eric Hobsbawm described, from the peasants' perspective, feudalism may have been "inefficient and oppressive," but it did provide
"considerable social certainty," especially since much of the land sold
was owned by the Catholic Church, which provided a self-contained
moral and political universe to its tenants and parishioners. Now, faced
with the removal of the old order and the sudden advent of market
economics, the French farmer experienced a "silent bombardment

which shattered the social structure he had always inhabited and left nothing in its place but the rich: a solitude called freedom."

The transition to modernity was wrenching enough in England, where economic liberalization had its fair share of opponents, as we have seen. In France, the disconnect between political leaders and the reality of the society they sought to transform was even starker. In many ways the French Revolution was, as Margaret Thatcher termed it, "a Utopian attempt to overthrow a traditional order . . . in the name of abstract ideas, formulated by vain intellectuals." Consider the revolutionaries' efforts to rationalize time itself, starting with the calendar. The twelve months were renamed, each divided into three weeks lasting ten days apiece, with ten-hour days, each of one hundred minutes comprising one hundred seconds. (French workers realized quickly that this "rationalized" schedule meant less frequent rest days.) And no longer would time begin at Anno Domini, the birth of Christ, whose divinity they doubted, but instead from the birth of the Republic itself. Still visible on ancient Egyptian temples is graffiti carved by Napoleon's invading troops with immortal messages marked *Year Six of the Republic*. The revolutionaries' hubris was remarkable: time, they contended, had begun anew.

In another attempt to impose the Enlightenment by force, they also sought to redraw the map of France. Virtually everyone agreed that the old, haphazard French provinces, with their overlapping dioceses and court jurisdictions of vastly unequal size and population, cried out for reform. As part of a reorganization that he argued would allow for rational administration, the cleric-turned-revolutionary Abbé Sieyès proposed slicing France into eighty-one square departments of equal size, with each square divided into nine local municipalities. Of course, his perfect Cartesian grid ignored rivers, mountains, and the interlinking road networks, trade routes, and cultural groupings that gave each existing region its identity. The new map did not correspond to the real France that its people knew and understood.

As the most famed critic of the French Revolution, the conservative Anglo-Irish statesman Edmund Burke compared the French story unfavorably with "the two principles of conservation and correction" that had defined England's Glorious Revolution. Burke was no reactionary. A ferocious critic of the abuse of power by the East India Company and a British defender of American colonists' rights, he believed in liberty and even in radical change at times, but only if it could be brought about organically, without upending society. Some aspects of the Glorious Revolution were genuinely radical, such as Parliament asserting its supremacy, deposing a despotic king, and declaring a Bill of Rights. But other elements of it were basically conservative, such as preserving England's monarchy and aristocracy, while empowering the merchant class and the underlying economic order. For Burke, without reform there is stagnation. But radical change without conservation of key elements of the past risks the disintegration of society.

NATIONALISM EN MASSE

How had the French Revolution come to this point, of rejecting liberalism and embracing dictatorship? It had begun with democratic, classical-liberal aspirations. But once war broke out in 1792, and the monarchies of Europe gathered to crush the revolution, radicalization escalated uncontrollably. Foreign foes, especially the hated Austrians, were depicted as bloodthirsty tyrants. Domestically, any opposition to the ruling clique of Jacobins was denounced as counterrevolutionary treason, a gift to the enemy. This was guilt by association: if you opposed the government of the day, you by definition supported royalism and wanted to re-enslave "the People."

Robespierre's descent into paranoia and murder exemplified the polarization and extremism that stamped the revolution. But populism, entwined with patriotic nationalism, was also indispensable in fueling revolutionary France's military success. The French Revolution would have been quickly crushed by its neighboring monarchies if the revolutionaries had not succeeded in fueling mass enthusiasm for an all-out war to save the republic and defeat tyranny.

In 1792, when the Austrian and Prussian armies met the mass of French conscripts defending the road to Paris, the royal forces expected a quick victory. After all, the allied kingdoms had the best troops in Europe: they were led by an elite aristocratic officer corps, men who had been trained at the finest elite military academies and who commanded professional soldiers and battle-tested mercenaries. Surely a poorly disciplined rabble of workers and peasants didn't stand a chance.

But to everyone's surprise, the French won. At this first military test, the Battle of Valmy, the revolutionaries—fueled by mass enthusiasm—overpowered a well-trained army. The next year, in 1793, the revolutionary legislature instituted the leveé en masse, a conscription order that raised a stunning eight hundred thousand troops in the first year. This measure was part of a whole-of-society effort to save the revolution. The Committee of Public Safety gave everyone a role: "The young men shall go to battle; the married men shall forge arms and transport provisions; the women shall make tents and clothing and shall serve in the hospitals; the children shall turn old linen into lint; the aged shall . . . preach the hatred of kings and the unity of the Republic."

The *levée en masse* raised millions of troops for France and saved the country. The old powers had to grapple with revolutionary forces that had been unleashed. Over the course of the next two decades, Revolutionary and Napoleonic France would defeat five anti-French coalitions, fighting almost single-handedly against the rest of Europe combined, drawing from the seemingly bottomless reserves of patriotic French citizens. The traditional monarchies had to adapt to the new reality or be destroyed.

French success did not just demonstrate the superiority of a national bureaucracy to draft millions of citizens into a war machine. It also showed the value of a patriotic call to arms. Peasants and laborers were being told a new narrative. Far from being a despised underclass at the beck and call of their noble betters, the workers were recast as the true heroes of history, the soldiers who would break the chains of despotism. No wonder Schama claims that "militarized nationalism was not, in some accidental way, the unintended consequence of the French Revolution: it was its heart and soul."

It turned out to be a short step from militarized nationalism to a charismatic demagoguery. Napoleon rose to power by offering a seemingly stabilizing force amid populist chaos. As dictator, he saw his role as safeguarding and cementing the revolution, lodging its legacy in his own person. "The Revolution is over," he said. "I am the Revolution." Shockingly, many ex-Jacobins and others on the left accepted him. Napoleon seized power claiming to protect the revolution but then turned its republican principles on its head, crowning himself emperor, and doling out royal titles to family and friends—putting his brothers on the thrones of Holland and Spain and a trusted general on the throne of Sweden. (The descendants of a common French soldier still reign in Stockholm today.)

After replacing the republic with a dynastic empire, Napoleon struck a bargain with the pope to return Catholicism to a central place in French society. France would embrace the old pillars of bloodline and church. Democratic idealists despaired. The great Romantic poet William Wordsworth had celebrated the early revolution: "Bliss was it in that dawn to be alive, / But to be young was very heaven!" Once Napoleon declared himself emperor, Wordsworth soured and decried history going backward, "the dog / Returning to his vomit." Equally disgusted by Napoleon's arrogant self-coronation, Ludwig van Beethoven—who had dedicated his Third Symphony to Napoleon and named it "Bonaparte"—struck out the name, retitling the composition "Eroica." Napoleon, endlessly self-aggrandizing and reactionary on many questions, including the rights of women, was no hero.

Later observers were less repelled by Napoleon. The historian Andrew Roberts gushed about him: "The ideas that underpin our modern world—meritocracy, equality before the law, property rights, religious toleration, modern secular education, sound finances and so on—were championed, consolidated, codified and geographically extended by Napoleon." The political scientist Francis Fukuyama identified the key achievements of the French Revolution as the rule of law, the neutral administrative state, and the civic code—all of which were actually Napoleonic reforms. But beyond legal changes, what was the main modern innovation of the revolutionary era? The answer is mass conscription: hundreds of thousands, even millions, of men under arms. The era of limited wars fought by small numbers of professional soldiers and mercenaries was over. Total war had arrived.

Conquest through raw military strength allowed France's revolutionary and imperial regimes to dodge the question of deep, underlying economic reforms. The Jacobins and Napoleon alike balanced France's books through plunder, not a modernized fiscal apparatus. Thus, the country owed its military success not primarily to its modernized state apparatus but to features that were extremely old-school. Indeed, thousands of years old, they would have been recognizable to the Roman emperors whose laurels and statues Emperor Napoleon imitated: charismatic leadership to build morale, individual strategic sense on the commander's part, and the expansion of a land-based territorial empire. At its height under Napoleon, the French Empire, including client kingdoms and puppet states, stretched from Spain to Poland, and incorporated most of western and central Europe.

We should not undersell Napoleon's merits. He was a tactical genius on the battlefield and had a keen logistical savvy, obsessed, for example, with supplying his men with adequate boots to keep pace on quick marches. He was in fact a modernizer. But he didn't bring about progress by allowing the deeper structures of society to improve organically. He declared it by fiat from above.

THE RISE OF STATISM

For all his administrative zeal and boundless energy, Napoleon exhibited several fatal flaws. His tendency to micromanage and his belief that trade was a zero-sum game hindered France's process of modernization. So did his attempt at stimulating innovation through mandates that made all scientists dependent on the state for patronage. These measures supported some technological breakthroughs in the short term. But in the long term, they cut off the kind of sustained private-sector connections that proved so essential in sparking the Industrial Revolution across the English Channel. Napoleon's subsidies and other protectionist measures were intended to nurture industry, but they combined with Robespierre's price regulations and economic controls to hamstring French competitiveness for centuries. All these policies shared a core feature: top-down centralization. The French after World War II called this model "dirigisme," the principle that the state should control and direct economic life.

Napoleon did much to cement this model when he created a trading zone he called the Continental System. This united most of mainland Europe into a single economic bloc to encourage trade to flourish inside the French imperial sphere of influence—and cut out his British enemy. This system has even been compared to a prototype of the European Economic Community. Yet calling the Continental System a free-trade zone gets it wrong; in reality, it was a protectionist project. The French Empire, along with its vassals and allies, was subject to onerous, arbitrary, and constantly shifting bureaucratic regulations. The British suffered a temporary setback and had to hunt for other export markets for their industrial textiles—and soon found eager consumers in the United States, Latin America, and Asia. As with the Spanish trying to squeeze the upstart Dutch with tariffs, an attempt at choking a rival with protectionism led the targeted power to go global.

Trade was another area where Napoleon's tendency to micromanage, which had served him well on the battlefield, backfired. The emperor concerned himself with exactly how much grain, olive oil, or brandy was being loaded or unloaded at various ports. His obsession with defeating Britain, that "nation of shopkeepers," led him to become a meddlesome, bureaucratic bean counter. Rather than opening up the space for private entrepreneurship, Napoleon burdened would-be business owners with an insane labyrinth of licenses.

Apart from the long-term harm done to the competitiveness of

French industry, Napoleon's ambition and aggression precipitated his own downfall. In 1810, Russia, refusing to accept being absorbed into the French-dominated Continental System, resumed trading with Britain. Furious at this slight by the tsar, Napoleon launched his disastrous invasion of Russia in 1812. The retreat from Moscow destroyed his Grande Armée of six hundred thousand that he had assembled from across Europe. Fewer than twenty-five thousand men survived the onslaught of Russian cavalry and the hardships of "General Winter." Intended as Napoleon's climactic conquest, the Russian campaign snapped the spine of French military power. Forced to abdicate, he was imprisoned on the island of Elba. Napoleon escaped captivity to return to France for one last military gamble, only to lose at the Battle of Waterloo in 1815.

FROM THE ASHES

The most poignant symbol from the Revolutionary and Napoleonic eras may be Paris's still-incomplete Arc de Triomphe. It was initially intended to be topped by a great statue that embodied the revolution triumphing over anarchy and despotism. But its designers endlessly wrangled over what symbol should top it: in one historian's words, "another chariot or an effigy of Napoleon standing on a pile of enemy arms or on a terrestrial globe, or a huge eagle, a statue of liberty or a gigantic star." The top of the arch stayed empty, as it remains today.

So too did the revolutionary French state have a void at the heart of its triumph. Inflamed by revolutionary spirit and regimented by Napoleon's tactics, France had conquered Europe. But to what end? Certainly not to defend a durable democracy in France. Just consider the crippling political instability that the revolution left in its wake. From 1792 to 1958, as I have noted, over a mere century and a half, France was governed by three monarchies, two empires, five republics, a socialist commune, and a quasi-fascist regime. (Meanwhile, since 1688, Britain can brag that it has had no unconstitutional or violent changes of government; enduring for more than a third of a millennium, it is the longest-lasting representative system on the Earth.) The French have lived through numerous other crises, uprising and near misses, even in modern times.

At first, some liberals elsewhere in Europe found inspiration in Napoleon's triumphal nationalism, given the way it so united and empowered France. They wanted their own national politics instead of being part of the vast multinational empires run out of Vienna and Moscow and Istanbul. The French model stirred imitators in the decades after Napoleon's reign, with populations rising up in present-day Italy, Hungary, Germany, and beyond. But those revolutions were nipped in the bud. The longer-term legacy of French nationalism in Europe was not to spread liberal values but to plant the seeds of identity politics. While some nationalist movements sometimes started out as liberal, many turned toward nostalgia and illiberalism.

Other European powers also reacted against the French Revolution's embrace of reason and its denigration of religion. The German states above all experienced a ferocious backlash to the cold rationalism of the Enlightenment, and its monstrous child, the revolution. The Right turned toward a new movement: Romanticism. In its most benign form, this meant angst-filled poetry and art that emphasized the heart over the head, like Goethe's *Sorrows of Young Werther*. The trend could be seen architecturally, too, in the "ruin craze" that spread through western Europe. Appealing to a romantic bygone era, aristocrats would hire architects to build bespoke ruins for their estates—a perfect expression of the nostalgic urge to reject modernity in favor of a past that never was. In the political realm, however, Romanticism lit the spark of a simmering, vengeful German nationalism that would eventually morph into fascism.

The more immediate backlash to the revolution came from the conservative monarchs who defeated Napoleon. Bent on preventing further revolutions, they pursued a reactionary agenda across Europe. This post-Napoleonic era, dominated by a coalition of great powers known as the Concert of Europe, lasted roughly 1815 to 1856 in its strongest form but lingered for decades afterward. It was defined by the archconservative Austrian chancellor Klemens von Metternich. In this era, right-wing conspiracy theory as we know it came into being. The leaders who had vanquished the French Revolution saw the shadow of the guillotine everywhere they looked. As implausible as it appears to us today, otherwise serious statesmen like Metternich made policy assuming that the secret cabal of the Knights Templar, the Illuminati, the Freemasons, linked by hidden cells of Jacobins, all joined together as parts of an insidious global network. If Italian rebels rose up against Austrian rule, surely this was linked to rumblings in Paris—or dissident nobles in Poland. It was, in the words of the historian Adam Zamoyski, an era of "Phantom Terror."

In another setback to liberalism, the French Revolution's violent legacy discredited rationalism and democracy. Much like twenty-first-century liberals who were labeled "communists" by their conservative opponents, many moderate reformers of the nineteenth century were tarred by association with the Reign of Terror. The memory of political purges undermined reforms of all kinds. Repudiating revolution meant not just rejecting the bloody guillotine but also obviously beneficial modernization. Zamoyski notes that Pope Leo XII, upon reclaiming political control over the Italian states that Napoleon had wrested from the Catholic Church, promptly "brought back the Inquisition" and "sent the Jews back to the ghetto." The pope also reversed other "revolutionary novelties" like street lights and vaccination.

More insidiously, Metternich's era revealed how a disproportionate fear of revolution can create a deadening counterrevolution that seeks to stifle any kind of democratic movement in the cradle. Metternich responded to calls for reform with crackdowns on students and universities. Even his fellow Austrian conservatives attacked his repression as an ultimately futile effort. A "forest of bayonets and the inflexible maintenance of everything that exists" is "the best way of bringing about revolution," one minister complained to the chancellor in 1833. The comparatively liberal British government saw the continent's monarchies as hopelessly backward. And indeed, by bottling up any reform at all, the restored monarchs ensured eventual revolution. In January 1848, Tocqueville gave a speech to the French legislature warning of a "volcano" of pent-up political energy. Within months, that volcano exploded.

REVOLUTIONARY VOLCANO

The Revolutions of 1848 are among the most extraordinary events in history. Across Europe, from north to south and east to west, from Scandinavia to Romania, Ireland to Italy, even in bucolic Switzerland, people rose up against autocratic rule, embraced liberal ideas and—at great risk to their lives and fortunes—protested against the ruling establishments in their countries. Nothing like it has ever happened since. The Revolutions of 1989 were confined to Eastern Europe. The Arab Spring of 2011 never reached beyond Arabic-speaking societies. 1848, the "Springtime of the Peoples," was a revolutionary shockwave that rippled through societies with dozens of different languages and ethnicities. Like the Arab Spring, the Revolutions of 1848 failed in the short run. But in the long run, they had deep and far-reaching effects.

Why did they happen? From Paris to Berlin to Vienna, the process of economic modernization continued apace, with coal and steam gradually displacing manual labor. In the early decades of the nineteenth century, peasants streamed into cities to become factory workers, undermining the model of artisanal production dominated by guild craftsmen. But atop this shifting foundation, Europe's rulers tried to lock in the same restrictive politics that had existed fifty years prior, before the French Revolution unsettled the equilibrium. That disconnect between economic modernization and political structure ultimately caused an upheaval.

In France, resentment toward the sluggish pace of reform under the restored monarchy led to a rerun of the French Revolution. In 1848, the government's ill-timed crackdown on political gatherings prompted mass street demonstrations in Paris, climaxing in the declaration of a Second Republic. Happily for the king, there was no guillotine this time around; the deposed Louis Philippe fled to a cushy retirement in England. But revolution was back on the agenda.

The uprising in Paris sounded a starting gun for reformers and revolutionaries across the continent. Educated, middle-class liberals had chafed at the deadening political climate since 1815. Meanwhile, agricultural failures pushed up the price of food, while unemployment in manufacturing soared, plunging much of Europe's working class into poverty. With intellectual leadership and masses of angry, unemployed workers, the news of revolution from Paris set off a societal explosion.

In the Austrian Empire's glittering capital, Vienna, a mob of students and workers demanded Metternich's ouster. The archconservative chancellor was fired and forced into exile, first to the Netherlands and then to England, which had remained a safe haven for heretics of all sorts. Austrian imperial rule was already straining to suppress liberal demands for reform and rein in the ambitions of its constituent nationalities: Hungarians, Croats, Czechs, Slovaks, Slovenes, and others, each contending for territory and pride of place. Only by pitting rival nationalities against each other was Austria's central government able to head off its revolutions in 1848, using Croat shock troops to crush Hungary's attempted independence.

A divided Germany was next up for revolution. At the time, it was a region, not a country, split into dozens of states as part of the German Confederation. But an idealistic young generation, inspired by French nationalism, dreamed of a united German people. Demonstrations in Berlin at first prompted concessions toward constitutional monarchy in Prussia. But then the revolutionaries tried to go even further, convening a self-proclaimed national legislature in Frankfurt where they declared a unified German state under the Prussian king, who they imagined sympathizing with their nationalist goals. Horrified at the sudden radicalization, the king rejected this offer of a "crown from the gutter." The liberal constitutional reforms were rolled back, as were plans for German national unity. In Italy, revolutionaries attempting a similar unification faced a severe setback when the pope declared his opposition. The forces of order defeated the revolutionaries on all fronts. All over Europe, conservative monarchs reasserted their authority and breathed a sigh of relief.

On the surface layer of politics, the Revolutions of 1848 were an almost unmitigated failure. Only in France did the new revolutionary government last—and even there, it was no victory for democracy. Napoleon's nephew won the first presidential election under the new republic and within three years had seized power in a coup before declaring himself emperor. But appearances were misleading. Whatever political structure they took, the governments that rose to power in country after country in the decades following 1848 increasingly converged on a common set of economic policies. They all promoted railways, trade, and the new model of industrial capitalism.

And by the 1870s, those countries that remained officially monarchical—such as Austria, Russia, and Germany—were forced to issue major liberal concessions. Pressured from the left, German leaders inaugurated a system of social welfare and adopted a federal parliament, the Reichstag, that exercised power over taxes and spending. Facing renewed unrest in Hungary, the Austrian Empire evolved into Austria-Hungary, a "Dual Monarchy" that elevated Hungarian nationalism to the heights of power. Even Russia, the most autocratic of Europe's great powers, abolished serfdom (de facto slavery of Russian peasants) and championed industrialization.

Italy in 1848 was among the least industrialized and most technologically backward of European societies. In the years after its failed revolution, Italy's struggle for *Risorgimento*—resurgence and national unification—showed the challenge of trying to modernize society while the old political order sought to preserve traditional values. The writer Giuseppe Tomasi di Lampedusa (the last prince of a Sicilian noble house) captured the spirit of the wrenching forces remaking Sicily in the 1860s in his 1958 novel, *The Leopard*. Seeing his own status threatened, the noble protagonist is memorably advised, "If we want things to stay as they are, things will have to change." To escape revolution, Europe's conservative ruling classes had to accept reform. But reform intensified structural changes in society.

After 1848, beneath the political surface, the foundations of society were changing. Even as old regimes clung to power, liberal aspirations of liberty and equality did not go away. The revolutionaries were crushed at the time, but their idealistic aims—ending royal monopolies on power, establishing and empowering parliaments, promoting freedom of speech, cultivating nationalism—were almost invariably adopted through gradual reform.

Not everyone was satisfied with piecemeal reforms, however. For radicals and discontents, the utopian dream of the French Revolution, that society could be radically transformed by fiat, never died. In fact, the revolution would be copied almost beat for beat some 1,300 miles to the east. One of the greatest ripple effects of the French Revolution through history was its Russian sequel.

A once-great land empire with vast resources and manpower but an unpopular and incompetent monarch faces economic collapse and military defeat—first being replaced by a moderate government, whose fumbles pave the way for a radical and murderous regime. The difference is that the French Revolution after 1789 unfolded in a series of largely unplanned escalations, while the Russian Revolution of 1917 was consciously strategized by Vladimir Lenin's inner circle, in imitation of the French Revolution as informed by Marxism. For Lenin, Marx's prediction of natural progression toward communism was too slow, too uncertain—so he called for a "vanguard class" of revolutionaries to accelerate history. We can therefore understand the Russian Revolution as an extremely similar process: a top-down revolution set in motion by radicalized elites, perpetrated upon a largely unmodernized agrarian society. In both cases, attempts to save the revolution from internal and external enemies unleashed a campaign of terror and narrowed bands of political acceptability, until one man reigned supreme over the state.

Like its French predecessor, the Russian Revolution devoured its children. After one member of Lenin's inner circle, Leon Trotsky, was accused of counterrevolutionary treason in 1927, he gave a speech in his defense. In it he developed the analogy between the two revolutions: "During the Great French Revolution, many were guillotined. We, too, had many people brought before the firing squad." The question Trotsky had for his accusers was "in accordance with which chapter" of the French Revolution were his rivals "preparing to have us shot"? He portrayed the Russian Revolution as being in danger of falling into the traps of moderation, à la the centrists that succeeded Robespierre, or "Bonapartism," meaning capture by an ambitious general. In exile, Trotsky would accuse his rival Stalin of being "the Bonaparte" whose militarized dictatorship had once again ruined a noble revolution's idealistic goals.

Communism endured much longer in Russia than radical republicanism in France, but its legacies were similar: a politically traumatized and economically dislocated society that had fallen behind its liberal-democratic rivals.

INDUSTRIAL SWALLOWS POLITICAL

Such was the fate of France. The fruits of the French Revolution for the country that birthed it seemed meager: hindered economic growth, uncompetitive industries, a shorn empire. French trade as a share of GDP plummeted from 20 percent to 10 percent from 1790 to 1820. Most damning, when Napoleon was deposed in 1815, France's level of industrialization had risen to match Britain's—as of 1780. Post-revolutionary France was left decades behind its rival.

Eric Hobsbawm in his magisterial history *The Age of Revolutions* explains why the French Revolution failed where the British Industrial Revolution succeeded. He invokes the Marxist concept of base and superstructure to show why the French economy, seemingly so well positioned for growth from 1789 to 1848, sputtered and stagnated. Heavy-handed regulation and price controls undermined the early liberal revolutionaries' attempts at modernization, he argued, while the "capitalist part of the French economy was a superstructure erected on the immovable base of the peasantry and petty-bourgeoisie." At its most fundamental level, in other words, the French economy remained decidedly premodern. Through Napoleonic conquest, the French Revolution brought rule of law and rationalized governance to swathes of western and central Europe, planting the seeds of later economic growth in many countries. It also kicked off a wave of "Atlantic Revolutions" from Spain to Haiti to Colombia. But it did not permanently enrich France.

Ultimately, the French revolutionary era ended by enshrining Britain's central place at the heart of the global political and economic order. The UK's unmatched naval, trading, and industrial primacy would only grow throughout the coming era. It would be Britain, not France, whose model of reformist, liberal politics and economics would inspire nineteenth-century modernizers across the world. Once again, Hobsbawm put it best: "The (British) industrial revolution had swallowed the (French) political revolution."

THE MOTHER OF ALL REVOLUTIONS

Industrial Britain

T HE INDUSTRIAL REVOLUTION "WAS PROBABLY THE most important event in world history," wrote Eric Hobsbawm, "and it was initiated by Britain." While one can debate the precise origins of the many transformations that are now collectively labeled the Industrial Revolution, no one can deny what the economist Deirdre McCloskey calls "the Great Fact": the unprecedented and exponential take-off in productivity that began with industrialization. This growth made possible almost every aspect of the modern world we take for granted today—rising incomes, burgeoning middle classes, universal education, mass politics, widespread technology, global communications, cheap and easy international travel and transport. The Dutch Revolution and its 1688 sequel modernized Britain, but Britain's Industrial Revolution modernized much of the world.

To understand just how dramatic a break from the past the Industrial Revolution was, look at the "hockey-stick" graph of world GDP over the past two thousand years. As you can see, it was century after century of almost zero economic growth, and then, around the mid-1800s, a dramatic spike in global per capita GDP. This growth was unevenly distributed, initially concentrated in the West, and, we now know, vastly damaging to the environment. But make no mistake.

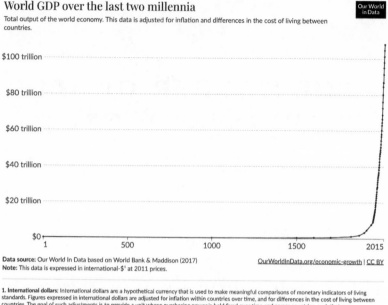

Inflation-adjusted world GDP, 0 to 2015 CE.

It created the modern world, with all its wonders, its cruelties, its hypocrisies, and its glories.

There is a vast literature that tries to explain why the Industrial Revolution began in Britain. Some historians argue that the country had certain unique qualities that spurred progress; others emphasize "coal and colonies," its vast supply of fuel plus its many markets and cheap labor abroad. My own sense is that while Britain was massively advantaged by abundant energy and its possessions in India and the Caribbean, it also boasted some special characteristics that fostered technological and economic innovation. Eighteenth-century Japan, for example, also had a vibrant textile industry, but it never took off like Britain's did. Consider one of the first inventions of the Industrial Revolution: the flying shuttle. Patented by John Kay in 1733, this simple device for quickly moving thread through a loom consisted of technology—wheels and weights added to a wooden body—that could have been deployed hundreds of years earlier. But by allowing just a single person to operate a loom, the flying shuttle greatly increased the productivity of weaving. Hundreds of such gadgets and machines were invented in Britain in the eighteenth century. Many of them, like the flying shuttle, had nothing to do with cheap coal. And all this progress in industry coincided with major innovations in farming, which sparked an agricultural revolution at roughly the same time. There were other countries that were ahead of Britain in science, but it was in Britain that the tinkerers, the mechanics, and the inventors flourished. And it was they, not the theoreticians, who launched the Industrial Revolution.

To be sure, coal was a great gift. The British Isles are rich in easily accessible deposits of the fuel. In the late 1500s, England was running dangerously low on wood for heating homes. Switching from wood to coal—in part an elite project to preserve royal forests for game hunting—was not easy. Coal mining was (and is) a dirty, dangerous, thankless job. Flooding was a particular hazard. But British ingenuity came to the rescue. In 1712, Thomas Newcomen developed a contraption that pumped water out; it was powered by a piston pushed by pressurized steam, and the ample coal present was burned to boil the water. James Watt greatly improved the design in 1776. That was the year Britain's North American colonies declared their independence, but the boon of industrialization meant that Watt's steam engine soon more than made up for the lost land. Even more so than it had for the Dutch, national power was decoupling from geography.

The steam-powered pump—the first practical and widespread use of steam engines—accelerated the production of coal, which then fueled more steam engines that were used to power textile factories and ultimately propelled the whole economy forward. By allowing machines to be driven not by men or horses but by an inanimate form of energy, coal unlocked human potential in hundreds of different ways. This energy revolution was the core of the Industrial Revolution, and without it, most of the material advances of the modern age would be impossible. Consider that by the end of the nineteenth century, one steam-powered locomotive did the same amount of work as around 1,300 horses. The ultimate consequence of the Industrial Age was that it let humanity break free from the limits of biology. From then on, civilization would be bound only by the limits of human ingenuity.

Britain was not magically blessed with more inventors than other countries. The Glorious Revolution had cemented two key pillars of English exceptionalism: parliamentary rule and market capitalism. Both were systems marked by continuous trial and error and both encouraged a culture of experimentation. In 1623, Parliament had passed a groundbreaking patent law that ended abusive and fraudulent claims to a monopoly over specific inventions, and instead rewarded the "true and first inventor" but limited the inventor's monopoly to fourteen years. This statute remained in force over centuries, and it became increasingly important in the eighteenth century as officials and judges required explanations of inventions to award patent protections. Because the original inventor was rewarded enough to incentivize innovation but could not claim exclusive use indefinitely, this system made it easier for others to adopt and improve upon new technology. Parliament even began paying inventors to disclose more information about their breakthroughs. In 1732, when Thomas Lombe's patent for silk manufacturing devices was expiring, Parliament refused to grant an extension but offered him the modern-day equivalent of $4 million to allow royal agents to inspect his machinery, construct models, and display them publicly for other weavers to learn from.

There is evidence that the flying shuttle was invented in France a year before Kay patented it in Britain. But French officials, dismayed by the disruptive employment effects of the new device, destroyed the machinery and appear to have banned it. Britain, by contrast, celebrated inventors and protected their intellectual property rights, giving these innovators the motivation to keep innovating.

Whatever the exact mix of causes, a seismic shift in the way we work and live began in Britain in the mid-eighteenth century. It supercharged that small island's power and influence, enabling the country to undertake another massive round of colonial land grabs and to spread its ideas far and wide. It enriched the motherland, made English a global language, and turned Britain into a model of political and economic liberalism for the world. Britain ruled the seas, dominated economics, and defined modern culture, sports, and leisure. So many of the features of today's world that we think of as normal—from football (what Americans call soccer) to tourism to the proverbial walk in the park—originated as practices of the British upper and middle classes.

ORDINARY LIFE TRANSFORMED

Even in the eighteenth century, before coal took off, raw cotton consumption in Britain expanded by a hundredfold, and labor productivity in the textile industry rose by a dizzying factor of 150. But then came the Victorian era, which in its strictest sense lasted from 1837 to 1901, Queen Victoria's reign. During the "Victorious Century," as one historian punningly called the broader period of British dominance, growth kicked into a new gear. Greater productivity meant higher incomes and more food on the table. From 1770 to 1870, real wages rose over 50 percent, even after adjusting for cost of living and inflation. The economic historian Brad DeLong has estimated that the average unskilled male worker in preindustrial London, circa 1600, earned enough to provide some three thousand calories of rough bread a day to his family, rising to five thousand calories by 1870. This was substantially higher than in other European countries, let alone the much poorer lands of Asia and Africa. Over the first half of the nineteenth century, British life expectancy rose by around 3.5 years, even during a period often remembered as bleak. It wasn't just that workers could supply their families with food and other necessities; improvements in health care and sanitation also lengthened lives.

The population of Britain boomed, both from natural increase and from immigrants drawn to opportunities there. The UK's first census, in 1801, counted just over ten million Englishmen. A century later, the population had more than tripled, topping thirty million. The growth in Britain's cities was even more spectacular. The 1851 census showed that, for the first time, the UK had become a majority-urban society—and by far the largest such country in history, dwarfing the Italian city-states and the Dutch Republic before it. London swelled to become the biggest city ever, more populous than China's great cities, or Rome at its height. From just 1 million in 1800, London's population ballooned to 3 million around mid-century and to an astounding 6.5 million by 1900. And many of Britain's second-tier cities—Liverpool, Manchester, Edinburgh—saw population explosions as well, in some cases growing tenfold in a few decades.

These growth figures can seem abstract today, but they represented the utter transformation of the average person's life into something we would now recognize. British industrialization revolutionized the human condition itself, drastically changing people's relation to time and space. Railroads annihilated distance, moving goods and people far faster than ever before. The first passenger train ran from Liverpool to Manchester, a journey that took four hours by coach and twenty hours by canal (that great modern transit revolution of the previous century, pioneered by the Dutch). By train, it took one hour and forty-five minutes. From the opening of Britain's first railroad in 1825, the country's rail network shot up to over twenty thousand miles of rail by 1914.

While train travel was initially a marvel available only to elites, it did not take long for its benefits to reach the masses—with a boost from the government. In 1844, a young member of Parliament and future prime minister, William Gladstone, introduced the Railway Regulation Act, which mandated that for every rail route in the country, there had to be at least one train every weekday that sold tickets for the steeply discounted price of a penny per mile. This cheap service, known as the "parliamentary train," made it possible for Britons of modest means to access the revolution in transport.

Vastly expanded travel demanded precise timekeeping. The Victorian era saw the advent of the ubiquitous pocket watch, not just a marker of wealth but also a connection to modernity itself. Before timepieces were mass-produced, virtually all human beings on the planet lived in vague chunks of time: "sunrise," "noonday," "dusk." Medieval Europeans largely relied on the tolling from the (often wildly inaccurate) village clock tower summoning them to church. In the 1600s, European governments began offering huge rewards for inventors who could devise ever-more-accurate timekeeping to determine longitude and keep navies on course, with brilliant scientists answering the call. Unfortunately, their proposed solutions—including a telescope-equipped helmet invented by Galileo for observing Jupiter's moons—were generally ingenious but impractical, unsuited to anyone but expert mathematicians and navigators.

In the era of railway schedules, the average person finally enjoyed accurate-to-the-minute timekeeping. Having a watch in your pocket or on your wrist was the nineteenth-century equivalent of the smartphone, an omni-use device that plugged you into the modern world. People who could keep time could catch trains and ferries, make appointments, and measure how much of their day they spent on various tasks. The clock took the murky chaos of everyday life and imposed order on it. The historian Daniel Boorstin called the clock the "mother of machines" for the way it unleashed technical ingenuity across society. To avoid the confusing flurry of differing local times, the Railway Clearing House (a kind of self-regulatory body for Britain's booming train network) inaugurated Greenwich Mean Time in 1847. It was an effective way to keep the UK's industrializing national economy in sync and its far-flung dominions operating in harmony. Technology hadn't just changed reality; it had also changed how people understood reality.

INVENTING LEISURE

Now that they could measure it, what did Britons do with their time? They worked defined hours, of course, but now more people could spend more time in *leisure*. Although the Industrial Revolution resulted in millions of workers performing repetitive tasks in harsh conditions, it also resulted in higher wages—which was why people left villages to work in factories to begin with—and fixed hours. Over time, it gave birth to the lifestyle we now associate with the global middle class, offering something previously available only to the very rich: income for consumption. Even earlier, in the eighteenth century, the upper middle classes had begun to buy tea, coffee, and sugar as the prices of those goods fell within their reach. But now other habits that had once been the prerogative of the aristocracy became more widespread. For centuries, young British gentlemen and ladies had taken the "Grand Tour": a months-long sojourn to mainland Europe to visit the great capitals and see the masterworks of Italian Renaissance art, take in French opera, ply Venice's canals, and hike amid the glory of the Swiss Alps. This was a gilded world available to the wealthy few. As industrialization fattened the pocketbooks of the middle class and lowered the barriers to travel, such luxuries became accessible to a much broader swath of the public.

Thomas Cook, a Victorian businessman, could justifiably claim the title of world's first modern travel agent. A member of the increasingly popular temperance movement, he wanted to provide people with more wholesome and less sodden pursuits than drinking away their disposable income. He hit upon the idea of travel packages, with train fare, lodgings, and food included. The first group tours he organized were modest weekend trips to Liverpool, Scotland, and the Great Exhibition in London, but eventually steamships would take his travelers on international trips that would have once been unimaginable. Even on the average "weekend" (a term that became commonplace in British English only around the 1880s), families could enjoy themselves closer to home. Taking the parliamentary train, they could visit the many new museums, libraries, and parks, and other amenities that had sprung up, consciously designed to offer working men a more edifying and sober alternative to the pub. For all of human history before the Industrial Revolution, the idea that a humble worker could go on a trip purely for pleasure had been laughable. Leisure had been for landed elites or wealthy merchants. Vacation for the average person was truly revolutionary.

Sports, too, took on a recognizably modern mold in the Victorian era. A French nobleman, Baron Pierre de Coubertin, was horrified by his home country's chronic instability, its constant coups and revolutions. His proposed cure? Sports. Enamored with elite English boarding schools, as chronicled in the 1857 novel *Tom Brown's School Days*, he sought to introduce to France their spirit of competition and fair play. Indeed, these elite schools had long been pioneers of sport, like the Rugby School, which lent its name to the game. In the words of the writer Ian Buruma, for Coubertin and other Anglophiles envious of Britain's industrial progress and educational system, "the British had achieved nothing less than a moral revolution, bloodless, without Jacobins or riots."A promoter of both internationalism and of cricket, rowing, boxing, and football, Coubertin saw sport as a way to take human competitiveness and channel it toward "peaceful rivalry" rather than "armed battle." Inspired by these ideas, he would go on to found the modern Olympics in 1896.

Even outside elite circles, up and down the social hierarchy, sports became ever more popular and organized. Football had been part of England's mass culture for centuries; a nobleman in King Lear insults another by calling him a "rascal" and "base football player." But now the sport became professionalized and lost the stigma of being a commoner's pastime. The oldest football clubs still in existence today—including Sheffield FC, founded 1857—marked the beginning of professional athletic teams as we know them. By the end of Victoria's reign, British sports had become truly global. A cricket craze swept South Asia, while football was adopted with enthusiasm across Europe and Latin America (though the behavior of some hooligans might test Baron Coubertin's hopes for sport as a more peaceful alternative to war).

No facet of life—how people worked, how they dressed, how they ate, how they spent their free time, and how they even thought about time and space—was left unchanged by Britain's economic transformation. Not even one of the oldest social arrangements in human history: that between men and women.

REVOLUTIONIZING "WOMEN'S WORK"

It was no accident that, after coal mining, the first area of the economy transformed by steam power was textile production. Making cloth had been an especially labor-intensive task for millennia. According to the historian Bret Devereaux, making textiles was "a major activity (indeed, *the* major activity) for probably around 40% of the population in most premodern societies—not merely almost all adult women, but girls too." By his estimate, making the clothing for a premodern farming family of six people took more than seven hours a day, a remarkable amount of labor to produce just a handful of outfits per person. Even when mitigated by labor-saving devices like the spinning wheel (invented in the late Middle Ages), untold hours were taken up with carding, spinning, weaving, darning, and sewing—until the Industrial Revolution.

Industrialization did not just set the world economy on pace to grow faster than ever before. It is not far-fetched to say that it was the first step to female liberation. Yes, many women crowded onto factory floors, exploited by bosses for wages far lower than their male counterparts. But the workers of Birmingham or Leeds in the early nineteenth century, much like the women of Dhaka or Hanoi in the early twenty-first century, were fleeing the poverty of rural life, not to mention the isolation and physical hardship. The wages for industrial working women were much higher than anything offered back in the village, if paid work was available there at all. And very soon, women realized that they needed to organize and demand better working conditions—and then rights—for themselves.

Women's shift from performing unpaid household labor to earning their own money upended both the workforce and the family. It took more than a century after women entered the industrial workforce

for them to earn the right to vote, but there was a clear connection between the two developments. As women participated in the
modern economy, they also became more educated, confident, and
politically active. Abolitionist societies, self-improvement clubs, and
eventually the suffragette movement—all of these organizations flourished among the new female urban workforce. In turn, once women
achieved some political power, they put themselves at the forefront of
broader efforts to protect downtrodden groups of all kinds—enslaved
people, child laborers, and underpaid workers. Women's liberation
may properly be called history's greatest social revolution, and it was
set in motion by industrialization, its greatest economic revolution.

DARK SATANIC MILLS

Despite all the wondrous accomplishments of the Industrial Revolution, the era was often seen as a fall from grace. An 1804 poem by
William Blake lamented how "England's green and pleasant land" had
been marred by "those dark Satanic mills." One hundred fifty years
later, J. R. R. Tolkien also tied industrialization to evil. In *The Lord
of the Rings*, the evil wizard Saruman, with his "mind of metal and
wheels," "does not care for growing things, except as far as they serve
him for the moment" and sets himself up as a budding industrialist.
In his greed, he clear-cuts forests and turns the idyllic preindustrial
Shire into a wasteland of ugly rowhouses, billowing brick chimneys,
and fouled rivers. Faced with depictions like these, who wouldn't side
with nature and the countryside against the encroachments of brutal,
mechanistic, soulless industrialization?

These depictions reflect a Romantic view of premodern societies as
pure and innocent. The truth, however, is that the world before the
Industrial Revolution was no Eden. For the vast majority of commoners, preindustrial Britain was far closer to hell than paradise. Rural
farming, near the level of subsistence—that is to say, the constant
threat of starvation—was the norm for almost all of history up until

the twentieth century. Disease, drudgery, and insecurity defined "the world until yesterday," to borrow a term from the anthropologist Jared Diamond.

The data I discussed earlier makes clear that while the workers of industrial Britain were exploited and poorly treated, they were still doing far better in material terms than their ancestors, or even their parents. The simplest proof comes from looking at the choices of ordinary peasants—and treating these choices with respect. Tens of millions of farmers, all across Europe, chose to leave rural poverty to pursue a better life in the cities. (Billions in the developing world have in recent decades made the same choice.) Yes, there were of course "push" factors. Enclosure displaced families, and new techniques reduced the demand for farmhands. But it wasn't as if the multitudes flocking to cities were all coerced or deluded. The pull of urban life was strong, and the Industrial Revolution materially benefited the workers who came, even if they did have to contend with unsafe conditions, cramped housing, harsh bosses, and longer working hours. None of this is to trumpet industrialization uncritically, or to take the side of Scrooge against Tiny Tim. The larger historical process was disruptive, wrenching, and traumatic—but over the long term, it produced a huge rise in standards of living for working people. "It is *not* the age of money-bags and cant, soot, hubbub, and ugliness," the British historian Frederic Harrison wrote of the nineteenth century. "It is the age of great expectation and unwearied striving after better things."

Even those who recognized the material progress of industrialism saw in it the seeds of moral collapse. The poet Oliver Goldsmith, writing "The Deserted Village" at the dawn of the industrial age in 1770, lamented how modernity had depopulated the countryside and killed the "humble happiness" that had marked the rural way of life. Now, he wrote, "Wealth accumulates, and men decay." Initially, such nostalgia was expressed mostly by conservatives, who saw the Industrial Revolution as the source of modern sin. But they were soon joined by ideologues of the left—most important among them, the architects of communism. Friedrich Engels, Karl Marx's collaborator and funder, inherited his family wealth from industrial textile mills, including one in Manchester. In 1845, after observing and managing such factories, Engels was inspired to write *The Condition of the Working Class in England*, which predated *The Communist Manifesto* by three years.

In many ways, Engels stamped the mid-nineteenth century with the dark view we still have today. It is hard to blame him. The mirror image of the dazzling machinery of the industrial age was the soot-stained faces of the workers whose back-breaking labor built it all. A visceral reaction was understandable. And Engels happened to be writing about a period when technology was booming but real wages remained stubbornly stagnant.

Yet this period, from about 1790 to 1840, was not the new normal of industrialization, as Engels and others feared. Rather, it was a short-term anomaly in history—so much so that the historian Robert C. Allen dubbed it "Engels' pause," a lull before workers' wages and living conditions took off. Various theories have been put forth to explain this interlude. During the early phases of the Industrial Revolution, the jobs were fairly simple, and workers faced steep competition when so many other workers were migrating from the countryside and even children were in the labor pool. Eventually, migration to the cities slowed, the government restricted child labor, and the factories became more complicated to operate, all of which boosted workers' bargaining power and helped them obtain higher wages. Another explanation is that it simply took time for all the new technology to be fully harnessed—and then for workers to share in the gains. Steam's full potential was unlocked only gradually, as it spread through the economy. At first, steam power could increase productivity merely within a given textile factory, since the rest of the economic infrastructure remained the same. Add railroads and steamships to deliver goods to and from the factory, however, and that factory became even more profitable.

As the world would see with the digital revolution, technological change enhances productivity and wages in fits and starts. But the more the new technology becomes ubiquitous, the more a country's economic structure changes, and the more its political leaders scramble to keep up with this jerky forward movement and the backlash to it. In the midst of this disruption, politics gets very turbulent.

LUDDITES AND LIBERALS

Economic advances do not magically produce political advances. Consider the defining political changes in early-1800s Britain: the implementation of free trade, which lowered food prices significantly, and the expansion of the franchise to some working-class men. Such reforms got through Parliament only after decades of intense, often radical agitation from below. The pressure came from various sources—weavers rioting against mechanization, philosophers advocating democracy, religious minorities demanding equal rights. This reformist push was rooted in economic and technological changes that created and empowered new interest groups. The story begins at Britain's moment of existential struggle against revolutionary France.

The chaos and violence of the French Revolution had tarnished the idea of reform across most of Europe, and Britain was no exception. Any appeal for liberalization, even for expanded rights for commoners or better conditions for the workers, became suspect. Demands for even modest reform were demonized by associating them with radical, revolutionary, and foreign ideas that had led to disaster. (It would become a familiar pattern: just as revolutionary France was invoked in Britain in the 1790s and 1800s to discredit the expansion of the welfare state, so was Soviet Russia in the United States in the 1950s and 1960s.) Determined to keep revolution at bay, especially at a time when Britain was defending itself against Napoleon, the British government greeted dissent with repression.

It was during this era that the infamous Luddites were born. Taking their name from a fictionalized rebellious apprentice named Ned Ludd, these Northern English weavers attacked the textile machinery they viewed as undermining their employment, wages, and social status as skilled craftsmen. Though later scholarship has contested how much the Luddites opposed industrial technology itself, rather than simply protesting poor working conditions, "Luddite" has become a byword for backward-looking people who resist technology's forward march. Anxious about any disruption to the war effort, the British government crushed the original Luddites mercilessly, dispersing their gatherings and executing some of their leaders. Parliament even passed a new law making the destruction of industrial machines punishable by hanging.

With Napoleon's defeat and banishment in 1815, British reformists felt emboldened, thinking their demands would no longer be seen as suspiciously French or treasonous. Their optimism was not unreasonable. After all, Britain should have been riding high: it had vanquished its traditional rival and was busy inventing astounding new machines and expanding its empire. Yet the end of the Napoleonic Wars did not bring a political thaw, and Britain plunged into decades of unrest. Beyond poor working conditions, there was much else to protest. Though a relatively liberal state compared to its continental contemporaries, Britain was far from a true democracy. It was more of a hierarchical oligarchy. Voting restrictions varied widely from district to district, but overall the electorate was tightly limited to those who paid tax or owned property. Before the 1830s, less than 2 percent of Britons voted. And the candidates were mostly wealthy landowners. From 1790 to 1820, some 75 percent of members of Parliament hailed from well-connected families boasting landed estates or had at least three relatives previously serving in Parliament.

Even worse, the apportionment of parliamentary seats had been decided centuries ago and not been updated since. Districts' boundaries were literally medieval. Much like the modern-day US Senate and the disproportionate power it grants to rural states, the British Parliament represented land and not people. Burgeoning industrial hubs like Manchester, Liverpool, Glasgow, and Birmingham had seen their populations increase by a factor of ten or even twenty from 1700 to 1850, and yet many such cities had little or no representation. Meanwhile, some rural districts had a member of Parliament despite having almost no voters. In these "pocket" or "rotten" boroughs, which had so few electors that they were in the pocket of easily bribed local dignitaries, many seats went for a century or more without a contested election. The most infamous of these districts, Old Sarum, near Salisbury, had under eleven voters—but still kept its two seats in Parliament. Another borough, Dunwich, on England's east coast, had literally been swallowed by the sea in earlier centuries—and also retained its two seats.

This status quo was just fine for the rural gentry who had always dominated British politics. But it was increasingly intolerable for the rising industrial classes—both the wealthy middle-class professionals and their working-class employees. In a Parliament run by lords and landowners, there was no place for bosses and factory hands.

Parliament, fearing further upheaval, maintained repressive measures like the suspension of habeas corpus even after the end of the Napoleonic Wars. But the drumbeat of discontent kept beating. One English printer, William Cobbett, dodged accusations that he was publishing a "newspaper" (which would need to be censored) by omitting news and publishing opinions only. By 1817, his self-deprecating "Two-penny Trash" was selling up to seventy thousand copies an issue. In this era, each copy might be read aloud by one literate friend to dozens of semiliterate or illiterate onlookers. Some historians suggest multiplying sales figures by a factor of twenty to get a sense of the true levels of exposure, meaning that as many as 1.4 million readers (out of a population of some 20 million) may have been receiving Cobbett's broadsides against the British state—a higher proportion than watch the evening news today.

This angst was not new; what was new was the ability to express it through more than rioting. Everyday Britons signed peaceful petitions made possible by widespread printing and expanded literacy, and they attended gatherings made possible by improved transportation. A novel set of social institutions—in the historian Emma Griffin's words, "the dissenting churches and their Sunday schools; the trade clubs and benefit societies; and mutual improvement societies"—gave working men the chance to get some education and learn how to exercise their power by organizing and mobilizing.

On August 16, 1819, as calls for reform reached a crescendo, a crowd of sixty thousand took to St. Peter's Fields, outside of the booming manufacturing city of Manchester, to demand an overhaul of Parliament. Beyond any of the demonstrators' specific requests, it was the sheer scale of the meeting that terrified Britain's leaders. This moment marked the beginning of modern mass politics in Britain. Local magistrates literally called in the cavalry, and saber-wielding soldiers on horseback dispersed the crowd, impaling and trampling innocent men, women, and children. Eleven people died, and hundreds were injured.

The antiestablishment press labeled the debacle at St. Peter's Fields "Peterloo," a play on Waterloo. But unlike Britain's greatest military triumph, this massacre was denounced as Britain's greatest shame. And yet the government doubled down on repression, requiring gatherings of more than fifty people to obtain approval from local magistrates and scrapping the "newspaper" loophole that had allowed seditious opinions to circulate. In the short run, Peterloo was a setback for the reform movement. But in a familiar pattern, many of its goals were eventually met—in this case, after just fifteen years. The reforms enacted were a credit to Britain's political system. While messy and ad-hoc, in the end it was responsive to voices from below.

REFORM TO STOP REVOLUTION

The death of King George IV in 1830 brought two elections in rapid succession, the second resulting in a landslide victory for the reform-minded Whig Party. A new era seemed to lie on the horizon. But when the overwhelming majority in the House of Commons passed a bill to overhaul Britain's electoral system, the upper chamber of Parliament, the House of Lords, rejected it out of hand. Representing the landed elites who were uncomfortable with rapid industrialization and the changes it wrought, the House of Lords would block reform for the next century.

With the parliamentary path to progress thwarted, a surge of popular unrest swept the country. Violence exploded across Britain's major cities, with rioters razing to the ground lords' and bishops' houses in an outpouring of anger against the landowning elite. Pro-reform fury combined with a second wave of Luddite unrest in the "Swing Riots" of 1830, a countrywide movement that destroyed threshing machines, a symbol of agricultural industrialization that farmhands felt threatened their jobs. Like the original Luddites, these protesters were not really as anti-technology as they were later portrayed to be; they mostly wanted better working conditions and more rights. This time around, their demands were again met with harsh repression. Britain seemed to be tearing itself apart at the seams—but the Lords stood firm. There would be no reform.

Thomas Babington Macaulay, a Whig politician and one of the most eloquent reformists, championed the rights of the newly numerous urban dwellers shut out from power in an impassioned and foreboding 1831 speech to the House of Commons. "Unhappily, while the natural growth of society went on, the artificial polity continued unchanged," he said. "Then came that pressure almost to bursting . . . the new people under the old institutions." Macaulay situated the struggle for the franchise within the sweep of history:

> All history is full of revolutions, produced by causes similar to those which are now operating in England. A portion of the community which had been of no account expands and becomes strong. It demands a place in the system, suited, not to its former weakness, but to its present power. If this is granted, all is well. If this is refused, then comes the struggle between the young energy of one class, and the ancient privileges of another.

He warned of past examples: in Rome, the plebeians' clash with the patricians, which led to civil war, the fall of the Republic, and the rise of the Caesars; in America, the colonists' war to cast off British rule; and in France, the repressed Third Estate's overthrow of the monarchy. From this history Macaulay drew the inescapable lesson: "Reform, that you may preserve."

Swayed by calls like these, the newly crowned William IV broke the impasse. Fearing more violence in the streets, and with the Whig leadership warning of French-style revolution, the king chose reform. The king reluctantly agreed to pack the House of Lords by using his royal authority to create fifty new peerages overnight, so that they could ram through the reform bill. The Lords were horrified at the idea of serving alongside upstart newcomers, and so they caved, letting the reform bill pass after two years of standoff. Though the House of Lords would stay unpacked and remain an obstacle to reform well in the future, mass democracy was coming to Britain, step by step.

It would be a long road. The actual terms of the Great Reform Act of 1832 were relatively modest. Most rotten boroughs were abolished, including the notorious Old Sarum. The smallest rural districts lost members of parliament, while previously unrepresented industrial towns gained them. The franchise was expanded modestly, to cover roughly 20 percent of England's adult male population (and a lesser proportion in Scotland and Ireland). Property requirements to vote remained, though they were reduced. There was still no secret ballot, with many rural electors continuing to cast their votes under the watchful eyes of local landlords.

To the more radical of the reformers, the provisions of the "Great" Reform Act were mere scraps thrown from the master's table. So just six years later, a group of parliamentarians and activists published the People's Charter, a manifesto calling for universal male suffrage, the secret ballot, the end of property requirements to serve in Parliament, and further rationalization of parliamentary districts. The Chartists, as these reformers were known, were thwarted in their efforts at the time, often violently. It would take almost a hundred years—until the end of World War I—for their demands to be fully met. But Britain's working class had found its voice.

Even as the Chartists looked ahead to universal democracy, powerful forces in Britain still looked back. A quirk of architectural history provides a fitting coda to the Great Reform Act. In 1834, two years after the bill passed, the Palace of Westminster, which housed Parliament, burned to the ground. An aghast duchess wrote of "the physical edifice crumbling along with the political edifice!" A debate began about its replacement. King William IV offered up Buckingham Palace, which he detested. Others suggested a neoclassical building, with columns and pediments evoking ancient Rome and Greece, but that style was in vogue in the United States and thus associated with the Americans' recent rebellion and republican form of government. Instead, from the old building's ashes rose the Gothic Revival structure we know today—a conscious effort to evoke a purer, more Christian Britain. So while Parliament began to reform itself for the modern era of mass democracy, it still cloaked itself in an imagined, nostalgic medieval past. And yet anchoring the complex was Big Ben, designed to be the most accurate clock in the world. This made the building not simply majestic but utilitarian, too, an embodiment of the industrial era's emphasis on efficiency and technological advancement. Progress and backlash, all mixed together.

FULL STOMACHS, NO REVOLUTION

Britain, in the throes of its Industrial Revolution, almost completely avoided the unrest that gripped the rest of Europe in 1848. How? The most common answer: reform and roast beef.

Through contentious battles over working conditions, electoral reform, rights for Catholics and Jews, and free trade, Britain had gradually updated its ossified and oligarchic politics. Equally important for defusing any revolution were high living standards. As early as the French Revolution, when Britain's industrialization was still just revving up, the Brits were famously well fed. After mobs rose up in Paris, patriotic British caricatures depicted the stereotypical

Englishman as a rotund, red-cheeked, beef-eating product of Britain's thriving middle class, complaining (as always) about "damn'd taxes." The French, meanwhile, appeared as pathetic, skeletal figures, none the better for whatever liberty they may have enjoyed on paper. While this was a gross exaggeration, Britons really did enjoy a higher standard of living. Cobbett, the radical printer, bemoaned the relative contentment of the British working class: "I defy you to agitate a fellow with a full stomache."

Widespread consumerism almost certainly helped suppress revolutionary tendencies among British workers. Like the 1950s middle-class American too busy buying a car or watching television to bother with communism, most Brits a century earlier were too busy enjoying their coal stoves and reading "penny dreadfuls" to pick up the pitchfork. And they weren't just getting richer through their labor: By the turn of the nineteenth century, this "nation of shopkeepers" had also become a nation of investors. About three hundred thousand

French Liberty, British Slavery.

people owned British government bonds, creating a broad stratum of British society with a vested interest in the national government's success. No wonder one prominent Chartist, a few years before the 1848 upheaval, cautioned Engels, "A revolution in this country would be a vain and foolish project."

To this traditional story, one must add some other factors that also snuffed out the revolutionary flame. As the historian Miles Taylor has demonstrated, Britain's far-flung empire helped the country enormously, mostly by giving it access to low-priced commodities. Colonies also offered distant locales where agitators could be exiled, although the practice backfired in Australia and the Cape Colony, where the arrival of radicals sparked new crises.

There was also repression closer to home. In 1848, the Whig government in Britain used thousands of policemen to disperse Chartist protests in London, along with 150,000 special constables as backup. Parliament also passed the controversial 1848 Alien Act, which targeted French and Irish migrants with the threat of deportation for antigovernment activism. So the story of British exceptionalism holds, but the entirely flattering version gives way to a more nuanced one.

LAISSEZ-FAIRE LEFT, ANTI-MARKET RIGHT

The most important political consequence of the Industrial Revolution was its scrambling of Britain's traditional left-right divide, leading the two sides to switch policies. When industrialization dawned, the Tories stood as the party of aristocratic privilege, rural protectionism, and benevolent welfare. They were skeptical of the heedless growth of modern capitalism and sought to preserve the world of village life against the disruptions of the market. The Whigs, for their part, began as the party of modernity, supporting free trade, merchants, and industrialization. When it came to welfare, they, like the modern free-market right, opposed handouts and thought the poor should be put to work.

Nothing better highlights the Whigs' laissez-faire flavor of reform than the New Poor Law. Fresh from their victory with the Great Reform Act of 1832, they instituted what we might call the end of welfare as they knew it. The Old Poor Law, a social safety net developed under Queen Elizabeth, was still on the books. It was a crude but effective system of dispensing funds to the needy, parish by parish. Rarely did aid recipients have to enter an institution that would change their behavior. In the spirit of Christian charity, the system was designed to alleviate grinding rural poverty (and, less charitably, to prevent public begging). Conservatives had long supported it. They felt that society owed help to struggling people, and that the Old Poor Law preserved the traditional order.

But progress-minded, market-oriented Whigs believed this welfare system hampered efficiency and economic growth. It incentivized indolence. The Whigs were already dismantling other vestiges of the Elizabethan economic system, such as apprenticeship laws, which restricted certain trades to guild members until 1814. In the same spirit of rationalization, the Whig-dominated Parliament passed the New Poor Law of 1834, eliminating the scattered system of village-based welfare. Instead, paupers were now sent to urban workhouses, prison-like facilities that served to both punish and rehabilitate their residents. Ideally, they would learn skills and have a work ethic drilled into them, all in an environment so unpleasant that people would want to leave quickly and find jobs. Charles Dickens famously depicted these nightmarish conditions in *Oliver Twist*.

The two parties' differing treatment of the poor was indicative of the broader political divide in the early nineteenth century, with the Whigs championing industrialization and the Tories chafing at it. The latter's cultural suspicion of capitalism drew its roots from Christianity, with its many warnings about the love of money being "the root of all evil." In the view of the conservative essayist Thomas Carlyle, the industrial world—with its cold rationality, heartless self-interest, and unshakable faith in progress—was hardly worth living in. The universe, he wrote in 1831, "was one huge, dead, immeasurable Steam-engine, rolling on, in its dead indifference, to grind me limb from limb."

The Victorian cultural critic John Ruskin likewise lamented the "mechanization" of labor, which he felt morally degraded workers through mindless, repetitive exertion. Ruskin explicitly attacked Adam Smith's vision of capitalism. Where Smith in *The Wealth of Nations* celebrated the division of labor in the making of the pin, with tasks efficiently separated into ever-simpler steps, Ruskin used the same example to underscore the evils of the new economy. "It is not, truly speaking, the labor that is divided," he wrote, "but the men," who were diminished to the point where "all the little piece of intelligence that is left in a man is not enough to make a pin." Artisans of past eras were craftsmen with freedom and creativity, like the stonemasons working on Gothic cathedrals who delighted in their individual craft and imagination. The industrial worker was reduced to a mere cog. Ruskin's work is one among an entire genre of jeremiads attacking the dehumanization of industrial Victorian society, a powerful strain of nostalgic, anti-capitalist conservatism.

At the start of the Industrial Revolution, the difference between the two parties seemed clear: the Whigs, somewhat on the left, stood for urban industry and all the change it brought, while the Tories, on the right, championed agriculture and traditional ways. But a battle over trade policy would shake up the old Whig-Tory divide.

THE FREE TRADE DIVIDE

Parliament had long regulated the importation of grain, or corn as it was often called at the time. In 1815, it passed a new Corn Law to shore up British farming, which was facing competition from abroad. The act placed such punishing tariffs on foreign grain that it effectively prohibited importing it, in order to prop up the price of domestic grain. At a time of rapid urbanization, this measure was a transparent handout to the large landowners who made up the Tory base—at the expense of the urbanites who made up the Whig base and had to pay more for food.

In the cities, the Corn Law was denounced as a scourge. Workers raged at high food prices; bosses fretted about the need to raise wages to match the cost of bread. They joined forces in the Anti-Corn Law League, a nationwide campaign of petitions and agitation to pressure Parliament into action. In 1846, their efforts bore fruit. The Conservative prime minister, Sir Robert Peel, bowed to pressure and pushed to repeal the Corn Law. Almost all Whigs supported him, while only a third of Tories did. It was enough to pass the repeal, thus inaugurating the era of Britain as a champion of free trade—but at the cost of splitting the Tory Party and bringing Peel down. Britain's political coalitions were beginning to fracture.

The dispute over the Corn Law caused the parties to realign in ways we would recognize today. Peel's downfall swept the Whigs into power. But their ascent quickly revealed the fissures within their party, between the champions of economic progress and the defenders of workers' dignity. Some Whigs had voted to repeal the Corn Law because they were true believers in self-regulating free markets. (The consequences of this pure laissez-faire ideology were laid bare during the Irish Potato Famine, when food continued to be exported to foreign markets even as the Irish starved by the millions.) But many Whigs preferred free trade not out of a belief in abstract economic theories but for the tangible benefits it bestowed on the working man. Later researchers would confirm: the repeal of the Corn Law helped the bottom 90 percent of British wage earners at the expense of the top 10 percent. In the case of the Corn Law, laissez-faire economics and workers' rights went hand in hand. But more often, the two were in tension. And so the Whigs began to question whether unfettered economic freedom was tenable in an industrial society, or whether it would lead to chaos as atomized individuals were ground down by the gears of markets and mechanization. They began showing more concern for the plight of the poor and called for greater regulation and more generous, less conditional welfare.

Among Tories, the repeal of the Corn Law split the party for decades, and set in motion soul-searching. Free trade had broken the economic power of the rural elite, whose agricultural goods sold at much lower prices. Never again would landowners have such a strong sway over British life. From 1809 to 1879, some 88 percent of British millionaires (in inflation-adjusted pounds sterling) were rural land-owners, members of the class that had long dominated Parliament. But from 1880 to 1914, only a third of millionaires came from landed wealth. The Tories took notice.

Rather than sneering at the new-money elites produced by the Industrial Revolution, the Right came to view factory bosses and financiers as allies against social upheaval and strikes by the lower orders. Wealthy industrial businessmen snapped up rural estates—and married aristocratic wives—to gain entry to British high society. This party reversal was a watershed in industrialization's transformation of politics. Rather than protect rural life against the inroads of modernity, the Tories—who had rebranded themselves the Conservatives, although they still went by their old name colloquially—transformed into champions of laissez-faire capitalism, with all its disruption. Meanwhile, the Whigs, evolving into a party calling themselves Liberals, grew increasingly divided over the contradictions between industrial economic growth and working conditions. The uneasy coalition between urban bosses and workers would fray and then snap altogether. Liberals would switch from being uncritical champions of the Industrial Revolution into the social-democratic, big-government Left that created large welfare states throughout the twentieth century.

An iconic scene in George Eliot's novel *Middlemarch* captured this transformation of Britain's political life. A group of tenant farmers, suspicious of a new railroad coming to their corner of England and emboldened "after swallowing their mid-day beer," attack a group of company agents scoping out the route. The rural ruffians don't have a revolutionary bone in their bodies, but they oppose railroads and all they represent, convinced they will be "good for the big folks to make

money out on . . . They'll on'y leave the poor mon furder behind."
Fred Vincy, a young gentleman, rides to the rescue of the railway
surveyors, fending off the pitchfork-wielding farmers with his whip.
In an earlier time, the local landowner might have been expected to
share his tenants' skepticism of urban businessmen and their novel
technology. But now, he takes the side of inevitable progress instead.
The rural gentry had made their peace with new money.

After Britain's political realignment, the arguments increasingly
employed by the left against capitalism mirrored those that had long
been wielded by conservatives when *they* were the ones suspicious of
the market. In 1928, by which point those divisions had crystallized,
George Bernard Shaw nicely captured the sentiment on the left. The
renowned Irish playwright was equally famous as a leftist ideologue,
and he wrote a runaway bestseller, *An Intelligent Woman's Guide to
Socialism and Capitalism*. In it, to describe the soul-crushing effect of
market capitalism, Shaw used the same example from Adam Smith,
the making of a pin, that John Ruskin had critiqued. Shaw also
quoted that haunting poem by Oliver Goldsmith; now it was the left's
turn to lament a world where "wealth accumulates, and men decay."
The right, for its part, began to celebrate the very forces it had long
decried, championing capitalism as its ranks swelled with those who
owed their newfound wealth to free markets. Industry was producing
a new aristocracy, one not built on inherited land but still able to play
a role in maintaining social order and stability.

CRYSTAL PALACE OR PANOPTICON?

The utilitarian philosopher John Stuart Mill started out as a free-
market enthusiast before turning into a skeptic and then an outright
opponent—making the same journey the broader left did. Mill came
of age during the high noon of the Industrial Revolution and mirrored the optimism that accompanied it. But as he matured, his sunny
outlook faded into despair.

In 1851, Britain seemed on top of the world. London proudly

hosted the Great Exhibition of the Works of Industry of All Nations, a showcase for British industrial genius and manufacturing might. Its centerpiece was the Crystal Palace, a vast transparent convention hall with high steel beams and the most glass that had ever been used in a single structure. For liberals and optimists, the Crystal Palace was modernity itself: light and airy, soaring to the heavens, promising transparency and openness in the industrial age. To pessimists, it embodied the false illusions of the industrial, hyper-individualistic modern age. The curmudgeonly protagonist of Fyodor Dostoevsky's "Notes from Underground," for one, considered the building hopelessly utopian. But most attendees were giddy with the promise of progress.

Mill's lifetime, which spanned from 1806 to 1873, was bookended by milestones in the Industrial Revolution and Britain's democratic evolution. When he was born, the adoption of steam power was accelerating, and he came of age with the opening of the first railroads in the 1830s and the 1832 Great Reform Act. The Whigs of that era embraced liberal openness in all its forms—including not just the abolition of slavery and the expansion of voting rights but also laissez-faire capitalism and the promotion of science and technology. By the time he died, discontent with industrialization's consequences was spreading, and the labor movement was gaining momentum. The meaning of liberalism itself had changed. The left had kept its social progressivism but abandoned its enthusiasm for unfettered industrialization.

Mill's own life was a grand experiment in liberal rationalism. His father, a Scottish-born historian, raised him with the goal of creating the greatest genius in world history, steeping him in philosophy from an early age. Mill started learning ancient Greek at age three and Latin at age eight, and by twelve had absorbed most of the classical canon. In his teens, he went for long walks with David Ricardo, the liberal theorist of free trade and comparative advantage. Mill's intellectual godfather—the Socrates to his Plato—was Jeremy Bentham, the founder of utilitarianism and in some ways the core thinker of the liberal politics that dominated during the Industrial Revolution. The young Mill learned at Bentham's feet, absorbing the maxim that the highest goal of life is promoting "the greatest happiness of the greatest number." Mill spent endless hours hobnobbing in London and Paris with his father's social set of famous philosophers, activists, scientists, and politicians. While this pressure-cooker atmosphere undeniably made Mill a high achiever, it also drove him into a depressive spiral. At age twenty, the young prodigy had a mental breakdown and even contemplated suicide. Mill emerged on the other side determined to break free from his father's strict upbringing and Bentham's long shadow. He sought out a greater connection to human emotion in the Romantic poetry of William Wordsworth and Samuel Coleridge.

It is perhaps no wonder that Mill chafed at an upbringing of unadulterated utilitarianism. There was a disturbingly mechanistic, unfeeling side to Bentham's philosophy. Perhaps the most enduring, and unsettling, of Bentham's thought experiments was the panopticon. A design for a prison, this dystopian structure was the dark mirror of the Crystal Palace. The blueprints envisioned a perfectly round building, with individual cells ringing an inner core where the guards would stand watch, monitoring the prisoners through peepholes. The overseers could supervise the behavior of the inmates, but the inmates could not see one another—or know when they were being watched.

It was a vision of maximal efficiency and order, with no privacy and no escape from work under the gaze of an all-seeing eye— utilitarianism infused with the cruelty of the New Poor Law's workhouses. As writers like Michel Foucault later pointed out, the panopticon achieved a new kind of total control in which the prisoner knew that his every move might be watched and thus internalized his captivity. It was a forerunner of techno-totalitarianism, the telescreens of *1984*, and the all-too-real wiretapping of the Stasi or KGB—or the facial-recognition cameras of modern-day China. With industrialization roaring in the late Victorian era, it was entirely unclear what kind of civilization the glittering new technologies would produce. A world of openness, free trade, human ingenuity, and universal prosperity—a giant Crystal Palace? Or a global panopticon, a closed,

ABOVE: *The Interior of the Crystal Palace.*

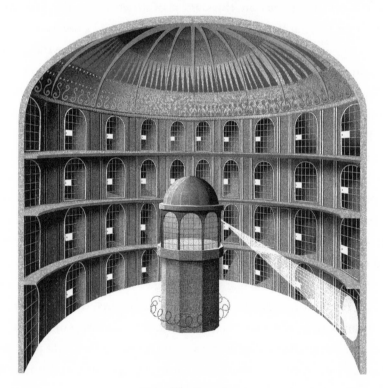

RIGHT: *The Panopticon.*

paranoid world of constant surveillance, hyper-efficient policing, and machine-like regimentation?

As Mill's thought developed, he broke with Benthamite orthodoxy by calling for the empowerment of workers. In his later years, Mill's works on political economy charted a path away from a society that abandoned the poor and vulnerable to one that protected them. That path took British liberalism away from laissez-faire and workhouses, toward labor unions and regulations, and ultimately toward the safety net endorsed by the Labour Party, which fully took up the Liberals' mantle as the UK's main left-wing party.

NEW POLITICS, OLD WOUNDS

Even as technological progress opened up new vistas, the undertow of older identity politics remained strong. Britain was no exception. As the country industrialized and modernized, the long-running conflict between Protestants and Catholics remained toxic. I touched on this issue earlier, but the full history goes back further and centers on Ireland, which had been conquered and colonized by Britain. Without delving into all the details, suffice it to say Catholics were long subjugated in Ireland, stripped of land and reduced to the status of tenant farmers, while in Britain they had to pay an extra tax and were forbidden to attend the best universities or serve in Parliament. The "Irish Question" was an ongoing wedge issue that many politicians, especially Conservatives, used to stoke anti-Catholic populism—the identity politics of its day.

As the common men of Britain demanded political rights in the early nineteenth century, so did Catholics specifically. In 1800, Parliament created the United Kingdom of Great Britain and Ireland, merging the Irish Parliament into the national Parliament in London. The Irish could now elect representatives to Westminster, but Catholics—the vast majority of the island's population—were prohibited from serving. Agitation over this issue led the Conservative government to pass a law in 1829 allowing Catholics to hold all but the highest public offices. But some Conservatives felt betrayed by the reform and pushed the party to become a more explicitly Protestant party. The Whigs (and then Liberals) at first benefited from disarray on the right—just as Republicans in the US benefited when the civil rights movement divided Democrats in the twentieth century.

This version of identity politics would come to destroy the greatest Liberal politician of the nineteenth century, William Gladstone. First elected prime minister in 1868, he hoped to stabilize Ireland by improving the rights of tenant farmers and eliminating the Anglican Church's status as the official church in Ireland. (This effort was part of a broader movement to "disestablish" the Anglican Church as the UK's state church, which met with opposition and birthed the comically long word "antidisestablishmentarianism.") Gladstone's fellow Liberals could agree to that limited reform. But when he went further and championed the idea of giving Ireland a measure of self-government, or "Home Rule," the issue cracked the party. "Unionists" in the Liberal Party wanted Ireland firmly under the thumb of London. The Tories welcomed these defectors, ushering in a two-decade period of Conservative dominance. Ultimately, Britain failed to grant Home Rule in time to placate Ireland, and in 1919, the Irish launched their war of independence.

It is tempting to believe that good things go together, that economic growth leads to political harmony. But in Britain's case, older sectarian divisions served to stoke populism even after centuries of industrial transformation. Then and now, technological progress did not make identity politics fade—indeed, it had the opposite effect. Having lost land and inheritance as the defining elements of conservatism, many Britons attached themselves to religion and empire. British workers buffeted by destabilizing forces were easy prey for scapegoating arguments that cheap Irish labor was undercutting their wages—the nineteenth-century version of the trope that Mexico and China are stealing Americans' jobs.

BRITANNIA TRIUMPHANT

"Self-satisfaction," remarked the historian Charles R. Morris, "is a dangerous sentiment for any competitor but may be understandable in the British case." Morris was writing about the years after Napoleon's fall. With France vanquished, Britain became the "hyperpower" of its time, not unlike the United States after the Cold War. It devoted only 2 to 3 percent of its gross national product to military spending and, on a strictly military level, was at most first among equals in Europe. But because it had financed the victorious side, Britain was the crucial player at the Congress of Vienna that organized European geopolitics after Napoleon's defeat. And Britain dominated the seas and much of the non-European world. The heyday of British industrialization was also the apex of the British Empire.

Britain's economic and technological prowess made itself felt in the geopolitical arena. The Royal Navy, the world's largest and most advanced fleet, secured truly global supply chains. Undersea telegraph cables, the first high-speed global communications system, linked Britain's colonies. The empire had grown greatly by the end of Victoria's reign, adding African territories that had been impossible to conquer before the advent of machine guns (to quickly crush non-European armies) and modern medicine (to protect against malaria and other tropical diseases). At the empire's height, it covered one-quarter of the Earth's surface, and one-quarter of humanity lived under British rule.

Imperialism was no doubt profitable to British industry. England did ban the import of cotton textiles from India in the early eighteenth century to protect its handloom weavers from cheaper and higher-quality Indian goods. But it was the invention of the spinning jenny, the water frame, and other such devices that made British textiles dominant. The historian John Darwin estimates that in the mid-nineteenth century, across British territories and informal empires such as in Latin America, industrially produced textiles were some *two hundred times* cheaper than the locally woven alternatives, making it impossible for indigenous weavers to compete. As the economists Mark Koyama and Jared Rubin have argued, the massive increase in incomes set in motion by the Industrial Revolution did not necessarily depend on the exploitation of non-European peoples.

Eighteenth-century Russia snapped up vast new territories in central Asia and Siberia, while Qing dynasty China absorbed what is now Xinjiang and Tibet—without experiencing any noticeable improvement in their economic growth. Conquest and industrialization do not always go hand in hand.

Yet at the peak of the British Empire's territorial extent, between World Wars I and II, the empire really did seem indispensable for Britain's prosperity. Even many left-wing thinkers agreed. Take the writer George Orwell:

> *The high standard of life we enjoy in England depends upon our keeping a tight hold on the Empire, particularly the tropical portions of it such as India and Africa. Under the capitalist system, in order that England may live in comparative comfort, a hundred million Indians must live on the verge of starvation—an evil state of affairs, but you acquiesce in it every time you step into a taxi or eat a plate of strawberries and cream. The alternative is to throw the Empire overboard and reduce England to a cold and unimportant little island where we should all have to work very hard and live mainly on herrings and potatoes.*

But in the decades after 1945, as Britain was shorn of its colonies, one by one, its economy grew *faster* than before. Post-imperial Britain had its problems, from strikes to stagnation. But "herrings and potatoes" it was not.

Britain had prospered mightily through the industrial era and, in large part as a consequence, won a global empire. The benefits of the empire are much debated. It brought vast resources and labor under British control, but it also consumed British statesmen and required massive expenditures to conquer and defend. As new economic competitors caught up economically, Britain found itself with growing overseas commitments and declining capacity to fund them—imperial overstretch. It would not be far off to call Britain the "world policeman" of the nineteenth century. The historian Paul Kennedy tallies up the many concerns consuming the country in 1895 alone:

> *The Cabinet found itself worrying about the possible breakup of China following the Sino-Japanese War, about the collapse of the Ottoman Empire as a result of the Armenian crisis, about the looming clash with Germany over southern Africa at almost exactly the same time as the quarrel with the United States over the Venezuela-British Guiana borders, about French military expeditions in equatorial Africa, and about a Russian drive toward the Hindu Kush.*

Meanwhile, other nations were jealous of Britain's empire and wanted their own place in the Sun. The greatest worry became something much closer to home: the rise of Germany. But Britain's strongest competitor actually turned out to be its one-time colony, cultural offshoot, and soon-to-be ally, the United States of America. And American power was rooted in its own industrial revolution that echoed many of the themes in Britain's march to modernity. But its political realignment took a bloodier and distinctly American path.

THE REAL AMERICAN REVOLUTION

Industrial United States

T HE AMERICAN REVOLUTION WAS CURIOUSLY UNREV-
olutionary. In a sense it was not even a *revolution*—that is, a
comprehensive social, economic, and political transformation—but
rather a struggle for national independence. True, the politics of the
country changed, with a monarchy being cast off in favor of a republican form of government. But the economic and social structures of
American society stayed largely intact after 1776. Plantation owners
continued to rule the South. Even up north, the "gentlemen revolutionaries" violently suppressed efforts to promote radical change—for
example, crushing Shays' Rebellion, an anti-tax revolt in Massachusetts. Before and after the Declaration of Independence, the individual
states retained much of the autonomy they had enjoyed as colonies.
Slavery endured. Women remained second-class citizens. Indigenous
people continued to lose territory as the ex-colonists moved ever more
aggressively into Native lands.

The American Revolution did emphasize liberty and equality,
but the United States' distinctive egalitarian culture (at least for free,
white men) was nothing new. That sensibility had existed since the
first colonists arrived in North America and was more a product of
the wide-open western frontier than a consequence of the American
Revolution. The task of trying to survive in the wilderness and seize

land from indigenous peoples fostered a spirit of cooperation. Plentiful land also allowed for a high degree of economic equality among whites. In 1774, the American colonies had greater income equality than their mother country, even when enslaved people are included in the calculations. Most crucially, at least in the North, there was no European-style manorial system of great estates and aristocratic privilege that had to be dismantled. America did not need a great social revolution to overcome feudalism; it simply never imported these relics of the Old World in the first place. This is what Tocqueville meant when he said that Americans "arrived at a state of democracy without having to endure a democratic revolution," and were "born equal, instead of *becoming* so."

Much of the American Revolution's spirit—against monarchies, in favor of individual rights derived from God and reason—may have been new and radical, but the basic political and social structure of society remained remarkably stable. Two of the greatest historians of the American Revolution, Edmund Morgan and Bernard Bailyn, argued that the revolutionaries were actually demanding a restoration of the rights that they had enjoyed as Englishmen before Parliament abrogated them. The political scientist Samuel Huntington argued that the American Revolution in essence extended a preexisting "Tudor polity," a weak and decentralized system whose councils, legislatures, and legal formulas the early colonists brought with them from seventeenth-century England. Even today, America's unusual system—which divides powers between different branches of government and different levels of government—bears the hallmarks of that Tudor system.

Socially, the American Revolution served more to reaffirm than subvert existing hierarchies. According to Bailyn, the American revolutionaries sought not to eradicate social or economic inequities but to "purify a corrupt constitution and fight off the apparent growth of prerogative power." After the Crown and Parliament had encroached too far, the revolutionaries pursued the narrow goal of severing this external connection. Far from trying to radically transform society like the French would do shortly, the American revolutionaries were trying to preserve it from forces they viewed as arbitrary and despotic.

But the United States would eventually get a real revolution. Once it reached American shores, the Industrial Revolution utterly remade American society, changing not only the forces of production but also basic relationships among people. Innovations in transportation, manufacturing, and communication reshaped daily life. The nation urbanized rapidly, the locus of work moved outside the home, and civic associations based on new identities sprang up. Regional disparities widened as locations with factories leaped forward. America's Industrial Revolution, which had proceeded in fits and starts since before the Founding, truly took off after the 1860s and also coincided with the biggest change in the young country's history: the end of slavery. And while it was not a direct cause, it is fair to say that industrialization massively shifted economic and technological power to the North, giving the Union an edge in the Civil War. Subsequent industrialization redefined political coalitions in the United States, creating the left-right divide we know today.

When one of the first railroad tracks was laid in the United States on July 4, 1828, the honor of breaking ground belonged to the only surviving signatory of the Declaration of Independence. Charles Carroll, age ninety-one, proclaimed, "I consider this among the most important acts of my life, second only to my signing the Declaration of Independence, if even it be second to that." For those few who had lived through both the American Revolution and the first stirrings of industrialization, it was genuinely unclear which event was more momentous. In the 2020s, with two centuries of hindsight, we can now say definitively: the Industrial Revolution changed American society more than the American Revolution did.

EAGLE ON THE HORIZON

How did America come to industrialize? In large part, it piggy-backed on British success. More accurately, it stole British intellectual property. In the late eighteenth and early nineteenth century, American factory owners tried mightily to lure British factory workers and managers across the Atlantic to reveal their techniques—so much so that the British (like the Dutch before them) put in place strict controls on the export of ideas and even restricted the emigration of trained industrial professionals. Charles Dickens raged as pirated copies of his works far outpaced legitimate sales in America, an experience that soured him on the country for decades. In 1791, the US government paid $48 to an English weaver to bring spinning technology to America, the first instance of state-backed manufacturing espionage that helped plant the seeds of infant industry. Twenty years later, American manufacturing would truly take off once Francis Cabot Lowell, a Massachusetts businessman, toured textile factories in Britain, memorized their designs, and set up the first modern cotton mills in the US. British industry was still the envy of the world, but it incubated inventions that could be deployed and refined by the entrepreneurs in the expanding United States. To shield the country's infant industries, meanwhile, the US government levied high tariffs on imports.

Starting in the nineteenth century, American inventors began to outpace their British counterparts, a sign of America's growing industrial potential. As early as 1807, Robert Fulton made history by operating the world's first commercially successful steamboat, carrying passengers up and down the Hudson River, making a sixty-two-hour journey from New York City to Albany and back. Even though the steamboat was first developed across the Atlantic, it was marketed and deployed widely across America's snaking waterways. Soon US inventors began churning out innovations in their own right. In 1844, Samuel Morse sent the first-ever long-distance telegraph message from the basement of the US Capitol ("What hath God wrought"), and two years later, in Cambridge, Massachusetts, Elias Howe received a patent for the first modern sewing machine—both marked improvements on older English ideas.

When the Civil War broke out, President Abraham Lincoln took advantage of the absence of Southern representation in Washington to bring forth not only a "new birth of freedom" but also a new birth of infrastructure spending. Lincoln had entered politics as a Whig, a faction inspired by Britain's own Whigs. Like its namesake across the pond, Lincoln's original party had championed government investment in infrastructure. A young Lincoln once expressed his ambition to follow in the footsteps of the New York governor, DeWitt Clinton, who had built the Erie Canal, and he later worked as a railroad lawyer. As president, he oversaw major federal spending to construct a transcontinental railroad, which was completed in 1869, four years after his assassination. Ultimately, Lincoln's investment in infrastructure—paired with rich natural resources from newly settled territories in the West and abundant labor from a wave of mass immigration—allowed the United States to modernize rapidly and become a global industrial leader. (In many ways, the Civil War, like other wars, accelerated technological development.)

America's Gilded Age—the late-nineteenth-century period of massive wealth creation—coincided with the height of Britain's Victorian era. The United States, knitting itself back together after the Civil War, soon became a greater industrial colossus than Britain itself. As prodigious as British manufacturing had been, US industry would come to dwarf it. By the mid-1880s, America surpassed Britain in iron and steel production. And US industrial strength kept growing. The manufacturing output of the United States in 1929 was twenty-eight times higher than it was in 1859, and US GDP overtook British GDP in 1916. For 135 years from the American Revolution to the eve of World War I, annual growth in the United States averaged an astonishing 3.9 percent—a feat unequaled in its endurance even by China and India, the growth engines of today.

In a sign of how industrial innovation was shifting across the Atlantic, by the 1860s most British homes were equipped with clocks manufactured in the United States. These American-made timepieces were so cheap that the British government accused the United States, not without reason, of "dumping"—illegally flooding the country with goods priced well below the market rate to undercut British producers—and began seizing the contraband. Dumping, intellectual property theft, abundant coal, and cheap labor were key ingredients in the growth of US industry in the late-nineteenth century—just as they have been for Chinese industry in the twenty-first century.

As seedy as the origins of America's Industrial Revolution may have been, there was no stopping the spread of ideas, inventions, and talent across the Atlantic to a hungry and eager country ready to deploy them at scale. By the end of the Civil War, the United States had built something genuinely new. The economic historian Brad DeLong explains that after 1870, innovation began to take on a novel, accelerated form in western Europe and North America. "The North Atlantic economies had invented invention," he writes. "They had invented not just textile machinery and railroads, but also the industrial research lab and the forms of bureaucracy that gave rise to the large corporation." Nowhere was this truer than in the United States, where the economy, fueled by these technological advancements, soared to new heights.

AMERICA TRANSFORMED

The bulk of America's economic growth was concentrated in its cities, which took off during this period. The share of Americans living in urban areas surged from 25 percent in 1870 to double that just fifty years later, with 1920 marking the first recorded year in which more Americans lived in cities than in the countryside. The poetry of Walt Whitman encapsulated the complexities of America's transformation. As Whitman himself moved into the city, he entered a new world: "Thrive, cities," he wrote in "Crossing Brooklyn Ferry," "bring your freight, bring your shows, ample and sufficient rivers." He celebrated the birth of industry: "Burn high your fires, foundry chimneys!" But Whitman also lamented industrialization's inequality and disruption, writing just four years later in another poem, "I sit and look out upon all the sorrows of the world, and upon all oppression and shame." His words reflect the exuberance and anxiety of modern America in its adolescence—at once optimistic and skeptical.

New York, already America's largest city by 1860, saw its population grow from around 600,000 in 1850 to 3.5 million in 1900. Much of this expansion came from the huge influx of European immigrants, who not only changed the city's density but also its culture. Many of these newcomers settled in distinct ethnic neighborhoods in New York and other cities in the industrial northeast, where they started businesses, built churches and synagogues, and joined social clubs. They formed trade unions and political organizations, the most famous of which was New York's Tammany Hall, the political machine that drew its strength from immigrant voters—especially the Irish—and maintained vast influence over the city's politics well into the twentieth century. This new wave of immigration turned America into a much more modern and diverse nation, as the arrivals tried to preserve their Old-World cultural identities while becoming American.

Rapid urban growth was not restricted to the Eastern Seaboard. In fact, it was Chicago that shot up the most in population in the late nineteenth century, establishing itself as a transportation hub. On May 10, 1869, when Leland Stanford hammered a symbolic golden spike into the ground at Promontory Summit, Utah, a transcontinental railroad at last united the eastern and western halves of the United States. As the logical midpoint between the vast, interconnected nation, Chicago served as a nexus between western raw materials and the eastern industrial machine that fed on them. And once the advent of the refrigerated railroad car in 1871 made industrial meat processing more tenable, most of the meat consumed by Americans ended up coming from Chicago's stockyards.

The South, meanwhile, was still recovering from the Civil War. The new wave of immigrants generally steered clear of the old Confederate states, with their sluggish economic growth and low wages (in part due to Jim Crow laws). Foreign-born people in 1870 were more than three times as numerous per capita in the North compared to the South. The South was also technologically backward, with field agriculture almost entirely unmechanized, performed by back-breaking manual labor. During the Gilded Age, a yawning gap emerged between the cities and rural areas, between North and South, between the coasts and the heartland, and between rich and poor within cities. And all these differences produced a new politics in the country.

The dramatic industrialization of the United States fueled, and was in part fueled by, the free-market ideology that reigned supreme at the time. Americans had always been suspicious of a strong state, including in economic affairs. But by the late nineteenth century, many espoused laissez-faire policies, a preference that bled into social views as well. When Edward Livingston Youmans, a champion of social Darwinism—the belief that people should be subject to the same evolutionary concepts like natural selection as plants and animals—and the founder of *Popular Science*, was asked what he would do to address social issues, he replied: "Nothing! You and I can do nothing at all. It's all a matter of evolution. We can only wait for evolution. Perhaps in four or five thousand years evolution may have carried men beyond this state of things. But we can do nothing."

It was the age of the robber barons, a time when men like John D. Rockefeller and Andrew Carnegie seized the commanding heights of the economy, consolidated power, and accumulated dazzling wealth. But the utter dominance they achieved raised the prospect of permanent monopolies. As some Americans acquired seemingly endless money and power, others could hardly make ends meet. Conditions were particularly appalling for the urban working class, famously captured in the late 1880s in "How the Other Half Lives," Jacob Riis's collection of photographs documenting Manhattan's tenements. The gross inequality that characterized the period inevitably led to backlash.

NO HOME FOR SOCIALISM

This backlash would take a somewhat different form in the United States than it did in Europe. Europe also experienced industrialization that hollowed out rural regions while swelling cities. European industrialists became fabulously wealthy, and white-collar workers emerged into an empowered bourgeois class, while European laborers suffered dangerous working and living conditions. On both sides of the Atlantic, some workers were drawn to socialism—a loose term, originally understood as collective ownership over the means of production—though the movement was far more cohesive in Europe. When Karl Marx and Friedrich Engels published *The Communist Manifesto* during the revolutionary upheaval of 1848, liberalism and nationalism were still the dominant ideologies at the time. But by the time Marx died, in 1883, socialism had become a potent political force across Europe. The ideology had first taken root in Britain. London, that nineteenth-century powerhouse of capitalism, even became home to the First International, a global network of socialists and communists that counted among its ranks Marx himself, then a little-known exiled journalist. With its strong union network and legacy of democratic political reforms, Britain was able to enact gradual social reforms—like public health mandates and regulations for safer factory conditions—that kept at bay more radical expressions of socialism. Later on, Liberals and socialists coalesced around the Labour Party, which became the dominant political party of the British Left by the early 1920s.

Working-class angst spread through continental Europe, too. By 1871, when the socialist Paris Commune briefly governed France's capital, viable socialist and democratic socialist parties had emerged across the continent. In Germany, where the recently unified nation-state leapt into industrialization, the Social Democratic Party became so powerful that it pulled society leftward, forcing Germany's conservative chancellor Otto von Bismarck in 1883 to introduce a social safety net including universal healthcare, lest his government be voted out of power. Once again, the Right learned to accept reform as the price of avoiding revolution.

By contrast, socialists in the United States in the late nineteenth century failed to band together in a powerful labor or socialist party, or even to meaningfully influence the policies of either of the two major parties. While American workers militantly resisted conditions of exploitation, their resistance took the form of factory strikes and boycotts, rarely straying into the political arena. Instead, for decade after decade in the United States, there was a bipartisan consensus on capitalism, with various political factions debating merely how open free markets should be or whether to champion the interests of financiers or farmers. The major third-party force became the Populist Party, small-scale agrarian capitalists who despised Wall Street and big business—not socialists arguing for the federal government to nationalize industries and abolish private property. Their demands were rooted in regional disparities: the economic interests of the Midwestern farming states arrayed against the economic interests of urban manufacturers and finance.

So why did the most industrialized country never produce a strong socialist contingent? For starters, America always lacked a feudal class structure. Its tradition of liberal individualism—supercharged by the heady economic boom of the industrial era—obscured the strict lines of class conflict that fed socialism. And while the plantation aristocracy in the South resembled a feudal elite, the peasants in this story were enslaved Black people, violently oppressed and excluded from wider American society. Even after slavery was outlawed, Black Americans were denied political rights, and ethnic and racial identities continued to shape political and social affiliations. These factors made lower-class unity difficult. In addition, white elites often took pains to sow divisions between Black and white members of the working class, reminding poor whites of their "higher" status and enlisting them in racial persecution.

For much of American history, politics in the country was riven by deep fault lines that existed largely outside the narrative of Left versus Right. Debates centered on federalism, with advocates of a strong central government sparring against those who wanted power to reside with the states. That Hamiltonian versus Jeffersonian debate, and all that flowed from it, consumed much of the energies of early American political life. At base, moreover, that debate was really about something else, with nearly every hot-button issue of the day— states' rights, executive overreach—in fact serving as a cover for a deeper divide over slavery. And so the United States followed its own peculiar path, until the Civil War, when slavery was abolished and the federal government was vastly strengthened. At that point, with the US economy primed for an industrial boom, American politics were remade and began to resemble the politics of Victorian Britain during its industrialization. This realignment, however, had a peculiarly American twist.

NEW IDENTITIES, NEW POLITICS

When industrialization kicked into high gear as the United States emerged from the Civil War, the Republican Party was both pro–big government and pro–big business. This combination might seem strange today, but an activist central government was in fact necessary to promote industrialization in a vast country. Industrialization in the United States would never have taken off as spectacularly as it did were it not for the large government investments in infrastructure projects, from the transcontinental railroad to the Panama Canal. Public spending at unprecedented scale was needed to break past the limits of geography and tie the sprawling republic together from Atlantic to Pacific. So the industrialists—overwhelmingly urban, Republican, and socially liberal—initially promoted a strong central government.

Meanwhile, the Democrats were wary of both industrialization and a strong state that could meddle in their local affairs. Heeding the wishes of their base of rural, socially conservative farmers, the Democrats pushed for states' rights. Particularly in the South, in the years following the Civil War, Democrats resisted centralized power, in part so that individual states could implement Jim Crow laws that enforced segregation and curbed Black voting rights.

But all of this changed once industrialization reached its peak. Politics is often the result of broader structural forces like economics and technology, and as industrialization upended existing social structures, it thrust new political considerations onto the table. "We are all peering into the future," Theodore Roosevelt wrote in 1895, "to forecast the action of the great dumb forces set in motion by the stupendous industrial revolution which has taken place in this century." Indeed, the Industrial Revolution rewrote the terms on which politics would be debated. Parties were forced to reframe their ideologies in relation to the market, differentiating more on economics than social issues, leading to a comprehensive realignment in the American political system.

Eventually, the Republicans, once the supporters of a powerful state, would become the party of laissez-faire economics, and the Democrats, once the proponents of a decentralized government, would champion a stronger state. Much like the realignment in the UK, the two major political parties in the US essentially swapped ideological visions with the advent of industrialization. While the two cases differ considerably—America never fully broke away from its particular and troubled history with race—on both sides of the Atlantic, industrialization ultimately produced a clearer split between a left-wing party and a right-wing party, divided over the modern economy and the role of the state. It is a testament to the sheer power of the Industrial Revolution that modern American politics was born during this era. The left-right split that emerged at the turn of the twentieth century would persist for well over a hundred years, only recently becoming complicated by new cleavages and forms of identity.

The political transformation that the Industrial Revolution set in motion in America would take place slowly, over the course of forty years. And similar to the way the Corn Laws sparked Britain's realignment, the American realignment also began with a dispute over farmers' interests.

CROSS OF GOLD

The backlash to industrial capitalism that fueled socialism in Europe led to the rise of populism in America. The seeds of populist discontent first emerged in the agricultural heartland and working-class industrial centers of the United States. Spurred to action by what they saw as grotesque inequality, populists railed against America's robber barons who had grown wealthy from the "hard money" gold standard system—whereby the value of the US dollar was fixed to a given quantity of gold—while laborers languished in poverty and debt. America's politicians were corrupt, they argued, while its financiers and industrial magnates were getting unjustly rich on the backs of the workers who were actually producing America's agricultural and industrial goods.

The Populist Party became one of the most successful third parties in American history. It controlled state governments, won electoral votes for the presidency, and elected dozens of lawmakers to Congress. Its closest brush with power came when it infiltrated one of the two mainstream political parties. In 1896, it nearly won the presidency when William Jennings Bryan, a fiery Nebraska politician, captured the Democratic presidential nomination. With his famous battle cry against bankers that "you shall not crucify mankind upon a cross of gold"—an homage to the populist quest to expand the money supply by adding silver coinage, thereby causing inflation and devaluing debts—he drew strength from the yeoman farmers and disempowered laborers whom America's Industrial Revolution had left behind. The Populist Party decided to nominate Bryan as its candidate, too. His candidacy panicked elites who feared that "soft money" would mean revolutionary change in the United States. *The New York Sun* even labeled him "William Jacobin Bryan."

Although Bryan lost the 1896 election (and subsequently the 1900 and 1908 elections), his energized populist base had exposed the soft underbelly of the prevailing economic orthodoxy. The Populist Party faded away, but populist backlash was here to stay. Bryan's own later career would show how America's homegrown anti-elite populism, unlike European socialism, drew much of its strength from those who saw their traditional values as threatened by modernity. In the Scopes "Monkey Trial" of 1925 that denounced the teaching of Darwin's theory as contrary to the literal interpretation of the Bible, Bryan helped prosecute the case. Instead of triggering a secular, Marxist-inspired working-class politics, in America the Industrial Revolution prompted a response that was rooted in traditional values and religious fundamentalism.

In 1900, L. Frank Baum published a children's story, *The Wizard of Oz*, that was also an allegorical tale in favor of populism. Perhaps that accounts for some of its enduring appeal. The American historian Henry Littlefield decoded the story in a brilliant 1964 essay. Dorothy lives in Kansas, a battered Midwestern farmland state. She follows the yellow-brick road (representing those advocating the gold standard) to the Emerald City, where Oz (the symbol for gold because it was weighed in ounces, abbreviated "oz.") reigns but turns out to be a phony. In the book, the magic shoes she wears are not ruby red, as in the movie, but silver, the magic metal for which the populists ardently advocated. Along the road, Dorothy meets up and allies with the scarecrow, representing the weak and frightened farmer, and the Tin Man, the dehumanized worker who has lost his heart. The villains are the wicked witches of the coasts, East and West, representing the cities with their financial and political power. And the cowardly lion is William Jennings Bryan, the fierce orator who could never actually get anything done, all talk and no action.

Bryan's challenge to the Gilded Age establishment did indeed fail. But in his wake, populists from the left and right would reemerge periodically in American politics, particularly during periods of profound economic and technological tumult. The co-opting of anti-elite agrarian populism by the Democratic Party signaled the first step toward America's party realignment, which would solidify over the next few decades.

THE 1896 REALIGNMENT

By the time Bryan secured the Democratic nomination for the 1896 presidential election, the chief debate in American politics was about economic policy. Hammering the same themes from his "Cross of Gold" speech, Bryan campaigned against the corruption of urban industrialists and the inequality facing rural farmers. While he still retained components of the Democrats' old coalition, including white supremacists in the South, he shifted the focus away from the racial attachments that once held the party together. Instead, his populist campaign was largely about resisting the unequal effects of industrialization. The Democrats, who had once vehemently opposed centralized state power, now began to realize that government intervention was the surest way to support those left behind by technological progress. This impulse to use the government to alleviate market inequalities would become central to the modern Democratic Party.

As Bryan established the Democrats as the critics of the industrial titans, his opponent in the presidential race, William McKinley, secured the Republicans as the champions of big business. Although Republicans had earlier wanted the government to invest in science and infrastructure on behalf of business, this changed with the 1896 election. When McKinley won it, Republicans grew more skeptical of government meddling. Meanwhile, as the twentieth century dawned, the source of capital for industrialization was moving from the public to the private sector—namely, through the business empires of Carnegie, Rockefeller, Morgan, and Ford. Lobbied by these magnates, Republicans argued that government intervention hindered technological progress and economic growth. The GOP had once favored centralized government authority, but now it embraced an anti-statist posture with laissez-faire economics at its core.

This realignment still retained distinctively American features. In the South, the Democratic Party saw the rise of the Populists as a great danger to white rule. The movement threatened to unite poor Blacks and whites into a coalition that would find a common enemy in the Southern landowners, and so the party set about breaking up that nascent alliance by playing up racial animus throughout the first half of the twentieth century. Lyndon Johnson (who had allied with white supremacists earlier in his career, before embracing civil rights) recalled this divide-and-conquer tactic: "If you can convince the lowest white man he's better than the best colored man, he won't notice you're picking his pocket. Hell, give him somebody to look down on, and he'll empty his pockets for you."

The year 1896 marked not only the crucial Bryan-versus-McKinley presidential race but also the *Plessy v. Ferguson* Supreme Court decision, which enshrined "separate but equal" racial segregation as constitutional. In the years following the decision, the South's Jim Crow system expanded, stopping Black Americans not only from voting but also from eating at the same restaurants, staying at the same inns, and using the same bathrooms as whites. If Black and white people were prevented from mingling, perhaps they would also be prevented from finding common economic and political ground.

Still, battles over the rights of Black people had been fading since the end of Reconstruction in 1877 as both parties accepted growing racial discrimination and focused instead on the crucial question of government intervention in the economy. Social issues were swept under the rug, thus perpetuating white supremacy. This bipartisan bargain was symbolized by photographs taken in 1913, on the fiftieth anniversary of Gettysburg, in which aged Union and Confederate veterans were shown shaking hands, old divides forgotten. The American political system was now defined by the same economic

Union and Confederate veterans shaking hands.

cleavages that existed elsewhere: The Democrats began to cohesively identify as the party skeptical of business and the Republicans as the party of free markets.

THE LAST PROGRESSIVE REPUBLICAN

There was one important exception to the stark division between Left and Right: McKinley's Republican successor, Theodore Roosevelt. Roosevelt was no radical, but he broke decisively with the laissez-faire ideology of his party. Much like Conservatives in Britain before that country's political realignment, he sought to curb the excesses of capitalism. His "Square Deal" program of consumer protection, union support, and antitrust measures battled robber barons and their monopolization of industries. "When I say I believe in a square deal I do not mean . . . to give every man the best hand," Roosevelt explained. "All I mean is that there shall be no crookedness in the dealing." The president did not seek to hinder economic growth, so long as everyone played by the rules. There seemed to him no greater offense than the arrogance of the new elites—in his words, the "wealthy criminal class"—who obfuscated their unethical business practices behind the free market.

Roosevelt himself was born into a stupendously wealthy family that owned vast estates on Long Island. But he drew a clear distinction between his type of "genuine aristocracy" and the "vulgar imitators," the robber barons of his time. Roosevelt's aristocratic heritage imbued him with a certain noblesse oblige that contrasted with the new titans of Manhattan's Millionaire's Row, with their ostentatious displays of wealth, underhanded manipulations of the market, and evident disregard for the public good. In many ways, Roosevelt resembled a European aristocrat, dismayed by the hustling and unethical behavior of the nouveau-riche businessmen suddenly dominating society. Among the old New York elite that the Roosevelt family embodied, there was a collective understanding that one's privileged status brought with it a moral responsibility toward the public. Many in this class recognized the disruptive nature of capitalism and the need for the government to help the masses.

Though Roosevelt had been McKinley's running mate against William Jennings Bryan in 1900, once McKinley's assassination thrust Roosevelt into the presidency, he in many ways took up the Populists' calls to crack down on big business. Roosevelt famously embarked on a program of "trust-busting," marshaling the power of the federal government to break up monopolies that had been taking advantage of the little guy. He got Congress to expand the government's regulatory authority over industries ranging from railroads to food. When a coal strike threatened a frigid winter for the nation, he intervened to reach an equitable arrangement between labor and capital, instead of breaking the strike as President Grover Cleveland had done in the Pullman Strike of 1894. Fundamentally, Roosevelt believed in capitalism, but he saw the government as a policeman of the free market.

Though his successor, William Howard Taft, would carry on some elements of his program—namely, trust-busting—Taft was cozier with big business, and Roosevelt would regret picking him as successor.

The divide between Roosevelt and Taft mirrored a broader rift in the Republican Party between economic conservatives and progressives, one that came to a head in 1909 over the issue of tariffs. Progressives within the GOP thought that import duties had gotten far too high, raising prices for ordinary consumers while serving the interests of big business—a similar argument to the one the Anti-Corn Law League had made in Britain. Conservative Republicans, however, proceeded to pass the Payne–Aldrich Tariff Act, which raised tariffs on certain goods even further. Though a supporter of free trade, Taft signed the bill, and progressive Republicans revolted. They contended that the bill prioritized business over the common man. When Taft proceeded to clinch the Republican nomination in 1912, this solidified the GOP as the firmly pro-business party. The progressive Republicans defected, with Roosevelt creating the Progressive Party and running as a third-party candidate.

The cleavage between Roosevelt and Taft ultimately handed the election to Democrat Woodrow Wilson, who ran on a progressive economic platform closer to Roosevelt's. Many progressive Republicans flocked to the Democratic Party, which solidified itself as the party of redistribution and regulation, leaving ardent pro-business types in the Republican ranks. America's party realignment was finally complete. The coming century of American life would be largely defined by political warfare between the Right, championing laissez-faire dynamism, and the Left, championing social security and stability. There was little room for Roosevelt's centrist synthesis.

THE MAKING OF MODERN AMERICA

In the opening decades of the twentieth century, a new kind of technological acceleration emerged in America. The Second Industrial Revolution, as it came to be called, saw petroleum replace coal as society's main source fuel, and the automobile displaced the train. If the United States sat in Britain's shadows for the First Industrial Revolution, it was the undisputed epicenter of this new industrialization. From the great black fountains of Texas oil geysers, to the whirring bedlam and mechanical precision of Detroit's factories churning out Model-T cars for the masses, America was forging the future (and, sadly, the environmental damage that accompanied it). A new managerial philosophy of "Fordism," of interchangeable parts and assembly lines, with workers made into ever more efficient cogs in grander and grander machines, began to sweep the world. The physical structure of the world we know—highways linking city centers to the single-family homes of suburbia—was beginning to take shape. To people alive at the time, it seemed as though the power of industrial efficiency yoked to high-tech machinery was empowering the individual with more speed, convenience, and autonomy than ever before. With private enterprise showering down its gifts—refrigerators, radios, vacuum cleaners—so freely, questioning the free market seemed ungrateful at best, heretical at worst.

Roosevelt's Republican successors now more or less embraced the pro-business ideology that was dominating right-wing politics around the world. The Republicans' free-market approach reached its apotheosis in the presidency of Calvin Coolidge. Coolidge, who took office in 1923, was known as "Silent Cal" for his subdued personality, dry sense of humor, and apparent passivity. The journalist Walter Lippmann described him this way: "Mr. Coolidge's genius for inactivity is developed to a very high point. It is far from being an indolent inactivity. It is a grim, determined, alert inactivity which keeps Mr. Coolidge occupied constantly." (When he died, the satirist Dorothy Parker quipped, "How could they tell?")

Yet Coolidge's lack of assertiveness was not a mere personality quirk; it was the central feature of his presidency. Inspired by the Puritan work ethic, Coolidge believed that individuals should take responsibility for their own success. The writer Irving Stone once commented that Coolidge "believed the least government was the best government; he aspired to become the least President the country had ever had; he attained his desire." Coolidge's staunch laissez-faire ideology positioned the Republicans as unambiguously pro-business. As he himself put it, "the chief business of the American people is business." His message fit the times. It was the Roaring Twenties, and American industry was exploding.

That same year in New York, the state's Democratic governor, Al Smith, was pushing for the opposite approach, one that redefined the Democratic Party. Smith envisioned a much more expansive role for government, urging voters to pass a $100 million bond issue to fund a wide array of public projects in New York, ranging from the construction of mental health facilities and schools to the expansion of workers' compensation programs. Smith was succeeded by Franklin Delano Roosevelt—Theodore Roosevelt's distant cousin—and although the two Democrats would become bitter rivals, FDR was in many ways Smith's ideological heir. Many of the government programs that Roosevelt would roll out as president in the New Deal era were first tried out in New York under Smith. Both politicians embraced an energetic and restlessly experimental approach to governing, one that put the state in the driver's seat.

Roosevelt won immense popularity by promising to fight on behalf of "the forgotten man at the bottom of the economic pyramid." The fires of the Populist Party still burned. But Roosevelt's new coalition was no longer rooted mainly in America's agricultural heartland. As industrialization swelled the size of cities and widened the gap between rich and poor, many urban workers were drawn to the Democrats' vision of a more active government. The Democratic Party began to resemble Europe's social democratic parties—which advocated regulated markets combined with welfare and redistribution—though it remained more moderate in tone and incremental in means.

Roosevelt had defeated Coolidge's successor, Herbert Hoover, a Republican who had started out his career identifying with the progressive wing of his party. As secretary of commerce in the 1920s, Hoover supported labor causes and encouraged cooperation between government and business. When it came to the role of the state, Hoover was committed to what Walter Lippmann called "mastery, not drift," meaning he wanted a government that intentionally aided prosperity as opposed to letting natural market forces play out on their own. Hoover is even said to have once told a journalist, "You know, the only trouble with capitalism is capitalists; they're too damn greedy."

But as president, Hoover tended to conform to the pro-market ideology that had captured his party. With the left-right realignment, there was no longer room for a Republican in the mold of Theodore Roosevelt and his Square Deal. And in the great test of his administration, the Great Depression, Hoover ultimately turned out to be more hands-off than not. The *New Republic* took him to task for his approach: "The historical role of Mr. Hoover is apparently to try the experiment of seeing what business can do when given the steering wheel. Mr. Hoover insists that there should be a steering wheel, but he will also let business do the driving."

When the Great Depression hit and Americans were urgently seeking economic relief, the Republicans' laissez-faire ideology proved inadequate. For the first time in decades, a Democratic president was elected with a large majority, and Franklin Roosevelt entered office in 1933 with firm control of both houses of Congress and an indisputable mandate. He immediately got to work during his first one hundred days in office. He evinced no cohesive ideological vision beyond trying to help people and earned a reputation for experimental, eclectic thinking. But what united his "alphabet soup" of reformist programs was that they rejected the previously unchallenged belief in the rightness of the market and embraced an active government that could provide stability and security against economic shocks.

Roosevelt's piecemeal reforms during his first year in office frustrated those who hoped for a more dramatic remaking of American society. Fortunately for them, Roosevelt dialed things up in the second year of his presidency. As he approached the two-year mark, he told Congress that "social justice, no longer a distant ideal, has become a definite goal." According to the historian David Kennedy, Roosevelt "now sought not simply recovery, nor merely relief." Rather, he wanted "something 'totally other' than what had gone before . . . something that would permit the steadying hand of 'that organized control we call government' to sustain balance and equity and orderliness throughout American society." Roosevelt's ambitions harkened back to the old progressive vision of his "Uncle Teddy." In 1935, in a move that would have made his relative proud, he signed the Social Security Act into law, setting the foundation for the modern welfare state.

This welfare state was uniquely American—less comprehensive and more committed to the market than what European social democrats advocated—but it nonetheless became ingrained into the ethos of the Democratic Party. The conservative Democrats of Grover Cleveland's era would barely have recognized the new Democratic Party. Indeed, the New Deal was initially conceived as a one-off emergency measure to counter the Great Depression's specific crisis, not a permanent ideological course correction. But FDR's newly dominant Democratic coalition was here to stay. The Democrats had evolved to become not merely the critics of laissez-faire economics but also the champions of the welfare state. And of course, all of this met ferocious pushback from the other side of the aisle.

The dividing line, between Left and Right on the economy and the role of the state, has defined politics for the past century, not just in Britain and America but around the world. I grew up in India in the 1960s and 1970s, and this divide was as meaningful there as it was in the West. At its peak during the Cold War, this dispute became a battle between extremes. Which was the proper model for society: democratic capitalism or authoritarian communism? That debate was over by the close of the twentieth century. While communism lost, it would not be correct to say that laissez-faire capitalism won. One might more accurately say (as the political scientist Sheri Berman has argued) that this battle was resolved in favor of neither free-market capitalism nor centralized state planning but rather a mix of the two.

Every advanced industrial country today combines capitalism with most of the welfare state measures advocated by the social democratic parties of Europe and the United States in the early 1900s.

With this ideological debate basically settled in favor of social democracy, a new one would emerge. The recent rise of a new populism has led new issues and new divides to seep into politics everywhere. Around the world, it has destabilized the old left-right coalitions, redefining how we understand politics itself. Supporters of government intervention in the economy are no longer found exclusively on the left. In fact, certain voices on the right are now the greatest champions of protectionist tariffs and the most ardent skeptics of large corporations. For them, "closed" economics has joined forces with "closed" politics—cultural chauvinism, fear of immigrants, and suspicion of modernity itself. Questions of open versus closed are becoming as important as left versus -right, if not more so. Why is this happening? This is a political revolution, like earlier ones, so what are the structural revolutions that have preceded it? To understand our own era's political reordering, we must look at the societal shifts that set it in motion: revolutions in globalization, information technology, and identity.

PART II

REVOLUTIONS PRESENT

6

GLOBALIZATION IN OVERDRIVE

Economics

I MAGINE FOR A MOMENT THAT YOU ARE A COAL MINER in rural America, coming from a family of miners with deep roots in the area. You take pride in the skill and grit it takes to do this arduous job. For several generations, your family has found stable work in the mines. Thanks to rising wages and better worker protections, your father was able to join the growing American middle class. You still believe your life will be better than that of your parents, and that your children's will be even better than yours.

A deep recession hits, starting on the coast—with financial panics and runs on banks—but quickly ricocheting through the American heartland. In short order, you are laid off. Your mine shuts down. You look for work elsewhere, but no one in your area seems to be hiring. When your mortgage comes due, you cannot pay it. With no income and no prospects for future employment in the industry in which you have spent your life, things spiral downward. You default on your mortgage. When you try to buy a smaller house, you are refused a loan. You are out of work, without a home, and disconnected from the land and labor that had brought you stability, community, pride, and purpose.

An upstart politician comes to town. He promises to cure the economic woes that have destroyed your American dream. He rails against the financiers on Wall Street and the ultrarich businessmen from the coasts, accusing them of gaming the system at your expense. If elected, he promises to rid American politics of its corrupt ruling class and return your job, your home, and your dignity. He reminds people that America was a great country but has been ruined by the greed and self-dealing of the establishment. He is going to make America great again.

This is not just the story of Donald Trump in 2016; it is also the story of William Jennings Bryan, whom we've already met, in 1896. During the Gilded Age, populists like Bryan surged to prominence. They challenged the laissez-faire orthodoxy and appealed to America's working class, a segment of society that was reeling from seismic shocks produced by the Industrial Revolution and a fast-globalizing American economy.

Those shocks also produced huge economic progress. For those who applied new technologies or worked in cutting-edge industries, the rewards were massive. And indeed, on the whole, society benefited from faster growth, a wider variety of cheaper goods, and the innovation that comes from competition. But for many, these new technologies—and the unusual world they heralded—promised nothing but pain and discontent. The industry most disrupted was probably agriculture, which in 1900 still employed almost half of the entire American workforce (it now employs less than 2 percent).

With expanding railroad networks, advances in refrigeration, and telegraph-enabled international coordination, agricultural goods increasingly began to trade on the global market. Europe gobbled up meat and produce from around the world. By 1870, western Europe imported more than two-thirds of all foodstuffs and raw materials sold on the world market. As mechanization increased crop yields, cheap agricultural goods flooded the market, and by the 1890s, global prices for wheat and cotton had dropped nearly 60 percent compared to just twenty years prior. This was a boon for the average consumer, who could now afford twice as much food on the same salary. And it benefited farmers in low-cost agricultural breadbaskets, like central and eastern Europe, along with the merchants, industrialists, and financiers who made the market function.

But for many farmers and workers in more advanced economies, this new trade network brought economic hardship. Sharp declines in prices led to steep drops in income. Plummeting incomes in turn caused consumers to become stingy and industrialists to become wary of new investments. In 1873, a full-blown financial panic broke out. Bankruptcies proliferated, spreading across industries and over borders in a matter of weeks. Production lines ground to a halt, even in the seemingly disconnected and immensely profitable businesses of iron, steel, and rail. With nothing to produce, businesses cut worker rolls, leading unemployment in the US to more than double from 1872 to 1878. For much of the late nineteenth century, the global economy was in depression.

In the United States, Britain, and other industrialized countries, millions of urban workers, already crammed into unsanitary tenement houses, were suddenly—and then persistently—out of work. They were disconnected from the traditional rural communities and jobs that had brought them and their families meaning for generations. And yet as economic depression in the agricultural heartland worsened, more and more people migrated to the slums of the great industrial cities in search of work. But their arrival only exacerbated the maelstrom of disease, hunger, and poverty that resulted from nineteenth-century urban life.

Technological progress and global trade fuel economic growth and raise incomes. But this combination also creates losers and unsettles societies, which often leads to a backlash following the inevitable crash or deep recession. That backlash then clears the way for politicians to channel anxiety, fear, and discomfort into anger—and sometimes solutions.

GLOBALIZATION AT FULL STEAM

For thousands of years, humans have searched for new lands, people, and markets—whether for farming, pilgrimage, conquest, commerce, or tourism. It was not until the industrialization of the nineteenth century, however, that the world became truly interconnected. Although adventurers had long plied the seas looking for glory and wealth, only in the 1800s did global supply chains truly displace local trade. As we have seen, British factories churned out high-quality goods at drastically lower cost and greater scale than artisans ever could by hand—goods that could now be shipped quickly and cheaply across the globe. Other countries, such as the United States and Germany, followed Britain's industrial capitalist model. As the political scientist Jeffry Frieden has noted, even for countries that were officially still kingdoms or empires, by the mid-1800s, "markets, not monarchs, were the dominant force."

Prior to the Industrial Revolution, conquest was often the most efficient—and sometimes the only possible—means by which nations could access foreign goods and resources. With the onset of industrial production and mechanized transport, trade became more profitable than war. In 1860, Britain and France concluded one of the world's first free trade agreements. Trade among advanced economies grew two to three times as fast as domestic production. From 1800 to 1899, trade as a share of global economic output increased eightfold. The expansion and interconnection of global markets demonstrably improved the material living conditions of practically every person in the world.

The expansion of commercial ties across the globe led not only to a greater exchange of goods but also to a greater movement of people. In 1873, Jules Verne's *Around the World in Eighty Days* captivated readers with fictional Phileas Fogg's speedy circumnavigation via train and steamship—a record-breaking feat that had once seemed unimaginable. We take for granted seven-hour flights from New York to

London and next-day delivery made possible by global supply chains. But long before planes were invented, the world was getting smaller.

DEFEATING DISTANCE

On February 15, 1882, the *Dunedin*, a British merchant ship outfitted with a brand-new coal-fired freezer, set sail from New Zealand laden with over five thousand freshly frozen lamb and sheep carcasses. This refrigeration machine pumped cool, compressed air into the *Dunedin*'s cargo hold. Ninety-eight days after setting sail, and after weeks passing through the humid tropics, the *Dunedin* arrived in London with just one carcass spoiled—a new record. Throughout human history, shipped foodstuffs had to be nonperishable—dried, salted, or otherwise preserved. The *Dunedin* changed that. Then came other improvements in transportation technology. Advances in the steamship and the steam-powered locomotive enabled producers to send mass-produced goods around the world, increasing global shipping capacity twentyfold over the nineteenth century. Between 1850 and 1900, steamships cut the cost of ocean transportation by more than two-thirds, and railroads cut the cost of land transportation more than four-fifths. Thanks to the revolution that these developments set in motion, we can now eat Maine lobster in London, Norwegian salmon in Tokyo, and Kobe beef in New York.

While transportation boomed, advances in communications technology were also bringing humanity closer together. For millennia, messages could only be sent via a courier on foot or horseback, or in mailbags carried on boats. But in the 1840s and 1850s, the telegraph allowed news to spread among world capitals faster than ever before. In 1858, when the first trans-Atlantic telegraph cable was laid, Queen Victoria sent American president James Buchanan a congratulatory telegraph. The queen's ninety-eight-word message took sixteen hours to transmit across the Atlantic, a journey that would have taken a steamship over a week to complete. Buchanan's response, which arrived in London the very next day, lauded the telegraph as a beacon of peace and harmony, an invention that would "diffuse religion, civilization, liberty and law throughout the world." By 1880, there were nearly one hundred thousand miles of suboceanic telegraph cables transmitting eight words per minute across the globe. It's not much of an exaggeration to compare the telegraph with the internet in its seismic impact on the way people communicated.

These technological revolutions did not merely remake individual societies; they created an interconnected world. International trade exploded, with the value of traded goods growing 260 percent between 1850 and 1870 alone. A global financial system emerged, with constant flows of information—prices of stocks, bonds, metals, and minerals—pinging back and forth across the planet. And global exchange was not the preserve of international bankers and merchants; it was a daily reality for hundreds of millions of people, shaping their jobs, their wardrobe, their reading material, and their diet. Immigration across oceans may be the most striking and durable transformation that the new globalization wrought. Brad DeLong makes the astounding observation that in the few decades from 1870 to 1914, "one in fourteen humans—one hundred million people—changed their continent of residence."

This was a sharp break from millennia of human existence. As Eric Hobsbawm explained, "History from now on became world history."

THE INVENTION OF INTERNATIONALISM

Economic globalization was accompanied by a new culture of internationalism. As the historian Mark Mazower argues, the changes seen in the mid-nineteenth century led to the "consciousness of the world as an interconnected whole." The very word *international* went mainstream during this period. The term was coined by Jeremy Bentham in 1780, and by 1850 the word had gained a suffix: *internationalism* became a buzzword on the lips of an entire new class of workers and managers.

Geopolitics transformed, too. The United Kingdom—the world's hegemon, thanks to its industrial strength—pursued a radically new type of foreign policy. Rather than seeking glory on the battlefield, Britain sought stability among the great powers in Europe, while working to secure its intertwined interests and values around the world. British naval power protected sea lanes across the planet, and the pound sterling became a kind of reserve currency, anchoring the new international financial system. It was during this late Victorian era that William Gladstone, the enthusiastic advocate of liberalism, served twelve years as Britain's prime minister. The UK, in his words, was building an international order predicated on the "equal rights of all nations" and a fundamental "love of freedom." In many ways, this nascent system was the world's first liberal international order.

As the leading economic power, Britain benefited from a Europe at peace. This was also the case for the nations on the continent, which had been torn apart by centuries of conflict, most recently the Napoleonic Wars. In the wake of Napoleon's defeat and the settlement forged at the Congress of Vienna, Europe could focus on fostering trade and prosperity. Of course, Britain and other European states were not content to let the rest of the world live in peace. For even most liberals at the time, the community of nations entitled to equal rights was only a small subset of the world's countries—the industrializing states of Europe and North America. Many of these countries—chief among them the United Kingdom—brutally subjugated civilizations across Asia and Africa. Even when Europeans did not formally colonize a place, they managed to exert their power in other ways. They forced markets open on advantageous terms, as Britain did when it waged the Opium Wars against China. They backed puppet rulers who protected foreign interests, as in Egypt, where the British wanted to ensure the flow of commerce through the all-important Suez Canal. Oppression and exploitation were the ugly side of the unprecedented expansion of global markets during the nineteenth century.

It wasn't just European great powers that acted this way. America forcibly opened up what soon became Asia's greatest economic power:

Japan. The country was an important rest stop for ships crossing the Pacific, and its islands were rich in coal deposits, its waters full of fish and whales. But for more than two centuries, Japan had closed itself off from the world, severely limiting trade, banning travel abroad, and harshly punishing any Japanese who attempted to import dangerous foreign ideas—especially the heretical religion of Christianity. As the Industrial Revolution swept across the West, Japan declined to adopt pioneering technologies. Then in 1853, a US Navy flotilla led by Commodore Matthew Perry steamed into Edo Bay, forcing Japan to open up. This style of globalization was not peaceful or voluntary, nor was it equally beneficial to all—a reality forgotten in the West but remembered by the rest.

TRADE WARS, SHOOTING WARS

In the last quarter of the nineteenth century, the boom turned bust, leading to a wave of backlash. In 1873, dual financial crashes in Vienna and New York sparked something unimaginable today—a twenty-four-year global depression, the first big economic downturn in modern history. This crash, now known as the Long Depression, sparked the first sustained reaction against globalization. It galvanized political outsiders—populists, socialists, and nationalists alike. It also led to a new, violent form of political expression. Human history had always featured violence, but it was not until the late 1800s that terrorism became widely used to make political statements. Beginning in 1878, an epidemic of high-profile successful and attempted assassinations broke out across the Western world. Between 1892 and 1901, five monarchs or heads of state were assassinated: the empress of Austria, the king of Italy, the prime minister of Spain, and the presidents of France and the United States. Historians would come to call this the Decade of Regicide.

Politically, the Long Depression helped the Right more than the Left. Some people were drawn leftward, and certainly there was a greater recognition that the socialist critique of capitalism had merit, since financial speculation and panics had immiserated ordinary people. But as socialism gained followers among Europe's working classes, its political successes prompted a more lasting and powerful counter-reaction from conservatives. Concerned that the traditional bonds within society were disintegrating, and that worker agitations would undermine Europe's *ancien* aristocratic and landed culture, conservatives turned nationalistic and militaristic. The polarizing pressures of socialism and conservative nationalism hollowed out the traditional liberal center, leading Benjamin Disraeli—Gladstone's Conservative rival and a two-time prime minister—to liken his country's Liberal leaders to "a range of exhausted volcanoes."

In the end, the winners of this struggle tended to be the conservative nationalists who often addressed domestic unrest by unifying or distracting people with nationalism and imperialism, like Germany's Bismarck and Italy's King Umberto I. They clamored for protectionism and mercantilism to promote the national interest. They blamed the chaos and unrest on foreigners, defusing the domestic class conflict brewing in working-class neighborhoods. Scapegoats were found. Jews faced pogroms in Eastern Europe and were demonized in France and Austria. In America, rioters attacked Chinese people in California and other western states, and in 1882, Congress passed its first major restriction on immigration, the Chinese Exclusion Act. Yes, all this has echoes in our times.

European colonial powers—including new entrants such as Belgium and Germany—stepped up the competition for supremacy in Africa, the Middle East, and Southeast Asia. As Britain's viceroy of India Lord Curzon put it, the world was "a chessboard upon which is being played out a game for the domination of the world." With their increasingly professionalized militaries and advanced technologies, Europe's colonial powers collectively achieved checkmate: in 1800, European countries controlled just 35 percent of the planet's surface; by 1914, they held 84 percent. Even Britain, which once promoted the "imperialism of free trade" that sought foreign *markets* rather than foreign *lands*, was now formally annexing vast swaths of Africa and

Asia. European empires used these territories to feed their industrial machines, focusing on labor-intensive plantation crops and extractive industries like gold and diamond mining.

Beginning around the 1890s, industrialized nations moved away from free markets and free trade. Trade still grew—the international economy had its own inexorable logic—but in many places, the politicians who supported economic openness were on the back foot. Instead, the most popular leaders were those who utterly opposed any kind of win-win conception of international relations. In 1890, the United States passed the McKinley Tariff; similar measures were taken in France in 1892 and Germany in 1897. Joseph Chamberlain, one of the most influential political figures of his age, urged Britain to junk its commitment to free trade in favor of imperial tariffs—an early version of what we now call "friendshoring"—creating preferential trade within the British Empire. That proved too complex and unworkable in a vast and varied empire that spanned a quarter of the globe, but Britain did adopt its own protectionist measures in 1902.

Watching this retreat from openness, journalist Norman Angell was moved to write *The Great Illusion*, his 1909 best-selling book that presciently warned politicians not to keep going down the path of nationalist conflict (earning him the Nobel Peace Prize in 1933). But some European leaders, like Bismarck and Austrian emperor Franz Joseph I, went down that path anyway. Western Europe and the United States increasingly relied on gunboat diplomacy and violent coercion abroad to fuel their industrial expansion, rather than competition through trade. This return to the logic of zero-sum mercantilism, colonial expansion, and shifting balances of power caused crisis after crisis—and then, in the summer of 1914, plunged Europe into all-out war.

THE END OF GLOBALIZATION

Four years of total war devastated Europe and shattered the nineteenth-century confidence in modernity, technology, and ceaseless progress. But a few years after the armistice, even in the US there was an urgent desire to go back to the good old days, a "return to normalcy" as Warren Harding put it in his 1920 presidential campaign. Soon, the boom times were back. The boozy parties and packed jazz halls so characteristic of the Roaring Twenties were the product of a roaring economy. In the United States alone, GDP grew by more than 40 percent, thanks in part to the mass production of automobiles and the spread of electricity. Calvin Coolidge, who occupied the White House for most of the decade, celebrated big business and capitalism, an approach that seemed in tune with the times. Movies and radio offered new forms of mass entertainment, creating truly global celebrities like Charlie Chaplin who became household names across the planet. Travel surged again, this time with better and bigger steamships and the fledgling but dazzling technology of airplane travel. For a while, Charles Lindbergh, who steered his plane across the Atlantic, might well have been the most admired man on the Earth. But then came the stock market crash of 1929, kicking off the Great Depression. Not only did the Depression upend the global economy and plunge millions into poverty, but it also killed any nascent faith in the market economy, at home or abroad.

The old doubts about free trade rapidly resurfaced, leading to high tariff barriers and a shift toward autarky, or economic self-sufficiency. In some countries that had once been trade-oriented, such as Germany, a new ethos of extreme national self-sufficiency arose, of a kind that is rare today (think Cuba or North Korea). Many countries invested heavily in domestic industries, building up industrial capacity and infrastructure in an effort to become fully self-reliant. In a Europe increasingly dominated by national, rather than continental, markets, everyone turned inward. Even in traditionally free-trading Britain and France, protectionism was on the rise. Britain instituted Imperial Preference, a system that lowered tariffs among Canada, Australia, South Africa, India, and other British colonies while raising them on the rest of the world. In France, the left-wing government jacked up tariffs of its own. The US, which already had high tariffs, raised them even higher.

In an open world economy, it is almost always cheaper to trade for a particular natural resource or industrial product than to take it by force. But with foreign markets locked away behind insurmountable tariff walls, conquest once again became thinkable and even profitable. In 1925, Adolf Hitler laid out an expansionist vision for Germany in *Mein Kampf*—*Lebensraum* (living space)—which was partly a means to ensure access to foreign agricultural goods and strategic minerals that high tariffs had cut off from the country. The Japanese faced an oil embargo that would have choked their economy to death. It would not be long until the German and Japanese ideologies of economic imperialism and cultural, national, and racial superiority pushed the world into total war once again.

GLOBALIZATION REBORN

World War II was at base a clash between liberal democracy and fascist autocracy, with the Allied victory representing the defeat of nationalism, protectionism, and militarism. By the end of the war, countries had recognized the dangers of closing themselves off to the world. The United States presided over the creation of a new world order, with FDR and then Harry Truman showing a particular dedication to openness and cooperation. Free trade blossomed anew, not least because of the tireless efforts of Roosevelt's secretary of state, Cordell Hull, who pushed trade as a way for nations to grow and prosper peacefully.

As Europe dug itself out of the physical, social, and psychological rubble of the war—aided in this task by American power and money—the pendulum swung firmly away from nationalism toward continental unity, even union. Winston Churchill, that old imperialist, proposed a "United States of Europe." The first step would be taken in 1952, with the creation of the European Coal and Steel Community, which established a single market for those essential commodities among Western European countries (including West Germany and France, no longer enemies). Autarky, which had seemed a legitimate road to prosperity in the 1930s, was now widely dismissed as delusional and dangerous.

A new liberalism—not the old laissez-faire liberalism of the nineteenth century but a social democratic form with some government intervention in the economy—was the order of the day. Free trade abroad was newly possible now that people at home had much greater protections from its vicissitudes thanks to expanded welfare states. Regulated markets, safety nets, and strong labor unions all allowed for much greater openness to international competition. And despite the Soviet Union's contestation of this formula throughout the Cold War, it proved so successful that it remains the dominant model today.

Of course, more than three decades of crisis and conflict from 1914 to 1945 had done grave damage. Much of Europe and Asia was in ashes, and nations that cast off the colonial yoke were woefully underdeveloped. Brad DeLong notes that by 1950, "the globalization cycle had been fully reversed," with international trade having plummeted to less than 10 percent of all global economic activity—a similar level as in 1800. It would take around sixty years for the world to return to pre-1914 levels of global exchange.

How it got there is the remarkable success story of globalization renewed. Learning from the failures of the interwar period, statesmen of the World War II generation placed greater emphasis on building strong multilateral institutions that could steward global markets and provide a forum for cooperation. Globalization would not just recover but eventually soar to new heights. And there was a crucial difference from the interwar years, when liberalism was on death's door: the open world that took shape as World War II ended had the undisputed anchor of a newly internationalist America.

The architect of this system was FDR. He envisioned an order rooted in great-power politics yet supportive of open markets, cooperation, and peace. For FDR, Woodrow Wilson's mistake had been to naively wish away great-power competition. That ethos was enshrined in the organization Wilson designed, the League of Nations, which treated all countries alike (and which the US refused to join, owing to Republican opposition). Roosevelt, by contrast, believed that the major powers had to be given a special seat at the table, hence the five permanent members of the UN Security Council—the victors of World War II. By investing in the UN and other new global governance institutions, championing global trade, and deterring new great power warfare, American power would underwrite the new world order.

Even some Republicans, long the standard-bearers of an "America First" isolationism, began to extol the virtues of internationalism. Henry Luce, the influential publisher of *Time* and *Life* magazines, captured this changing sentiment in his era-defining essay "The American Century." Published in *Life* in February 1941, before America entered the war, Luce's essay declared a new age in which an active United States would promote democracy and capitalism across the globe. His arguments reverberated widely, winning over voters— and the statesmen who would rebuild the world after the war. By 1945, when representatives of the Allied powers met in San Francisco to sketch the outline of the United Nations, a broad consensus was crystallizing around the virtues of liberal internationalism and multilateral institutions.

A new economic order sprang to life, one supported for the first time by a global set of rules and regulations undergirded by new institutions: the UN, the International Monetary Fund, and the General Agreement on Tariffs and Trade (the forerunner to the World Trade Organization). Those rules and regulations began to take shape in a 1944 conference of more than seven hundred representatives from Allied countries. Over three weeks of negotiations in Bretton Woods, New Hampshire, in the foothills of the White Mountains, delegates designed a system of international monetary regulation meant to address the structural weaknesses of the interwar years and supercharge economic recovery. They agreed that global financial stability would be underpinned by the US, with other currencies pegged to the dollar and the dollar convertible for gold.

The Bretton Woods System, as it came to be known, enabled one of the swiftest and most profound economic expansions in history. At the close of World War II, every advanced economy lay in ruins (oftentimes literally), with the sole exception of the United States. And yet by 1964, Western Europe's per capita output had doubled, and by 1969, Japan's had grown by a factor of eight. Even the United States, which wasn't growing from a low base, saw its per capita output rise by 75 percent by 1973. By that year, when the Bretton Woods System collapsed after the US ended gold convertibility, global GDP had increased more than 200 percent from its prewar level—nearly the same percentage increase as during the second Industrial Revolution, from 1820 to 1914, when the modern economy was born.

THE JET AGE

Once again, this new burst of globalization was spurred by profound advances in transportation. For most of the twentieth century, cargo was shipped much as it had been in the nineteenth century, in barrels and sacks unloaded from one vessel and onto another, with marginal improvements in efficiency thanks to cranes and other similar tools. In 1956, however, an entrepreneur from North Carolina, Malcolm McLean, catapulted shipping into the future with his invention of the container ship. He loaded the *Ideal X*, a decommissioned oil tanker, with fifty-eight truck trailers lifted directly off the ground by cranes. The ship carried the shipping containers from Newark to Houston, where fifty-eight semi trucks were waiting to reattach the trailers and zip the goods to their final destination.

With his labor-saving innovation, McLean cut the loading and unloading time of shipped cargo by more than three weeks. As a result, the cost of freight suddenly dropped by 97 percent, down to a minuscule 16 cents per ton. This was an even more profound change to global trade networks than the one heralded by the *Dunedin*'s first shipment of refrigerated meat. From then on, it became cheaper to ship goods to and from ports around the world than it did to transport them by truck from port to their final destination.

By 1973, trade accounted for two or even three times as much of advanced economies' GDP as it had in 1950. Of course, the Cold War limited how truly global this new wave of globalization could be. Stalin forbade any Eastern Bloc countries from accepting American aid via the Marshall Plan, and for decades East-West trade remained tiny.

Revolutions in transportation technology also ushered in a new era of human mobility. In the 1860s, the journey from New York to San Francisco—via steamship, with an interlude by rail across the Isthmus of Panama—took around 30 days. Before World War II, some commercial airlines flew across the Atlantic, but few passengers preferred the deafening noise, multiple stops, and hefty costs over the relative luxury and affordability of ocean liners. Practically all transoceanic travel took place by boat, with coal-powered passenger ships taking days or even weeks to make their crossings. Then, in 1958, Pan Am—the premier global airline through much of the twentieth century—flew its first trans-Atlantic passenger route on a jet airliner, the Boeing 707. The Jet Age had begun.

International tourism soared as new technologies made long-distance flight ever cheaper, faster, and easier. By 1965, one year after a Pan Am 707 flew the Beatles to America for the first time, tourist arrivals across the globe exceeded 110 million—nearly five times the figure from just fifteen years earlier. By the early 1970s, jumbo jets plied the skies, touching down in as many as 160 countries. International arrivals practically doubled every decade. By the 2010s, there were upwards of one billion tourist arrivals per year.

This unprecedented mobility of people, goods, and capital was not just for the 1 percent. The growing middle classes of Europe, America, and (soon) East Asia reaped the rewards of globalization in the form of cheap goods, accessible travel, peace, and prosperity.

NO ALTERNATIVE?

In the years after World War II, Western governments invested heavily in welfare programs. Voters cheered politicians for providing both economic growth and domestic stability. Welfare spending across all of the advanced economies rose on average from 27 percent of GDP in 1950 to 43 percent in 1973. Labor movements stayed strong, with anywhere from one-third to two-thirds of workers in these countries belonging to unions. Thanks to seemingly ever-expanding economic opportunities, unemployment rates averaged around 3 percent, significantly below the 8 percent average of the interwar years. The French called the three decades after World War II *Les Trente Glorieuses* (the glorious thirty), and what was achieved was indeed magnificent: the coexistence of openness and stability, fueling economic growth across the globe. With lower trade barriers, smart regulations, and strengthened safety nets, the West had found the Goldilocks formula.

But over time, the golden age began to wane. Governments overspent and overregulated, borrowing more money to make up for growing deficits. Unions, in turn, demanded higher wages to make up for rising inflation. By the 1970s, the balance between economic dynamism and social welfare had gotten off-kilter. Growth had slowed, inflation had risen, and the state was increasingly intervening in the economy, with governments eventually imposing strict price controls on staple goods like bread, milk, and soap. In much of the West, top marginal income tax rates exceeded 70 percent. Oil shortages, caused by Middle East geopolitics, exacerbated the situation. The result was a painful combination of stagnation and inflation: stagflation. The world economy was in the doldrums.

With every major contraction of globalization, the economic and political orthodoxy of the day is rejected anew, and the crisis of the 1970s was no exception. Voters balked at active government intervention and social welfare spending and flocked to a new generation of laissez-faire conservatives like Ronald Reagan and Margaret

Thatcher. Inspired by the work of economist Milton Friedman, these politicians emphasized monetary policy over fiscal policy and championed the deregulation of private markets. Unlike the solution preferred in the 1930s, when leaders doubled down on nationalism and protectionism, this new generation sought to unshackle markets and trade. In other words, *more* markets and *more* globalization. There was a rising cultural conservatism—against the women's movement, racial integration, and secularism—but the Right was led by *economic* conservatives, who harnessed the furies of their cultural confederates for their own purposes.

Thatcher and the Conservatives swept to power in Britain's 1979 general election, having pledged to revitalize Britain's sluggish economy and put an end to labor unrest. In 1980, Reagan achieved a similar feat in the United States, winning in a landslide election on a promise to fundamentally restructure the American economy. In office, both Thatcher and Reagan implemented a new economic approach that would later be termed "neoliberalism." They championed privatization and deregulation while promising balanced budgets. Reagan, for his part, failed to deliver on that last promise, instead tripling the national debt during his tenure. But because high interest rates—set by American, British, and other European central banks to fight stagflation—made government bonds attractive to investors, he and other neoliberals could have their cake and eat it, too. They cut taxes but increased spending, making up the gap by borrowing, made ever less painful as interest rates declined. Foreign governments and investors stepped in to finance much of the West's government spending. That, along with neoliberals' embrace of free trade, knitted together the world economy even more.

International economic flows were further stimulated by the birth of the modern finance industry. Across the West, the state lost power to the financial sector, which became bigger than ever before. In the United States, the powers of the Federal Reserve Board and the Federal Deposit Insurance Corporation to manage credit and supervise banks were rolled back, allowing financial institutions to operate largely autonomously. Britain undertook a similar move. In the 1930s, there had been a general consensus that the Bank of England needed to be brought under state ownership to control credit, but by the late 1970s, markets had taken over that function. This all enabled a system that was more profitable and more efficient, but also much riskier, ultimately setting the stage for the 2008 global financial crisis.

Neoliberal reforms were implemented in practically every economy across the globe—often under duress. After a series of economic implosions across the developing world in the 1980s, the IMF and World Bank rode to the rescue, but their loans came with conditions. Governments were required to make major macroeconomic and political reforms along the lines of what came to be known as the Washington Consensus, a set of policies designed to unleash market forces. In order to receive much-needed loans from the IMF, developing countries were urged to transform into free-market liberal democracies. For most financially insolvent states, there was—as Margaret Thatcher famously quipped—"no alternative."

In many places, reforms helped spur growth. In Argentina, for example, after economic collapse in the 1980s, neoliberal policies in the 1990s encouraged foreign investment that fueled almost a decade of steady GDP growth. But the Washington Consensus also increased inequality, widening the gap between the beneficiaries of globalization and those it left behind.

GLOBALIZATION GOES INTO HYPER-SPEED

The seismic event of the late twentieth century was the fall of communism. In 1989, Eastern Europe's Soviet-aligned states collapsed, and two years later the Soviet Union itself broke apart. Socialism as an economic and political system had finally been discredited. As the Iron Curtain fell, new states in the former Soviet bloc clamored to join international markets, and to do so as liberal democracies. The neoliberal reforms of the 1980s had unleashed global capital and tied economies together more than ever before, and now socialist

economies were fading into history. In just a few short years, the
world had entered a new era of hyper-globalization.

Money—in the form of bank loans and international investments—
rocketed around the world. The uptick had already begun in the
1980s as the financial sector took off. Between 1985 and 1987 alone,
the annual volume of international bank lending grew by 62 percent.
But in the 1990s, banking expanded even further. Governments tore
down barriers to capital flows, and financiers took advantage of the
spread of computers and other new communications technologies like
the internet and fiber-optic cables to quickly track market fluctuations
and find new investment opportunities. As the historian Adam Tooze
notes, the entire financial sector went through a fundamental restructuring, turning away from the traditional deposit-oriented banking
system and instead focusing on high-liquidity lending. From 1990 to
2000, the world's ten largest private banks went on a spending spree,
increasing their share of total global assets from 10 percent to 50 percent. Profits exploded. In 1983, the American financial sector represented only 10 percent of all corporate profits; by the mid-2000s, that
figure had increased to around 40 percent, surpassing manufacturing
as the most profitable American industry.

Eager to reinvest their new surpluses into faster-growing areas,
advanced economies thrust capital into emerging markets. The EU
poured hundreds of billions of dollars of structural investment funds
into the nascent democracies in Eastern Europe in the 1990s, in a
series of programs that Tooze equates to a modern-day Marshall Plan.
Private investors also flocked to the region: by the end of the 1990s,
nearly half of all Eastern European manufacturing capacity was owned
by Western European corporations.

The effects on the region were profound. Just look at Škoda, the
Czech Republic's largest automobile manufacturer and one of the
most important industrial conglomerates in Central Europe. State-
owned since 1948, its reputation as a premier global manufacturing
company had suffered during the Cold War due to poor quality and
substandard designs. After communism collapsed and Czechoslovakia

transitioned to democracy, Volkswagen Group, a stalwart of West Germany, bought the struggling automobile manufacturer. In 1991, Škoda made 172,000 cars, selling 26 percent of those in thirty foreign countries. Just nine years later, it made 435,000, sending 82 percent of these abroad to more than seventy countries. Today, Škoda is one of Volkswagen Group's most profitable subsidiaries, second only to Porsche.

There were thousands of similar success stories in the 1990s, as the sudden entrance of so many nations into the capitalist system generated seemingly limitless growth. This wasn't just an Eastern European story. The entire world was enjoying the fruits of hyper-globalization. For the first time ever, the production of high-quality goods became a truly global phenomenon. Consider the story of Intel. Founded in 1968 in a small valley just south of the Bay Area that would—thanks in large part to the company's success—come to be known as Silicon Valley, Intel was for decades the most important microchip manufacturer in the world. It opened its first foreign factory in Malaysia in the early 1970s, and by the 1990s, it was relying on a network of manufacturing, assembly, and product-development facilities across the globe, mostly in Asia at first but then also in countries outside the region, such as Costa Rica. One study found that Costa Rica's GDP grew by 8 percent in the two years after Intel began manufacturing there—the highest growth rate in Latin America and the country's largest GDP increase in thirty years.

For many developing nations, the hyper-globalization of the 1990s didn't just mean reaching Western levels of economic performance; some even began to out-compete the West, playing the game of globalization better and cheaper. By 2007, developing nations were responsible for more global output than advanced economies were, and their share has only grown.

The world as a whole was producing far more than it ever had before. Compared to 1980, global GDP had nearly doubled by 2000 and more than tripled by 2015. From 2000 to 2007, per capita income grew at its fastest rate in history. Global trade increased by 133 percent between 1990 and 2007, with emerging markets accounting for half of this growth. Cheap yet decent-quality goods from Japan, South Korea, Vietnam, and China flooded American and European markets, boosting the economies of the exporting nations and lowering prices for Western consumers. This influx was facilitated by large multinational retailers like Walmart and major manufacturers that offshored production. Only with the hyper-globalization of the 1990s could a low-wage worker in rural America purchase the latest Nike sneakers, designed in Oregon and manufactured in China.

And as always, this new round of globalization had political consequences as well, with economic and political liberalization going hand in hand. Rising middle classes around the world demanded democracy, and the failure of statist economic policies discredited authoritarianism. In the 1970s, only 8 percent of countries were considered liberal free-market democracies; by the end of the 1990s, more than 30 percent of countries were. In 1988, there were few consolidated, mature liberal democracies outside of those in Western Europe, the United States, Canada, Australia, and Japan. By 2010, liberal democracy had become the norm in every region but North and Sub-Saharan Africa, Central Asia, and the Middle East. From its origins as a small cluster of countries nestled along the North Atlantic, the free world had grown to include almost 112 states with some level of real democracy.

ORIGINS OF OUR DISCONTENT

The hyper-globalization of the 1990s was the apotheosis of liberal democracy and global capitalism. All competing ideologies and economic systems seemed to have lost legitimacy and support. As the political scientist Francis Fukuyama put it famously, it was "the end of history." Human civilization had reached its highest stage.

But soon there began a backlash, which is still manifesting itself across the globe today. Many of the nations most celebrated for their transition to liberal free-market democracy have slid backward—look at Vladimir Putin's Russia, Viktor Orbán's Hungary, Recep Tayyip Erdoğagn's Turkey, Narendra Modi's India, or, up until recent elections, Jarosław Kaczyński's Poland and Jair Bolsonaro's Brazil. Much of this reversion, fueled by homegrown resentment toward globalization and its associated values (including liberalism and cosmopolitanism), can be traced precisely to the transitional moment of the 1990s.

In the West, the development of free-market liberal democracy, which in many respects traces its roots to the Dutch Republic in the sixteenth century, has been long, slow, and organic—and even now, it wobbles at times. Because the developing world did not have the time to slowly develop its institutions, democratization in the 1980s and '90s was swift and shallow. Countries emphasized market reforms over political and social transformations. Elections were easy to put in place—the rule of law and the protection of individual rights, less so. Developing countries adopted and adapted new systems from the West, from freely elected representative assemblies to supreme courts to financial regulatory bodies, but oftentimes with little or only a cursory understanding of how they should work in practice. Countries failed to embed the protections and freedoms promised by liberalism. The masses, in turn, did not know what to expect or demand from this new system and, in many cases, were left to weather the disruptions of market liberalism with no institutional insulation to protect them.

In the post-Soviet world, civil society failed to establish deep roots, and politicians struggled to adhere to an independent rule of law. The rapid and often corrupt process of privatizing state-owned industries created a handful of extremely wealthy oligarchs with newfound political power but failed to improve the living conditions of the masses. In many cases, they actually worsened. (In Russia, life expectancy fell and crime spiked during the 1990s.) Regular people failed to internalize the values of liberalism because they were given little time to understand it. Politicians failed to construct resilient democratic institutions, receiving little support from the West on how to do so effectively. Boris Yeltsin, who as Russia's first president oversaw its reforms in the early 1990s, aptly summarized the problem: the new liberal democratic and free-market institutions were "beautiful structures and beautiful titles with nothing behind them."

In the West itself, globalization's discontents have ripened in the very shadows of its success. Through the 1980s and much of the 1990s, it seemed that integration was nourishing a new era of continual growth. Recessions, endemic to capitalism, would be short, contained, and managed through new tools: good monetary policies and a sustained commitment to openness. But in the late 1990s, a currency crisis in East and Southeast Asia ricocheted around the world, leading to the first worries about the volatility of unfettered globalization.

The crisis began in 1997 when the Thai government, having run out of the foreign reserves needed to peg its currency to the US dollar, was forced to float its currency instead. Foreign investors got skittish and pulled their investments from Thailand. Because international capital markets had grown so large, and because they operated twenty-four hours a day, the result was a massive capital flight. Trouble in Thailand caused investors with interests elsewhere in East and Southeast Asia to pull their money, too. Unemployment skyrocketed in Thailand and South Korea and rose across the region as the crisis cascaded. Poverty in South Korea doubled, and GDP in Indonesia and Thailand fell by double-digit or near double-digit percentages.

The IMF and most creditor countries offered a package of financial stabilization similar to the one they had offered Latin American countries in the 1980s, but this time the result was not consistent GDP growth but prolonged economic contraction, sustained wage losses, and decreased export competitiveness. As the crisis worsened, lenders in advanced economies feared their investments in developing countries outside Asia were also unsafe. They preemptively withdrew their capital, thereby making a regional downturn go global. Although the Asian financial crisis lasted only two years and was largely contained to the developing world, it showed that globalization was not just dynamic, but disruptive—and that the pain was not spread equally.

One of the first major antiglobalization protests in an advanced economy occurred in Seattle in 1999, as the World Trade Organization held its annual meeting. The protesters demanded a slowdown to the hyper-globalization of the 1990s and a return to some degree of national protection. They railed against the unregulated expansion of multinational corporations, demanded better safeguards for workers, and even advocated for new global rules on sustainable development. At the time, many people dismissed their concerns as those of a disaffected, extremist fringe—crunchy hippies, joining forces with outright anarchists. But in retrospect, the Battle of Seattle, as it was later dubbed, looks less like an isolated flare-up from the embers of a dying leftism and more like a harbinger of things to come. In the decades after Seattle, antiglobalization activism increased exponentially.

CHINA SHOCK OR GLOBALIZATION SHOCK?

Today, many blame the current antiglobalization backlash on the so-called China shock, the influx of cheap manufactured goods from a newly market-oriented China in the 1990s. Seemingly overnight, "Made in China" had replaced "Made in the USA" on practically every basic consumer good. These Chinese imports undercut American manufacturers, so the argument goes, shuttering factories and decimating local communities.

China's entrance into the global economy really was a shock to the system—just not the negative one most assume. On December 11, 2001, after nearly fifteen years of negotiations, China formally entered the World Trade Organization. The country's accession came on the heels of its massive economic expansion. Since the early 1980s, China's economy had grown by at least 9 percent every year—the fastest and most sustained rate any major economy had ever experienced. This period of unimaginable growth was made possible by Deng Xiaoping, China's modernizing leader. But it was subsidized in large part by eager foreign investors. Throughout the 1990s, China was the second-largest recipient of total foreign direct investment and, by the end of the decade, accounted for close to one-third of all such investment in developing countries.

Trade with China boomed. In the late 1970s, China engaged in roughly $20 billion in foreign trade; by 2000, that figure had sky-rocketed to $475 billion. In 2001, the year China joined the WTO, it accounted for 4 percent of global exports; by 2010, it accounted for 10 percent and had become the definitive leader in global exports—a position that has only grown stronger since. China quickly became the world's top supplier of low-cost goods.

It is true that unemployment soared in American manufacturing towns as low-cost Chinese goods outcompeted American ones. Many jobs were actually lost to automation, not trade, but some of the losses were indeed caused by low-wage competition from China. Yet blaming China for the ills of globalization misses a more fundamental point. Japanese, South Korean, and Taiwanese manufacturing took off in the 1980s yet failed to produce the same kind of backlash. Why?

The answer is that China's rise as a powerhouse of production hap-pened to coincide with the natural decline of American manufactur-ing. In 1966, the economist Raymond Vernon outlined the five stages of any important product's life cycle: introduction, growth, maturity, saturation, and decline. During the first three stages, production is clustered near where the product was invented. By the time a product enters the latter two stages, it is almost always produced elsewhere or supplanted by technological change. By the 1990s, the production of many basic consumer goods—from clothing to toys to bicycles—had entered the saturation or decline stages.

As a result, many manufacturing communities in heartland Amer-ica had already begun to hollow out before the China shock. Middle-class incomes were stagnating, and many of the reliably good low- and medium-skilled jobs were leaving the regions that had traditionally depended on them. Low-cost goods were now "Made in China," and high-wage manufacturing of new high-tech goods, like semiconduc-tors and computers, was moving to Silicon Valley and other clusters of innovation. What's more, "Made in China" is itself a simplification. Fifty percent of all goods traded in the world are intermediate goods—that is, components of a final product, like the more than two hundred parts that go into an iPhone. The device itself might be classified as Chinese-made but in fact, hundreds of the parts, gadgets and chips within it were produced in India, Taiwan, South Korea, Malaysia, Vietnam, Sri Lanka and Thailand—and then assembled in China. The China shock would be better described as the "globalization shock." Had China not existed, most of the jobs lost to it would have been lost anyway, to machines and a combination of other low-wage countries.

Of course, for the tens of thousands of people whose wages flatlined or whose jobs were lost, it made no difference who the true culprit was, and obscure economic theories provided little solace. It's not hard to see why those who lived in single-industry regions that were outcompeted by foreign producers or displaced by automation might blame China—which took the lion's share of global manufacturing—for their sense of dislocation. The columnist Thomas Friedman, one of the earliest and most ardent advocates of globalization, presciently noted that "it is when people or nations are humiliated that they really lash out." Indeed, much of the backlash from globalization would come from perceived humiliation and stagnation from those who felt left behind.

UNDERSTANDING THE SHOCK

Nevertheless, the backlash to globalization is not a simple matter of economics, the poor revolting against the rich. Nor does it arise from some natural aversion to openness. Most people like being connected to others. But human psychology is also concerned with status. As the world becomes more interconnected and transparent, the gaps between the haves and the have-nots become more obvious. Even if you may be better off than your grandparents on every metric, seeing others living even better makes it easier to feel resentful. As Alexis de

Tocqueville remarked some 150 years ago, it is relative deprivation, not absolute deprivation, that sparks revolt.

As a matter of absolute gains, Americans have advanced significantly from where they were in, say, the 1960s and '70s. The size of the average American home has grown by nearly 1,000 square feet, from 1,525 in 1973 to 2,467 in 2015—and while most houses back then lacked air conditioning, nowadays almost all homes are equipped with it. In 1960, 22 percent of American households did not have a car; today, only 8 percent remain without access to a car, and over 50 percent of households have two or more. Air travel has become much more accessible for American families, with domestic flights costing about half of what they did in 1979. Food has also become much cheaper, consuming about half as much of the average household's income as it did in 1960. The cost of clothing has plummeted even more. In 1960, the average American household spent 10 percent of its budget on clothes, compared to a little over 3 percent today.

People's lives are better today in all sorts of other intangible ways. Information and entertainment that used to cost huge sums of money are now free and available to anyone. Even education and healthcare, whose costs have skyrocketed, are nonetheless available to more people than ever before. In 1960, just 8 percent of Americans graduated from college. Today, that number is up to 38 percent. Twenty-five percent of Americans lacked health insurance in 1960, versus about 10 percent today. And the vast majority of Americans are receiving care of a quality that would once have been unimaginable. Ultrasound was not commercially available back in 1960, while CAT scans and MRIs were years away. Miracle drugs from statins to antidepressants have come on the market, and cancer treatment has progressed to the point that today the disease kills less than one-third of patients within five years of diagnosis compared to half in the 1970s.

Yet all of these areas are secondary to a human being's self-worth, which hinges on one's status, one's place in a community, one's ability to find a partner and support a family. White working-class men—Donald Trump's base—have seen well-paying jobs that used to confer status dry up. Women have more autonomy now and are outpacing men in educational attainment. A wave of immigration has diversified the country, eating into whites' political power. White American's economic dominance has been eroded, too. They still earn significantly more than Black and Hispanic Americans, but the gap has narrowed. Over the last three decades, the median white income has risen 35 percent, but Black Americans are making 51 percent more and Hispanics 46 percent more. These are trends worth celebrating, but they hardly seem so if you are feeling a sense of relative deprivation and stagnation.

In the United States and beyond, a sense of powerlessness has also emerged, as societies have become more complex and day-to-day activities require greater technical expertise—further distancing the elite from the masses. Time and again, antiglobalization movements crop up in the wake of a serious financial crisis, precisely because the failure of the system generates mistrust toward those who manage it. As the historian Quinn Slobodian has noted, much of the architecture of globalization was designed in a profoundly undemocratic fashion, with most institutions intentionally lacking any connection to the voting masses. Global rule-making bodies such as the IMF and the EU often bypass electoral politics altogether, an approach the political scientist Helen Thompson has called an "aristocratic" reining in of "democratic excess." This might have been good for growth, but it stoked rage and conspiracy theories about "globalist elites."

Economic dislocation always produces anxiety, and this anxiety always spills over into politics, culture, and society. This is what the anthropologist Karl Polanyi meant when he wrote that markets are not self-contained enterprises but instead exist within a social and political framework. The market economy can never be fully insulated from social pressures. And the bigger the shock, the more society will want to protect itself from the next one.

THE 1990s BOOM GOES BUST

Our current moment of discontent solidified after the 2008 financial crisis. The seeds of that crisis were sewn in the 1990s, as overoptimistic lenders and financiers looked for easy money amid the globalization boom. Money was cheap, and everyone wanted in on the debt-financing game. Household debt in the US alone ballooned, growing from 61 percent of GDP in 1990 to nearly 100 percent in 2007. This proved unsustainable; it was only a matter of time before the 1990s boom went bust.

Overinflated mortgage lending accounted for much of this growth in household debt, and by 2007 many Americans could no longer afford their homes. As mortgage defaults began to cascade across the nation, major financial institutions struggled to cover their vast liabilities. Most banks tottered on the edge of bankruptcy. Many folded entirely, and those that survived did so only because they were bailed out by the government. The United States led the response by extending credit to foreign countries and implementing quantitative easing at home, a monetary policy that essentially amounted to the Federal Reserve purchasing toxic assets from troubled lenders. These steps stabilized the financial system, but they did little to help people who had lost their houses or their jobs.

Knowing what we do now about the cycles of globalization, we should not be surprised that those hurt most by the financial crisis wanted to jettison the '90s-era economic orthodoxy that they thought caused it. If economics superseded politics in the neoliberal period—with political parties across the world converging on economic policy—the 2008 financial crisis ushered in a new era in which politics superseded economics.

As many lost faith in the managers of globalization, various strains of populism popped up across the political spectrum. At first, much of the frustration from the 2008 financial crisis reinvigorated the Left, kicking off the Occupy Wall Street movement in 2011, for example, and enhancing the appeal of politicians like Bernie Sanders through his 2016 presidential bid. Ultimately, however, it was right-wing populists that proved most alluring to those disaffected with globalization.

These antiestablishment forces had existed since hyper-globalization began, but they had largely remained fringe movements. The 1992 independent presidential candidacy of Ross Perot, for example, combined economic heterodoxy with nationalism. Railing against globalization and deficit spending, the Texas billionaire promised to reject the North American Free Trade Agreement and balance the budget. Similar concerns, coupled with anxiety about immigration in previously homogenous European societies, spurred the founding of the UK Independence Party in Britain in 1933 and the growth of the National Front in France around the same time. But before the financial crisis, none of these movements had gained widespread national standing.

Afterward, they surged to prominence. Workers hurt by the crash wanted to unwind globalization, and they gravitated to right-wing populist parties. In 2014, the UK Independence Party (UKIP) won its first seat in Parliament. It would become Britain's third most popular party in 2015, winning 13 percent of the national vote. A year later, UKIP would significantly aid the successful "Vote Leave" campaign, building on widespread protectionist impulses, general skepticism toward the European Union, and rising anti-immigrant sentiments across the country. The result was the infamous Brexit, the United Kingdom's exit from the European Union.

The French National Front had a similar string of successes in the 2010s, winning 15 percent of the vote in 2011 district elections under its charismatic new leader, Marine Le Pen. The following year, Le Pen managed to place third in France's presidential election. In 2014, her party won nearly 25 percent of the votes in elections for the European Parliament, shocking pundits across the continent. The next year, seeking to rebrand the National Front, Le Pen expelled her own father—Jean-Marie Le Pen, the party's founder and long-time leader—whose racist comments and downplaying of the Holocaust had long caused embarrassment. The younger Le Pen became an even more serious contender in France's 2017 presidential election, channeling the spirit of Islamophobia and protective French nationalism. She came second in the first round, and though she lost badly to Emmanuel Macron in the runoff, she had successfully injected skepticism of immigration and Islam into French political discourse, leading Macron's government to take a remarkably hard line on those issues.

In the United States, no viable new party emerged, but an insurgent faction within the Republican Party blew through American politics like a hurricane. The Tea Party arrived on the scene in 2009, demanding lower taxes and decrying the size of the national debt. The energy animating the Tea Party contributed to the "shellacking" of Democrats in the 2010 midterm elections (as Barack Obama memorably put it), and the movement successfully pulled the Republican Party to the right. Insurgent candidates like Marco Rubio and Rand Paul rode the wave into office, and many traditional conservatives also adopted the populist rhetoric that had propelled Tea Partiers. Ultimately, much of the broader GOP absorbed the Tea Party's ideas and ethos, blazing a path for Donald Trump to emerge as a political force in the 2016 election. Trump himself never identified as a Tea Partier, but his anti-elite, anti-globalist, ethno-nationalist rhetoric resonated deeply with Americans who felt left behind by globalization.

Around the world, each populist party that rose in the wake of the Great Recession has a unique appeal based on long-running dynamics in its country; it is hardly possible to speak of a "populist international." Yet these parties do share some key similarities that distinguish them from their liberal opponents. Like many right-wing populist parties we know from history, today's antiestablishment movements espouse an exclusionary vision of "the people," leaving out many groups they deem as foreign or corrupted. And their platforms have emphasized social cohesion, a sense of belonging to and duty toward the in-group, often to be achieved at the overt expense of minorities.

These movements decry openness as they lament the breakdown of traditional economic structures and social norms in their contemporary societies. They each peddle in forward-looking nostalgia—contrasting a bleak present with what they consider the good old days. They blame working-class economic dislocation on open migration patterns and international industrial competition. It makes no difference that these narratives are mostly untrue or simplistic. What matters is that these antiglobalization parties have successfully tapped into the social and economic anxiety of millions who, like many before them, feel disabused of the promises of globalization and stand ready to disavow its champions.

THE PENDULUM SWINGS TOO FAR

Whereas the free-market Washington Consensus reigned supreme for much of the past few decades, today a new economic consensus is forming, this one around state intervention. As inequality has climbed and intersecting crises have laid bare the vulnerabilities of interconnection, people across the political spectrum have begun to question the logic not only of unencumbered free markets but also of globalism itself. While the policy prescriptions on the left and the right differ in important ways, many on both sides share a desire to put the brakes on globalization and prioritize national interests once again. Governments have begun to restrict international trade and investment and take a more active role in the economy. Nationalist sentiment is festering under the surface as countries prioritize economic resilience over growth. Whereas the old consensus in the West centered on an open global system and celebrated shared prosperity, the new one sees China's rise as coming at Americans' expense and tries to remedy the ills of the globalized order.

Donald Trump brought this view into the mainstream and swung US policy in that direction, but a more sophisticated version of this new consensus was put forward by Joe Biden's national security advisor Jake Sullivan. In April 2023, he argued that although free trade and open markets fostered growth, growth was not the only goal the United States should pursue. In the era of hyper-globalization, he asserted, policymakers had ignored the need to keep domestic manufacturing alive, reduce inequality, create a more resilient economy, and they failed to recognize that China was not just an economic competitor but a geopolitical one, too. In other words, America opened up its economy to the world, but American workers, as well as American national security, suffered as a result. While some interpreted the speech as heralding a new course, Sullivan was only putting a strategic gloss on policies that the United States had lurched toward under the previous administration. Trump slapped tariffs on China, as well as on US allies. He banned the Chinese telecom company Huawei from the US and tried to block TikTok. He restricted certain US exports to China and curbed investment going both ways. He rejected the Trans-Pacific Partnership, a trade deal President Obama had struck with Asia-Pacific countries. President Biden generally kept Trump's policies in place and sometimes expanded them.

In fact, even before Trump was elected, the United States had been moving away from free trade. The economist Adam Posen writes that since 2000, the US "has increasingly insulated the economy from foreign competition, while the rest of the world has continued to open up and integrate." He adds, "The country suffers from greater economic inequality and political extremism than most other high-income democracies—countries that have generally increased their global economic exposure." Globalization is an easy bogeyman for rising inequality and job displacement across the United States, but the timing doesn't support this accusation, since these trends predate the recent acceleration of globalization. We should therefore be skeptical of a new consensus that globalization alone is to blame for people's economic woes—and that the solution is to undo it.

It is true that moving too far in the direction of laissez-faire economics causes grave problems. But moving too far in the opposite direction yields its own troubles. Navigating these currents is becoming increasingly difficult in an interconnected world. And it is made even harder by the other structural revolution that has accompanied globalization, perhaps the most dramatic one we are undergoing.

INFORMATION UNBOUND

Technology

N OTHING SPOILS A TECH DEMO LIKE AN ACCIDENTAL death. The year was 1830, and the occasion was the debut of the world's first intercity railroad, between Liverpool and Manchester. As dignitaries milled about, a local member of Parliament, William Huskisson, one of Britain's most ardently pro-railway politicians, walked on the tracks to shake the hand of Prime Minister Arthur Wellesley. Huskisson didn't realize just how fast one of the new trains—*Rocket*, which could travel at thirty miles per hour, unthinkably fast for the era—was barreling toward him. Panicking at the sight, he got stuck on the tracks. It was the end of the line for William Huskisson. Rail's coming-out party had been marred by one of the first-ever train fatalities.

The idea that such fast transportation could soon be accessible to everyone was groundbreaking, but at the time, headlines focused on the tragedy resulting from this terrifying new technology. Today, with the digital revolution that has unfolded since the 1970s (the Third Industrial Revolution) and the rise of artificial intelligence and biotechnology in the 2020s (what some are calling the Fourth Industrial Revolution), the world is again changing faster than ever—and many people feel like they'll be the ones stuck on the tracks.

The twenty-first century has few true Luddites calling for technology to be rolled back. But beneath the surface of digital marvels lies a world of disruption, upheaval, and dissent. Many of the tensions of our times—between prosperity and instability, between interconnection and atomization, between progress and backlash—are at least partly a result of these technological transformations. It's no coincidence that populism's appeal has grown in a world rapidly reshaped and destabilized by innovation. The gains to productivity and human flourishing from the information technology revolution have been immense. But we should hardly be surprised that the ride has been bumpy so far, perhaps even bumpier than previous ones, because this revolution upends not just physical limits but mental and biological ones. It changes who we are.

Ironically, the roots of this change—a transformation that seems too fast, too confusing, too chaotic—emerged from what seemed like a period of slowdown and stasis. The 1970s are often remembered as a time of malaise. In politics and culture, the idealistic crusades of the '60s had flamed out into frustration. Economically, stagflation seemed to be the new normal. The economist Robert Gordon's sweeping *The Rise and Fall of American Growth* chronicles the astounding century from 1870 to 1970, from the Gilded Age to the Computer Age, when new technologies modernized American life and pioneered the lifestyle we now associate with the middle class around the world. As we have seen, it was Britain that overwhelmingly enjoyed the fruits of the original Industrial Revolution—steam, rail, and mass-produced textiles—beginning in the late eighteenth century. And it was the United States that was the chief innovator and leading beneficiary of the Second Industrial Revolution beginning in the late nineteenth century, making advances in energy, materials, chemicals, and automobiles.

The United States continued to build on that progress into the middle of the twentieth century, remaking itself to the benefit of almost everyone within its borders. Americans enjoyed longer-than-ever lifespans thanks to new medicines. They ate more abundant and varied food produced by industrial agriculture. They lived in new suburbs and cities interlinked by rail, highways, and airlines. These transformations were largely physical. You could see the countless cars on the road, the dishwashers and televisions in homes, the cities lit up by electrification, the sprawl of urban areas, the gigantic combine harvesters trawling through fields of wheat and corn. In arguably the greatest feat of engineering in human history, in 1969 the men of the Apollo 11 mission landed on the moon, marking new heights of American technological ingenuity.

Yet in the following years, America fell back to Earth. The explosive growth of the postwar years petered out. Getting to the moon was an exciting achievement, but space wasn't a new frontier that could actually be settled and developed. On the ground, the rate of change slowed, and Americans settled into the humdrum rhythms of modern life. The way people commuted to work, the way food got to their plates, the way their homes were powered—these changed little over the subsequent decades. In the words of the economist Tyler Cowen, it seemed that America had already eaten "all the low-hanging fruit of modern history." The country had experienced a one-off burst driven by harnessing fossil fuels and developing land, along with a healthy dose of human ingenuity. It was an explosion that couldn't easily be replicated.

For all the malaise of the '70s, however, it would turn out to be a period of hidden progress. A storm of technological change was quietly gathering in a part of California that would soon become known as Silicon Valley. This revolution would not transform the physical landscape like past ones; it would be a digital revolution, built on invisible bits and bytes. But it would change the world like nothing before. Technology in prior revolutions changed the physical world; the digital revolution would change the mental world, expanding information, knowledge, analytic capacity and with it our definition of what it means to be human. Whatever the quantitative impact of the information revolution we are living through, this *qualitative* impact on the human psyche is vast and ongoing.

THE JETSONS GOT IT WRONG

The rise of the internet and personal computing is sometimes termed the Third Industrial Revolution. This revolution has been both faster and more widespread than the first two, and yet subtler, taking place largely in the realm of information. The first computers were developed in World War II as code-breaking tools for American and British military intelligence. These were behemoths of vacuum tubes and circuitry that filled whole rooms. With the invention of the computer chip came the first personal computers, compact machines built by companies like Hewlett-Packard and Xerox. What we now call the internet began not with private firms but with a Pentagon project, ARPANET, a network designed to link researchers at West Coast universities with their colleagues around the country. From the time it went online, in 1969, ARPANET steadily branched out to more universities and labs in the 1970s and 1980s. Then, in 1989, English computer scientist Tim Berners-Lee, working at the CERN particle physics lab in Geneva, devised the combination of systems that drive the modern internet: hypertext links that allow users to move from one text to another, transmission control protocols that connect computers of all types to the same information, unique domain names for each website. He called it the World Wide Web, though at first it was only available to scientists within CERN. Two years later, as all eyes were on the collapsing Soviet Union, a potentially even more momentous change quietly took place in Geneva: the Web was opened to the whole world, inaugurating the internet as we know it today.

In 1990, no country on the Earth had even 1 percent of its population using the internet. Today, 93 percent of Americans are online, as are some 70 percent of Asians and Middle Easterners. Even in the world's least-developed regions, sub-Saharan Africa and South Asia, roughly a third of people use the internet. Every day, over three hundred billion emails are sent from more than four billion users around the world. Think about how many decades it took for railroads to diffuse across the world in the nineteenth century, or for automobiles to become ubiquitous in the twentieth. At the turn of the twenty-first, personal computers and smartphones (minicomputers in our pockets) went mainstream in just twenty years. Technological adoption within the internet happens even faster. It took almost four years to get one

First electronic computer.

hundred million people worldwide to use Facebook, over two years to get that same number on Instagram, and just two months to get one hundred million people using ChatGPT.

As impressive as the shift from the physical to the digital has been, many skeptics, even some in the industry, consider it a disappointment. In the oft-quoted words of Peter Thiel, the founder of PayPal and Palantir: "We wanted flying cars. Instead we got 140 characters." On a surface level, Thiel is right. We are a far cry from the vision of the twenty-first century in the 1962 animated television series *The Jetsons*. Eagle-eyed fans have noted that George Jetson, the patriarch of this archetypal futuristic family, was born in 2022. But the world today looks nothing like the Jetsons' world: no flying cars, no sentient robotic maids, and (not even for Elon Musk) no interplanetary vacations.

And yet, what do we have that the Jetsons did *not* have? While some predictions were correct—video calls, for example—the more profound implications of the digital transition were unforeseen. The technology that underpins our age is radically different from those that preceded it. It has fomented a revolution of the mind. It has dramatically expanded access to information, connecting nearly everyone on the planet, and making it easier for ideas of all kinds, good and bad, to spread.

Rather than changing our physical world, the info-tech revolution has created an entire new world—a digital world, full of universally accessible knowledge, the digitalization of almost every industry, endless mediums for entertainment, and new kinds of social connections. So while modes of transportation have not advanced as some predicted, think about what you can now do on an airplane flight or train ride that would have been pure science fiction to the travelers of the 1960s: instantly access virtually any movie, TV show, or book; talk to a friend or loved one; conduct your business (if you are a white-collar worker) nearly as effectively as if you were in the office.

Quality of life has substantially improved for all, even while the many free goods and services made possible by the digital revolution are not fully captured in conventional metrics like GDP. Take the music industry. From 2004 to 2008, total revenue from music sales dropped from $12 billion to $7 billion. But it wasn't as if people listened to less music; they merely did so in a new way. Over that same period, single-track downloads increased nearly tenfold from around 143 million to 1.4 billion, with songs now widely accessible through a variety of digital platforms.

Similarly, anyone with access to the internet today can get lost in the depths of Wikipedia, which in 2023 had around one hundred times as much information as the printed *Encyclopedia Britannica*, formerly the premier source of English-language generalized knowledge from its first publication in 1768 through the late twentieth century. But unlike the printed *Britannica*, Wikipedia is free. The difference in usage is staggering. In 1990, eleven years before Wikipedia was founded, 117,000 copies of *Britannica* were sold worldwide. Today, Wikipedia gets over 1.5 billion unique visitors every month. Indeed, one of the most striking features of this revolution is how it has transformed leisure time. In the year 2013 alone, Facebook users collectively spent around two hundred million hours each day on the platform. As the scholars Erik Brynjolfsson and Andrew McAfee have pointed out, this is ten times as many person-hours as were needed to build the Panama Canal. In this comparison we see a microcosm of the shift from industrial to information revolution—from the physical realm to the life of the mind.

EVERY MAN A KING

After World War I, a brilliant young economist named John Maynard Keynes described the world of economic and technological advancement that the war had destroyed. "The inhabitant of London could order by telephone, sipping his morning tea in bed, the various products of the whole earth, in such quantities as he might see fit, and reasonably expect their early delivery on his doorstep." Pointing to the easy availability of transport, communication, and news, he noted that this was an age when the middle and upper classes had "comforts, conveniences, and amenities beyond the compass of the richest and most powerful monarchs of other ages."

Had Keynes lived to see the information revolution, he would have looked around in awe. The average American can now summon just about anything imaginable—a pen, a pomegranate, a Peter Pan costume—to their doorstep within days or even hours. Information and money can move across the planet within seconds. All it takes is the push of a button or a verbal command to a digital servant like Alexa. No wonder over 70 percent of book sales, over 40 percent of clothing sales, and 15 percent of all retail sales in the US now take place online. The effortlessness of listening to any song among millions on Spotify or streaming any movie ever made are advances so large as to defy comparison. No monarch ever had that kind of entertainment at his fingertips.

Despite all the hand-wringing about the digital age, the truth is that for the average person, the everyday good far outweighs the bad. People can work in flexible ways, freeing them from the tyranny of fixed hours and physical offices. Grandparents can FaceTime their grandchildren who live far away. Anyone can pull up a video to learn a new skill. Students can do their homework without having to go to a library and check out a book. We can work, connect, play, read, and watch everywhere and anywhere. We don't often think about the genuine pleasure our technology brings us, but our actions reveal just how attached we are. We keep using it, every day of our lives.

Yet the easy and instantaneous nature of our online existence also increases angst and impatience with the complexities of civic life. In the face of one-click ordering on Amazon, messy systems like liberal democracy, with its frequent gridlock and inefficient bureaucracy, seem clunky. Consider Donald Trump's pledge to cut through the Gordian knot of stalled politics. "I alone can fix it," he declared. His communication style was made for the times. As soon as he had a thought, he simply blasted it to the world on social media. His Twitter feed was a steady stream of shocking statements, frequently unhinged but rarely boring. Trump first became a public figure through tabloid newspapers and reality TV, but it was the internet that catapulted him into the White House. He was able to speak directly to his followers and dominate the ever-shortening news cycle. And his simplistic policy prescriptions—solve illegal immigration by building a wall (and making Mexico pay for it), restore American manufacturing by imposing tariffs (that other countries would supposedly pay for)—promised a kind of instant gratification at no cost, something people have come to expect in the internet era.

Writing in the 1960s, the media scholar Marshall McLuhan—known for his adage "the medium is the message"—predicted that the challenges posed by new electronic media would be almost impossible to recognize. He declared, "I am in the position of Louis Pasteur telling doctors that their greatest enemy was quite invisible, and quite unrecognized by them." Recognizing the reality of Pasteur's germ theory was key to making medical advances. Today, we have taken that first, diagnostic step: recognizing the potential downsides of the internet to rewire our brains, shorten our attention spans, and feed the resentful parts of ourselves. But we have not yet moved on to developing effective treatments for what ails us; no equivalent to a vaccine is yet in the offing. So for now, we get enormous gains from information technology—but admittedly, at a steep price.

BOWLING ALONE

When the internet first gained popularity in the 1990s, there was a revival in utopian dreaming: the world had never been so interconnected, the possibilities for new social bonds never so boundless. Today, a young gay person in a rural community in the United States, with no peers or role models to confide in, can escape from a judgmental reality to find support and guidance on Facebook and Instagram; a religious minority in a tribal region of Pakistan can find camaraderie through distant relatives on WhatsApp. Indeed, new online networks have undeniably been an immense boon for those who are isolated or stigmatized in their community.

But as the digital revolution has created new forms of communal engagement, it has accelerated a rot within society. Digitalization has decimated local communities, and traditional affiliations have weakened as younger generations have shifted their lives online. Was this a Faustian bargain? We have gotten convenience and efficiency at the cost of losing civic engagement, intimacy, and authenticity. In this we again hear the echo of the poet Oliver Goldsmith: "Wealth accumulates, and men decay." Amid such dislocation, people are drawn to fringe online communities—or even reject modernity itself, turning away from liberal democracy, economic growth, and technological progress.

It did not happen overnight. In his 2000 book *Bowling Alone*, the political scientist Robert Putnam described the decline of shared community in American suburbia after the 1950s. Voluntary associations had been the backbone of American society since the time of Tocqueville. But Putnam found Rotary Clubs, church groups, and adult sports leagues had atrophied. Today, most Americans cannot name a single "local person of influence," signaling a deterioration of their communal ties. Social media has facilitated more and more online connections, but Americans have become increasingly lonely. The number of American men who say they have more than ten close friends has fallen from 40 percent in 1990 to 15 percent in 2021. Alarmingly, the number who said they had *no* close friends rose from 3 to 15 percent. In 2023, US Surgeon General Vivek Murthy issued a report on the growing public health crisis of loneliness, documenting that its ill effects are comparable to smoking fifteen cigarettes a day.

The psychologist Jonathan Haidt has argued persuasively that social media is partially to blame. Into the void left by eroded communities, the internet has promoted unhealthy behaviors and connections. Since 2012, indicators of teen mental health—suicide attempts, hospitalizations for self-harm, self-reported feelings of anxiety and depression—have gotten significantly worse. This is roughly the same time that young people transitioned from flip phones to smartphones and when social media took the addictive form we recognize today. In 2009, Facebook instituted its iconic "like" button and Twitter rolled out its "retweet" function. With these dopamine triggers of virtual popularity, online life in many ways came to subsume in-person relationships. These bonds of online association are weak and can sometimes even be malevolent.

In late 2017, Reddit shut down a forty-thousand-member "involuntary celibate" or "incel" support group, for "people who lack romantic relationships and sex." What started out as a forum for lonely people had quickly turned rancid, with men raging against women who wouldn't sleep with them and even advocating rape. Harm from these communities manifests offline, too. Elliot Rodger, a twenty-two-year-old self-proclaimed incel, shot three women at a sorority house near UC Santa Barbara in 2014. In a YouTube video uploaded before the attack, he had promised "retribution" for female rejection.

For every innocuous use of the Internet—"Birdwatchers of Greater Tuscaloosa, unite!"—there are other forums that serve as incubators of radicalism. Many adults, living lives of greater isolation, have gone online and found a sense of shared purpose in the increasingly virulent politics of the day. As disturbing and fantastical as some conspiracy theories can be—dark visions of globalist cabals and child sex rings hidden in pizza shops—such worldviews may provide a perverse kind of comfort, a coherent narrative to replace randomness. Rather than helpless atoms at the mercy of anonymous forces, these true believers cast themselves as tragic heroes of their own story, victims of enemies who can be identified and defeated. In their version of events, the hollowing out of their towns and the decline in steady careers were not the result of generation-long shifts in economic and technological structures but rather the outcome of reversible decisions by sinister global elites.

This psychological reaction is not a new phenomenon. In the twentieth century, the political philosopher Hannah Arendt argued that totalitarian ideologies gained so much traction only because societies were so atomized. Imperialism and capitalism had brought wealth to European nations but destabilized traditional hierarchies and left many people without social affiliations. As a result, people were drawn to ideas that provided a clear sense of identity and simple explanations for an increasingly complicated world. In the final pages of *Origins of Totalitarianism*, Arendt wrote, "What prepares men for totalitarian domination in the non-totalitarian world is the fact that loneliness, once a borderline experience usually suffered in certain marginal social conditions like old age, has become an everyday experience of the ever-growing masses of our century." Unfortunately, the digital revolution has not only exacerbated the forces of loneliness and atomization but also empowered those who seek to exploit them.

SOMEWHERE, ANYWHERE

So, which is true? The glittering facade of "every man a king"? Or the societal decay of "bowling alone"? The answer: both, with the two effects distributed highly unequally. The digital economy, for all its promise, has caused inequality to spike to levels not seen since the Gilded Age.

As the world shifted under their feet, many American politicians have often acted as though we still live in the manufacturing-dominated world of the 1960s. Barack Obama in 2012 and Hillary Clinton in 2016 made the usual Democratic appeals to organized labor. But in each election, union members voted more Republican than in 2008. Although they would never phrase it this way, most Democratic politicians' implicit message to a laid-off worker made redundant by globalization and technology goes something like this: "Your old job isn't coming back, so your best hope in the digital economy is to retrain for an entirely different career in a new city or state. Your children should make sure to get a better education than you did and search for new centers of growth, far away from you." This is efficient economics but bad politics. It tells people that to make it in the new world, they need to fundamentally alter who they are. (Biden has taken a different approach, with a series of policies designed to revive manufacturing. This is inefficient economics but good politics.)

The digital revolution accelerated the shift in employment away from manufacturing and agriculture and toward the service sector. In the process, it unknit many communities. Over the past few decades, incomes for most working-class and rural people have not in fact drastically declined, even if they have stagnated compared to their educated, urban peers. But the reconfiguration of America's geography has undermined the community structures that once sustained the social life and culture of small-town America. The mom-and-pop store? Gone, unable to compete with Amazon. The corner arcade? Displaced by online gaming. The local movie theater? Run out of town by Netflix. These are all examples of what venture capitalist Marc Andreessen meant when he declared, "Software is eating the world." Brick-and-mortar businesses find that digital technology has a very real-world impact.

A small town, with its mom-and-pop businesses, is for its inhabitants a unique place—a "Somewhere" in the words of British writer David Goodhart. It shapes the life of many of its denizens, who define themselves in a way that would have been familiar centuries earlier, as people from that place—whether it is Alabama or Shropshire or

Toulouse. But increasingly, young men and women in such places are leaving to get educated and find white-collar work, clustering with their peers in globally linked metro regions, and joining a deracinated class of "Anywheres." Anywheres, writes Goodhart, define themselves not by their place of birth but by their education or profession. Those acquired characteristics shape their lives. As the young "somewheres" become "anywheres" this further hollows out the towns they leave behind and magnifies a winner-take-all concentration of talent. The beneficiaries of the high-tech globalized economy derive their identity from aspects of their life that are malleable—education, profession, passions. But not everyone wants to be a free-floating "Anywhere." Many people derive their sense of identity and life satisfaction from their roots, from being grounded in a specific geography—"Somewhere."

A new generation of populist Republicans have picked up on the idea of the Anywheres as disloyal, even "anti-American." These Republicans resent self-satisfied urbanites who disrespect their hometowns by moving to the East or West Coast. When Josh Hawley launched his Senate campaign in Missouri against Claire McCaskill in 2018, he railed against "coastal elites" who look down on the American heartland as "flyover country." Campaigning for Senate in Ohio in 2022, *Hillbilly Elegy* author J. D. Vance decried the "toxic" message for young boys and girls that they should move out of their hometowns. Never mind that many of these supposed champions of small towns themselves sought opportunity by moving to major universities or big cities (Hawley and Vance both have law degrees from Yale). The truth is, the urge to move up is strong, and that often means moving away from Somewhere.

HOW THE OTHER HALF LIVES, 2.0

Household incomes have grown robustly since the digital revolution. But averages conceal a lot of fantastic wealth and economic pain. And for many, the numbers don't convey the instability wrought by all this fast-moving change. They lament the dissolution of community ties and shuttered small businesses. Growing swathes of the country now face economic desolation, a world away from the glittering (and unaffordable) superstar cities.

These disparities are constantly displayed on social media. As more and more people share their personal lives online, a hyper-awareness of the lifestyles of the global elite grows. Call it "How the Other Half Lives, 2.0." The original 1890 Jacob Riis exposé used the novel technology of photography to show, in excruciating detail, the squalid living conditions of Manhattan's tenement dwellers. Confronted with these images, elites felt a responsibility to help the masses. They instituted regulations to reduce crowding and ensure proper sanitation.

Today, smartphones and social media have created a similar awareness of inequality, but in the reverse direction. Rather than guilty elites learning of the masses' plight, this time it is regular people who have grown acutely conscious of the lifestyles of the rich and famous. From trailers and tiny apartments in the United States—or remote villages in the Global South—anyone with a $100 phone can gaze with envy, longing, and resentment on the way elites spend their money. Italian villa getaways, ritzy rooftop parties, and immaculately composed Zen gardens flit by with the swipe of a thumb.

This dynamic is actually most pertinent in the developing world, where the gulfs in lifestyle between elites and average people are the most stark. The resulting resentment may have helped spark and sustain uprisings like the Arab Spring. For instance, in November 2010, WikiLeaks began releasing diplomatic cables from the US Embassy in Tunis that exposed the corruption of then-Tunisian president Zine el-Abidine Ben Ali. The Arab Spring took off in Tunisia one month later. Similarly, as early as 2009, outlets wrote about how Syrian dictator Bashar al-Assad's wife "had been flaunting her designer wardrobe on Facebook," all while her country suffered from poverty and repression. (A British newspaper labeled her "The First Lady of Hell," a phrase quickly taken up by social media.) This sentiment fueled public discontent in Syria, culminating with the Syrian civil war in 2011.

Our fixation with glamorous lifestyles has always existed—newspapers wrote about lavish balls and opulent mansions during the Gilded Age—but today, many celebrities' lives are on full display. Comparing one's ordinary life to that of the rich is easier than ever, causing understandable envy and resentment. Perhaps more galling, even workaday elites—not celebrities but software engineers or financial professionals—have raced ahead. McAfee and Brynjolfsson explain the problem well: "There's never been a better time to be a worker with special skills or the right education, because these people can use technology to create and capture value. However, there's never been a worse time to be a worker with only 'ordinary' skills and abilities to offer, because computers, robots, and other digital technologies are acquiring these skills and abilities at an extraordinary rate." Income inequality in the United States since the start of the digital revolution has risen steadily. Over the past fifty years, household incomes have grown three times faster for the top 20 percent of earners than for the middle quintile.

This inequality has helped fuel populism on the right and left—not just rage at billionaires and corporations but also an entire class of global elites that are seen as corrupt and self-serving.

THE NEW PRINTING PRESS

Even as wealth has become more unequally distributed, one of the great sources of power and wealth through the ages has become democratized: information. You are one click away from knowing practically anything. It's not only the consumption of information but also the production of it that has been democratized. Social media and the decentralization of media sources have brought new voices to the fore, allowing anybody, regardless of education or status, to participate in the global conversation.

This is not the first time technology has flattened the production and consumption of content. As the historian Ada Palmer has said of Gutenberg, "Many moments in the print revolution he unleashed were terrifying as well as good." But, she adds, the numerous new forms of media that have appeared since the 1400s "show us that democratizing expression always aids the democratization of power, aids community organization, civil rights movements, justice, human dignity and flourishing"—at least, one might add, overall and in the long term. But in the short term, the transformations may cause great chaos. Remember what followed the invention of the printing press in Europe: a century and a half of religious wars.

The democratization of information on the internet has already transformed politics. Twitter helped facilitate protests during Iran's "Green Revolution" of 2009, an early Middle Eastern tremor presaging the real quake: the Arab Spring of 2011. By allowing people to circumvent traditional media channels and oppressive government controls, the internet provided an unprecedented level of transparency, enabled the rapid spread of dissent, and mobilized people across borders toward collective action. Millions of people across the Arab world demonstrated against corruption, economic mismanagement, and dictatorial abuses—the largest multinational wave of democratic uprisings since Europe's revolutionary year of 1848.

Yet the mutually supportive relationship between democratic politics and information technology proved tenuous, and cracks soon appeared. Social media may be useful for rapidly generating energy and attention, but when it comes to building sustained movements, its fragmented, leaderless nature makes real long-term political change hard. Every one of the democratic movements to emerge from the Arab Spring has since been suppressed. In the United States, Occupy Wall Street's left-wing flare-up fizzled out without any major policy victories in Washington. An equally important flaw of internet-assisted movements is that while they are democratic in some sense, their anonymous, mob-like nature can also make them susceptible to illiberal tendencies. In France, the Yellow Vest protests against a proposed fuel tax increase came together fast in 2018, but they soon devolved into scattered, leaderless bursts, many of which turned violent or xenophobic.

Authoritarian states have bristled at the internet's ability to feed grassroots movements and have tried to clamp down through aggressive censorship apparatuses. The greatest example is China's Great Firewall, a fairly comprehensive internet censorship regime that keeps a lid on most dissent. Not only does China automatically block subversive content—searches for "Hong Kong independence," "Dalai Lama," and "Tiananmen massacre" turn up nothing—but it also recruits ultranationalist netizens into an online mob called the "50 Cent Army," so named for the small payments they receive for each comment denouncing Western values and praising Xi Jinping. Across Chinese social media platforms, public posts that take a stance against the regime are frequently flooded with a barrage of comments expressing unwavering support for the Communist Party and condemning those who disagree as traitors.

Back in 2000, President Bill Clinton dismissed China's attempts to censor the internet as doomed. "Good luck!" he said. "That's sort of like trying to nail Jello to the wall." China's Great Firewall has tested Clinton's hubris, proving more effective than many thought possible. Yet even under these extremely repressive conditions, neither the Great Firewall nor the party's online lackeys can stop dissent from percolating. Consider the anti-lockdown protests that arose across China's major cities in the fall of 2022. And outside of China, authoritarian regimes like the one in Vietnam have found it harder to censor social media. Governments, even democratic ones, are getting savvier at censorship. India and Turkey routinely shut down the internet during crises to keep dissent from spreading. Russia since launching its full-scale invasion of Ukraine has tried to replicate China's online surveillance state, with limited success. Social media is a powerful force for free expression but governments have also found new ways to tame it.

It's hard to feel optimistic about social media's democratic promise these days. New information technology has tended to empower marginalized voices, but also extreme ones. And it has been difficult to translate dissent into real power. Liking something on Facebook is just high-tech virtue signaling. And another disturbing trend has emerged in Western democracies: in the name of giving voice to the voiceless, many end up silenced.

OLD TRIBALISM, NEW NETWORKS

In 2021, the commentator Noah Smith observed, "Social ostracism is as old as the hills. Social media is not." In other words, being stigmatized for unpopular beliefs is nothing new. Just think of Socrates being disparaged and ultimately executed for his subversive views. The term "ostracism" actually comes from ancient Athens, which had a formal voting process to banish people from the city. Throughout the rest of history, dissidents and iconoclasts found themselves purged and punished for heresy, wrongthink, or other kinds of nonconformity. For most of humans' existence on the Earth, it has been the norm to harshly enforce the bounds of acceptable belief. Those who stretch or go beyond those bounds—the Galileos and Gandhis—are met with harsh consequences.

The punishments today may be far less severe, but technology has radically altered the scope and setting of unpopular speech. Consider a town hall meeting, direct democracy in the traditional New England style, sometime in the 1940s—say, the man standing up and speaking out in the iconic Norman Rockwell painting *The Freedom of Speech*. The speaker surely shared a huge amount of social and cultural background with his audience. Everyone in the room was white and from the same town. They likely grew up together and were overwhelmingly Christian, many of them attending the same church. Even if they disagreed with him, the speaker could hear and respond—if the audience began to stir and mutter in their seats, the speaker could tell that his message was not being received well.

In today's online echo chambers like Twitter, there is no such commonality. Being told to "read the room" when discussing controversial topics implies that the interlocutors—separated as they may be by distance, borders, cultures—are nonetheless part of a communal online

Freedom of Speech.

space with shared norms. No wonder that early internet dreamers' attempts to construct a digital, universal culture have been beset by obstacles.

Marshall McLuhan coined the term "global village" in the 1960s to describe the world's increasing interconnection. By the 1990s, with the Cold War over and globalization at full tilt, this term conjured a rainbow world, hands joining together in a Kumbaya circle, the internet knitting the world into a seamless whole. But McLuhan was not so optimistic. He feared a technologically connected community where perfect strangers would act like village busybodies: nosing into one another's business, peering through one another's windows, and enforcing an ever-narrower range of social conduct. Is this not the online world of today? In certain left-wing online circles, writing stories from a perspective outside of your identity group could get you denounced for appropriating others' lived experiences. On the other side, posting a picture in a mask during the pandemic could get you blacklisted from swathes of the conservative internet. It's the tyranny of a passionate minority—small groups of online zealots who seek to control discourse.

The information revolution has empowered the most irresponsible and inflammatory members of our societies, and their views are often crazy, sometimes dangerous. The Left has members advocating open borders, justifying ecoterrorism, and even demanding the abolition of police. But the Right appears more susceptible to online conspiracy theories: think of QAnon followers, anti-vaxxers, climate deniers, white supremacists. True, fringe movements have always existed—in the sixteenth century, some Protestant zealots were so convinced that the end was nigh that they took over an entire German city and slaughtered anyone who opposed them. People have believed all kinds of conspiracy theories about witches, Jews, Masons, UFOs, JFK, and the Beatles. But the internet concentrates conspiracy theorists and thus massively enhances their power. Alex Jones created a multimillion-dollar business based on delusions about staged shootings, satanic globalist cabals, and gay frogs—and had Donald Trump courting him.

With an assist from Russia and other nasty actors, these online channels have accelerated the spread of misinformation, broadly eroding public trust in the democratic process. Polls consistently find that around two-thirds of Republicans believe that the 2020 presidential election was fraudulent and illegitimate. Election skepticism spread partly through traditional means, of course, but social media certainly helped embed the "big lie" into the American public.

The misinformation problem will only be exacerbated by advancements in artificial intelligence. More benign uses of generative AI can create, in seconds, artworks that have never been painted (say, a Rembrandt portrait of Dwayne "the Rock" Johnson) or music that has never been sung (a Sinatra cover of Taylor Swift). But this technology can easily be put to much more malicious ends. So-called deepfakes have sprung up during the war in Ukraine, with one video, for example, purporting to show Putin announcing that Ukrainian forces had invaded Russia. This video was quickly debunked, but as deepfakes increase in quality and frequency, the problem will only get worse.

The inability to adjudicate between truth and falsehood has already intruded on the world's largest democracy, India. In the southern state of Tamil Nadu, where the nationally dominant Bharatiya Janata Party has struggled to make inroads, an audio clip was released of a rival politician discussing his party's corruption. The accused politician dismissed the audio as a deepfake, but expert analysts were unable to definitively say whether the clip was real. We can easily imagine how deepfakes could similarly destabilize American politics. On the eve of a presidential election, a video surfaces online allegedly showing one candidate accepting a bribe from a Chinese Communist Party official. Mainstream media and fact-checkers label it fake, but half the country, egged on by their party leader, come to believe the incident is true.

We should be on guard for such dangerous disruptions—but not lose our heads and act as though technology is solely to blame. Alas, human nature has proved all too susceptible to paranoia, conspiracy, and delusion with far more old-fashioned methods. Consider *The Protocols of the Elders of Zion*. This crudely written anti-Semitic pamphlet appeared in 1903 and circulated for decades, fueled pogroms across Europe, and became part of the guiding ideology of Nazism. Or take the Jonestown Massacre of 1978, which killed almost one thousand people. The mass poisoning was organized offline through age-old cultish proselytizing. Social media and AI may well accelerate the spread of hate and madness. But terrible ideas can go viral by whatever means, high tech or low tech.

ROBOTS AREN'T STEALING YOUR JOBS (YET)

For most people, the greatest threat from technology is not the proliferation of hate groups online, nor being "canceled" or censored. Rather, it is the fear of losing their jobs to automation. It's not just blue-collar workers who are getting nervous about automation:

when Hollywood actors and writers went on strike in 2023, their key demands concerned the possibility that studios would use AI-generated actors or dialogue.

There's no doubt that some occupations have already been affected by the machine age. Consider cashiers, who have seen their numbers shrink with the rise of self-checkout at the grocery store. But outside of a few experimental Amazon stores, cashiers are far from being eliminated entirely. Some customers will always prefer a human touch, and stores will always need people to oversee the machines. In 2018, Britain's House of Commons released a report on automation and employment in another prosaic workplace, the humble car wash. Yet another account of jobs lost to robots, bemoaning the diminishing opportunities for the working class? No. In fact, the report was not about automation; it was about *de*-automation. From 2006 to 2016, Britain lost over 1,100 automatic car washes, while an estimated 10,000 to 20,000 hand car washes sprang up. Consumers preferred hand car washes because they were actually cheaper and more convenient despite being performed by humans. (The report focused on concerns that hand car washes violated environmental and labor laws.)

Car washes are not a major source of employment, but the broader point is that humans are still far from being replaced by robots. Even after the shock of the Covid-19 pandemic, the effect was not to shunt vast numbers of low-skilled manual laborers out of the workforce. Rather, as society reopened, the economy suffered from a labor shortage amid a demand for workers that was unprecedented in modern history. Employers drove fierce competition for employees, even for entry-level and unskilled workers. Some restaurants went so far as to offer signing bonuses; others were so short-staffed that drunk employees were merely sent home instead of being fired. The much-feared future, of machines taking away millions of jobs and bringing about "the end of work," simply has not come to pass—at least, not yet.

Some jobs have certainly been eliminated, but many others have been created. And for some workers, technology has not replaced them but has augmented them with a kind of physical or mental prosthetic. And we are still only in the early stages of these collaborative robots (called "cobots" in manufacturing parlance). Imagine the possibilities: A farmer glances at a tablet displaying a satellite image of her fields, supplemented by drone footage—and she controls several harvesters, all from one platform. A doctor gets nudged toward performing a different surgery by a machine-learning tool that has scanned through millions of prior cases, looking for patterns. A factory foreman surveys an assembly line composed half of robots and half of technicians, coders, and engineers who direct, repair, and support the machines. Already, these sectors have been improved by digitalization, streamlining processes and training workers more effectively. Software has also given rise to entirely new fields, from video games to social media to app development, creating new and different kinds of jobs.

But concerns remain, and in the long term, AI-induced unemployment may come to pass. Andreessen may have said software was "eating the world" back in 2011, but with the advent of ChatGPT, venture capitalists Paul Kedrosky and Eric Norlin argue that software can "finish eating." ChatGPT is itself software; it's cheap, powerful, and could disrupt a host of industries. It can answer all kinds of questions and write everything from marketing materials to news articles to legal documents. It can also supercharge existing software. For instance, Salesforce has integrated the technology into its tools so that when a sales rep is put on a new account, ChatGPT can provide an overview of the company, find contact information for the right people, and compose a personalized email—and then make the email less formal if needed. Instacart launched a ChatGPT feature that suggests a recipe, turns it into a shopping list, and adds the items to your online cart. Chatbot software can even be used to create *other* software. After all, chatbots generate writing, and computer code is a kind of writing. So now someone can build their own software simply by feeding prompts to ChatGPT. Andrej Karpathy, a cofounder of OpenAI (the company behind ChatGPT), proclaimed, "The hottest new programming language is English." All of this suggests much more software in the world, which means many more jobs may be disrupted or automated.

It's not just white-collar jobs in marketing, law, or programming. Imagine AI that is connected to robots. Many blue-collar jobs have proved too complex to automate, but a "thinking" robot might be able to handle them. The most-anticipated example is probably self-driving cars, which would not only transform personal transportation but would also render truck drivers, bus drivers, and Uber drivers obsolete. The technology is still in its early days, but some day, it could eliminate driver jobs that almost four million Americans hold—mostly men, mostly without college degrees. Conservative TV host Tucker Carlson has opined that he would ban driverless trucks to protect these blue-collar jobs.

This kind of neo-Luddism is not confined to the right. In 2017, Bill Gates proposed a "robot tax," which would force firms to pay the IRS when they replace a human worker with a machine (which is, among other problems, pretty unworkable). In 2022, the Biden administration contributed $684 million to modernize ports nationwide, after shipping backlogs had snarled global supply chains, but on the condition that no technology be installed that resulted in a net loss of jobs. This approach is literally counterproductive, choosing inefficiency over productivity. It recalls a story the economist Milton Friedman told about a visit he made to an Asian country in the 1960s. He toured a site where a canal was being constructed, and he was puzzled to see the workers using shovels rather than mechanized tractors and excavators. He queried a government official, who answered, "You don't understand. This is a jobs program." Friedman said, "Oh, I thought you were trying to build a canal. If it's jobs you want, then you should give these workers spoons, not shovels."

Fears about automation are understandable, and never more so now that AI has made huge breakthroughs. But over the course of history, technology has, in the long run, created more jobs and made our lives better. Refusing to use it would be foolish. If it does finally bring about "the end of work" then we will need to fundamentally rethink society. In 1930, John Maynard Keynes predicted that productivity would rise so much that his grandchildren would have to work only fifteen hours a week. It sounds like the kind of utopia Marx envisioned, where a person may "fish in the morning, hunt in the afternoon, rear cattle in the evening, and criticize after dinner . . . without ever becoming hunter, fisherman, herdsman or critic."

Let us not get carried away by our imaginations or fears, though. In the long run technology has never caused mass unemployment before, and as of now, Keynes and Marx have been way off the mark on this subject. Of course, politicians may find it hard to resist voters who demand that the government protect their jobs. But leaders should not stand in the way of technological progress. They should try to foster the creation of new jobs and industries rather than insisting that workers dig with spoons rather than shovels.

As AI develops, however, it will change our basic understanding of human capacity. Eric Schmidt, Daniel Huttenlocher, and Henry Kissinger point out in *The Age of AI* that ever since the Enlightenment, human beings have seen the human mind as unlocking the mysteries of the universe. Human rationality explained phenomena that in earlier eras was viewed as the product of divine forces. The Sun rose in the sky, for example, because the Sun god rode his chariot across the heavens. But AI is so complex, its data sets so vast, and its calculations so numerous that no human can even understand how it came to its conclusions. As AI's abilities improve, we will have to trust that the computer knows best, placing our faith in AI just as the pre-Enlightenment humans placed their faith in God. UCLA's Ken Goldberg similarly argues that when the Copernican Revolution took the Earth out of the center of the universe, it essentially put reason and human intelligence at the center. A new revolution is on the horizon—when artificial intelligence surpasses human intelligence and forces us to reassess our own place.

BIOLOGY GETS SMART

Along with AI, we are witnessing another aspect of the Fourth Industrial Revolution that could be just as transformative: the bioengineering revolution. In many ways, the two are intertwined. Take the "protein folding problem"—predicting the three-dimensional structure of amino acid sequences that make up the proteins that organisms need to function. This was considered one of the hardest challenges in biology since the 1960s. In 2020, researchers armed with an AI tool called AlphaFold essentially solved protein folding, unlocking an untold number of breakthroughs in biotechnology.

More broadly, the biotechnology revolution can be seen as another facet of the information revolution, one that deals not with bits and bytes but with the nucleotides of DNA and RNA that encode the structures of life forms. For more than three billion years, evolution was steered only by the forces of natural selection, which led some mutations to survive and others to die out. But today, humans are taking control of nature. The rise of modern biotechnology allows scientists to directly interfere with DNA inside living cells, engineering organisms and even engineering humans. As Jennifer Doudna, a pioneer of the revolutionary CRISPR gene-editing technology, and biochemist Samuel Sternberg have written, "for the first time ever, we possess the ability to edit not only the DNA of every living human but also the DNA of future generations—in essence, to direct the evolution of our own species."

In 2000, when the Human Genome Project had finished its rough draft of the entirety of genetic code found in human DNA, President Bill Clinton announced, "Today, we are learning the language in which God created life." In the ensuing two decades, the cost of sequencing a human genome dropped from $100 million to under $1,000. A process that used to take years now takes days. At noon on Friday, January 3, 2020, a Chinese research team received a test tube containing the DNA of the novel coronavirus. By 2 a.m. on Sunday, they had mapped out the virus's genome.

Thousands of miles away, two struggling, little-known biotech companies were about to have their moment. Massachusetts-based Moderna had faced growing skepticism from investors about its fanciful scheme of creating vaccines based on messenger RNA, or mRNA. In 2019, a German mRNA-focused company, BioNTech, had raised just over half as much money as it had hoped for. Suddenly, the coronavirus pandemic allowed the two companies to prove their vision. DNA is a huge master file that is stationary in a cell's nucleus; mRNA essentially takes little snapshots of DNA to transmit the instructions for making proteins. This particular virus, scientists quickly discovered, had certain spike proteins on its surface that, if disrupted, would inhibit its ability to multiply. Armed with the virus's genome, the companies could create a "mugshot" of that spike protein, using mRNA to plaster that mugshot all over our bodies. When the actual virus comes along with its spike protein, our immune system recognizes it and is already prepared to fight off the virus. This was the theory, at least.

It proved to be a smashing success, saving tens of millions of lives. And the speed at which the vaccine was developed was breathtaking. In April 2020, the New York Times projected that at the typical pace for new vaccine development, shots would be going into arms by the end of 2033. To meet the goal of creating a Covid vaccine by mid-2021, the Times said, would be to "achieve the impossible." The Moderna and Pfizer-BioNTech vaccines began to be administered before the end of 2020.

But what science giveth, politics taketh away. Though a majority of Americans would eventually get vaccinated, a vocal, angry minority refused to get the vaccine. They denounced vaccine mandates as a tyrannical form of government overreach. There were prominent anti-vaxxers on both sides of the aisle, but conservatives in particular used the issue to whip up the Republican base. J. D. Vance, for example, called Biden's vaccine mandates "naked authoritarianism." No amount of coaxing or explanation from experts could convince some people, who might refuse the vaccine and other cutting-edge drugs, yet would take hydroxychloroquine or ivermectin, which quacks claimed were miracle cures. Misinformation like this spread around the world, as did outright conspiracy theories like the belief that Bill Gates, who helped fund the vaccine, was using it to implant microchips in people.

Resistance to the vaccine reflects dangerous levels of polarization but also a broader mistrust in elites. Experts failed the public in the Iraq War, the financial crisis, and even early on in the pandemic, telling people not to wear masks. But technology has exacerbated mistrust. Tom Nichols, author of *The Death of Expertise*, argues that the world has become so complex that the average person doesn't understand how things work, feels helpless, and comes to resent experts. And with endless information just a click away, people think they can find out the truth for themselves and dispense with the experts. Never mind that it might take a true expert to successfully "navigate through a blizzard of useless or misleading garbage" that proliferates on the internet. So when it came to vaccines, though most people rejoiced at this marvel of human ingenuity, a significant part of the population rejected the advice of experts. They felt uncomfortable about a vaccine produced so quickly and with such a novel technique.

A similar skepticism can be seen in people's attitudes toward genetically modified organisms, or GMOs. With today's technologies and farming methods, meeting the world's expected food needs in 2050 would require farmland the size of Africa and South America combined. GMOs can help farmers grow more food with fewer resources, allow crops to withstand a changing climate, and even make the crops more nutritious. In the 1950s, the papaya ringspot virus nearly wiped out the entire production of papaya on the Hawaiian island of Oahu. A scientist at Cornell who grew up in the region saved the industry by creating a genetically modified papaya that was immune to the virus. This innovation was widely adopted by papaya producers. Today, 80 percent of Hawaiian papaya is genetically engineered.

There's a less happy ending to a story about rice, a staple crop that is the only source of food for many poor people in Asian countries.

Every year, vitamin A deficiency kills a million people worldwide, mostly children, and leaves as many as half a million blind. When scientists in 2000 engineered a new strain of rice rich in vitamin A, they hoped their invention, Golden Rice, would go a long way toward solving that problem. But GMOs have caused anxiety around the world, and many governments have prohibited their use. One incident in the Philippines aptly captures this backlash: in 2013, anti-GMO activists uprooted life-saving Golden Rice plants, while dismayed farmers looked on. The reactionaries were protesting a technology they saw as part of a conspiracy to subordinate local agriculture to multinational corporations. As of this writing, Golden Rice has not achieved anything like the widespread adoption needed to save millions of lives. Many still fear the consequences of tinkering with plant and animal genes, even though humans have long practiced selective breeding, a clumsier version of genetic engineering.

When it comes to tinkering with our own genes, we do have to be very careful because of the societal implications. But from a health perspective, gene editing could be a godsend. CRISPR can be used to replace specific mutations that cause diseases and has already shown great promise in curing patients with sickle cell anemia. Researchers hope CRISPR will someday be deployed to fix mutations that cause more complex genetic disorders or increase one's likelihood of cancer. This could be done before a child is even born. In 2018, Chinese scientist He Jiankui shocked the world by announcing that he had used CRISPR to modify the genetic code of two twins' embryos to make them resistant to HIV—and that these babies had already been born. The scientific community universally condemned this reckless meddling with the human genome without proper oversight or consideration of the risks, and Professor He was jailed and disgraced. But this technique may gain broad acceptance in the future because of its incredible potential to prevent disease.

This revolutionary technology will need to be carefully regulated. We are closer than ever to reaching Aldous Huxley's *Brave New World*, where babies are engineered for particular physical and mental characteristics. If you think people resent elites now, just imagine if the rich can pay extra to have perfect children. Such a world would challenge one of the bedrock premises of classical liberalism: that all men and women are created equal.

So while CRISPR and other biotech developments hold unbelievable promise, they will, like AI, also force a powerful reckoning of what it means to be human. The scholar Yuval Noah Harari argues that for all the social, political, and economic changes over the millennia, *Homo sapiens* have not changed much physically or mentally—until now. The combination of the twin revolutions in biology and computing will allow human beings to expand their physical and mental capacities. The result, he says, will be the creation of a godlike superman: *Homo deus.*

BEYOND DYSTOPIA

The future is starting to come into view. Technology could transform society in ways we can't even fathom today. Neal Stephenson is a prescient science fiction author who coined the terms "metaverse" for a virtual world and "avatar" for a person's digital self. He has also imagined how AI might transform the human experience. In his 1995 novel, *The Diamond Age*, a "smart" AI-powered storybook helps a girl escape from poverty, serving as a one-on-one tutor with infinite patience who encourages her when she loses hope. When many people think of AI and digital worlds today, their minds may turn to bleak dystopias like *The Matrix*, or the more mundane fears of video-game addiction and virtual reality displacing real life. But Stephenson's story—and real-life startups creating AI-powered one-one-one tutoring—show some of the more optimistic possibilities of artificial intelligence. In earlier eras, it was only the aristocratic few who could afford a private tutor—if AI makes it possible for anyone to receive individually tailored education, it's another example of "every man a king."

But revolutionary change is by definition highly disruptive. The information revolution has radically reshaped the world, and further progress, on a potentially larger scale, will be scary. Many jobs will go away, even as overall productivity will rise, generating greater wealth that could help all. Norms will be broken, but we can hope that everyone's quality of life will improve. There are real concerns about privacy and real questions about how the government should regulate companies and itself when it comes to the most advanced technologies. But these are not insoluble problems; we can have the benefits of digital life and also protect our privacy and our democracy. And if we can develop thoughtful rules around the AI and bioengineering revolutions, we will not lose our humanity, either. Indeed, we may come to appreciate it all the more. It will, however, lead to even greater changes in our conception of ourselves and our sense of what is distinctively human about us.

For all the technological doomsaying, we often lose sight of its vast potential. The ancients longed for devices that could free them from drudgery and bondage. In Aristotle's *Politics*, he imagined a sort of utopia where slavery and servitude might wither away: "If each tool could perform its task on command or by anticipating instructions, and if like the statues of Daedalus or the tripods of Hephaestus— which . . . 'entered the assembly of the gods of their own accord'— shuttles wove cloth by themselves, and picks played the lyre, a master craftsman would not need assistants, and masters would not need slaves." Today, we are ever closer to Aristotle's vision, a world where we will have to ask ourselves: what are human beings for, if not work and productivity? And if computers with AI can be better analytic machines than human brains, then what does that leave for humans? We will probably start defining our distinctive features as those that cluster around emotions, morality, and above all sociability—our ability to work, play, and live with other humans. "Man is by nature a social animal," said Aristotle in that same book two thousand years ago. Perhaps we are returning to that ancient wisdom.

No country is even close to universal abundance delivered by automation. But technological revolutions have already created greater productivity and wealth, which has slowly turned political battles away from economics as the defining battleground. The old left-right divide focused on big-versus-small government has given way to considerations of dignity, status, and respect. We are thinking differently about what defines us at our core—and how that definition translates into the broader social and political realm.

REVENGE OF THE TRIBES

Identity

A S THE FRENCH RANG IN 1968 WITH CHAMPAGNE AND
fireworks, their president struck a celebratory tone. "It is impossible to see how France today could be paralyzed by crisis as she has in the past," declared Charles de Gaulle, a man who had led Free France during World War II, created the nation's Fifth Republic, and was now presiding over the country's long postwar boom. But only five months after his New Year's message, Paris seemed like it had returned to the time of the Revolution. The broad boulevards of the French capital were blocked by makeshift barricades built from uprooted trees and defaced street signs. Economic life ground to a halt. Student activists occupied university buildings to challenge traditional hierarchies of power within the academy and beyond. On May 30 alone, almost a million Parisians—including both student protesters and supporters of the president—took to the streets. Defying the conformity of the older generations, youths covered Paris in graffiti such as "It is forbidden to forbid!" The day before, President de Gaulle had abruptly fled to a West German military base, perhaps fearing for his physical safety. A country that had known its share of violence and chaos was once again on the brink.

By the summer of 1968, the revolution had reached the heart of America. As the Democratic Party prepared for its national convention in Chicago that August, the city was brewing with the anticipation of violence. In the months before, the two biggest icons of the American

Left—Robert F. Kennedy and Martin Luther King Jr.—had been shot dead. For several years, a culture of dissent had been emerging, opposing everything from racism to war to drug laws. A generation was rising up against traditional norms, hierarchies, and authorities. In Chicago, as Democratic politicians rallied around the establishment candidate, Vice President Hubert Humphrey, the mood outside the convention hall turned sour. Half a mile away, police chased young protesters through the broken windows of the Conrad Hilton Hotel, clubbing anyone they could get a hand on. Tear gas even penetrated Humphrey's hotel suite. "The whole world is watching!" chanted protesters while TV cameras broadcast the unrest across the globe.

The world watched, and the revolution spread even further. Over the course of 1968, a global protest movement rippled through countries as diverse as West Germany, Mexico, and Japan. It swept through democracies and dictatorships, capitalist and communist countries alike. In the West, students protested against the excesses of consumerism and the free market; in the east of Europe, they rallied against communism. In Rome, in front of the city's main university, police battled thousands of student protesters who threw rocks and overturned cars. In Prague, Russian tanks rolled through the cobblestone streets, crushing under their treads the reformists' slogan of "socialism with a human face."

More than half a century later, the specter of 1968 still evokes emotions like no ordinary year. As the political commentator David Frum has written, there are two contrasting narratives about the era: "In the children's myth, Americans huddled frozen and miserable . . . until the brave, joyous protesters of the 1960s liberated them. In the parents', a golden age of patriotism and duty was wrecked by draft-dodging, pot-smoking, hippie-turned-yuppie lowlifes." This divergence of perspectives still shapes American political ideologies today.

In more ways than one, 1968 prefigured the two great trends that would reorder Western politics—the rise of identity politics and the growing polarization that accompanied it. The Democratic Party passed sweeping civil rights legislation in the wake of King's assassination and nominated Humphrey, who was, despite the protests, the most socially liberal candidate in its history. As the more culturally conscious "New Left" rose to prominence across the Western world, blue-collar workers slowly began to drift away from traditional left-wing parties. Race riots became commonplace, social issues rose to prominence, and middle-ground consensus broke down in favor of dogmatic fervor on both ends of the spectrum. In a matter of a few years, the revolution of the 1960s radically changed the culture, breaking with centuries-old mores around hierarchies of gender, race, and authority. From abortion access to housing protections, voting rights to equal employment laws, the '60s set in motion a sweeping set of reforms. Almost every contemporary social movement, from #MeToo and Black Lives Matter to the conservative fight against critical race theory, is wrestling with ideas that were first articulated in that decade. Where politics was once overwhelmingly shaped by economics, politics today is being transformed by identity.

The '60s didn't achieve the political revolution longed for by its most ardent proponents. In France, the communist takeover feared by de Gaulle failed to materialize. If the spring of 1968 recalled the Jacobin fervor of the early 1790s, then the summer brought back vague memories of the Napoleonic counterrevolution that followed in its wake. In July 1968, de Gaulle's party won 74 percent of all seats, as French voters firmly rejected the radicalism of the activist Left. By the end of the year, workers had returned to their factories and students to their classrooms. Conservatives continued to occupy the Élysée Palace until 1981. In the United States, law-and-order Richard Nixon defeated Humphrey in 1968, and two years later in Britain, the Conservative Party swept into power. The '60s failed to forge a lasting consensus around a shared agenda of social reform. Instead, it exposed new cultural cleavages that became the new battle lines of politics.

THE HIERARCHY OF NEEDS

Revolutions can erupt from desperation and despair, as in France in 1789. But a different kind of revolution can originate from a state of abundance—and that is the case of the identity revolution. As the political scientist Ronald Inglehart put it, societal needs, much like individual ones, follow Abraham Maslow's "hierarchy of needs." At the bottom of the pyramid are food, security, and housing. For most of human history, these have been the ends to which all societal activity is directed. But once these material needs are satisfied, people shift their focus to higher-order demands: abstract values of personal freedom and self-expression. Put another way, when revolutions in economics and technology generate improvements in living standards—along with dislocation and disorientation—they tend to produce revolutions in identity as well. Once detached from their traditional roles in the economy and society, people respond with either hope or fear. Formerly marginalized groups perceive the change as liberating and reach for newfound dignity; those at the top fear losing the status they already have.

The 1960s and '70s saw the swiftest and most radical identity revolutions of the twentieth century. By 1968, the Western world had reached a turning point, thanks to the postwar economic boom brought about by globalization and technological progress. Young people, who had come of age free from the horrors of war and hunger, were dissatisfied with a society run by out-of-touch elites. They yearned for greater individual rights and a more inclusive vision of citizenship, one that extended to those historically left behind. In Europe, as Mark Lilla notes, protesters still largely saw themselves as waging class war, not culture war. And ironically, with cultural divides not yet at the center of political contention, social change was much faster and more permanent in the Old World. Abortion, for instance, was rarely politicized.

As a new consensus formed in the 1980s and 1990s around economics, culture began to replace it as the main political battle line. In the United States, people began to focus more on their personal identities—race, religion, gender—than on their class, sowing the seeds of a culture war that continues today. The process took longer in Europe, but it, too, succumbed to polarization and identity politics, mostly driven by immigration. By the 1990s, a new kind of identity revolution had taken hold. This was a slow revolution, a tectonic shift rather than an earthquake. Again, structural change preceded political revolution: after the fall of the Berlin Wall, an even faster pace of globalization and technological change ushered in a new golden era of free-market politics. Once the Left jumped aboard the neoliberal bandwagon, the Right confronted an acute crisis of how to differentiate itself. Conservatives realized they would need to double down on identity politics if they wanted to distinguish themselves from an increasingly moderate center-left.

Some right-wing leaders sensed early on where the wind was blowing. In 1992, firebrand Republican presidential candidate Pat Buchanan roared, "There is a religious war going on in this country. It is a cultural war, as critical to the kind of nation we shall be as was the Cold War itself, for this war is for the soul of America." The coming decades would prove him correct.

PROLETARIANS UNITED

Today's political divide between leftist yuppies and conservative blue-collar workers would strike any nineteenth-century observer of Western politics as strange. In 1848, Karl Marx and Friedrich Engels wrote in *The Communist Manifesto* that "the history of all hitherto existing society is the history of class struggles." If lacking in historical nuance, Marx's assessment of contemporary European politics was broadly on point. Since the dawn of the Industrial Revolution, they had indeed been defined by constant conflict between the working-class left and the bourgeois right. This divide continued for a century after the publication of the *Manifesto*. Factory workers banded together to fight for better wages, shorter hours, and safer working conditions—as we have seen. Meanwhile, the US also had strong labor movements and fierce economic debates over policies such as tariffs, though with the added dimension of race complicating everything.

It was not until after World War II that a consensus was reached, at least within the West. The formula for success was democracy plus markets plus the welfare state. In Europe, conservatives and social democrats had learned to avoid the extreme left-right polarization of the interwar era and instead embraced a more cooperative style of governance. In the United States, the Great Depression and the war effort fostered broad agreement on the need for government involvement in the economy. Even President Dwight Eisenhower, a Republican, supported almost all of FDR's "socialist" programs, from Social Security to marginal tax rates above 90 percent. Put simply, the Right, once bitterly opposed to the welfare state, now accommodated itself to it.

Of course, the supposed mid-century utopia—with low inequality and little political polarization—was built on racial exclusion. It is no accident that much of this "heyday of American social democracy," as the historian Dorothy Sue Cobble termed it, coincided with Jim Crow. Throughout the first half of the twentieth century, both parties had tacitly agreed not to challenge the foundations of white supremacy. In the 1930s, only 4 percent of Black Americans were eligible to vote. Meanwhile, the Immigration Act of 1924 appeased nativists by effectively banning all immigrants who weren't white and northern European.

White Southerners conditioned their support for the redistributive policies of the New Deal program on the continued subjugation of Black Americans. No wonder New Deal legislation banned domestic workers and farm workers—who were largely Black—from unionizing and receiving Social Security benefits. In return, the South rewarded Roosevelt handsomely. In the 1936 presidential election, he won 97 percent of the vote in Mississippi and 99 percent in South Carolina.

By the 1950s, racist redlining policies in the North and legal segregation in the South meant that white and Black Americans lived separate lives. As economic growth ballooned, white Americans could pursue the American dream from the safety of their suburban Levittowns. America seemed to have reached a stable equilibrium. In 1950, the American Political Science Association published a report titled

"Toward a More Responsible Two-Party System." Its conclusion? What American democracy needed was less compromise, more party cohesion, more distinct party platforms—in short, *more* polarization.

Soon enough, that wish would come true. Consensus on economic policy opened the door for social issues to come to the fore. The dominance of white men would be undone. These changes would bring America much closer to fulfilling its founding ideals, but they would also bring chaos into the streets.

AMERICA'S COMING OF AGE

In the 1950s, many American families would gather around the TV every Monday night for the weekly airing of *I Love Lucy*, the most popular show of the decade. Yet by the following decade, the image of harmonious family life depicted in *I Love Lucy* seemed utterly outdated. "Your sons and your daughters / are beyond your command," sang Bob Dylan in 1964. Young men now wore Beatles-inspired mop tops and swapped their slacks for denim jeans.

The year 1964 also marked the start of large-scale US involvement in the Vietnam War, a conflict that devastated Vietnam physically and tore the US apart culturally. Young Americans, many of whom were drafted into military service, became passionately opposed to US involvement in the war. Some fled to Canada. Others expressed their anger by marching, burning their draft cards, staging hunger strikes, or occupying university buildings. Some Vietnam veterans publicly threw away the medals they had won for valor. The Weather Underground, a far-left domestic terrorist group, went further, bombing targets including the US Capitol, the Pentagon, and the State Department.

As the youth of America protested the war, they came to rebel against an entire older culture they considered too conservative. In 1967, a hundred thousand young Americans gathered in San Francisco's Haight-Ashbury neighborhood for the rock-and-roll, psychedelics-fueled "Summer of Love." Two years later, nearly half a million flocked to the Woodstock music festival, where Jimi Hendrix's warped rendition of the national anthem seemed to embody the changes afoot: a bending of the rules, a newfound freedom of self-expression, a willingness to challenge the strictures of American politics.

Before long, the social changes pioneered by the counterculture movement had left their mark on the country. By 1971, 35 percent of Americans thought the concept of marriage was obsolete. A more permissive approach to drugs also took hold in an astonishingly short time. In 1967, only 5 percent of Americans had ever tried marijuana. By 1979, 51 percent of high school seniors admitted to having smoked pot in the past year.

At the same time, Americans rapidly lost trust in traditionally revered institutions—from the church to the government. The percentage of American Catholics attending weekly mass shrank from 75 percent in 1957 to 54 percent in 1975. In 1958, 71 percent of Americans trusted their government to do the right thing almost all or most of the time. Twenty years later, only 29 percent felt the same. After the government's lies about Vietnam and then the Watergate scandal, the American public no longer gave their leaders the benefit of the doubt. At the outset of the protest movement of the '60s, the student organizer Jack Weinberg had told the country, "You can't trust anyone over 30." By the 1970s, it seemed like few people trusted anyone anymore. The collapse of faith in authority and institutions has created a fertile breeding ground for populism, conspiracy theories, and a "post-truth" world.

EUROPE'S QUIET REVOLUTION

In Europe, as in America, change was spearheaded by a new generation that prioritized political participation and freedom of expression over traditional authority. This was what Ronald Inglehart called a "postmaterialist generation," preoccupied with personal self-realization rather than material possessions or safety. In 1970, Inglehart surveyed people across six Western countries. Among those who had

grown up during World War II, materialist values outranked postmaterialist by as much as three to one. But "postmaterialism" dominated
the cohort of people between the ages of fifteen and twenty-four, who
had been born after the war. Which category one belonged to was an
extremely accurate predictor of how one felt about the student movement. Out of those who favored "materialist" values like order and
price stability, only 16 percent supported student protests. Of those
who prioritized "postmaterialist" values such as political participation
and freedom of speech, 71 percent did.

In Europe, even with fascism discredited by World War II, the underlying structures of authority—in business, academia, and government—
had remained largely intact in Axis countries like Germany and Italy.
Fighting communists became a priority as the Cold War deepened,
which meant putting the fight against fascists on the back burner. In
West Germany and Austria, rehabilitated Nazis returned to positions
of power in government and society. Even more so than in the United
States, the emerging divide between student revolutionaries and their
detractors was a titanic struggle between the generations.

Perhaps nowhere was that gap as stark as in West Germany, where
young people revolted against a generation of leaders who had been
complicit in the atrocities of the Holocaust. In short succession, both
leaders of the West German government in 1968—President Heinrich
Lübke and Chancellor Kurt Georg Kiesinger—were revealed to have
been affiliated with the Nazi regime. At the Christian Democratic
Union's party convention, an activist named Beate Klarsfeld walked
up to the podium, slapped Kiesinger across the face, and shouted
"Nazi!" The left-wing militant Gudrun Ensslin put things in terms
that became emblematic of the rift tearing through the country: "This
is the Auschwitz generation, and there's no arguing with them!"

As youth of the '60s aged into positions of authority, cultural change
followed swiftly. Throughout the '60s and '70s, Europe experienced
an unprecedented wave of secularization. Between 1963 and 1976, the
number of annual divorces in West Germany more than doubled. In the
Netherlands, the percentage of Catholics attending weekly mass fell by

half between 1965 and 1975. In fact, secularization went much further in Western Europe than in the United States. Among Western European Christians, less than a quarter today believe in God with absolute certainty (compared to 76 percent of American Christians). Abortion laws changed accordingly. Before the 1970s, Iceland was the only non-communist European country to have legalized abortion. But then, in April 1971, the French magazine *Le Nouvel Observateur* printed a petition signed by 343 women—including the feminist philosopher Simone de Beauvoir and the actress Catherine Deneuve—publicly admitting that they had had illegal abortions and demanding changes to the penal code. As cultural norms shifted, European countries liberalized their abortion laws in rapid succession. In 1975, France removed penalties for abortion; West Germany followed suit in 1976 and Italy in 1978.

In a matter of years, the New Left—new in that it prioritized social issues over class conflict—transformed Europe's cultural sphere, winning hearts and minds much more successfully than its American counterpart. This sea change in public opinion forced the Right to compromise on a variety of social issues. With the culture wars having been preemptively settled in favor of the Left, and with politics still largely a fight between classes over economic issues, Europe's cultural conservatives were rapidly losing ground. As a result, Europe saw far less of the cultural backlash that was convulsing the United States. In addition, European multiparty systems proved more adept at accommodating diverging identities and interests, removing some of the partisan tensions that roiled America. By the 1980s, for example, left-leaning German voters could choose between the social democrats, centrists, and Greens. This range of options prevented some of the friction and polarization plaguing America's two-party system.

THE SILENT MAJORITY

By contrast, polarization came to split America in two. It started when the ties between the American working class and the political Left began to come apart. In 1948, white, working-class voters had been

12 percent more likely than the general population to vote Democratic. By 1968, the ground had shifted under Democrats' feet: that year, white, working-class Americans opted for Democrats by only a margin 3 percentage points higher than all voters. And by 1972, they were 4 points more Republican than the entire electorate. 1968 had changed the basic rules of US politics. America experienced a backlash to the 1960s that was bigger and longer-lasting than anything in Europe. Why? Because it touched on the most sensitive area of American politics and social relations: race.

"I am invisible," the Black novelist Ralph Ellison had written in 1952, "simply because people refuse to see me." By the 1960s, Black Americans were demanding to be seen. The saga of the civil rights movement is familiar to many—from the bus boycott inspired by Rosa Parks to Martin Luther King Jr.'s "I Have a Dream" speech to the "Freedom Summer" voter registration drive. In 1954, the Supreme Court declared school segregation unconstitutional; a decade later, the Civil Rights Act outlawed racial discrimination. President Lyndon Johnson earned the lasting hatred of his fellow Southern Democrats by ramming through the Voting Rights Act of 1965, which finally guaranteed Black Americans' right to vote. The same year, the Johnson administration abolished the "national origin" immigration quotas that favored people from Protestant northwest Europe, ushering in a new era of immigration from Asia and Latin America.

But at every step of the way, progress was followed by backlash. The story of the civil rights movement is also that of the lynching of Emmett Till, the harassment of the Little Rock Nine, the assassination of Martin Luther King. Pro-segregation extremists stopped at nothing to stem the tide of racial equality. While Martin Luther King Jr. enjoys near-universal reverence today, many whites at the time were deeply skeptical of the charismatic civil rights leader. On the eve of his assassination, nearly 75 percent of Americans held an unfavorable view of him. After his death, almost a third thought he was to blame for his own murder. Just imagine how whites felt about militant groups like the Black Panthers.

So the identity revolution of the 1960s was almost immediately followed by a massive backlash, creating a vicious cycle of political polarization. In the United States, groups that had long been on top— men, whites, Christians—suddenly felt their dominance slipping. The more that women or racial minorities demanded equality, the more white men felt threatened. An identity politics around whiteness and masculinity began to pick up steam across the country.

For even if social change seemed ubiquitous, many of the reforms propagated by the student generation still seemed radical to a majority of Americans. The image we have of the '60s and '70s—long-haired hippies in tie-dye, rolling joints—had little to do with the lived reality of most Americans at the time. To many, the ecstasy of Woodstock seemed as far away as the moon landing one month earlier. And though we today recall the anti-Vietnam War movement as an overwhelming success, the war long remained popular among large segments of the population.

Those Americans feared that the country they knew was disappearing. In the 1968 presidential election, Richard Nixon capitalized on this general unease by declaring himself a champion of "the great majority of Americans, the forgotten Americans, the non-shouters, the non-demonstrators"—what he would later call "the great silent majority." At Kent State University in 1970, armed national guardsmen fired on a crowd of student peace activists, killing four. Today, the iconic image of a distraught fourteen-year-old girl kneeling over a dead body is remembered as a symbol of sheer brutality. At the time, however, most Americans thought the students had provoked the carnage. The Silent Majority was real.

So, alas, was their core complaint: crime. A variety of factors in this period led crime rates to soar—a surfeit of young men born during the baby boom, suburbanization and "white flight" that hollowed out cities, the spread of drugs, the emptying of mental institutions. Rising crime strengthened support for strict "law and order" policies. In Martin Scorsese's 1976 movie *Taxi Driver*, the young Vietnam veteran Travis Bickle drives through the filthy streets of New York

City, which are teeming with prostitutes and criminals. After Travis kills two men at a brothel to rescue a child, the press treats him like a hero. The film captured the spirit of the times, a period when the initial excitement about newfound freedoms had given way to a yearning for normalcy and order.

The introduction of affirmative action and "forced busing"—integrating school districts by transporting students away from their home neighborhoods—made racial integration seem unsettling even to white moderates. One young Democratic senator called busing "an asinine concept" in 1975. (His name is Joe Biden.) By the late 1970s, up to 91 percent of white Americans opposed busing. (Efforts to integrate housing also failed, and American cities remain strikingly segregated to this day.) As the liberal novelist and activist Norman Mailer recounted, speaking about himself in the third person with surprising candor, "It was a simple emotion and very unpleasant to him—he was getting tired of Negroes and their rights." If *Taxi Driver*

The Soiling of Old Glory.

captured the era's obsession with law and order, another movie from 1976 hinted at the rising tide of white backlash. *Rocky* features the Italian-American working-class hero Rocky Balboa, who challenges and defeats the ostentatiously wealthy Black heavyweight champion Apollo Creed. It was the highest-grossing movie of the year.

The struggle around race proved so intense that it led to a fundamental realignment of the American party system. Black Americans had been a key constituency of the GOP since the Reconstruction era. As Frederick Douglass once remarked, "the Republican party is the ship and all else is the sea." In 1932, Black Americans favored Herbert Hoover over Franklin Roosevelt, two-to-one. Slowly but surely, however, their allegiance shifted. FDR would win over many Black voters, and JFK and LBJ would cement their support by backing civil rights legislation. In the 1964 presidential election, the Republican candidate, Barry Goldwater, garnered just 6 percent of the Black vote.

Even though Goldwater lost in a landslide, the 1964 election pointed the way toward a viable new strategy for conservatives. Republicans focused on drumming up support among white Southerners, in large part by playing into their deep-seated fears of racial integration—the "Southern strategy," as it was known. Just four years after Goldwater pioneered this new approach, Richard Nixon perfected it. In 1968 virtually the entire South defected from the Democrats, going for Nixon or the segregationist "Dixiecrat" candidacy of George Wallace. The day he signed the Civil Rights Act, Johnson remarked, "Well, I think we may have lost the South for your lifetime—and mine." While white Southern Democrats like Carter and Clinton would go on to win many states in the region, Johnson was largely right. No longer the unshakable foundation of the Democratic Party, the South evolved into the most Republican region in the country.

Attracting Southern whites meant jettisoning the Republican Party's mantle as the party of racial equality. While Nixon had garnered 40 percent of the Black vote in his 1960 candidacy, his share of support among nonwhite voters fell to 13 percent when he ran in 1972. The civil rights movement put an end to the "big tent parties" of the prewar era in which economics determined politics. Southern segregationists had sat alongside Northern liberals on the Democratic side, linked together by economic policy. No more. Conservatives moved into the Republican Party and liberals into the Democratic Party.

After a long history of slavery and segregation, the civil rights movement had finally integrated Black Americans into their country's political life. But instead of ushering in a postracial era of reconciliation, these advances prompted a backlash so powerful that it fundamentally reorganized American politics. For the first time since the end of Reconstruction, American parties were now divided along the lines of race rather than economics. And the heated fights over integration that began in the 1960s were a harbinger of the culture wars yet to come.

THE PROBLEM THAT HAS NO NAME

The civil rights movement served as a powerful catalyst for other social revolutions. From sit-ins to boycotts to marches, Black civil rights leaders had pioneered a model for other marginalized groups to voice their own grievances. Chief among those groups was the feminist movement. It is worth emphasizing the seismic nature of the shift in gender relations that gained force in the 1960s and 1970s. For thousands of years, domination of women by men had been a fundamental feature of human society. Other groups had risen or fallen at various times, with one dominating the other, but when it came to gender relations, virtually everywhere on the Earth, the story was the same: men controlled women. As the feminist philosopher Simone de Beauvoir put it in *The Second Sex*, women "have always been subordinated to men, and hence their dependency is not the result of a historical event or a social change—it was not something that *occurred*."

Women's rights activists had celebrated an early success with the passage of the Nineteenth Amendment in 1920, guaranteeing women the right to vote. Yet suffrage had done little to change the lived reality of women across the country. As is so often the case, technological progress played a role in paving the way for social change. In 1957, the Food and Drug Administration approved the use of what would later become the first contraceptive pill, and in 1965, the Supreme Court struck down state bans on the sale and use of contraceptives for married couples in its *Griswold v. Connecticut* decision. By then, 63 percent of married couples under forty-five were using contraception, a quarter of whom were using the pill.

It was against this backdrop in 1963 that the journalist Betty Friedan published her groundbreaking treatise, *The Feminine Mystique.* For her 15-year Smith College reunion, Friedan had been tasked with surveying her classmates about their lives. Behind the happy facade of middle-class family life, many of these women, graduates of an elite women's college, were deeply unfulfilled. In *The Feminine Mystique*, Friedan called this phenomenon "the problem that has no name."

Her book landed like a bombshell, selling nearly three million copies within the first three years of publication. Not unlike what Harriet Beecher Stowe's *Uncle Tom's Cabin* had done for slavery in the 1850s, *The Feminine Mystique* served as a rallying cry awakening a generation to the plight of women in America. Friedan joined with around thirty women from across the country to found the National Organization for Women—an activist group explicitly modeled after the successful example of the National Association for the Advancement of Colored People.

Groups like the National Organization for Women spearheaded a "second wave" of feminist activism that no longer contented itself with voting equality. Feminists now advocated equal opportunity laws, abortion rights, and state-provided child care. They set out to remake the image of what a woman's life could—or should—look like. "Women's liberation" proceeded at a heady pace. After *Griswold* protected the use of contraception in marriage, the Supreme Court soon extended that right to unmarried couples, and then in 1973 recognized a right to abortion in *Roe v. Wade.* By that time, the "sexual revolution" was in full swing. In 1964, the majority of American women still reported being virgins when they got married, and only about one marriage in twenty ended in divorce. By 1975, 88 percent of college women reported being sexually experienced, and the number of yearly divorces had more than doubled.

Many critics decried these shifts as representing nothing less than the death of the nuclear family. But let us not forget that amid all these changes, women's material situation progressed dramatically. Among Friedan's generation, holding a college degree was a rarity, and those who did more often than not went to college for the "Mrs." degree—to find a suitable husband. Not so after 1967: the percentage of American women with a college degree rose from 8 percent to 23 percent toward the end of the millennium. Over the same period, the percentage of stay-at-home mothers more than halved. From the '60s onward, laws and attitudes shifted and kept shifting, demonstrating that even deeply ingrained power relations are not immutable. Even if women today are still vastly underrepresented at many levels of power, progress continues. Women made up 2 percent of US senators in 1990 but 25 percent in 2023. By the early 2000s, women in the United States were outperforming men in terms of educational attainment, from high school to professional degrees.

While the feminist movement of the '60s and '70s was largely focused on the plight of white, middle-class women, it inspired other groups that had long lived at the margins of society. Other identity-based groups followed on the heels of the feminist movement. In the 1960s, "homophile" activists began to express their sexual identity more openly. Queer Americans had long been persecuted. Senator Joseph McCarthy's witch hunt against alleged communists in the 1950s had gone hand in hand with the "lavender scare"—a moral panic about the supposed menace of gay men in positions of power.

But toward the end of the '60s, the tide slowly started to turn against the bigotry of the McCarthy era. In the wee hours of June 28, 1969, police raided the Stonewall Inn on Christopher Street in New York City. Gay bars had long been targeted by authorities, but this time, gay and lesbian patrons, as well as drag queens and trans people, fought back. They hurled coins, rocks, and bricks at the uniformed

intruders. Unrest continued for several days, during which time activists founded the Gay Liberation Front. The movement declared itself
part of a larger liberation struggle, aligning itself with various anti-
capitalist, anti-imperialist, and anti-racist causes.

Public attitudes toward homosexuality were stubbornly slow to
shift. In 1987, 75 percent of Americans still thought homosexual
behavior was "always wrong," five points higher than in 1973. But
as with civil rights and women's rights advocates, gay rights activists
had begun to change the conversation—and started to make more
traditional Americans deeply uncomfortable.

A NEW GREAT AWAKENING

If the '60s was the era of white backlash to the civil rights movement,
then the '70s was a time of Christian backlash to women's liberation
and gay rights. In the early 1960s, religion still played a unifying role
in American life, with a coalition of Black Baptist preachers, main-
line Protestant churches, Catholic dioceses, and Jewish congregations
rallying together in support of civil rights (even as many Southern churches backed segregation). But by the 1970s, religious groups
nationwide had fractured along the same lines of culture war that
divided the country as a whole: abortion, contraception, feminism,
and gay rights. In a trend that would intensify with time, religiosity
became associated with the Right, and secularism with the Left. As
church attendance dwindled, religious conservatives rallied to defend
what they perceived as America's traditional Christian values.

The '70s thus saw a widening divergence between religious and
secular Americans. On the one hand, the percentage of Americans for
whom religion played a "very important" part in their lives dropped
dramatically, falling from 70 percent in 1965 to 52 percent in 1978.
But on the other hand, among some Protestants, people who perhaps
felt threatened by the decline of traditional American values, there
was a renewal of faith. A more fervent and politically active brand of
Christianity emerged with surprising force and speed. When Jimmy

Carter ran for president in 1976 as a "born-again Christian," the term was unknown to most Americans. Four years later, all three top contenders for the presidency—Carter, Ronald Reagan, and John Anderson—identified as born-again Christians or evangelicals.

While some Americans abandoned the faith of their parents and socialized across religious lines, some Protestant groups increasingly siloed themselves. Concerns about racial integration and progressive curriculums led to a massive exodus of white Christians from public schools to private religious institutions. In 1954, there were only 123 non-Catholic parochial schools in the United States; by 1970, there were about 20,000. Conservative Christians were building their own society within a society.

They were also upending partisan politics. Before 1973, there was no difference in rates of weekly church attendance between Democrats and Republicans. By 1992, the partisan divide between churchgoers had widened to 11 percent. Before 1973, abortion was not a wedge issue, with voters of both parties equally split on the question. As late as the 1976 election, both presidential candidates—Gerald Ford and Jimmy Carter—identified as pro-life. But by galvanizing conservative voters, *Roe v. Wade* set in motion a longer-term process that made abortion a key point of contention between the parties. By the time the 1980 election rolled around, Reagan had secured the support of the National Right to Life Committee by pledging to support a constitutional ban on abortions and to oppose government funding for abortions.

Anti-abortion activism was accompanied by a broader backlash against the women's rights movement. During the "first wave" of feminist activism in the early twentieth century, supporters of women's suffrage could be found in both parties. Until 1971, in fact, Republicans were more likely to cosponsor women's rights legislation than their Democratic counterparts. First Lady Betty Ford, a Republican, was an outspoken advocate for the proposed Equal Rights Amendment, which would have enshrined equal rights for women into the Constitution. But in the mid-1970s, conservative activists launched a large-scale campaign that turned public opinion against the amendment. Activists like Phyllis Schlafly warned that the Equal Rights Amendment would discriminate against housewives and force women into military conscription. In some ways, Schlafly pioneered the "trolling" tactics of today's right-wing activists, hell-bent on irritating the left with deliberately inflammatory statements. "I'd like to thank my husband, Fred, for letting me be here today," Schlafly began many of her speeches. "I like to say that because it irritates the women's libbers more than anything." From the mid-'70s on, the GOP held to a conservative line on women's issues.

Ronald Reagan harnessed the energy of the religious right and made it a core part of his coalition. In 1979, Jerry Falwell Sr., the televangelist founder of Liberty University, launched the Moral Majority, a lobbying group that soon became synonymous with the alliance between conservative Christians and the GOP. The organization would go all-in on Reagan and help shape his platform. Christian Voice, a conservative advocacy group founded in 1978, implored supporters to "Bring God Back to American leadership and elect Ronald Reagan President of the United States."

Reagan, the Hollywood star who would become the first divorcé to occupy the Oval Office, may have seemed like an unlikely darling of the Christian right (as with a more recent divorced entertainer-turned-president). But Reagan managed to speak to the anxieties of Christian America like no other. During his campaign, Reagan sat for an interview with the prominent televangelist Jim Bakker, who criticized Carter for not governing like an evangelical. Reagan replied, "Do you ever feel that if we don't do it now, if we let this become another Sodom and Gomorrah, that we might be the generation that sees Armageddon?" Evangelicals felt more under cultural siege than ever before, and they were determined to fight back. They turned out in force to elect Reagan.

The religious Right's hold over the Republican Party has only grown stronger since. By the 1990s, Catholics, historically a core Democratic voter bloc, were now more likely to support the GOP. In

2020, 71 percent of white churchgoers voted for Donald Trump. Now that politics was focused on the culture wars, religion had become one of the biggest dividing lines in American life.

RISE OF THE THIRD WAY

The "Reagan Revolution" was about more than the marriage between conservative Christians and the political right. Reagan also brought free-market ideology back into the White House. Earlier in his career, Reagan liked to read Austrian economist Friedrich Hayek on long train rides. Initially a staunch Democrat and president of the actors' union, Reagan was converted to Republicanism in no small part by reading Hayek, whose 1944 treatise *The Road to Serfdom* presented a biting critique of socialist command-and-control policies. (Though the book's central prediction—that governmental interference in economics inevitably leads to dictatorship—has proved to be wrong. Northern European countries like Denmark and Sweden have large welfare states and yet are among the freest in the world.)

In the early postwar decades, Hayek seemed to be fighting a losing battle. Social democracy was the order of the day on both sides of the Atlantic. But by the time Reagan ran for president in 1980, Hayek and other neoliberal intellectuals were in vogue. Tax-and-spend policies seemed useless in the face of the dangerous mix of inflation and stagnation that bedeviled the United States in the 1970s. Neoliberals had an easy answer to a seemingly intractable range of problems: less government. And at least in the short run, that answer seemed to work brilliantly. Whether it was thanks to the free-market policies of "Reaganomics" or the Federal Reserve's tightening of the money supply, inflation was tamed and economic growth was restored. Voters rewarded Republicans with three back-to-back terms in the White House.

When a Democrat was finally elected, in 1992, he came to office with ambitious progressive goals. Bill Clinton had campaigned on the promise of universal healthcare. But "Hillarycare" (so named for the First Lady's fierce advocacy for the bill) crashed and burned in Congress. In 1994, Democrats received a stunning blow in the midterm elections: for the first time in forty years, the Republicans captured both houses of Congress. Clinton, a pragmatist if there ever was one, knew he had to change tack. The moderate Arkansas Democrat brought in his trusted consultant Dick Morris, a political mastermind who would later become a Republican strategist. Morris helped devise the administration's strategy of "triangulation," which meant finding a popular, centrist middle ground between rabid slash-and-burn Republican policies and unpopular big-government Democratic policies.

Clinton pivoted to the center with astounding success. He signed nearly three hundred trade agreements (most notably NAFTA), deregulated the telecommunications industry, and repealed key provisions of the Glass-Steagall Act, which had restricted the banking industry. Alan Greenspan, who served as chairman of the Federal Reserve during the Clinton administration, hailed Clinton as "the best Republican president we've had in a while." That was unfair. In fact, Clinton was the most prominent member of a new generation of pro-growth "New Democrats," who broke with their party's old commitments to taxing and spending. He did toughen welfare requirements (infamously boasting that he had "ended welfare as we know it"), but he also fundamentally believed that smart and limited government intervention could help markets function more smoothly. All this was done in the service of a better, more effective social safety net and an expansion of opportunities for the less fortunate in the country. The poorest Americans saw their lot markedly improve during the Clinton years.

In Europe, what was called neoliberalism was ascendant. Margaret Thatcher—Reagan's political soulmate in Britain—championed deregulation and privatization. Across the English Channel, the movement to privatize national industries gained a following among such unlikely leaders as François Mitterrand, France's socialist president. Europe's left had no recipe to respond to the popularity of free-market economics. Instead, it followed the path blazed by Clinton's New Democrats—and was handsomely rewarded. By 1994, the UK's Labour Party had lost four elections in a row. When Tony Blair was elected as its leader that year, he rebranded the old workers' party as "New Labour." Under Blair, New Labour pursued a centrist "third way" between capitalism and socialism that essentially embraced the consensus around deregulation and privatization. When asked about her greatest political achievement, Thatcher is said to have replied, "Tony Blair." Blair and Clinton, both well-spoken and charismatic, won overwhelming electoral victories in large part by co-opting the economic policies of their conservative opponents. With the main parties converging on economics, the main political battleground would have to lie somewhere else.

THE CENTER DOES NOT HOLD

In Europe, populists responded by harnessing a widespread sense of lost autonomy felt across the continent. Economically, the Washington Consensus around neoliberal reforms insulated global capitalism from democratic demands and created the impression of an unresponsive globalist elite. Politically, the transfer of state power to a faceless EU bureaucracy caused Europeans to feel they had lost agency. Culturally, mass migration made white Europeans feel like strangers in their own land, a trend that would only intensify in the decades to come. These developments reinforced one another, fueling dislocation and priming individuals for the flames of the culture war that right-wing populists assiduously stoked.

Backlash against immigration wasn't new to Europe—an undercurrent of resentment had long simmered under the surface of polite politics. After World War II, for example, West Germany actively recruited "guest workers" from southern and southeast Europe, most notably Turkey. By 1973, around 10 percent of Germany's active labor force was foreign-born, and native-born Germans were beginning to grumble. The United Kingdom also saw rising numbers of immigrants arriving from its former colonies. British discontent quickly turned toxic. "It is like watching a nation busily engaged in heaping up its own funeral pyre," the Conservative politician Enoch Powell groused in his infamous "Rivers of Blood" speech in 1968. While Powell was sacked from his cabinet position for his comments, polling at the time suggested that 61 percent of Britons believed immigration harmed the country while only 16 percent felt the country benefited.

Yet only after 1990 did the backlash against immigration truly come to the fore. When the Berlin Wall fell in 1989, doors opened to immigrants from across the continent. Refugees from the Balkans fled to the rest of Europe throughout the 1990s during the Yugoslav Wars. In 1995, the Schengen Agreement effectively abolished borders between most European Union member states. Publics took notice of the uptick in immigrants: in the decade after 1989, the percentage of Germans who viewed asylum and immigration as their number one concern grew from 10 percent to 70 percent.

The impending sense of doom over a lost identity was compounded by national governments' willingness to relinquish power to the European Union. By many measures, the European Union was a huge success, bringing unprecedented growth and economic stability to large parts of Europe. But emotionally, the EU always struggled to bridge the gap between its sterile Brussels bureaucracy and the passions of European publics. From the outset, Europeans were less than enthusiastic about the idea of giving up national sovereignty. In 2003, a study found that 89 percent of national elites—elected politicians, senior civil servants, media leaders, and others—thought their country had benefited from EU membership, compared with only 52 percent of the general public.

Many citizens felt a loss of control over their own affairs—a feeling made more immediate by the rise in global trade, new structures of political authority, and widespread immigration. Populist parties across Europe readily capitalized on this sense of unease. Silvio Berlusconi became Italian prime minister in 1994 and again in 2001, supported by the anti-immigration party Lega Nord, whose leader became a minister in his government and called for the navy to use cannons to sink boats carrying illegal immigrants. In France's 2002 presidential election, the far-right National Front stunned the world by coming in second place.

For decades after World War II, the European center had held together. The center-right and center-left factions were united in their support for European integration and increased immigration, even as they differed on economic policies. But as integration and immigration sped up, this consensus came apart. The historical left-right divide was being replaced by a new cleavage between open and closed politics on issues like trade or immigration. Just as the star of protectionism rose in the age of globalization, and neo-Luddism emerged in a time of profound technological change, populist nationalism drew strength from the identity revolution by capitalizing on a new sense of unease. As this populism seeped into the political mainstream, traditional class alignments broke down. By 1999, for instance, Austria's far-right Freedom Party had won over most of the country's manual laborers. Across Western Europe, the average share of the vote earned by mainstream political parties dropped—falling from almost 80 percent in the 1970s to less than 60 percent in the 2010s.

EUROPE'S TIPPING POINT

By the mid-2010s, Europe, like the United States, had reached a tipping point. In 2015, Europe recorded over a million irregular migrants—migrants who came through illegal means. This was twice as many as over the preceding five years combined. The bulk came from the greater Middle East, with many fleeing ISIS in war-torn Iraq and Syria. A Syrian boy named Alan Kurdi came to symbolize the plight of these desperate refugees after his family attempted the treacherous journey across the Mediterranean and his dead body washed ashore in Turkey. Europe seemed to rise to the challenge of accepting so many migrants. "We can do this!" said German Chancellor Angela Merkel, reflecting the spirit of the times. Germany took in an astonishing 2.14 million migrants in 2015, a record high.

But as the numbers of asylum seekers kept rising, an initial outpouring of support was quickly drowned out by voices of opposition. Soon, right-wing populists were winning big across the continent. Germany hadn't had a far-right party in its parliament since 1945, but many Germans rejected Merkel's welcoming approach. In 2017, the Alternative for Germany (AfD) suddenly became the third-largest party in the Bundestag. Farther north, the far-right Sweden Democrats—an outgrowth of that country's neo-fascist movement—also surged in popularity. Jimmie Åkesson, who had called Islam "our biggest foreign threat since World War II," led the Sweden Democrats, a right-wing populist party, to its best result yet in the 2018 elections, winning over 17 percent of the vote. In Britain, the UK Independence Party was also stoking fears of unchecked migration. In the 2015 British parliamentary elections, it garnered the third-most votes. The following year, its raison d'être became a reality when the country passed a referendum to leave the European Union.

Europe's right-wing populists focused on immigration as their key wedge issue. In fact, populists from France's Marine Le Pen to the Netherlands' Geert Wilders took left-wing positions on some social issues, framing their beliefs as part of a broader opposition to Muslim immigration. "The freedom that gay people should have—to kiss each other, to marry, to have children—is exactly what Islam is fighting against," Wilders told Dutch voters in 2016. Instead of assailing gay marriage and abortion rights, and risking alienating the socially liberal mainstream, European populists drew from an even deeper well of cultural anxiety.

The Right warned that neighborhoods with large Muslim populations, from the banlieues of Paris to the Molenbeek suburb of Brussels, had become breeding grounds for Islamic fundamentalism. In 2015, the French novelist and firebrand Michel Houellebecq published a novel, *Submission*, describing a dystopian France flooded by immigrants and subjugating itself to sharia law. Such fears had been gripping Europe even before the migrant crisis broke out. The Swiss voted to outlaw the construction of minarets in 2009, and at least seven European countries have banned the burqa in public places.

COMING APART

Donald Trump would feel right at home among European populists. But in the United States, with its entrenched two-party system, it's nearly impossible to launch a successful third party. So Trump did one better than his European counterparts: he captured one of the two main parties and rode it into the highest office in the land.

The GOP's populist turn emerged from a dilemma the party faced in the 1990s. At the start of Bill Clinton's presidency, when he pursued some typical Democratic policies—raising taxes and pushing universal health care—the strategy was clear. Newt Gingrich focused on economic issues in his "Contract with America," a legislative agenda for Republicans to campaign on in the 1994 midterm elections. It advocated a balanced budget, tax cuts, and welfare reform, and denounced Clinton's "New Democrats" as the same old big spending Democrats of yesteryear. The result was one of the greatest Republican electoral triumphs ever, with Gingrich becoming Speaker of the House.

But when a chastened Clinton responded by pivoting to the economic center, Gingrich had to pivot, too. How was the Right to distinguish itself now? To counter Clinton's winning formula of centrist pragmatism, Republicans launched a new phase of the culture war. In 1996, Gingrich sponsored the Defense of Marriage Act, which strictly defined marriage as the union of a man and a woman. The closer to the center the left tacked on economics, the further to the Right conservatives moved on culture—denouncing gays, feminists, and liberals as the enemies of "real America." In a 1994 memo to fellow party members, Gingrich provided a list of words to use when describing the other party: "betray, bizarre, decay, destroy, devour, greed, lie, pathetic, radical, selfish, shame, sick, steal, and traitors."

Gingrich now leaned into this scorched-earth strategy, using tactics that foreshadowed the Republicans' path toward extremism: in fighting the treacherous liberals, no weapons could be off limits. They would have to use radical means for conservative ends, exploiting and exacerbating America's distrust of its elites.

In Gingrich's narrative, Clinton was not a moderate Democrat but an extreme liberal, an elitist, with loose morals, out of touch with everyday Americans. Gingrich spent much of his time on the dais chastising Clinton for his extramarital transgressions, even though he himself was having an affair at the same time. The era of hyperpolarization had begun. Gingrich brought a generation of radical conservatives into Congress and triggered two government shutdowns.

But Gingrich overstepped, and his firebrand style ended up alienating many Americans. The impeachment of President Clinton was unpopular. Voters punished Republicans in the 1998 midterms, leading Gingrich to resign. Clinton left office with the highest final approval rating of any president since polling began. When George W. Bush came into office, his "compassionate conservatism" was a conscious departure from the radicalism and nastiness of the Gingrich era. Bush's signature domestic achievement was a typical Republican economic policy: tax cuts. Bush, who had won some 44 percent of the Latino vote in 2004, even championed an immigration bill so moderate he couldn't muster enough Republican support to pass it.

It took an economic collapse and the election of a Black president with the middle name Hussein for populist Republicans to make a resurgence. The 2008 financial crisis did more than tarnish the Bush dynasty. As we've seen, it eroded people's remaining faith in American elites across the board. Only a month after Barack Obama's inauguration, CNBC's Rick Santelli delivered an impassioned rant against the president's foreclosure relief plan from the floor of the Chicago Mercantile Exchange. "This is America!" fumed Santelli. When Santelli spontaneously proposed having "a Chicago Tea Party in July," he could hardly have expected the enthusiastic reception from conservatives around the country.

Although the Tea Party was originally formed in opposition to Obama's "socialist" bailouts, this loose grassroots coalition did not follow a strict fiscal conservatism. In a 2012 survey, 89 percent of Tea Party supporters said Obama had expanded the government's role too much, but 62 percent actually expressed approval for Social Security and Medicare. At a South Carolina town hall, an enraged senior citizen told a Republican representative to "keep your government hands off my Medicare."

Throughout Obama's presidency, racial resentment was an inescapable factor shadowing political opinion. Racist conspiracy theories abounded. Donald Trump famously stoked the suspicion that Obama was born in Kenya, and before Obama finally released his birth certificate, over 40 percent of Republicans believed he was born abroad (and many continued to believe it). Late into his presidency, 43 percent of Republicans were still convinced that Obama was secretly Muslim. Trump, as a candidate and as president, leaned into racial animus and xenophobia, bringing the party along with him. Fiscal conservatism and free-market reforms were out. Tariffs, Muslim bans, and border walls were in.

Trump's own evolution in some ways embodies the Republican Party's ideological journey away from Reaganism. In 1987, the real estate mogul was calling for reducing the deficit, promoting peace in Central America, and supporting nuclear disarmament negotiations with the Soviet Union. (He did even then have an unusual obsession with making countries like Japan and Saudi Arabia pay the US for protection.) Unlike other Republicans, Trump said in 1999 that he supported universal healthcare and a wealth tax. But what thrust him into the political limelight were his baseless claims about Obama's birth certificate. And what ushered him into the White House was a grim warning about the twin threats of immigration and globalization. Always the master marketer, he tried and tested all kinds of policy stances, discarding what didn't work and keeping what did.

In many respects, Trump's rise to power, rather than a hostile takeover, was the product of the Republican Party's decades-long soul-searching exercise. The Reagan formula—free markets and spreading democracy—was dead. The path blazed by populists from Pat Buchanan to Newt Gingrich had led the party toward Donald Trump.

The mainstream GOP's positioning on immigration and trade had long been out of step with its electorate. In 2013, the Republican base revolted against an immigration reform bill introduced by the "Gang of Eight," a bipartisan coalition of senators that included Marco Rubio and Lindsey Graham, both of whom would later convert to Trumpism. By 2016, the Republican electorate was ready for something different. When Trump rode down Trump Tower's golden escalator to announce his presidential candidacy, many establishment conservatives were appalled—but many more working-class conservatives were ecstatic that someone was finally standing up against the social changes that had enraged them for decades. Strong borders, law and order, and a war against "political correctness"—these were all popular with the Republican electorate. Trump was the culmination, not the cause, of the identity politics revolution that had swept through Western democracies.

TRIBALISM IN AMERICA

On cultural issues, the United States is today more divided than other major Western countries. If one were to split the United States into two countries—one blue, one red—the blue part would look much like Northern Europe's havens of secularism and social democracy, while the red would have more in common with conservative religious societies like Poland or Turkey. In a 2020 Pew Research Center poll, 65 percent of Americans on the right thought their country would be "better off in the future if it sticks to its traditions and way of life," while just 6 percent on the left agreed. This 59-percentage-point gap contrasts with a 19-point gap in France, where the left still holds tradition in higher esteem. In a 2018 poll, 71 percent of American conservatives thought religion should play a larger role in society, compared to only 29 percent of liberals. That divide is 17 points wider than the one in Poland, another deeply polarized country that has fought its own battles over abortion and LGBTQ rights.

Cultural polarization almost invariably brings with it political polarization. When Trump clinched the Republican nomination in 2016, he pulled off a genuinely shocking feat. What followed in November was in some ways less surprising. Those who had voted Republican in the past overwhelmingly opted for Trump in 2016 (and again in 2020), even though he was a very different candidate from the typical GOP standard-bearer. Party affiliations have become so deeply ingrained, so tightly interlinked with deeply held personal identities, that switching parties now amounts to abandoning one's tribe. Partisans may rage that the opposing party is immune to reason, no matter how high the scandals pile or how low their leader falls. But is it any wonder that people would sooner look away from reality than repudiate their own sense of group identity?

It thus becomes less surprising that both Republican elites and voters who at first opposed Trump so quickly fell in line once he secured the nomination. Among Republicans, his approval ratings throughout his presidency never fell below 77 percent. A solid majority of Republicans either strongly or somewhat believe the former president's lie that the 2020 election was stolen. For centuries, wars were fought over religious divisions, but today partisans on both sides of the aisle tell pollsters they would be more disappointed if their child married outside their political party than outside their religion. Politics is now about supporting your team and affirming your tribal identity, come what may.

THE IMMIGRATION WARS

In the 2016 presidential election, the bubbling cauldron of social and demographic change that followed successive waves of immigration finally boiled over. Older working-class whites perceived an existential threat to their status. The percentage of America's population that was foreign-born, which had hit a low point of 4.7 percent in 1970, had nearly tripled to over 13 percent. In the 1970 midterm elections, a whopping 92 percent of voters had been white. By the time Trump launched his candidacy, whites made up only 74 percent of voters. Meanwhile, many of Trump's most enthusiastic fans reported feeling like strangers in their own countries. So as the country became more diverse, American conservatives sought a return to a world gone by.

As in 1968, age was a major separator between left and right in 2016. Older Americans struggled to wrap their heads around trends like gay marriage and ethnic diversity. Barack Obama's victory in 2008 epitomized this generational gap: for the young, Obama's election seemed like the natural outcome of an ongoing struggle for racial equality, while for the old, the election of a Black president with an unfamiliar name was a radical departure from the world of their youth. If you compare voters who supported both Obama and Hillary Clinton to voters who supported Obama but then defected to Trump, there is one issue on which the two groups diverged most: immigration. As in Europe, the embrace of a right-wing populist in the United States was part of a backlash against demographic changes that were quite literally changing the face of the nation. The populist revolt that has rocked the Western world in recent years is about more than economic dislocation.

Immigration may be a stand-in for all kinds of changes associated with globalization and modernization more generally. It is hard to see the globalization of goods and services. But large-scale immigration comes with visible and visceral change—suddenly, the people around you start looking different, talking in different languages, attending different houses of worship. Anti-immigrant sentiment can have some basis in economic self-interest. But those who fervently oppose immigration are rarely competing directly with immigrants for jobs. Rather, they genuinely believe that their country and culture are under threat and want to protect a way of life that they cherish. Those fears then become the basis for paranoia and conspiracy theories about the "Great Replacement" peddled by the likes of Tucker Carlson and other demagogues. Keeping immigrants out becomes a symbol for stopping all sorts of unnerving changes.

DEATH OF GOD

Another trend unsettling American conservatives, beyond demographic transformation, is secularization. Northern and Western Europe rapidly secularized after World War II. America got less religious, too, but to a lesser extent. But in the past few decades, things changed quickly. While the portion of the religiously unaffiliated remained flat between 1972 and 1991, it rose from 6 percent in 1991 to 23 percent in 2018. Between 2007 and 2020, the United States registered the biggest drop in religiosity of forty-nine countries surveyed. Back in 1982, 52 percent of Americans said God played a very important role in their lives, while only 23 percent thought so by the time Trump took office. Even in America, Nietzsche's declaration seems to have come true, just a bit later than the rest of the West: "God is dead, and we have killed him."

America's recent secularization has been fueled by its political polarization and vice versa. In the 1980s, as we have seen, the Christian right became firmly enmeshed in the Republican Party. The subsequent waves of political polarization in the 1990s and 2010s collapsed previously distinct categories of identity. Partisan affiliation now aligned closely with ideology, race, and faith. Polarization and secularization reinforced each other. The politicization of Christianity on the right led secular Americans not only to vote left but also to abandon religion. Church attendance among Democrats dropped significantly when gay marriage and abortion were at the top of the political agenda. Meanwhile, Christians as a whole became more Republican as they sought to protect their country from an increasingly godless left.

As a result, secularization has divided Americans even further. On the question of whether being Christian is an important aspect of being a citizen, there is a 23 percentage point gap between those on the left and the right, compared to only 7 percentage points in the United Kingdom, where religion plays a much smaller role in public life. In 2009, white evangelicals in the United States were twice as likely to be Republican than Democrat; ten years later, they were almost four times as likely. Rapid secularization has added fuel to the fire of the raging culture wars. It hasn't just galvanized the Christian right; the secular left has struggled to replace religion with an alternative source of meaning and has redirected its fervor into politics. Liberalism's great strength throughout history has been to free people from arbitrary constraints. Its great weakness has been the inability to fill the void when the old structures crumble.

A GREAT AWOKENING?

All of these shifts, taken together, make many conservatives feel like strangers in their own land. This alienation is exacerbated by the constantly shifting goalposts of the culture wars. While pundits are quick to point out that the American right has radicalized in its rhetoric and strategy, the data suggests it is Democrats who have changed their *minds* the most. In 1994, only 32 percent of Democrats and 30 percent of Republicans believed immigrants strengthened the country. By 2017, the percentage of Republicans who thought the same had actually risen slightly—while the share of pro-immigration Democrats had skyrocketed to 84 percent.

This trend extends to many of the thorniest issues in the American culture wars. Overall, the country has become much more tolerant over the past twenty-five years: approval for interracial marriage, for example, increased from 64 to 94 percent. But on some social issues, segments of the left have outpaced the rest of the country. White Democrats tend to hold opinions on race and racism that are consistently to the left of even the average Black voter, in a phenomenon the journalist Matt Yglesias has termed the "Great Awokening."

Young Democrats are progressive to an extreme. Since 2010,

Gallup polls have consistently seen around half of American youths express a favorable opinion of socialism. In a 2020 poll, 64 percent of college students backed the movement to defund the police, a position held by just 34 percent of all Americans. Universities across the United States have seen a return to campus activism that recalls some of the radicalism of the 1960s, with students shouting down speakers, occupying buildings, and staging protests against perceived racism and discrimination.

Fearing the perceived cultural extremism of the modern Left, Republicans have turned to political radicalism in a last-ditch effort to win elections no matter what, to arrest what they see as further cultural decline. The tragic asymmetry of contemporary American life is this: the Right often punches above its weight in politics but yearns for cultural power. The Left owns the culture but constantly pines for political power. It chafes at what it perceives to be built-in advantages for Republicans: the rural tilt of the Senate and Electoral College, gerrymandering in the House, a conservative-dominated Supreme Court, and other anti-majoritarian features of the American constitutional system. It tries to use its cultural power to shape politics—a dangerous and often illiberal quest. The Right, meanwhile, looks at the Left's built-in advantages in the media, universities, Hollywood, even large corporations, seeing them all as founts of a new and radical progressive ideology.

With outsized political power despite their shrinking numbers, whites and churchgoing Christians feel that the culture war— "wokeness," cancel culture, secularization, the decline in traditional patriotism, the growing acceptance of alternative sexualities— constitutes an existential crisis. Trump's inroads among Black, Latino, and Asian voters in 2020 signaled that the conservative base may not actually be shrinking; social conservatism, low taxes, and hostility to "socialism" and anti-wokeness have broad appeal. But whether conservatives are actually shrinking in numbers is beside the point. The cultural dominance of the left makes Republicans *feel* that they are under attack and have to fight back.

CULTURE WAR MAKES STRANGE BEDFELLOWS

Increasingly, personal identity is the battlefield on which the twenty-first century's polarized politics are fought, not only in the West but around the world. And now this cultural battlefield has merged with actual battlefields. These same gale-force winds of modernization produced in the Arab world a violent Islamic backlash. Many parts of the Middle East had been politically stagnant—with little progress in political, civil or social spheres—and as economics, globalization, and technology entered those lands, this bastardized modernization provoked a virulent response in the form of politicized religion. If the problem was a failed, Western-style modernization, the Muslim fundamentalists' solution was: Islam. Like the social backlash in much of the world, in the Islamic world it has taken on a strikingly anti-feminist, even antifemale character.

For Russian conservatives, Moscow has always been the "third Rome." After the fall of the capitals of Christianity in the West (Rome), and the East (Byzantium), the Russian Orthodox Church was, to them, the guardian of true Christianity. Vladimir Putin's reactionary dream of a new Russian empire is tied up with this image of himself as the last defender of Christian morality in the face of a decadent, secular, gay-friendly West. Two weeks after the Russian invasion of Ukraine, Patriarch Kirill I, the head of the Russian Orthodox Church, bizarrely invoked gay pride parades as part of the reason for the war in Ukraine. A few weeks later, Putin griped that the West was trying to "cancel" Russian culture the way *Harry Potter* author J. K. Rowling had been canceled for her views on transgender people.

In China, likewise, Xi Jinping's ideology, though officially communist, is increasingly synonymous with right-wing cultural grievances. The Chinese government has positioned itself against feminism, LGBTQ culture, and the claims of racial and ethnic minorities, in favor of male breadwinners and a Han Chinese majority. Male television anchors have been warned not to dress, sound, or act in "effeminate" ways. Some China watchers have quipped that the nation is experiencing America's 1950s all over again: rapid highway construction, ubiquitous smoking, workplace sexism, and geopolitical hubris.

Moscow and Beijing both feel they must defend their culture by cracking down on liberalism at home and strengthening their countries' military apparatus to project power abroad, which will help weaken the forces of global liberalism led by the United States of America. This cultural balancing against the West is just one part of a revolution in geopolitics, one that has produced the most dangerous and unpredictable international environment since the Cold War.

THE DUAL REVOLUTIONS

Geopolitics

M ORE THAN 2,400 YEARS AGO, IN THE *HISTORY OF the Peloponnesian War*, one of the earliest and greatest histori-ans, Thucydides, described the fundamental reason for war between the two leading city-states of his time. "It was the rise of Athens and the fear that this instilled in Sparta that made war inevitable," he wrote. Growing in strength, Athens was emboldened to expand its military and diplomatic ambitions, bumping up against those of then-dominant Sparta. Sparta grew increasingly jittery and felt a fierce need to defend its status. The result: the Peloponnesian War, which devastated both powers, ended Greece's golden age, and opened the door for the Romans to conquer the Greek world. Structural changes don't just lead to power shifts within nations; they also lead to power shifts *among* nations. Those shifts produce new ambitions and anxi-eties, which often end in war.

This phenomenon—of a rising power threatening to displace an established power, ultimately leading to war between them—is a familiar story. The historian Paul Kennedy describes the pattern over the course of five hundred years in his magisterial *The Rise and Fall of the Great Powers*. More recently, the political scientist Graham Allison's work has sparked fierce debate over the "Thucydides Trap." Allison documents sixteen different cases in which a rising power challenged a ruling power over the past five centuries, ranging from the ascendant

Habsburg Empire contesting French power in the early sixteenth century to an expansionist Japan threatening American dominance in the twentieth century. Of these cases, twelve ended in war. The big question today, of course, is this: Are America and China destined to go down the same path? Were they to do so, it would make for a turbulent and bloody twenty-first century.

The changes that we are witnessing on the world stage today could be described as a geopolitical revolution. Geopolitical revolutions are rare, and we are living through the third major one in modern history. The first was the rise of European nations above all others, beginning in the fifteenth century. It produced the world as we know it now: commerce and capitalism, global trade and great-power diplomacy, the scientific and industrial revolutions. It also led to the prolonged dominance of the nations of the Western world and the colonization and domination of most non-Western countries across the globe. The second great power shift, which began in the final years of the nineteenth century, was the rise of the United States. Once it industrialized, America soon became the most powerful nation in the world. Crucially, it became stronger than any likely combination of other nations, which made it the decisive geopolitical player in the twentieth century. It defeated three efforts by a rising power to establish hegemony. In World Wars I and II, American intervention proved decisive in defeating Germany. During the Cold War, America organized and led the successful coalition that contained the Soviet Union until it collapsed.

For the last thirty years, that second power shift went into overdrive as we saw something unprecedented in modern history: a single power dominated the globe without any serious challenger. After the Cold War, Russia was weak, China was still too underdeveloped, and the other major powers (Britain, France, Germany, Japan) remained close American allies. During this Pax Americana, globalization and liberalization benefited the whole global economy, which grew dramatically. But those forces ended up driving the third great geopolitical shift of the modern age—the waning of the Pax Americana.

This shift is not so much the decline of the West as the rise of the rest, the economic ascent and growing self-confidence of many non-Western countries. I first explored this phenomenon in *The Post-American World,* and the trends have only intensified since that book was published in 2008. The central player in the geopolitical revolution has been China, which in a single generation moved from economic and technological irrelevance to the leading edge. We have also witnessed a resurgent Russia, which not only profited from the insatiable demand for natural resources in a growing global economy but also felt threatened by the spread of Western power and ideas. Ironically then, the Pax Americana created conditions that produced the two biggest challenges to American hegemony: China's rise as a peer competitor and Russia's return as a spoiler. The current geopolitical revolution could be seen as a familiar tale of rising and established powers that ends inevitably in war.

But today's shift takes place in a world transformed by another revolution—that started in the realm of ideas. This one is a liberal revolution, supercharged by US hegemony, that has changed the way that countries interact with one another. When scholars speak of liberalism as an ideology in international relations, they don't mean left-wing policies but rather a respect for liberty, democracy, cooperation, and human rights. This view is often opposed to realism or realpolitik, which place a premium on raw power and self-interest. It might seem overly hopeful to claim that things have changed so much from the familiar pattern of power politics as they have played out since Thucydides's time. But they really have. Since 1945, the world has been organized in new ways that emphasize rules, norms, and values. There are now thousands of international agreements with rules that govern the behavior of countries and international organizations that create forums for discussion, debate, and action.

As we saw earlier, there has also been an explosion of trade, investment, travel, and communication among nations. The levels of interdependence are unprecedented. Before World War I, countries did trade with one another, but less so and through simple bilateral arrangements. The "trade openness index," the sum of global exports and imports divided by world GDP, stood at about 30 percent in 1913. Today, it is just under 60 percent, where it has plateaued since the mid-2000s. (The pandemic did reorient trade flows but doesn't seem to have dented overall trade in the long run.) Now money, goods, and services all crisscross the world in complex ways—often going back and forth several times before a final product is released. Countries that were once bitter enemies, like South Korea and Japan—and even countries that are rivals today, like the United States and China—are deeply intertwined economically. Mass travel has taken off and become a major global industry. In 2019, before the pandemic, there were 1.5 billion international trips, and preliminary data for 2023 suggests that the number has nearly bounced back. This astounding interconnectedness may allow for new kinds of relations between nations, ones that somewhat constrain the usual power politics that have played out for millennia.

I am not naive; I know that in extremis, power trumps all, politics trumps economics, that many global rules and norms are routinely broken, that international organizations are often toothless. The United Nations General Assembly, for example, is mostly just a talking shop. Real power still resides with nations. But consider what the world was before 1945—a true realpolitik jungle—and the impact of this liberal revolution becomes unmistakable. We have moved from centuries of ceaseless conflict to what the historian John Lewis Gaddis has called the Long Peace, the longest period in modern history without great-power war—almost eighty years and counting. Since 1945, the annexation of territory by force, once a common occurrence, has become vanishingly rare—which is why Russia's invasion of Ukraine stood out as a sharp anomaly. France and Germany went to war three times in eight decades and then, after World War II, got knitted into a European order in which a war between those two powers became unthinkable. In the early 1990s, watching

East Asia's economies boom, I asked Lee Kuan Yew, the brilliant and tough-minded founder of Singapore, whether as countries in his region rose to power, they would repeat Europe's history of armed conflict. *No, he replied, we in Asia have seen what war did to countries like Vietnam. And we have seen what trade and cooperation have done in Southeast Asia.* In effect, he was saying, we can learn from the past and choose a mutually beneficial future. And in fact, despite heady economic growth, contested borders, and historical grievances, East Asia has remained at peace.

Countries are intertwined through trade and investment. Liberal ideas, values, and practices have spread. Rules pertaining to specific issues, often practical solutions that help all states, have become more and more common, creating a web of treaties, laws, and norms that govern all kinds of nooks and crannies of international life. And democracy and rule of law, once the preserve of a handful of countries nestled in the North Atlantic, have proliferated across the world. It's true that there are still many unfree countries, and that interdependence has failed to tame all geopolitical tensions, as the US-China relationship demonstrates. (Though it is worth noting that there has been no war between the two countries despite all the friction.) Democracy, after surging forward for decades, is now in a real recession, with many countries backsliding. The phenomenon of "illiberal democracy" that I identified in the 1990s has become a growth industry. Nonetheless, looking at the broad sweep of history, it is still undeniable that there has been a liberal revolution in international affairs over the last century, one that broke with centuries of realpolitik.

These dual revolutions—the return of great-power politics and the ascension of the liberal international order—are taking place simultaneously, and how they play out will determine the future of the world. One plausible path would be a reversion to realpolitik, but that would mean the collapse of globalization and a return to nationalism and competing blocs. We have seen this kind of backsliding before. Or we could see the forces of interdependence push nations

Countries that are democracies and autocracies, World

Political regimes based on the criteria of the classification by Lührmann et al. (2018) and the assessment by V-Dem's experts.

Our World in Data

Closed autocracies

Electoral autocracies

Electoral democracies

Liberal democracies

Data source: OWID based on Lührmann et al. (2018); V-Dem (v13)   OurWorldInData.org/democracy | CC BY
Note: The share of closed autocracies increases a lot in 1900 because V-Dem covers many more countries since then, often colonies.

1. **V-Dem:** The Varieties of Democracy (V-Dem) project publishes data and research on democracy and human rights. It relies on evaluations by around 3,500 country experts and supplementary work by its own researchers to assess political institutions and the protection of rights. The project is managed by the V-Dem Institute, based at the University of Gothenburg in Sweden. Learn more: Democracy data: how do researchers measure democracy? The 'Varieties of Democracy' data: how do researchers measure democracy? The 'Varieties of Democracy' data: how do researchers measure human rights?

Democratization in the world from 1900 to 2022.

to pursue peace, build stronger economic ties, and cooperate more closely on issues of mutual concern like climate change. That would take extraordinary leaders in the most important countries acting in concert to create a shared vision for the future. Most likely, the world we are going to live in will lie uneasily between the two scenarios, with geopolitical tensions existing side by side with cooperation and economic ties. Interdependence will sometimes serve as a restraint on geopolitical adventures but at other times will be weaponized by one country to gain an advantage over others. Managing these twin revolutions is going to be complex and dangerous, with the constant risk of collapsing into war.

ROOTS OF PAX AMERICANA

The world of rivalry and realpolitik has been with us since time immemorial. The world of a rules–based liberal order is relatively new. Like so many liberal ideas, it emerged from the European Enlightenment—and arguably, from the Netherlands first. In 1625, Hugo Grotius, a Dutch diplomat and jurist, wrote *On the Law of War and Peace*, which laid out the notion of international law based on natural rights and reason, rather than shared religion. More than a century and a half later, the paradigmatic Enlightenment philosopher Immanuel Kant, writing amid the bloodshed of the French Revolution, published an essay titled "Toward Perpetual Peace." Kant described what was needed to achieve the conditions of permanent peace, not just the temporary absence of war. His ideas sound strikingly contemporary. He argued for a world of economically interdependent republics, where citizens preferred trading to fighting and had the power to determine policy. He sought a federation of free nations governed by law rather than might, a precursor to the idea of international organizations like the UN. Kant envisioned a future that was rooted in the rights of human beings as opposed to the self-interest of states.

For a while, these ideas stayed just that—ideas. But then came the superpower of the nineteenth century, the United Kingdom, which was infused with a Protestant sense of mission. It began to see itself as pursuing not just its naked self-interest but also its values and ideals. To be fair, it often did pursue naked self-interest and act viciously, but there were flashes of benevolence in its approach. British power provided global public goods like "freedom of the seas," a concept first developed by Grotius. In practice, this meant that the Royal Navy suppressed piracy, which protected peaceful vessels conducting trade, no matter which flag they flew. Britain also used its sea power to protect freedom more literally. Once it abolished its slave trade, it aggressively enforced that ban on its own subjects and even on other countries. By 1860, the Royal Navy's West Africa Squadron had seized some 1,600 slave ships, freeing 150,000 people in the process. Britain was the first great power to actively raise moral issues with other countries and to place weight on the idea of international law and a rules-based international order. In fact, one of Britain's main motivations for entering World War I was that it felt honor-bound to uphold its commitment to its ally Belgium, which was facing German aggression. A realist would have made an accommodation with Germany, as the historian Niall Ferguson argues Britain should have done.

William Gladstone, the Liberal politician who served four stints as Britain's prime minister in the late nineteenth century, gave a series of famous speeches during the run-up to the 1880 elections. He advocated a foreign policy animated by the "love of freedom" and "the equal rights of all nations." He denounced the oppression of ethnic minorities under Ottoman rule. He even raised the plight of villagers in far-off Afghanistan, where Britain and Russia played their geopolitical Great Game, the nineteenth century rivalry over influence in central Asia:

> Remember the rights of the savage, as we call him. Remember that the happiness of his humble home, remember that the sanctity of life in the hill villages of Afghanistan among the winter snows, is as inviolable in the eye of Almighty God as can be your own. Remember that He who has united you together as human beings in the same flesh and blood, has bound you by the law of mutual love; that that mutual love is not limited by the shores of this island, is not limited by the boundaries of Christian civilisation; that it passes over the whole surface of the earth, and embraces the meanest along with the greatest in its unmeasured scope.

In office, Gladstone was far less idealistic in his policies. But his ideas and rhetoric would cast a long shadow. It was a short intellectual journey from Gladstone to a man who admired him greatly, Woodrow Wilson.

Wilson viewed America as a force for good in the world as

Gladstone did Britain, and he was also deeply influenced by Kantian ideas. After World War I, he tried to build a lasting peace by setting up the first major global organization, the League of Nations. But Wilson—a sometimes-cold idealist with no real feel for practical politics and human relations—badly bungled the diplomacy abroad and at home. He ended up presiding over a vengeful peace that left Germany embittered and outside the international order. Back home, the Senate refused to have the US join the League, leaving the new international body without the support of the world's most powerful nation. Global order veered onto a dark path. Debt crises, hyperinflation, the Great Depression, and the rise of fascism all followed, and Wilson's hopes were devoured in the inferno of World War II.

From the ashes of that war, however, came another effort to build a liberal international order. This time, the architect was a politician far more skillful than Wilson: Franklin Delano Roosevelt. Roosevelt had been assistant secretary of the navy under Wilson and visited Paris briefly during the 1919 peace negotiations. He shared Wilson's ideals but believed Wilson had been too idealistic in his methods. So FDR searched for a way to ground those ideals in the realities of power politics. His vision for the United Nations enshrined the great powers' status and influence, giving them a stake in a stable world, one in which they had a privileged position. He achieved much of his vision, though the onset of the Cold War quickly threw a wrench into those plans.

The phrase "the American Century" has come to define the world order that the United States shaped after World War II. As noted before, the influential magazine publisher Henry Luce coined the term in February 1941, urging a very reluctant America to take on the mantle of global leadership. After Pearl Harbor, the country steadily grew more comfortable with Luce's vision, but it is worth recalling what the post–World War II era looked like. America was not the undisputed hegemon across the planet. Even after 1945, France and the United Kingdom still had formal empires and thus deep influence in large stretches of the globe. The Soviet superpower contested Washington's influence in every corner of the planet. Remember that the phrase "Third World" derived from the tripartite division of the globe: the First World being the US, its Western allies, and Japan; and the Second World being the communist countries. The Third World was everywhere else, with every nation forced to choose between aligning with the US or USSR. America was, of course, economically and culturally dominant, but for much of the world's population, from Poland to China, the century hardly felt American. The "liberal international order" in its founding era covered a zone limited to North America, Western Europe, and a few Asia-Pacific countries.

After the Cold War, the liberal order expanded fast as dozens of countries moved away from communism, socialism, and planned economies. Even then, however, US supremacy was initially hard to detect, and most observers missed it. In 1990, British prime minister Margaret Thatcher argued that the world was splitting into three new political spheres dominated by the dollar, the yen, and the deutsche mark. Henry Kissinger's 1994 book *Diplomacy* predicted the dawn of a new multipolar age. Certainly in the United States, there was little triumphalism. The 1992 presidential campaign was marked by a sense of weakness and weariness. "The Cold War is over; Japan and Germany won," the Democratic hopeful Paul Tsongas said again and again. Observers of Asia's economic rise began speaking of "the Pacific Century." Even those who saw that the world was moving toward free markets, free trade, and democracy did not necessarily see America as gaining strength because of it.

There was a notable exception to this analysis, a prescient essay in *Foreign Affairs* by the conservative commentator Charles Krauthammer: "The Unipolar Moment," published in 1990. But even this triumphalist take was limited in its expansiveness, as its title suggests. In a follow-up *Washington Post* column, Krauthammer predicted, "The unipolar moment will be brief." He argued that Germany and Japan, the two emerging "regional superpowers," were already beginning to pursue foreign policies independent of the United States. Policymakers outside the US welcomed the waning of unipolarity, which they assumed was imminent. In 1991, as the Balkans began to tear themselves apart, Jacques Poos, the foreign minister of Luxembourg, declared, "This is the hour of Europe." He explained: "If one problem can be solved by the Europeans, it is the Yugoslav problem. This is a European country, and it is not up to the Americans." But it turned out that only the United States, leading the NATO alliance, had the combined power and influence to intervene effectively and end the wars in Bosnia and Kosovo.

Similarly, beginning in 1997, when a series of panics sent Asian economies into a tailspin, only the United States could stabilize the global financial system. It organized a $120 billion international bailout for the worst-hit countries, resolving the crisis. *Time* magazine put three American technocrats—Treasury Secretary Robert Rubin, Federal Reserve Chair Alan Greenspan, and Deputy Treasury Secretary Lawrence Summers—on its cover with the headline, "The Committee to Save the World."

Against most expectations, the three decades after the Cold War were a period of Pax Americana. The United States led not only politically, economically, and militarily, but also ideologically. Democracy became the dominant political system around the world. Holding elections and opening up the economy were seen as best practices for nations. This is what Francis Fukuyama meant when he described "the end of history" in 1992—the end of a long debate about the evolution of politics. (He did *not* say that major historical events like wars or terrorism had ended, as those who read only the title often assume.) For those who grew up in these decades, it may have seemed like the Pax Americana was natural and permanent. The Washington Consensus, embracing free trade and free markets, was not just something pushed by American policymakers onto reluctant foreigners. It was in fact a consensus view among academics, intellectuals, and journalists—and when countries adopted some of these ideas, they did get growth and dynamism, most vividly seen in China and India in the 1990s and 2000s.

But we were living through a rare period, one characterized by the absence of great-power politics and the uncontested power of America. The US share of global GDP and military spending towered over every other nation. Even Japan and Germany, close allies that could have been economic competitors, spent much of the period after 1989 consumed with internal troubles—Japan suffering through its long economic slump and Germany busy absorbing its Eastern half. Now we are seeing the return to a world of multiple great powers—and this geopolitical revolution is transforming international relations along every dimension. It began not with the rise of China and the return of Russia but something broader and more benign: the rise of the rest.

THE RISE OF THE REST

When historians record the narrative of our own era, decades from now, the dominant trend in today's world will surely be "the rise of the rest." After centuries of lagging behind the West, being colonized by it, and then remaining marginal in global power politics, many once-poor countries rose to wealth and power. Over the last two decades, countries outside the industrialized West have seen growth rates that were once unthinkable. While there have been booms and busts, the overall trend has been unambiguously upward. So-called emerging markets made up just a third of the world economy in 1990. Today they make up close to half. And this rise has created a new international dynamic, one that resists easy characterization. Scholars debate whether the world is unipolar, bipolar, or multipolar. But the reality is that regardless of whether these newcomers rate as great powers, many of them are acting forcefully in their own interest and resisting being corralled by larger powers. In today's world, more and more nations seek to be free agents. Not all of them can achieve that, but enough can succeed and produce a more free-wheeling international system.

We live in a post-American world. That is not to say we have seen a dramatic decline of American power. The US economy remains the largest in the world by far, comprising about a quarter of all global output—more than the next two countries, China and Japan, put together. Since the 1980s, the American share has remained surprisingly stable, even after 2008, as the US recovered faster and stronger from the global financial crisis than many of its peers. America's military is utterly unparalleled, spending more on defense than the next ten countries combined.

While American power has not declined, American influence has. Influence is ultimately the ability to get others to do what you want them to do. Global influence is determined only partially by hard power like military size and GDP; it is also measured by one's relative standing in the world. So while America might still be strong, its relative predominance has waned. From 2000 (on the eve of China's entry into the World Trade Organization) to 2022, the American economy went from being 750 percent larger than China's to just 40 percent larger. Countries from India to Saudi Arabia to Turkey to Brazil have also seen their economies grow faster than the US economy in that period. In all these countries, you see societies that are stronger economically, prouder culturally, and bolder geopolitically. They have become more confident, seek greater influence, and refuse to be bullied by Washington (or Beijing for that matter). This new reality might not produce a genuinely multipolar world—the US and China are head and shoulders above the rest—but the superpowers of the twenty-first century are less able to dominate other countries the way Washington and Moscow once did.

You can see this shift even in soft power: a country's sway over ideas and agendas, its ability to serve as a model. During the 1980s, when I would visit India—where I grew up—most Indians were fascinated by the United States. Indian elites were obsessed with American politics, ideas, art, and culture. America defined modernity for them. But many Indians' interest in America did not operate at a lofty level. I remember some people asking me about Donald Trump, then simply a celebrity real estate mogul. He was the symbol of American wealth: rich, flashy, crass, larger than life. In those days, if you wanted to find the biggest and shiniest of anything, you looked to America. People in foreign countries even began to follow American basketball and football. But today, modernity is being defined differently. When you travel to Singapore or Beijing or Dubai, for example, you feel as if, in some crucial aspects, you are visiting the future: the cities not only have gleaming, high-tech infrastructure, but the people also have a sense of pride in their past growth and achievements still to come. As for Trump, of course now people everywhere ask me about him—not because he is a symbol of America's wealth but because he is a symbol of the country's dysfunction.

Culture follows power. As emerging nations have blossomed, they have begun prizing their own culture. They have created their own versions of celebrity tabloid culture, which was once provided by the West. Read India's newspapers or watch its television—you'll see coverage of dozens of Indian businessmen who are now wealthier than the Donald of the '80s, indeed richer than many billionaires in America today. The Ambani family in Mumbai ranks in the world's top ten richest families, but there are dozens of other non-Americans on these lists as well. The top five tallest skyscrapers in the world are currently in the Gulf States, Malaysia, and China. Korean pop culture in music, television, and movies now dominates much of East Asia and is even big in the West. In India, Bollywood and an energized version of television-friendly cricket leave little space for Hollywood and almost none for any American sports. America is no longer the only place where the future is happening.

It wasn't just that others rose—there was a loss of faith in America, too. How did the US lose its sheen? As I noted in the introduction, the first blow was the Iraq War, which cracked the image of America's seemingly invincible military. The world's sole superpower, with a monster defense budget, could not succeed against a ragtag group of insurgents. Revelations of civilian casualties and torture at CIA black sites further undermined America's reputation as a champion of human rights. Then came the erosion of US economic legitimacy with the 2008 financial crisis, a disaster unleashed by the much-storied American financial sector. The Washington Consensus was now suddenly questioned around the world. The coup de grâce was the crisis in America's political and moral legitimacy brought about by the presidency of Donald Trump. Americans are much more divided on their view of Trump than the world is; most people outside the US see him as a dangerous demagogue. (There are some notable exceptions, such as the populations of Kenya, Israel, and the Philippines.) Even before Trump's tenure, many people worldwide had stopped regarding the American political system as worth admiring or emulating. America's present reality combines towering strengths—technological innovation, world-leading universities, strong demographics—with glaring weaknesses, from gun violence to drug overdoses to persistent inequality.

RISE AND RESURGENCE

The rise of the rest was already coming into view when I wrote *The Post-American World*. But the ensuing years have brought a veritable revolution in geopolitics, with China and Russia contesting America's influence and creating a new global landscape.

China's rise was the greatest economic story of our time, and now economics is transforming geopolitics. The future of the international system hinges on a basic question: Does China want to destroy the system or simply get rich and powerful within it? Under Mao, it clearly wanted the former, funding revolutionary movements across the world and boycotting most international organizations. But after

Deng Xiaoping took the reins in the late 1970s, China decided that it wanted to be rich and respected, not roguish and revolutionary. It grew powerful within the existing order. Today, it is the second-largest funder of the UN and pays on time and in full, unlike the US. It covets leadership positions in the UN. It contributes more peace-keeping troops to the UN than the other permanent members of the Security Council combined. During the 2008 financial crisis, China acted in concert with the US and other leading countries to stabilize the international economy.

The previous generation of Chinese leaders believed in pursuing a quiet, "peaceful rise" in which their country accommodated itself to the prevailing American-led international order. President Xi Jinping seems to have a different view. With America weakened by its war on terror, the global financial crisis, and populist chaos, Xi sensed an opportunity to overturn America's unrivaled status. He has begun to speak of the East rising and the West declining. In October 2017, he gave a speech to the 19th Communist Party Congress that reflected his interpretation of what he saw as new structural realities. "China's international standing has risen as never before," he proclaimed, adding that the nation was "blazing a new trail for other developing countries to achieve modernization." Xi heralded "a new era . . . that sees China moving closer to center stage and making greater contributions to mankind." In other speeches, he appeared to be saying that China would become the new guarantor of the global trading system as America turned inward toward protectionism. These statements suggested a benevolent kind of Chinese leadership. But some of China's recent behavior indicates it would not be such a benign hegemon. It has taken military action against India over disputed territory, demanded that Australia kowtow to it on a series of issues from Huawei to Hong Kong, and asserted that long-recognized international waters in fact belong to China. In country after country, China has funded vast infrastructure investments, but often with onerous repayment conditions. It has also showered favored autocratic governments with high-tech surveillance equipment, while dangling promises of aid to induce minor countries to cease recognizing Taiwan. Back in 2010, when Southeast Asian nations protested Beijing's actions, Yang Jiechi, who would become Xi's top foreign policy official, responded bluntly: "China is a big country and other countries are small countries, and that's just a fact."

Of course, China's attitude toward the international system is not set in stone. Beijing will be watching the winds and assessing how other countries are moving, whether toward greater integration or away from it. Its own policies will be shaped by the actions of other nations, especially in the Global South, which it sees as its natural audience. Mao had a strategy of "encircling the cities from the countryside," which in the Chinese Civil War meant turning the poor rural majority against the urban minority. In the Cold War, it meant rallying the underdeveloped Third World against the small clique of rich capitalist societies. Today, Xi is trying to do the same with his outreach to the developing world.

For these countries, geopolitics is important, but so is development. They will want to balance both, finding ways to cooperate economically with China while also maintaining some kind of geopolitical relationship with the United States—investing in their economic future but buying insurance, as it were, against Chinese domination. And while China and the United States are becoming more adversarial in many ways, they too are part of a deeply intertwined global economy that has a dynamic of its own. Thus in recent years, tensions have risen, but trade hasn't fallen all that much. Over the last decade, adjusting for inflation, US-China trade in goods has in fact plateaued, not plummeted. Many of the United States' largest companies, from General Motors to Apple to Nike, need the Chinese market, and China needs American consumers for its economic growth. Those consumers also benefit. The so-called "Walmart Effect"—the availability of low-priced goods of every kind to Americans—is largely a result of imports from China. Even America's growing green economy owes something to China. Those solar panels you see everywhere have become so affordable because most are made in China. (This may change somewhat with the Biden administration's Inflation Reduction Act, which subsidizes domestic solar manufacturing.) And then there is the nearly $1 trillion worth of American debt that China holds. While the deeply intertwined relationship may continue to fray, it isn't likely to unravel anytime soon.

THE SPOILER STATE

If China is the challenger, Russia is the spoiler, the great power most determined to break the rules and norms of the existing international system. Under Vladimir Putin, Russia has become a resentful nation, convinced that during the Pax Americana it has been cheated of its empire and glory. Fortunately for Putin, the early part of his tenure saw a steady rise in oil prices, which had caused Russia's GDP to almost double from 2000 to 2007 and sent vast quantities of cash into the Kremlin's coffers. A newly enriched Russia looked around its region with a much more opportunistic gaze. Putin had already consolidated control at home. Sitting atop the "vertical of power" he had created, he began a serious effort both to restore Russian influence in its historical sphere of influence and counter Western interests and ideals. What followed—military interventions in Georgia and Syria, funding for populist and pro-Russian political groups in Europe, electoral interference in the US and other democracies, cyberattacks— were all in service of these goals. Fomenting instability also happens to benefit Russia because international tensions raise the prices of oil and other essential commodities that are the lifeblood of the Russian economy and budget.

Putin's war in Ukraine, beginning in 2014 and then kicking into high gear in 2022, is the most brazen action he has taken. After the Soviet Union's demise, Russia never fully accepted the independence of Ukraine, which represented the most painful reminder of its lost empire. By 2022, Putin was convinced that the West was in retreat and NATO was feckless. The invasion that year was the first full-scale land war in Europe since World War II. To punish Russian aggression, Washington and its allies turned the very interdependence of the open trading system against Moscow. With a speed unimaginable just weeks earlier, Russia was surgically cut out of global financial networks. Key Russian banks were blocked from accessing SWIFT, the system undergirding the vast majority of cross-border flows between international banks. Hundreds of billions of dollars in Russian assets held overseas were frozen.

Punishing as these sanctions were, the war's consequences were far more dire for everyday Ukrainians. A world unaccustomed to interstate war looked on in horror as Russia bombarded Ukrainian cities, millions of refugees fled their homes, Ukrainian harvests rotted in ports, and both sides dug themselves into World War I-style trenches. Poor people around the world were also impacted as a key breadbasket turned into a war zone and global food prices skyrocketed.

Despite its brutality, Russia has proved unable to defeat a nation that is a fraction of its size and has a much smaller army. Ukraine has the benefit of considerable Western backing, but it has also outdone Russia in high-level strategy and the determination of its troops. Russia's forces suffered because Putin has prized loyalty over competence among his subordinates, because he allowed corruption to fester in Russia's military apparatus, and because he threw its troops into the meat grinder to fight an unjust war. That is not to say Russia doesn't have a formidable military, but it has been overestimated, as has much of Russia's power. While Russia can still inflict tremendous damage (especially if it ever used its massive nuclear arsenal, the world's largest), it is weak in many other ways. Many economic and social measures suggest a country in inexorable decline. One stunning statistic provides a case in point: a fifteen-year-old Russian boy today has the same life expectancy as a fifteen-year-old boy in Haiti. Remember, Russia is an urbanized, industrialized society with levels of education and literacy comparable to, and perhaps even exceeding, other European countries. But alcoholism, depopulation, poverty, unemployment, and a kleptocratic political elite have created a society ill-equipped to compete as a modern nation. In any case, despite its decline, Russia is powerful and motivated enough to keep sowing chaos and is big enough to do so. The Russia-Ukraine War is the most tragic illustration of the return of realpolitik to the world stage.

TOO STRONG, TOO WEAK?

What led to this breakdown of geopolitical stability? Were the rise of China and the return of Russia inevitable results of economics, or were Western mistakes to blame?

As far as Russia's aggression, some realists have argued it was provoked by the steady growth in the number of NATO members after the Cold War. During the debate over NATO expansion in the 1990s, I was a somewhat skeptical voice on the issue. I was in favor of admitting the major Eastern European countries—Poland, Hungary, and the Czech Republic—but then pausing precisely to consider Russian interests and sensitivities. And I believed then and believe now that George W. Bush's decision at the Bucharest Summit in 2008 to open up the possibility that Ukraine might join NATO but not make a formal offer was the worst of both worlds—enraging Russia without giving Ukraine any path to security. But it is worth recalling that in the 1990s, the countries of Eastern and Central Europe were all traumatized, still recovering from a half century of domination by Moscow. They were desperately seeking an anchor, and to have left them entirely unmoored would have created a zone of instability in the heart of Europe.

Even without NATO expansion, Russia may have invaded Ukraine (many in the region think it might have done so even sooner). Ukraine had long loomed large in the Russian consciousness. Russia traces its history to the medieval state known as Kievan Rus, whose capital was Kiev, and much of Ukraine was under Moscow's rule for over three hundred years. When Putin famously called the collapse of the Soviet Union "the greatest geopolitical catastrophe of the century," he went on to explain why. It was because millions of Russians were no longer part of Mother Russia—a view that sees Ukrainians as Russians (albeit second-class ones) and Ukraine as a subordinate part of Russia. After a period of weakness in the 1990s, when Russia still waged two bloody wars to keep Chechnya, Putin set himself the goal of restoring Russian power, which inevitably meant returning Ukraine to the motherland.

The Soviet Union was the world's last multinational empire, and a quick glance at history teaches us what usually happens when such empires collapse: the imperial power undertakes bloody efforts to hold on to their former territories. The French waged a brutal war to keep Algeria, which they saw as a core part of France. They tried to hold on to their colony in Vietnam, as did the Dutch in Indonesia. The British killed more than ten thousand people in Kenya during the Mau Mau rebellion. Putin's foray into Ukraine can be seen as a war of imperial restoration. Before and after his invasion, he elaborated at length on his belief that Ukraine is not a "real" country but more properly thought of as a part of greater Russia. Still, many lay the blame for this war on the United States, for having been too strong and assertive in its Russia policy.

When it comes to China, the consensus goes the other way—that Washington was too weak and submissive. America welcomed China into the international system and opened the floodgates of trade and investment, so the argument goes, without regard to China's exploitative economic practices and authoritarian tendencies. This was done in the belief that China would moderate and become a responsible democracy. The new Cold Warriors who want total confrontation with China claim that this decades-long policy of "engagement" was naive and failed. After all, China did not turn into a liberal democracy.

In reality, Washington's policy toward China was never purely one of engagement, and its core aim was not to turn China into Denmark. The policy was always a combination of engagement and deterrence, sometimes described as "hedging." Since the 1970s, American officials concluded that bringing China into the global economic and political system was better than having China sit outside it, resentful and disruptive. But Washington coupled these efforts to integrate China with consistent support for other Asian powers as a balancing mechanism. It kept troops in Japan and South Korea, deepened ties with India, expanded military cooperation with Australia and the Philippines, and sold arms to Taiwan.

To a large extent, this balancing act worked. Before Nixon's overtures to Beijing, China was the world's greatest rogue state, funding and giving political support to insurgencies and guerilla movements across the globe from Latin America to Southeast Asia. Mao Zedong was obsessed with the idea that he stood at the vanguard of a revolutionary movement that would destroy Western capitalism. There was no measure too extreme for the cause—not even nuclear apocalypse. "If the worst came to the worst and half of mankind died," Mao explained in a speech in Moscow in 1957, "the other half would remain while imperialism would be razed to the ground and the whole world would become socialist." By comparison, China since the time of Deng Xiaoping has been a remarkably restrained nation on the international stage, neither going to war nor funding armed insurgents anywhere in the world since the 1980s. Viewed in this light, America's bipartisan China policy worked remarkably well.

But Xi Jinping has initiated a much more assertive foreign policy. He has overturned much of the Chinese consensus that fueled his country's success, scrapping Deng's diktat "hide your strength and bide your time" and Hu Jintao's promise of a "peaceful rise." There is little hidden or peaceful about Chinese clashes with Indian troops in the Himalayas, pressure on South Korea to drop a US missile defense system, and naval exercises menacing Taiwan. Perhaps it was inevitable that this day would come, after China had bided its time long enough and was ready to flex its muscles. China feels it deserves to be treated as the great power that it is.

We cannot be sure what the world would have looked like had Washington pursued very different policies toward both China and Russia. The alternative scenarios are tempting. Could a humbled, democratized Russia have been integrated into the liberal order, like postwar Germany? Would it have made a difference if US policymakers had recognized and responded to Chinese ambitions earlier, before Beijing grew so powerful? Would that have resulted in a China that looked more like a rising Japan in the 1980s, economically threatening but much less of a geopolitical danger? But it is ironic that some of the high priests of realpolitik, who would usually argue that clashes between great powers are the inevitable result of competing national ambitions, still blame American actions—in one case for being too tough, in the other case too weak. At the end of the day, changes in domestic leadership and the global balance of power were arguably more crucial in stirring Moscow and Beijing into action. After bouncing back from its '90s-era weakness, a revived Russia was likely to seek vengeance for losing the Cold War. For its part, China was never going to meekly accept a modest status after surging to become the world's second-largest economy. Unlike Japan, it was not depending on Washington for its security, nor was it constrained by its history. Xi's "Made in China" announcement, setting out the goal for China to dominate leading sectors of the economy and to be largely self-sufficient in those areas, came in 2015, well before Trump's tariffs and Biden's technology bans. The unipolar moment could not last forever. History had to return.

DICTATORSHIPS IN DANGER

It is easy to see a world of open trade, free markets, and open technology as benign, even virtuous, if you are an American or a Pole or a Singaporean. But it does not look that way to someone like Xi Jinping. After all, all these forces spur economic modernization, which produces a middle class, who increasingly have the freedom to work, move, make money, and consume information and entertainment. They are emboldened and ask for even more. Autocratic regimes fear for their hold on power and crack down. When two other East Asian autocracies, South Korea and Taiwan, went through rapid industrialization, it led to growing middle classes and calls for greater political freedom—prompting the regimes to crack down, often violently. Though the regimes clung to life for a few more years, soon they had to open up to real elections. China has now shown that, if the regime hangs tough, there is nothing inevitable about democratization following economic growth. But the task Xi has set for himself is immense: to put a lid on any further reform, even as he watches society transform around him.

Amid Xi's drive for political control, there has been perhaps an even more important structural change: the end of China's golden age of growth. From the beginning of Deng's reforms in 1978 through Xi's ascension in 2013, China's GDP growth averaged an astonishing 9.9 percent per year. Under Xi, it has dropped to 6.2 percent. Part of this is due to the Covid-19 pandemic and decisions made long ago, like the one-child policy, which caused the demographic challenges China faces today. And a slowdown had to come eventually. China may have reached the end of "catch-up" growth; the epochal movement of hundreds of millions of peasants from villages to cities can only happen once. China is now at risk of falling into the same middle-income trap that has plagued similar developing economies as their wages rise and competitiveness wanes.

But Xi's statist turn has not helped, and growth has slowed even further over the last few years. Even after the lifting of "Zero Covid" restrictions, China's economy did not roar back to life as many anticipated. The economist Richard Koo has warned that China may be at risk of "Japanification," a downward spiral of real estate debt and diminished competitiveness, while Zongyuan Zoe Liu points to the

"Four D's" crippling Chinese growth: demand, debt, demographics, and decoupling. In other words, insufficient consumer demand, overreliance on government borrowing, a labor force that is too small to support an aging and shrinking population, and decoupling from Western economies—together, these trends make for a substantially gloomier economic outlook than seemed likely even a few years ago, when China was riding high. (The climate of fear around the "China threat" often overlooks these trends. Washington can and should compete with Beijing—but it does not need to imagine that China is ten feet tall.)

Again, not all of China's problems can be laid directly at Xi's feet. Yet why did he turn so abruptly away from the policies that had brought China prosperity and prestige across the planet? There are signs that it was precisely because he saw that economic liberalization was transforming China profoundly—in a way that concerned him gravely. He believed that the Communist Party was on the verge of irrelevance in a society dominated by capitalism and consumerism. His nightmare seems to be a China that follows the Soviet Union's path: the party loses faith in itself, begins a process of reform, and is ultimately shoved aside by the societal forces it unleashes.

So Xi has taken a series of steps to weaken the private sector: cracking down on tech companies, humbling billionaires, propping up state-owned enterprises. He has become a more Maoist leader, creating a cult of personality, reviving elements of communist ideology, purging many officials from the party on corruption charges, and ramping up virulent nationalism. He has tightened the screws of Communist Party control and repression, putting Uyghurs into reeducation camps, crushing Hong Kong's autonomy, and even tracking dissidents abroad to intimidate them or have them arrested. He has eliminated term limits put in place by Deng to avoid another Mao-like despot. Governing by committee is gone, replaced by one-man rule. The scholar Elizabeth Economy argues that Xi's reforms amount to a transformation of Chinese society equivalent in scale to Mao's collectivization and Deng's moderation—China's "third revolution." While much of that revolution is responding to what is happening internally in China, some of it is triggered by fears of outside influences, by a world being made by America and the West.

CULTURAL BALANCING

China and Russia both feel that the liberal international order does not serve their interests—indeed, that in some ways it threatens them. America's efforts to expand the sphere of democracies whether in the Middle East or Asia seemed to justify those fears. But more recently, American values at home have also come to seem threatening. It is not only America's liberal democratic political system that Putin and Xi are trying to resist, but also its social liberalism.

Russia has always wanted Western technological and economic prowess but has been far more ambivalent about Western values. When Peter the Great traveled incognito to the Dutch Republic in 1697, he did so first and foremost to learn the ways of modern shipbuilding from the technological frontrunner of the age—not to study their liberal politics or tolerance of minorities. Three centuries later, when Russian leaders signed a Partnership and Cooperation Agreement with the EU in 1994, they did so more out of economic interest than from feelings of cultural kinship. From the nineteenth century onward, there was a strong belief that the communal, rooted life of the Russian peasant was superior to the cosmopolitan rootlessness of the Moscow and Saint Petersburg elite (as seen in Tolstoy's biting depictions of aristocrats in *War and Peace* and *Anna Karenina*). A "real" Russian almost by definition distrusted all things foreign.

For all that has changed since the time of the tsars, in many ways Putin's governing ideology echoes the traditional principles of "orthodoxy, autocracy, and nationality"—in other words, loyalty to Russia's distinct religion, ruler, and culture. The revival of these values in modern Russia was in some sense a backlash to the Western ideals of diversity, democracy, and globalism that reigned supreme in the 1990s. Consider one example of these old-school Russian values, coming from an unexpected corner: Russia's biker movement. It originated in the late 1980s as a quasi-libertarian gang inspired by Western individualism, embracing counterculture and opposing Soviet dictatorship. Decades later, bikers morphed into nationalistic and religious conservative thugs who wear icons (of the Virgin Mary and Stalin alike) and do Putin's bidding, roughing up dissidents and protesters. One group, the Night Wolves, sees their mission as defending "Holy Russia," which is "the last bastion of true religion," against diabolical Western influence.

Putin also encourages old-fashioned norms of patriarchy and masculinity. Western observers may scoff at his manly stunts, from riding horses bare chested to plunging into icy waters. But he clearly revels in a certain kind of machismo, even using it in foreign policy. When Angela Merkel visited Putin's dacha in 2007, he deliberately intimidated the dog-phobic chancellor with his giant black Labrador. More recently, Putin has even portrayed Russia's military actions in Ukraine as part of an effort to prevent the decadent West from imposing sexual deviancy on Russian society, where "mother and father" would be replaced by "parent number 1, parent number 2, number 3." For Putin, the flight of Western companies and pro-Western Russians after the invasion of Ukraine has in many ways been a welcome development, for it has purged the country of what he considers alien values. Doubling down on the culture war, in December 2022, Putin enacted a measure prohibiting the representation of LGBTQ relationships in any media. In July 2023, he signed another law criminalizing all hormone treatments and surgeries used for gender transitions.

In the minds of people like Putin and Xi, liberalism is a form of ideological hegemony, an outgrowth of America's post–Cold War geopolitical hegemony. Xi's China is if anything even more determined than Russia to block Western contamination. It would not be too strong a claim to say that, in response to this threat, Xi has launched a softer and tamer version of Mao's Cultural Revolution.

China's original Cultural Revolution lasted from 1966 to 1976, with purges and unrest that killed hundreds of thousands, imprisoned or displaced millions more, and hounded many intellectuals into suicide. Mao called upon legions of "Red Guards," passionate youths who were eager to build China into a utopia, to smash the "Four Olds": old customs, culture, habits, and ideas. Among those "olds" were the Confucian dogmas of patriarchy, hierarchy, and harmony that had shaped Chinese culture for millennia. Now chaos reigned. Workers insulted party bosses; children denounced their parents; students defied, beat, or even killed their teachers. It was as close to a pure social revolution as anything in human history—a total inversion of China's traditional order.

The madness unleashed by Mao traumatized the young Xi Jinping. His father, a top party official, was disgraced, jailed, and humiliated. Even the elder Xi's own wife was forced to publicly denounce him. Fifteen-year-old Xi was sent away to a remote village, at times living in a cave and working as a ditch digger, an exile that would last seven years. Today, Xi's own version of the Cultural Revolution is actually a cultural *counterrevolution*: conservative, nostalgic, traditional.

Xi's Chinese Dream—"the great rejuvenation of the Chinese nation," in his words—embraces nationalism, the primacy of the majority Han ethnic group, and the traditional social order. Under his leadership, China has persecuted ethnic minorities, repressed religious groups, and turned away from the instruction and use of English. The country has also swerved back toward promoting patriarchy. Mao, for all his near-genocidal mismanagement and tyranny, is still remembered in part for his feminist proverb, "Women hold up half the sky," and for welcoming more women into universities and the sciences.

Under Xi, government policies prioritize family unity over female choice. A so-called "cooling-off law" passed in 2021 has stymied attempts at divorce (separations dropped more than two-thirds in the months after its implementation), with judges advising the unhappy couples to try to work it out and come back later. Even though China is now desperate to juice its birth rate and reverse the disastrous effects of the one-child policy, unmarried women are prohibited from freezing their eggs, although men may preserve their sperm. Meanwhile, pro-LGBTQ organizations have been shuttered, and regulators have cracked down on Chinese celebrities seen as effeminate "sissy men" who follow the gender bending ways of K-pop and Western stars. Through all of these conservative shifts, Xi is attempting to control not just the economy but also the fabric of Chinese society. He wants to preserve a distinctive and homogeneous Chinese culture, with a sense of civilizational cohesion to resist Western liberalization.

Xi's top political advisor, an ideologue named Wang Huning, sees liberalism itself as the Communist Party's nemesis. In an account by the pseudonymous China watcher N. S. Lyons, Wang appears as a grand vizier counseling whole generations of leaders, from Jiang Zemin to Hu Jintao—but it is only Xi who has elevated him to China's inner sanctum, giving him a seat on the seven-man Politburo Standing Committee. In the aftermath of the reformist 1980s that birthed the Tiananmen Square democracy protests, Wang won a fellowship to spend six months traveling the United States, "like a sort of latter-day Chinese Alexis de Tocqueville," in Lyons' words. What Wang found in America disgusted him. Revolted by drug use, homelessness, crime, and corporate overlordship, he recoiled against liberal modernity itself. His memoir about these travels, *America against America*, has guided Chinese policy for three decades. When Wang returned to China, he became the sharpest opponent of political reform and looser party controls. No longer an idealist, he saw modernity in its American form as a dangerous solvent breaking down all of society's cherished sources of meaning.

This rationale explains why the Chinese celebrities who embraced supposedly "nihilistic" Western culture have been targeted. It explains why Xi has recoiled from allowing China to become a fully open, freewheeling consumer society, as in the Western model. In other words, Xi recognizes that globalization and fast-paced growth can fuel his country's strength, but at the price of disrupting established norms and empowering individuals to express their own identities. He wants to keep the fruits of growth, but regulate the pace of these societal changes—or stop them entirely. History suggests that, in the long run, this is not a winning strategy.

The cultural clampdown in China—and the one in Russia—should be seen as a conservative backlash to the liberal revolution transforming our world. China and Russia are rebelling against the liberal international order because they want to contest not only the West's hegemony of power but also its hegemony of ideas, both of which threaten them.

NEITHER LIBERAL NOR INTER-NATIONAL NOR ORDERLY

Does this Sino-Russian challenge mean that the liberal international order is doomed? Not yet. Voltaire said of the Holy Roman Empire that it was neither holy, nor Roman, nor an empire. The historian Niall Ferguson says the same of the liberal international order—that it has been neither liberal, nor international, nor orderly. And it's true that we often puff up this international system. It has been only somewhat liberal and open, it is embraced by most but not all of the world's great powers, and it has not prevented many small wars and conflicts, even as it has prevented major wars from breaking out. And yet, the post-1945 arrangement, with its alphabet soup of organizations—UN, IMF, UNESCO, UNICEF, WTO—has grown from modest beginnings to encompass more and more of the world, especially after the end of the Cold War. Its flexibility is one of its strengths. It has accommodated itself to a variety of regimes—from Nigeria to Saudi Arabia to Vietnam. It has survived all manner of crises, wars, and state collapses because it provides an overarching framework that encourages (but does not guarantee) peace, stability, and civilized conduct among nations. It has weathered communism and Islamic terror. And it has proved so enduring because at the end of the day, most countries and most people strive for peace and stability, an open world in which they can trade and prosper.

Today, the fundamental challenge this world order faces is that the country that imagined, constructed, and sustained it—the United States of America—no longer has the capacity or desire to play that hegemonic role. The American public is more ambivalent than ever before about maintaining their country's global role. More important, though America is still the pivotal player, it is not supreme anymore. "The rise of the rest" has created a world with many more active players, none willing to simply follow Washington's dictates, each vigorously pursuing its own interests. So a new post-American era is forming. But what will that look like? Will it be possible to sustain a liberal international order without a liberal superpower? The present international system evolved over two centuries during which the two dominant nations, Britain and America, both embraced Enlightenment ideals of freedom, democracy, liberty, the rule of law, and human rights (admittedly, sometimes more in aspiration than in practice).

The order's greatest task, of course, will be to manage Russia's revanchism and China's rise. But there are other problems it will have to deal with as well. Climate change, pandemics, terrorism, and the proliferation of unpredictable new technologies all require cooperation across the planet. We will need a mix of strategies to meet these challenges—some deterrence, some intervention, some coordination—or else we will witness the steady erosion of what order exists. Growing nationalist competition would return us to what the neoconservative scholar Robert Kagan has called "the jungle" of international life, where there are few rules, norms, or values, and a great deal of violence and instability.

Preserving the international system first and foremost means facing down Russia's aggression. It is the most immediate threat to that order, and it must not stand. At stake is the most fundamental rule underpinning international stability, which has been almost universally upheld since 1945—that borders are not changed by force. Unfortunately, Russia has not been isolated from the world in the wake of its invasion of Ukraine; it still maintains good relations with much of the planet. But it has been isolated from most of the richest and most productive countries. It faces a future of technological decay, economic stagnation, and diplomatic weakness as it increasingly becomes a vassal state of China. These facts do not ensure that Ukraine, even backed by the world's wealthiest nations, will prevail in its fight. North Vietnam was no economic dynamo and enjoyed far less outside support than its noncommunist rival to the south, and yet it won the Vietnam War. Ukraine will have to win on the battlefield, or at least achieve enough there to broker a lasting peace for itself. But either way, Russia seems to have sealed its own fate, and it is not a future in which Russia becomes a vibrant, advanced nation, able to present itself and its system as a model for other countries.

China poses a different and much broader challenge. It is likely to remain, for decades to come, the world's second-largest economy, technologically advanced, with a powerful military, a huge population, and a culture of achievement and innovation. In purely hard power terms, we are moving into a world that is bipolar. The United States and China dwarf all other nations by traditional economic, technological, and military measures. But China remains much weaker in many ways, especially when it comes to translating power into influence. It enjoys virtually no alliances, has little agenda-setting capacity, and is viewed suspiciously by most of its neighbors and an increasingly large part of the globe. Its economic model is sputtering, and its demographic trends are gloomy. Still, it has substantial resources to draw on, far more than any country other than America.

That does not mean conflict is inevitable. If China and the United States move toward a confrontational, zero-sum relationship, that will in all likelihood result in the unwinding of globalization, the division of the globe into economic and security spheres, and the fracturing of the open international order. There are some signs that we are entering such a world. High-end technologies like AI models and chips are already becoming decoupled, with separate "free world" technology platforms and Chinese ones. But we can find a way to live in peaceful albeit energetic competition with China, an outcome most of the world would fervently choose.

Crucially, there is the rest of the world to think about. The United States will confront the reality that Europe's economic growth depends on good commercial relations with China. In Asia, almost all countries have China as their largest trading partner. China is the largest external trading partner for South America and Africa. All these countries would like to maintain strong trading relations with China, use more affordable Chinese technology, and receive all the aid, loans, and technical know-how that the country offers. At the same time, many are wary of China and want strong geopolitical ties with the United States, too. In effect, they want to order à la carte from the international menu, choosing some American and some Chinese items. If Washington or Beijing insists on a prix fixe—you can only be close with America if you reject China, or vice versa—nations will find themselves in an impossible bind. The failure of economic sanctions to deter and then cripple Russia should remind us that the world economy is a vast space, and many countries will happily trade with anyone, no matter what America wants or does.

Washington needs a strategy toward Beijing that mirrors the complexity of the relationship, one in which China is part competitor, part customer, part adversary, part collaborator. Take technology. Over the past few years, the US has tried to curtail China's access to the very highest level of technology that could be used for its military (for example, the most sophisticated computer chips) while leaving China free to buy most items (such as regular computer chips). Citing national security concerns, the US has also limited China's ability to sell certain technologies and buy certain companies. The Biden administration describes this policy as putting a "high fence" around a "small yard" of the most important technologies. It's a sensible idea, but it's easier to state in theory than to maintain in practice. Politicians will compete with one another to ban ever more Chinese products, and US companies will lobby to keep out the competition. Expect to hear arguments as to why Chinese cars are a national security threat to America.

Is there a stable equilibrium in which the two countries can coexist as competitors? Under Xi, China's objectives are unclear. China does not act like Russia—a defiant rogue state trying to burn the house down—but it often acts in ways that erode the order's foundation. Xi wants a more insular political system, a more self-sufficient economy, and a society that is less influenced by Western sensibilities and culture. The dynamic now at work is already leading to higher tensions, which could then lead to actions and reactions, misperceptions and miscommunications. In the process, the United States and China would edge toward more and more hostility, and perhaps even, for the first time in nearly eighty years, a great-power war.

Among developing countries, no nation will have as much impact on the US-Chinese rivalry as India, the world's most populous country and fifth-largest economy (and climbing). India is gaining strength and becoming an indispensable counterweight to China. But other middle powers could also play a critical role in pushing back against Beijing—from Saudi Arabia in the Middle East to Indonesia and Vietnam in Southeast Asia to South Africa, Nigeria, and Kenya in Africa.

For now, however, it is important to recognize that the West remains strong. The coalition supporting Ukraine—America, Canada, Europe, the East Asian democracies, Australia, Singapore, and some others, what one might call "the West Plus"—comprises almost

60 percent of global GDP. With the Ukraine crisis and the Russian threat, Europe has become more unified, and the West Plus is more closely allied than ever before. Holding the alliance together will be a challenge, but no greater a challenge than the Cold War, when many countries sought to find a third way between the US and the USSR. But if successful, the West Plus could bolster and expand the zone of peace and freedom.

The diplomats who founded the European Union were steeped in history and determined to ensure that war did not break out again in Europe. Today's European leaders are beginning to infuse their day-to-day decisions with a similar sense of historic responsibility. Ever since its founding, the European Union has dreamed big but has never managed to overcome its divisions and act as a coherent unit. If Europe finally becomes a strategic player on the world stage, that could change—which would be the biggest geopolitical consequence of Russia's invasion.

The United States, for its part, must also act in a more historically minded way and remember the main lesson of the last century: an international system in which the most powerful player retreats into isolation and protectionism will be one marked by aggression and illiberalism, whereas a system with an engaged superpower can safeguard peace and liberalism. So who will fill the leadership vacuum left by waning American hegemony? The US could make common cause with a more unified Europe, along with Japan, South Korea, Australia, and Singapore—perhaps joined on occasion by India, Turkey, and some others. Instead of having one hegemon uphold the international order, it would be enforced by a coalition of powers united around shared interests and values.

ILLIBERAL DEMOCRACY, ABROAD AND AT HOME

Beyond the challenge of shoring up a liberal order internationally, there is the possibly greater challenge of defending the liberal project *within* societies—and the two are connected. Think about India. Its economic take-off has been accompanied by a surge in a homegrown version of populist nationalism—called Hindutva, a form of Hindu supremacy. Narendra Modi's India encapsulates a larger, global problem America will have to confront: how will it approach potential allies whose own nationalist politics have illiberal overtones?

Back in 1997, before Viktor Orbán and Vladimir Putin took office, while the West was cheering as countries across the globe were holding elections, I identified the phenomenon of "illiberal democracy": a system practiced in countries like Russia and Slovakia, Peru and the Philippines, where elected leaders were abusing power, depriving people of their rights, and hollowing out the essence of classical liberal, constitutional government. Since then, unfortunately, that list of democratic backsliders has gotten much longer. Western allies such as Turkey and Hungary have regressed significantly; other democracies like Israel and India are still vibrant but have seen concerning developments. Some places that I had identified early on, like Russia and Belarus, have morphed into dictatorships that hold rigged elections. According to data from Freedom House, liberal democracies have been declining in quantity and quality for the past sixteen years—a downturn the sociologist Larry Diamond has called a "democratic recession."

Populist strongmen around the world often claim that the values of an open society—pluralism, tolerance, secularism—are a Western import. They say they are building an authentic national political culture that is distinct from Western liberalism. And it is possible that the erosion of cosmopolitan and liberal ideas in these societies will reveal that they rested on an elite that was educated or inspired by the West, that underneath a less tolerant nationalism lay in wait. India's first prime minister, the Harrow- and Cambridge-educated Jawaharlal Nehru, once told the American ambassador, "I am the last Englishman to rule India." The country Nehru and his fellow post-independence leaders created was built on values they drew from deep associations with Britain and the West. Their India was a secular, pluralistic, democratic, and socialist state. I was the first to celebrate when India jettisoned much of its socialist heritage, which had caused untold dysfunction and corruption. But socialism is not the only imported Western idea that countries are now second-guessing. All kinds of Enlightenment ideas—freedom of press, independent courts, religious tolerance—have been fading in countries like India, Turkey, and Brazil. It's true that Russia and China stir up anti-Western discontent in other countries, but they are exploiting a backlash that already exists. In many places, the Enlightenment project—of which the liberal international order is a crucial part—is seen as a legacy of Western dominance.

Of course, in the West itself, there are people who reject the Enlightenment project. Many voters are opting for populists who present themselves as being in total opposition to the established order and its embedded values. With all the change and transformation that has occurred, people are overwhelmed, anxious, and fearful of a future that could mean more disruption, dislocation, and the loss of the world that they grew up in. Some are ready for radicalism even if that means burning the house down. This strain of illiberalism may well be the greatest threat to progress that we face.

CONCLUSION

THE INFINITE ABYSS

I N 1929, AT THE PEAK OF THE ROARING TWENTIES, AND after decades of heady economic and technological accelerations that rival what we have recently gone through, the influential American journalist Walter Lippmann wrote a bestselling book, *A Preface to Morals*. It tackled what he saw as the central problem of the age. For Lippmann, the revolutions that produced modern life in the mid-twentieth century had also had a huge psychological impact. People were left without the faith, tradition, and community that had long been their anchors. As he wrote, "By the dissolution of their ancestral ways, men have been deprived of the sense of certainty as to why they were born, why they must work, whom they must love, what they must honor, where they may turn in sorrow and defeat." Lippmann began his book with an epigraph from Aristophanes: "Whirl is King, having driven out Zeus." In other words, custom and order had been replaced by chaos. There could be no new canon of beliefs, no new authority that replaced what had been displaced because, Lippmann argued, "the acids of modernity are so powerful that they do not tolerate a crystallization of ideas which will serve as a new orthodoxy into which men can retreat." Or as Marx and Engels wrote in the quote that serves as epigraph for this book, "All that is solid melts into air, all that is holy is profaned."

The theme of this book has been ceaseless action and reaction, progress and backlash. Even the most successful revolutions that produced lasting prosperity, like the Dutch, British, and American examples in this book, generated deep resistance. The failed French Revolution led to a fear of radical change, casting a shadow that persists to this day and is the origin story of modern-day conservatism. Today, we see the push-pull dynamic even in the arena of international politics. After years of globalization and integration, Xi and Putin worried that their countries were slipping from their grasp, becoming more influenced by a set of global values, and they moved to reassert national interests and culture over cosmopolitan ones. Similar impulses motivate Donald Trump, the Brexiteers, Viktor Orbán, Jair Bolsonaro, and their populist fellow-travelers across the globe. They attack the ideas and institutions of liberalism at home—the established parties, the courts, and the press—because they worry that the acids of modernity are corroding the old way of life. Even the Dutch, progenitors of classical liberalism, show strains of this illiberal populism with the recent victory of Geert Wilders.

The crisis of global liberalism has not emerged in a vacuum. It is the result of rapidly transforming societies and leaders who capitalize on fears of all this change. In fact, for most people, globalization and the digital revolution have changed the world in myriad positive ways. These forces have democratized technology, unleashed innovation, raised life expectancies, spread wealth, and connected the far corners of the planet. Few people on the Earth today—perhaps none—would be better off growing up one hundred years ago. (Among other things, your lifespan on average would be half as long as it is now.) But the forces that modernize societies so much so fast are also, by definition, profoundly disruptive. Improvements often upend traditional ways of living, leaving many people feeling unmoored. Material progress can lift standards of living on average, but it might also shatter individual communities and people. Identity revolutions that feel like a liberation for some are deeply unnerving to many. As private corporations gain efficiency and scale by transcending national borders, people pocket the low prices but feel powerless.

Archbishop Desmond Tutu, who played a pivotal role in guiding

South Africa from apartheid to democracy, once wrote, "To be human is to be free." We all want to be free. We want choice, autonomy, control of our lives. There are mountains of evidence for this assertion across the ages—going as far back as the Israelites fleeing Pharaoh. More recently, we've seen East Germans slipping past the Berlin Wall, Arabs demanding democracy, North Koreans sneaking through the border to the south, migrants rushing into America and Europe, and Ukrainians sacrificing their lives to live in the free world. And yet, we also know that when human beings embrace freedom, they can end up feeling profoundly ill at ease. The very forward movement they celebrate makes us feel unmoored. Freedom and autonomy often come at the expense of authority and tradition. As the binding forces of religion and custom fade, the individual gains, but communities often lose. The result is that we may be richer and freer but also lonelier. We search for something, somewhere, that will fill that sense of loss, the emptiness that the French philosopher Blaise Pascal called "the infinite abyss."

Throughout history, governments have often defined what makes a meaningful life and directed people to work toward it. During the Middle Ages, the highest calling was to serve the glory of God and his chosen defender, the monarch. Later, for many it became service to the Fatherland or the communist cause. Only a few countries—Iran, North Korea—are still organized in this way, around a state-directed ideology, because the results of that approach have been almost universally disastrous. The liberal state, by contrast, does not tell its citizens what makes a good life; it leaves that to each individual. Instead, it puts in place a set of procedures—elections, free speech, courts—to help secure liberty, fair play, and equality of opportunity. Modern societies protect your life and liberty so that you may individually pursue happiness and fulfillment, defining it as you please so long as you do not impinge on anyone else's ability to do the same. But that freedom can be unnerving. The Danish philosopher Søren Kierkegaard said, "Anxiety is the dizziness of freedom." Constructing one's own meaning of life is not easy—much simpler to consult the Bible or the Quran. The rational project of liberalism is seen by many as a poor substitute for the awesome faith in God that once moved human beings to build cathedrals and write symphonies. Nor can it summon men to arms as easily as the trumpet calls of nationalism.

When describing the triumph of liberal democracy in the book-length version of his famous essay, "The End of History?," Francis Fukuyama added four words to his trademark phrase so that the title read, "The End of History and the Last Man." Fukuyama's worry was that although victory over communism would leave Western societies rich and tranquil, it would also make everyone passive—a "last man." The phrase comes from the German philosopher Friedrich Nietzsche, for whom the last man is quiet and complacent, desiring only peace and order so he can pursue his own comforts. Nietzsche contrasts him with the powerful, creative *Übermensch*—superman—who molds the world to his will. Fukuyama's fear was that the liberal project stripped human beings of a sense of striving, ambition, and desire for recognition, which are essential motivators of human behavior. The image Fukuyama conjured up after the victory over communism was of people with no great ideological cause to defend, who would spend their days pursuing their material needs and wants—and feeling empty, alone, and depressed.

Into this void step populism, nationalism, and authoritarianism. They offer people what the German-American scholar Erich Fromm called an "escape from freedom." A distinguished psychologist who studied the rise of fascism, Fromm argued that once human beings live through the chaos of freedom, they get scared. "The frightened individual seeks for somebody or something to tie his self to; he cannot bear to be his own individual self any longer, and he tries frantically to get rid of it and to feel security again by the elimination of this burden: the self." In explaining his own illiberal ideology, Hungarian prime minister Viktor Orbán has argued that liberalism is too focused on the individual and his ego. "There are certain things which are more important than 'me,' than my ego—family, nation, God," he told Tucker Carlson in 2023. Orbán's policies (purportedly) aim to put those things on a pedestal and, in Fromm's words, "eliminate the burden of the self." Taking a page from the same playbook, Vladimir Putin implores Russians not to follow the West's siren song of individual self-expression but instead help make Russia great again. Xi speaks in similar tones about China's great project of national rejuvenation, which celebrates Chinese culture as distinct from Western individualism. Even in the West, populists speak of the paramount importance of God, country, and tradition. These ideas have powerful resonance. As the social psychologist Jonathan Haidt has argued, left-wing morality addresses only two of the five foundational (and likely evolutionarily evolved) principles of morality: care and fairness. Right-wing morality includes other values too: loyalty, authority, and sanctity. Those three values are what drive Republican voters to, for example, fume over NFL players who kneel for the national anthem or people who say racism was central to the founding of the US. They want leaders who will stand up for those values of devotion, order, and purity. These atavistic impulses have generated much energy throughout history, though also, let us not forget, much cruelty and oppression.

Will populist ideology fill the hole in the heart created by modernity? I doubt it. In the end, as much as human beings are unsettled by the consequences of freedom for all, they still want it for themselves. They show this every day in all kinds of ways. All the forces that are changing society—Lippmann's "acids of modernity"—are the consequence of human beings making free choices. After all, churches would not sit empty if people decided to show up to pray. Small towns and communities would not be hollowed out if young people stopped leaving for better jobs at higher wages. The online revolution would not have put brick-and-mortar stores out of business if consumers spurned the convenience of buying with a click and instead went to their local shops. Family ties would not be loosening if people stayed close to their kin and always married within their faith. *We* are the acids of modernity, choosing to act in ways that, in aggregate, create a world that leaves many feeling disquieted.

One of the most insightful accounts of this dynamic comes from the journalist Alan Ehrenhalt, who grew up in the 1950s on the South Side of Chicago. As he recounted in his book *The Lost City*, a tight-knit web of communities sustained and enriched life when he was a boy, and he went back to understand why they had disappeared. He arrived at a simple answer: choice. In the old days, people were locked into their neighborhood because local banks were the only place you could get loans, local factories were the only place to get jobs, and local leaders were the only people who would help you get both. Attending church was a religious duty but also a civic and economic benefit because the priest could put in a good word with the banker. As the economy became less tethered to local contacts and connections, and people found other, better prospects, they moved. Even among those who stayed, technology changed things, sometimes in surprising ways. Ehrenhalt remembered the rich community life of stoops, where everyone hung out during summers, or group trips to the movie theater. Once air conditioning arrived, people sat outside less, and as television sets became ubiquitous, those communal outings to the movies also waned.

Community is formed and maintained by hierarchy and constraints. We gain much when we shake off authority and escape from coercion, but inevitably we lose community. And when we lose it, we miss it and remember it with heightened nostalgia. Lippmann described how a person accepted the ways of the world in the old days: "When he believed that the unfolding of events was a manifestation of the will of God, he could say: Thy will be done." That changes when a person lives without faith: "When he believes that events are determined by the votes of a majority, the orders of his bosses, the opinions of his neighbors, the laws of supply and demand, and the decisions of quite selfish men, he yields because he has to yield. He is conquered but unconvinced." In other words, a person can submit to the realities of modern life but still reject any justification for those realities—say, the closure of a factory or the influence of alien cultures. And being unconvinced, that person can be seduced by some ideology that attacks his bosses, his neighbors, elites, all of whom are part of a grand conspiracy to force him to yield, to become the victim of their evil designs. He is free and yet he feels coerced—and searches for some way to fight back.

WHAT IS TO BE DONE?

Almost everywhere across the world, we can see the effects of this loss of faith in God, religion, experts, politicians, institutions, and norms. Often it can take a nasty form, blaming the breakdown of the old ways on those who look different, speak in foreign accents, or worship unfamiliar gods. Some scholars have found that underneath much of the populist rage in the West lie fears among an older, whiter population of a looming demographic transformation of the country, a "great replacement." Many of our recent demagogues have used rhetoric and advocated policies that exploit these anxieties and fears. But it would be a mistake to explain all such reactions as merely racism. There is a broader uneasiness about a changing world, a loss of certainty, and the collapse of community. This malaise requires serious thought and response.

Some part of that response involves specific policies and programs that strengthen communities and help people feel less adrift and insecure. Programs like free preschool, subsidized child care, and paid parental leave can bolster family life. Building local infrastructure, investing in education facilities, and promoting civic participation can make individuals more connected to their towns and localities. Today's colleges and universities should try to create communities centered around learning and the free exchange of ideas, rather than seeking relevance by attaching themselves to political causes that have little to do with their core mission. Reasonable regulation of markets coupled with wealth redistribution can reduce the precarity felt by the working class. Joe Biden is the rare Washington politician who has genuine concern for non-college-educated Americans, given his roots in that world. Many of his policies and spending programs help the parts of America that feel left behind. A substantial portion of the investments initiated by the Inflation Reduction Act are going to counties with below-average wages and below-average college graduation rates, most of them solid Republican districts.

Consider, however, the long-term trends. In the decade after 2010, by one estimate, the fifty-three largest American metro areas saw 71 percent of all population growth, two-thirds of all employment growth, and three-quarters of all economic growth. The twenty biggest cities accounted for 50 percent of all job growth. Changes in work patterns after the pandemic might slow this pace, but they are unlikely to reverse it altogether. We will need ways to create communities that bind together ever more disparate parts of the country. I have long advocated some kind of universal national service in the United States as one way of doing just that. The decades after World War II are remembered as ones when the country worked better and with a stronger sense of unity because the shared experience of wartime service bound together a generation of Americans. As Mickey Kaus noted in his book, *The End of Equality*, John F. Kennedy, one of America's richest heirs and a graduate of Choate and Harvard, captained a PT boat in the Pacific theater with fellow crew members who were mechanics, factory workers, truck drivers, and fishermen. Today, if the sons and daughters of financiers and software engineers taught in public schools, worked in national parks, and served in the armed forces alongside the children of construction workers and schoolteachers and farmers, over the years that might bridge some of the gaps in understanding and heal America's intense polarization.

Economic measures will not entirely solve a problem that is largely cultural. We need to create an immigration regime that is seen by all as rules-based and fair. Climate change, poverty, and political instability are all producing waves of migration to the West that are unmanageable. In 2022, there were 2.4 million unauthorized crossings of the southern border of the United States. Many migrants pay cartels to get them to the US border and then, having arrived, claim asylum status, which allows them to stay in the US and have their cases heard over a lengthy period of time. Some slip into the shadows of the American economy. Similar dynamics are at work in Europe. Asylum policies—born in the aftermath of the Holocaust—were designed for a small number of people who were personally facing harsh persecution because of their identity, faith, or political views. Now the system is buckling under strain from the constant flood of people fleeing all kinds of crises. And no single issue animates modern populism as much as these waves of uncontrolled migration and the sense that they are causing anarchy. It is not too strong to claim that Syria's refugee crisis accelerated the rise of Europe's populist Right. As the writer David Frum put it, "If liberals insist that only fascists will enforce borders, then voters will hire fascists to do the job liberals refuse to do."

One can think of other policy initiatives and adjustments for times like these. But they seem small bore when one thinks about the profound psychological character of the changes now taking place. One statesman who foresaw some of those changes was Singapore's founding father, Lee Kuan Yew. I had the opportunity to speak to him on several occasions over the final two decades of his life and was struck by a theme he returned to again and again. People often praised him for moving Singapore from poverty to prosperity in a single generation or for practicing a deft foreign policy. But he felt that his greatest achievement was having created a nation out of a polyglot population of Chinese, Malays, Indians, and others on the sandbar that is Singapore. That nation-building experiment required a determined focus on his vision of multiculturalism, which meant enforcing mixed housing and schooling so that people did not live in ethnic enclaves but raised their children together in shared spaces. *We needed to build a common civic culture,* he told me.

Yet Lee also encouraged these communities to retain their languages, rituals, festivals, and faith. He worried that in rapidly developing East Asia, too many had forgotten where they came from. "We have left the past behind," he said, "and there is an underlying unease that there will be nothing left of us that is part of the old." He described the experience of Malaysians who moved to Australia and Canada in the 1960s and 1970s because they wanted their children to have the best education possible at a time when Malaysia was shifting from English-language education to instruction in Malay as the primary language. "The children grew up, reached their late teens and left home. And suddenly the parents discovered the emptiness of the whole exercise. They had given their children a modern education in the English language and in the process lost their children altogether." To this day, Singapore's leaders try hard to have their citizens stay rooted in their communities and cultures so they don't turn into deracinated yuppies. They are trying to maintain a highly functioning advanced economy and meritocracy, but one filled with people who think of themselves as "Somewheres" rather than "Anywheres." Yet there is a delicate balance between giving people access to new opportunities and preserving their traditional identities.

Lee's story about Malaysian parents will sound hauntingly familiar to immigrants everywhere. No matter how much you insist that your children learn and maintain the language and traditions of the old country, they are living and growing up in a new world and are inevitably shaped far more by that new culture than by the dribs and drabs of the old one that parents push onto them. In fact, the story of change and progress—and loss and backlash—that I have been telling in this book through hundreds of years of history can be told metaphorically through the lives of immigrants who come to a new place because they want to embrace all the economic and technological improvements it offers. They adapt and succeed and raise their children, who enjoy opportunities that were unimaginable in their ancestral land. But as they age and retire, they miss the culture and community that they left behind. Some listen to the old music and watch the old movies, others gather in small groups of like-minded immigrants with similar experiences, and still others find ways to spend more and more time back in the old country. They long for the place they had once eagerly left behind.

Can you build the kind of bulwark against modernization in the way that Lee Kuan Yew imagined? For a while, it seemed that Japan offered a solution to these problems. It consciously sought to keep capitalism at bay, reducing the inevitable tendency toward inequality. It retained many core elements of its traditional culture. Despite labor shortages, it took in few immigrants. And, in fact, Japan is that rare advanced industrial nation with little right-wing populism. The ruling Liberal Democratic Party continues to reign, now in its seventh decade. But Japan has paid a price. The economy became less dynamic and innovative. The society remains hierarchical and patriarchal. And the labor shortages have begun to bite. The country has begun making changes on all fronts but has a long way to go.

The truth is, we are all increasingly leaving some of our culture behind. Even among white working-class Americans, there is a feeling of alienation. In a 2016 survey, nearly half of them agreed with the statement, "Things have changed so much that I often feel like a stranger in my own country." Everything seems to be in flux. People are on the move everywhere, leaving their homes, arriving in new places, making new lives, and meeting new people. Intermarriage means admixture. The children of a mixed marriage must choose parts of different cultural traditions, and by the act of choosing they are already breaking down the authority and hierarchy of the old cultural order. This is all part of a thrilling human adventure to smash barriers and prejudices and embrace our common humanity—at a deeper and personal level. So the admonition to simply "hold onto your past" as you rapidly enter the future seems unlikely to work. In fact, so many countries are now building "universal nations," encompassing people of all races, castes, and creeds, and allowing those who once sat in the shadows to walk with pride in the gleaming light of day.

FAITH IN FREEDOM

Liberalism's problem in many ways is that it has been too successful. It has been and remains the principal force for political modernization across the world. Look at what life was like centuries ago—monarchies, aristocracies, church hierarchies, censorship, official discrimination by law, and state-run monopolies. Over time, all of these traditions and practices have cracked and crumbled because of the powerful appeal of liberal ideas—celebrating individual liberties and rights, opposing tyranny and state control, empowering ordinary people. Liberal ideas in economics—respecting private property and using open markets, trade, and free exchange—have taken hold almost everywhere across the planet, though often with important adjustments to ensure greater economic equity and fair play. But liberalism is not a perfect system, and its shortcomings and excesses provide ample fodder for its enemies to attack it. This is a fight with deep historical roots.

The push and pull of politics worked best in places like the Netherlands, Britain, and America, where liberals argued for more freedom, openness, and individual rights. They faced opposition, which often took the form of conservative forces who wanted to preserve the old order. But over time, as the contestation of party politics worked its magic, both liberals and conservatives mellowed, and the countries found a way to move forward—perhaps more slowly than the liberals wanted but faster than the conservatives hoped. Change happened with the grain of society rather than against it. That organic, bottom-up revolution succeeded where the French Revolution failed. The French approach was to impose radical ideas from above, with little thought to where the country was in its development. It resulted in dramatic disruption, social chaos, widespread violence—and, ultimately, dictatorship.

As the French Revolution shows, one side of the aisle does not have a monopoly on virtue. That would be a profound misreading of history. I have used the term "liberal" to denote someone who wants to expand liberty and defend the rule of law. Conservatism is not inherently in opposition to this kind of liberalism. Conservatives have had a long and honorable place in history, taking the perspective of continuity and caution. They often accept the need for change but worry that going too far, too fast will rip the fabric of society. The totemic conservative figure, often invoked by modern conservatives, is Edmund Burke, a British member of Parliament who, as we saw earlier, earned fame for eloquently opposing the French Revolution. But Burke was in fact a liberal in the classical sense. He had argued passionately in favor of the American Revolution and had made his name attacking Britain's corrupt rule in India. He believed that the French Revolution was too radical, a movement based in abstract theory, not drawn from society. The revolution claimed to be liberal but was in fact deeply illiberal. Burke warned that it would end in violence and anarchy, and he was correct.

The prominent modern conservative George Will is also a classical liberal. In his book *The Conservative Sensibility*, he contends that conservatism is an ideology that tries to conserve liberalism. For him, the original conception of government laid out by the American founders was a set of classically liberal ideas and principles, which he believes true conservatives ought to protect. Indeed, Republicans and Democrats have both traditionally been proponents of this kind of classical liberalism, though one side tends to think a less invasive government fosters liberty and prosperity, while the other thinks a more active government is needed to protect people's rights and promote equality of opportunity. Each side can go too far, but each has its value. Both reject the backward-looking illiberal ideology of an Orbán or Trump, who conjure up the older European idea of what Will calls "throne-and-altar" conservatism, a truly reactionary worldview that borders on authoritarianism and that Will rightly says has no place in the modern world. There is no greater proof of success than the fact that liberalism has become something even conservatives treasure.

Today, the task for those who embrace the Enlightenment project, celebrate the progress we have made so far, and want to continue to move society forward is to learn from the struggles of the past. Don't succumb to hubris and believe that every theoretical advance in rights is pure virtue and should be implemented today. Don't treat the nation as a guinea pig for your latest scheme. Don't impose change from above. Instead, work within the fabric of society, with actual communities and people, to educate, persuade, and convince them of your cause. Don't give up on freedom of speech just because at any given moment you despise a message that is spreading far and wide. Don't be seduced by identity politics—which is fundamentally illiberal, viewing people as categories rather than individuals. Moving too quickly and too forcefully will often cause more backlash than progress. Accept that compromise is an inevitable aspect of democracy—indeed, that it is a virtue because it takes into account the passions and aspirations of others.

Consider the 1960s and 1970s in the West, particularly in America. There were so many major advances for liberty, like the end of the formal Jim Crow laws. As I argued earlier in this book, perhaps the most important and enduring change was the emancipation of women, who in almost every society in history had lived as second-class citizens. (The backlash to that dramatic advance infuses all reactionary movements, from Islamic fundamentalism to Christian conservatism.) But along with these waves of progress there was also excess, radicalism, and violence. In just eighteen months during 1971 and 1972, there were some 2,500 bombings on American soil, perpetrated by radicals who had lost faith in the possibilities of reform within the system. The Weathermen and the Black Panthers in America and the Red Brigade in Europe did not further progressive causes but instead produced a backlash that lasted for decades. In our own isolated and atomized times, the desire for revolution (or as is often the case, counterrevolution) is just as palpable. The Right's disdain for core aspects of the liberal project is frightening and poses the greatest danger. But many on the left also want to dispense with some of liberalism's rules and procedures—most notably free speech—and simply get to the "correct" outcome. They want to ban those who have "wrong" ideas from speaking. They want to achieve racial equality by quota or decree. They want to use education or art to achieve political goals rather than educational or artistic ones. Convinced of the virtue of their ideas in theory—say, the rights of asylum seekers—they are comfortable pushing this abstract notion of virtue onto a reluctant society. But top-down revolutionary actions, from the uncompromising left or the reactionary right, often cause more turmoil than progress.

At the end of the twentieth century, the philosopher Isaiah Berlin reflected on the danger of those who fervently believe that they have the answer and are impatient with liberalism's focus on rules, procedures, and compromise. It serves as a cautionary note to those with illiberal tendencies on the right and left:

> *If you are truly convinced that there is some solution to all human problems, that one can conceive an ideal society which men can reach if only they do what is necessary to attain it, then you and your followers must believe that no price can be too high to pay in order to open the gates of such a paradise. Only the stupid and malevolent will resist once certain simple truths are put to them. Those who resist must be persuaded; if they cannot be persuaded, laws must be passed to restrain them; if that does not work, then coercion, if need be violence, will inevitably have to be used—if necessary, terror, slaughter. . . . We must weigh and measure, bargain, compromise, and prevent the crushing of one form of life by its rivals. I know only too well that this is not a flag under which idealistic and enthusiastic young men and women may wish to march—it seems too tame, too reasonable, too bourgeois, it does not engage the generous emotions. But you must believe me, one cannot have everything one wants—not only in practice, but even in theory. The denial of this, the search for a single, overarching ideal because it is the one and only true one for humanity, invariably leads to coercion. And then to destruction, blood—eggs are broken, but the omelette is not in sight, there is only an infinite number of eggs, human lives, ready for the breaking. And in the end the passionate idealists forget the omelette, and just go on breaking eggs.*

Extremism may feel satisfying, but gradual reform more often produces enduring change. If liberals can understand that time is on their side, and that their opponents are not always evil or stupid, they might find that they are able to gain broader acceptance and that progress will be made—steadily, albeit slowly. Those who seek to restrain these disruptions, for their part, should recall how resisting any change at all can simply bottle up frustration until it erupts in revolution. Rather than preserve every aspect of the status quo, better to follow the lead of the British conservatives who, after 1832, made their peace with the Great Reform Act's gradual democratization, according to the credo, "Reform, that you may preserve." The leading British Conservative of the late nineteenth century, Benjamin Disraeli, embraced the new working-class voters—and sought their political support, which he often got. Most conservatives today accept and defend most of the advances in opportunities and benefits—for workers, the elderly, women, and minorities—that their predecessors had bitterly opposed at the time they were first proposed. For his part, President Biden seems to understand the logic of compromise as well. Fearing another populist-nationalist explosion like 2016, he has accepted the need to pivot the neoliberal consensus toward some modest, reformist versions of certain populist policies: spurning new trade deals, subsidizing American manufacturing, even constructing a small strip of Mexican-American border wall. His argument, I suppose, is that it is better to give a little for the sake of preserving the overall liberal project than to hold fast and risk its collapse. It is a long journey toward a more perfect union.

The greatest challenge remains to infuse that journey with moral meaning, to imbue it with the sense of pride and purpose that religion once did—to fill that hole in the heart. One reason fast-paced change never produced communist or fascist revolutions in places like Britain and America is that some of the old elements of society—religion, tradition, community—were ballasts in the storm of change. The historian Gertrude Himmelfarb called this the "moral capital of the Victorians," the reservoir of tradition that stabilized a fast-changing society. Lee Kuan Yew would understand and endorse that idea. But growth, technology, urbanization, secularization, and intermarriage are all corroding those old anchors. The new ways have to give purpose to help keep people from drifting. Community has to form around the ideas and practices of liberalism. For instance, the European Union is today seen as a soulless bureaucracy in Brussels, but it is in fact the embodiment of a grand idea, that nations which warred against each other for centuries now live as one closely tied political community. "That idea of Europe deserves songs written about it, and big bright blue flags to be waved about," wrote the singer-songwriter Bono. And surely all these liberal ideas—freedom, individual rights for all, religious liberty, democracy—should be able to fill our chests with pride, give meaning to our lives, and make us all realize that we are not "last" men and women, idling away our time on the Earth.

In his magisterial television show *Civilisation*, the great art historian Kenneth Clark asked why a civilization like Rome—that was once dominant, technologically advanced, cultured, and prosperous—could collapse into the barbarism of the Dark Ages. He concluded that beyond the material causes, there was a mental one: "It is lack of confidence, more than anything else, that kills a civilisation. We can destroy ourselves by cynicism and disillusion, just as effectively as by bombs." Modern civilization has given ordinary human beings greater freedom, wealth, and dignity than any before it. It has empowered billions of people in all kinds of ways. If it collapses, and the new dark ages arrive, it will be because in our myopia, our internecine squabbles, and our petty rivalries, we lost sight of the fact that we are the heirs to the greatest tradition in history, one that liberated the human mind and spirit, that created the modern world, and whose greatest achievements are yet to come.

ACKNOWLEDGMENTS

W HEN I LOOKED AT THE ORIGINAL CONTRACT FOR this book, I was startled to realize I signed it ten years ago. It's taken a while, partly because along the way, I decided to write two short books, one on a liberal education and the other on the post-pandemic world. But it's mostly taken me time to read, research, and think about what became an ever-more expansive topic. Even before Brexit and the election of Donald Trump, it was becoming clear to me that political debates were charting a new course, and I wanted to uncover the deeper forces underneath this shift. (The original title for the book was *Beyond Left and Right*.) I have always been interested in how and why countries developed differently over time. My 2003 book, *The Future of Freedom: Illiberal Democracy at Home and Abroad*, analyzed emergent populism, the threats to democracy, and the often bumpy road of modernization—though the trend has gotten darker and more complex in the two decades that followed.

Along this extensive journey, I leaned on a brilliant group of associates to help me. Since 2019, Jonathan Esty has been my main researcher on the project, driving the historical research and editing the manuscript as it evolved. He is now a PhD student at the Johns Hopkins School of Advanced International Studies. Andrew Sorota, fresh from Yale, picked up the baton in 2022, sharpening the philosophical direction of the project and pushing tirelessly to ensure the book got over the finish line. Jonathan and Andrew have been true intellectual partners, critiquing drafts and offering suggestions that always improved the book. They've also worked with me on other projects at Schmidt Futures, the innovative philanthropic venture set up by Eric and Wendy Schmidt where I serve as a senior advisor.

In the final stages of polishing the book, I asked two people whose judgment and intelligence I value highly to vet the manuscript—Jonah Bader, a producer on my show at CNN, and Stuart Reid, executive editor at *Foreign Affairs* and now an acclaimed author in his own right. They both took time out of their busy schedules to review the manuscript and ask just the right questions to strengthen the thrust of the book.

For exhaustive research and editing on the Globalization and Identity Politics chapters I thank Nick Cohen and Johannes Lang. Nathalie Bussemaker was a meticulous and thorough fact checker of the entire manuscript, and Andrew Moore was an excellent sounding board for ideas. The four of them also work at Schmidt Futures.

Several others assisted with supplemental fact checking and copyediting, including Victoria Hsieh, Anna Miller, Selina Xu, Claire Zalla, and Katia Zoritch. I am also grateful to those who helped me in the decade that I have been thinking about, reading, and researching this book. John Cookson did excellent work on British politics and trade policy. Gavan Gideon dove into Dutch and English history. Scott Remer researched theories of nationalism. Adham Azab translated French archival sources that informed my discussion on the origins of Right and Left.

Needless to say, none of these people bear responsibility for any of my mistakes, nor do I mean to imply that they agree with everything I have written.

Drake McFeely has been my editor for more than twenty years, over the course of five books, and is my indispensable and patient friend, philosopher, and guide in these efforts. Alas, this will be our last book together because Drake is hanging up his hat after an amazing career at Norton, where he was, for many years, chair and president. Stuart Proffitt, the legendary editor of Penguin Press, once again agreed to publish the book in Great Britain and the Commonwealth. His comments are always a treasure, even when they are critical. He sensibly urged me to have a subtitle for the book, which clarifies its scope for the reader. My agent, Andrew Wylie, continues to amaze me with his perseverance. (He gets the prize for quickest response time to an email.) Thank you to Drake's assistant editor, Caroline Adams, who kept us on track throughout the process, and to Charlotte Kelchner, who copyedited the manuscript fast and well.

I'd like to thank my staff at CNN. Melanie Galvin manages my professional life expertly, keeping several balls in the air and never letting one drop. Jennifer Dargan helps arrange my media appearances, and Chris Good handles my newsletter and social media accounts. Tom Goldstone is my trusted partner and friend who runs my weekly show, with the help of Jessica Gutteridge, and Dan Logan ably leads my documentary unit. They oversee teams of top-notch producers, production assistants, and interns who collaborate with me on a daily basis to create programming of the highest caliber. The show would also not be possible without the many editors, crew members, technical staff, makeup artists, and others at CNN. The list of individuals is too long to name, but know that I deeply appreciate the work you do every day. My sincere thanks also to my research assistant Claire Zalla, and to David Shipley, Mike Larabee, Christian Caryl, and the rest of the opinion team at the *Washington Post* who make my weekly column a reality.

Working on an intensive project like this makes demands on one's family and friends. I'd like to give a special thanks to Eric Schmidt, who not only funded research support for the book through Schmidt Futures but has also been a great friend and thoughtful interlocutor over the years. Thanks to my family: my children, Omar, Lila, and Sofia, my ex-wife, Paula, my brothers Arshad and Mansoor, my sister Tasneem, and their spouses, Ann, Rachel, and Vikram.

I've dedicated this book to all the people who mentored me as I moved through life, in India and America, from school to college to graduate school and then in the working world. I firmly believe that luck plays a large role in anyone's success, but part of getting lucky is having people who take the time and effort to teach you, guide you, and give you opportunities to grow. I would not be where I am today without all of them.

NOTES

INTRODUCTION: A MULTITUDE OF REVOLUTIONS

1 **"'Poli,' a Latin word":** Emily Herbert, *Robin Williams: When the Laughter Stops 1951–2014* (London: Blake, 2014), "Twenty Great Robin Williams' Jokes."

3 **almost all the living nominees:** Bob Dole, the nominee in 1996, being the sole exception who, at the age of ninety-two, did endorse Trump in 2016.

4 **"open versus closed":** "Full text of Tony Blair's speech to the TUC," *Guardian*, September 12, 2006.

6 **"sudden, radical, or complete change":** *Merriam Webster Online*, s.v., "Revolution."

11 **"my teacher":** Howard W. French, "The History of Tough Talk on China," *Wall Street Journal*, December 10, 2016.

12 **polarization reached a peak:** see Laura Paisley, "Political Polarization at Its Worst since the Civil War," *USC Today*, November 8, 2016; and Rachel Kleinfeld, "Polarization, Democracy, and Political Violence in the United States: What the Research Says," Carnegie Endowment for International Peace, September 5, 2023.

12 **"holiday from history":** George F. Will, "The End of Our Holiday from History," *Washington Post*, September 12, 2001.

16 **"The older order changeth":** Alfred, Lord Tennyson, "Morte d'Arthur," Poetry Foundation.

19 **"opposite camp":** Louis-Henry-Charles de Gauville, *Journal du Baron de Gauville, député de l'ordre de la noblesse, aux Etats-généraux depuis le 4 mars 1789 jusqu'au 1er juillet 1790* (Paris: Gay, 1864), 20.

20 **"polarization of the Assembly":** Timothy Tackett, *Becoming a Revolutionary: The Deputies of the French National Assembly and the Emergence of a Revolutionary Culture (1789–1790)* (University Park: Pennsylvania State University Press, 2006), 201, quoted in John Richard Cookson, "How French Racehorses Are to Blame for U.S. Partisan Politics," *National Interest*, July 7, 2016.

CHAPTER ONE: THE FIRST LIBERAL REVOLUTION

25 **a boomlet of books:** See Thomas Cahill's books on the Greeks, Jews, and Irish; and Arthur Herman, *How the Scots Invented the Modern World: The True Story of How*

Western Europe's Poorest Nation Created Our World & Everything in It (New York: Three Rivers, 2001).

26 **earliest flourishing of classical liberalism:** See: Jonathan I. Israel, *The Dutch Republic: Its Rise, Greatness, and Fall; 1477–1806*, The Oxford History of Early Modern Europe (Oxford: Clarendon, 1998); and Simon Schama, *The Embarrassment of Riches: An Interpretation of Dutch Culture in the Golden Age*, 1st ed. (New York: Knopf, 1987).

26 **"the top performer":** Angus Maddison, *Dynamic Forces in Capitalist Development* (Oxford: Oxford University Press, 1991), 30.

28 **Venetian Empire:** Wantje Fritschy, *Public Finance of the Dutch Republic in Comparative Perspective* (Leiden: Brill Academic, 2017).

28 **glassmakers on Murano:** See "Murano Glass," *Scholarly Community Encyclopedia*, citing David J. Shotwell, *Glass A to Z* (Iola, WI: Krause, 2002), 586–87.

30 **Military Revolution:** Geoffrey Parker, *The Military Revolution: Military Innovation and the Rise of the West, 1500–1800*, 2nd ed. (Cambridge: Cambridge University Press, 1996).

31 **90 percent of the indigenous populations:** This story is ably told in Jared M. Diamond, *Guns, Germs, and Steel: The Fates of Human Societies* (New York: W. W. Norton, 1999). The economic historian Brad DeLong has recently appraised the ongoing debate over the merits and limitations of Diamond's account, proposing that perhaps the better full list of key variables for Western dominance would be "Guns, Germs, Steel, Coal, Slavery, Seaborne Empires, Peninsulas, Mountain Ranges, Rainfall, and Chance," see: Brad DeLong, "Guns, Germs, Steel, Coal, Slavery, Seaborne Empires, Peninsulas, Mountain Ranges, Rainfall, & Chance: Jared Diamond's 'Guns, Germs, & Steel' After Twenty-Five Years," *Brad DeLong's Grasping Reality*. See also: William H. McNeill, *Plagues and Peoples* (New York: Anchor, 2010).

33 **"terps":** Johan A. W. Nicolay, "Terp Excavation in the Netherlands," *Encyclopedia of Global Archaeology* (2014): 7271–73.

34 **"private control of the land":** Jan de Vries, "On the Modernity of the Dutch Republic," *Journal of Economic History* 33, no. 1 (1973): 191–202.

34 **over half:** Jan Luiten van Zanden, *The Long Road to the Industrial Revolution: The European Economy in a Global Perspective, 1000–1800* (Leiden: Brill Academic, 2009), 98–100.

34 **four times that of Paris:** Russell Shorto, *Amsterdam: A History of the World's Most Liberal City* (New York: Vintage, 2014), 178.

36 **"looked like a hell":** Letter from Richard Clough to Thomas Gresham, Antwerp Wednesday 21 August 1566, from *Relations politiques des Pays-Bas et de L'Angleterre sous le règne de Philippe II*, 4th ed. J.M.B.C. Kervyn de Lettenhove (1885) 337–39; 341–44.

37 **"Christ's own body":** Nicholas Sander, "A Treatise of the Images of Christ and of His Saints, 1566," collected in Robert S. Miola, *Early Modern Catholicism: An Anthology of Primary Sources* (Oxford; New York: Oxford University Press, 2007), 59.

38 **distributed power:** I am painting with a broad brush. The Dutch were repressive and brutal in building their overseas empire, conscripting hundreds of thousands of enslaved laborers to toil on plantations in Indonesia and elsewhere. But it is still true that the Netherlands' domestic governance, compared with other major countries at the time, was distinctive along the lines I have described.

38 **superior ships:** Oscar Gelderblom, "The Golden Age of the Dutch Republic," in *The Invention of Enterprise*, ed. David S. Landes, Joel Mokyr, and William J. Baumol (Princeton, NJ: Princeton University Press, 2010), 161.

39 **twelve tons per sailor:** Jan Lucassen and Richard W. Unger, "Shipping, Productivity and Economic Growth," in *Shipping and Economic Growth 1350–1850*, ed. Richard W. Unger (Leiden: Brill Academic, 2011), 7:31.

39   **half those of their competitors:** Tim Blanning, *The Pursuit of Glory: The Five Revolutions that Made Modern Europe, 1648–1815* (New York: Penguin, 2008), 188.

39   **merchant fleet of 568,000 tons:** Blanning, *Pursuit of Glory*, 96.

40   **city's dockyards:** Robert K. Massie, *Peter the Great: His Life and World* (New York: Wings, 1991), 180–86.

41   **40 warships, 150 trading ships:** Blanning, *Pursuit of Glory*, 98.

41   **"richest corporation in the world":** Blanning, *Pursuit of Glory*, 98.

41   **"greatest Treasure":** Sir William Temple, *Observations upon the United Provinces of the Netherlands* (London: Edward Gellibrand, 1676), 99–100, quoted in Marjolein 't Hart, "Cities and Statemaking in the Dutch Republic, 1580–1680," *Theory and Society* 18, no. 5 (1989): 663–87.

42   **Counter-Reformation:** Matías Cabello, *The Counter-Reformation, Science, and Long-Term Growth: A Black Legend?*, unpublished.

42   **one-third of Amsterdam's merchant community:** Oscar Gelderblom, "The Golden Age of the Dutch Republic," in *The Invention of Enterprise*, ed. David S. Landes, Joel Mokyr, and William J. Baumol (Princeton, NJ: Princeton University Press, 2010).

42   **perseverance and drive:** Alexandra M. De Pleijt and Jan Luiten Van Zanden, "Accounting for the 'Little Divergence': What Drove Economic Growth in Pre-industrial Europe, 1300–1800?," *European Review of Economic History* 20, no. 4 (2016).

43   **most densely populated:** Kees Klein Goldewijk, "Three Centuries of Global Population Growth: A Spatial Referenced Population (Density) Database for 1700–2000," *Population and Environment* 26, no. 4 (2005): 343–67, 356.

43   **56 percent of the population:** Paul Kennedy, *The Rise and Fall of the Great Powers: Economic Change and Military Conflict from 1500 to 2000* (New York: Random House, 1987), 69.

43   **figure for France:** Liam Brunt and Cecilia García-Peñalosa, "Urbanisation and the onset of modern economic growth," *Economic Journal* 132, no. 642 (2022).

43   **the world's first-ever system of public street lamps:** Israel, *Dutch Republic*, 681.

44   **an eighth of Amsterdam's working population:** Oscar Gelderblom, "The Golden Age of the Dutch Republic," in *The Invention of Enterprise*, ed. David S. Landes, Joel Mokyr, and William J. Baumol (Princeton, NJ: Princeton University Press, 2010), 159.

44   **"the pursuit of private gain":** Karel Davids, "Openness or Secrecy? Industrial Espionage in the Dutch Republic," *Journal of European Economic History* 24, no. 2 (1995).

45   **58 percent of all tax revenues:** James D. Tracy, *The Founding of the Dutch Republic: War, Finance, and Politics in Holland 1572–1588* (Oxford: Oxford University Press, 2008), 312.

46   **"least regard for his rank":** Israel, *Dutch Republic*, 2.

46   **"seedbed of theological, intellectual, and social promiscuity":** Israel, *Dutch Republic*, 2.

46   **"idea of liberalism":** Shorto, *Amsterdam*, 274.

48   **"mounting spiral":** Israel, *Dutch Republic*, 612, 633.

49   **driving at least 150,000 to flee France:** Philip Mansel, *Louis XIV: King of the World* (Chicago: University of Chicago Press, 2020), 562–63.

CHAPTER TWO: THE GLORIOUS REVOLUTION

51   **"A revolution strictly defensive":** Thomas Babington Macaulay, *History of England from the Accession of James II* (1848), Volume 2, Chapter 10.

52 **"collapsed more spectacularly":** Walter Scheidel, *Escape from Rome: The Failure of Empire and the Road to Prosperity* (Princeton, NJ: Princeton University Press, 2019), 363.

52 **witenagemots:** Not to be confused with J. K. Rowling's magical parliament, the *Wizengamot*.

53 **"community of taxpayers":** Scheidel, *Escape from Rome*, 365.

53 **30 to 50 percent of Europe's population:** James W. Wood et al., "The Temporal Dynamics of the Fourteenth Century Black Death," *Human Biology* (2003), cited in Sharon N. DeWitte, "Age Patterns of Mortality During the Black Death in London, A.D. 1349–1350," *Journal of Archaeological Science* 37, no. 12 (December 2010).

53 **still hotly debate:** See inter alia: Guillaume Vandenbroucke, "From Ye Olde Stagnation to Modern Growth in England," *Economic Synopses*, no. 3 (2023); Mark Bailey, "Society, economy and the law in fourteenth-century England," University of Oxford; Gregory Clark, "Microbes and Markets: Was the Black Death an economic revolution?" *Journal of Demographic Economics* 82, no. 2 (2016): 139–65.

54 **bourgeois virtues of Prudence and Temperance:** Deirdre N. McCloskey, "Bourgeois Virtues?," *Prudentia*, May 18, 2006. For much more on the bourgeois virtues, see: Deirdre N. McCloskey, *The Bourgeois Virtues: Ethics for an Age of Commerce* (Chicago: University of Chicago Press, 2007).

55 **"huge reservoir of conservative and reactionary forces":** Barrington Moore, *Social Origins of Dictatorship and Democracy: Lord and Peasant in the Making of the Modern World* (Boston: Beacon, 1993), 30.

55 **didn't actively oppose:** Eric Hobsbawm, *The Age of Revolution* (New York: Vintage, 1996), 51.

55 **trades other than farming:** Patrick Wallis, Justin Colson, and David Chilosi, "Structural Change and Economic Growth in the British Economy before the Industrial Revolution, 1500–1800," *Journal of Economic History* 78, no. 3 (2018): 27.

56 **one in eight English men:** Christopher Brooks, "The English Civil War and the Glorious Revolution," in *Western Civilization: A Concise History* (Portland: Portland Community College, 2019).

56 **killed some 150,000 total:** "By its end, around 62,000 soldiers were dead, and perhaps 100,000 more had died from war-related disease": Jonathan Healey, *The Blazing World: A New History of Revolutionary England, 1603–1689* (New York: Knopf, 2023), 203.

56 **ended in victory:** His son, Charles II, would continue these schemes. Samuel Pepys' diary records: "I find . . . that for a sum of money we shall enter into a league with the King of France . . . and that this sum of money will so help the King that he will not need the Parliament," "Wednesday 28 April 1669," *The Diary of Samuel Pepys*.

56 **"lascivious Mirth and Levity":** "September 1642: Order for Stage-plays to Cease," in *Acts and Ordinances of the Interregnum, 1642–1660*, ed. C. H. Firth and R. S. Rait (London: His Majesty's Stationery Office, 1911), 26–27. British History Online.

57 **strict and austere:** "Overview of the Civil War," UK Parliament.

58 **execution of Charles I:** Howard Nenner, "Regicides," *Oxford Dictionary of National Biography*, September 23, 2004.

59 **"Shewing how they were first Bred":** D. F., *The Dutch-mens Pedigree: or A relation, shewing how they were first bred, and descended from a horse-turd, which was enclosed ina butter-box. . . .* London: Printed in the year 1653. And are to be sold at St. Michaels Church door in Cornhill.

60 **"the Devil shits Dutchmen":** "Friday 19 July 1667," *The Diary of Samuel Pepys*.

60 **"with victory on their side":** "Monday 29 July, 1667," *The Diary of Samuel Pepys.*

60 **disaffected nobles and merchants:** Steve Pincus, *1688: the First Modern Revolution* (New Haven, CT: Yale University Press, 2011), 233–34.

61 **turning point:** As for the Dutch, after William's death in 1702, they decided to make do without a Stadholder for a while, cementing the Netherlands' republican form of government. The Republic lasted another century before being destroyed in the French Revolutionary Wars: At the 1815 Congress of Vienna, the Netherlands was reborn as a kingdom with the House of Orange officially becoming Dutch monarchs, a status they still hold today.

62 **"move beyond identity politics":** Pincus, *1688: The First Modern Revolution*, 94.

62 **political give-and-take:** England would become perhaps the first society in human history to permanently stay within what scholars Daron Acemoglu and James A. Robinson call "the Narrow Corridor": a path between tyranny and anarchy. See: Daron Acemoglu and James A. Robinson, *The Narrow Corridor: States, Societies, and the Fate of Liberty* (New York: Penguin, 2019).

63 **would repay its debts:** Douglass C. North and Barry R. Weingast. "Constitutions and Commitment: The Evolution of Institutions Governing Public Choice in Seventeenth-Century England," *Journal of Economic History* 49, no. 4 (1989): 803–32.

63 **English prosperity:** John Brewer, *The Sinews of Power: War, Money and the English State, 1688–1783* (Cambridge, MA: Harvard University Press, 1990), 154–55.

63 **1689 Act of Toleration:** For more on religious toleration, see Mark Koyama and Noel D. Johnson, *Persecution and Toleration: The Long Road to Religious Freedom* (New York: Cambridge University Press, 2019).

63 **Bank of England:** Israel, *Dutch Republic*, 630.

64 **15 percent of its starting capital:** Mansel, *King of the World*, 318.

64 **Huguenot surnames:** "Huguenots and the World of Finance: Part One," Huguenot Society, April 25, 2022.

65 **restricting the flow:** Karel Davids, *The Rise and Decline of Dutch Technological Leadership* (Leiden: Brill, 2008), 153–54.

65 **new guilds:** Israel, *Dutch Republic*, 1014.

66 **essential precondition:** Maine's ideas were expanded upon by the economist Deirdre McCloskey's thesis of the "Four Rs" that gave us the modern world— reading, reformation, revolt (in the Netherlands), and revolution (in England in 1688) culminated in late seventeenth-century England in the fifth and ultimately decisive "R," the revaluation of the bourgeoisie, an "R-caused, egalitarian reappraisal of ordinary people," cited in Scheidel, *Escape from Rome:* 489.

67 **first drink of tea:** Sidney W. Mintz, quoted in Jan de Vries, *Industrious Revolution* (New York: Cambridge University Press, 2008), 31.

67 **2,450 calories a day:** "Daily supply of calories per person," 1800, Our World in Data, citing S. Broadberry , B. Campbell, A. Klein, M. Overton, and B. Van Leeuwen. (2015). British Economic Growth, 1270–1870. Cambridge: Cambridge University Press and Table 1.2 from Fogel, R. W. (2004). The escape from hunger and premature death, 1700–2100: Europe, America, and the Third World (Vol. 38). Cambridge University Press.

67 **"working manufacturing people of England":** Daniel Defoe, *The Complete English Tradesman* (1726), chapter 22, quoted in Robert C. Allen, *British Industrial Revolution in Global Perspective* (New York: Cambridge University Press, 2009), 25.

67 **60 to 80-percent:** Scheidel, *Escape from Rome*, 382.

68 **multiplied by 10:** Scheidel, *Escape from Rome*, 369.

68 **all other nations' fleets combined:** Hobsbawm, *Age of Revolution*, 106.

69 **"physical, moral, and intellectual":** The most famous Whig historian, Lord Macaulay, began his 1848 *History of England* by declaring "the history of our country during the last hundred and sixty years is eminently the history of physical, of moral, and of intellectual improvement."

CHAPTER THREE: THE FAILED REVOLUTION

74 **"Every man":** Herbert Butterfield, *Christianity and History* (New York: Scribner, 1949), 11.

75 **relatively peaceful:** The Dutch waged the Eighty Years War against their Habsburg overlords, and saw their fair share of coups at home, but still managed to craft a political order that was far less violent than the European norm of the era. And although England's 1688 Glorious Revolution saw remarkably little bloodshed, it followed the much-bloodier English Civil War of 1642–51.

75 **over 80 percent:** Mansel, *King of the World*, 634.

77 **proliferation of rumors:** Robert Darnton, *The Revolutionary Temper: Paris, 1748–1789* (New York: W. W. Norton, 2023).

78 **at his sire's feet:** Simon Schama, *Citizens: A Chronicle of the French Revolution* (New York: Knopf, 1990), 1028.

78 **six thousand National Guards:** Schama, *Citizens*, 1031.

79 **"ever-memorable vengeance":** "The Proclamation of the Duke of Brunswick, 1792," in *Readings in European History*, ed. J. H. Robinson (Boston: Ginn, 1906), 2: 443–45.

80 **slumped to 15 percent:** Malcolm Crook, *Elections in the French Revolution: An Apprenticeship in Democracy, 1789–1799* (Cambridge: Cambridge University Press, 2002), 85. Crook notes that although the requirement that voters must be taxpayers was removed, domestic servants and others considered "dependents" were still excluded from the voter rolls in 1792.

80 **abysmal 8.7 percent:** Lemarchand Guy, "Sur les élections pendant la Révolution: Patrice Gueniffey," *Le nombre et la raison. La Révolution française et les élections.* In: *Annales de Normandie*, 47ᵉ année, n°5, 1997. Etudes médiévales. Journées d'histoire du droit—1996. pp. 607–12.

81 **preaching idealistic measures:** For a treatment of Robespierre the man—populist, intellectual, idealistic, and unforgiving—see this biographical portrait by the late novelist Hilary Mantel, best known for depicting other ruthless men in the halls of power, including Thomas Cromwell and Henry VIII in Wolf Hall: Hilary Mantel, "'What a man this is, with his crowd of women around him!'," *London Review of Books*, March 30, 2000.

83 **wielder of the guillotine:** See the illustration on p. 82: Anonymous, *Robespierre guillotinant le bourreau*, Louvre, Paris, France. This satirical cartoon depicts Robespierre trampling on the Constitutions of 1791–1793, and, having guillotined everyone else in France, ends by "guillotining the executioner."

83 **seventeen thousand:** Of cases where a victim was officially condemned to death, some 59 percent of the Terror's victims were workers or peasants, 24 percent middle class, 8 percent nobles, 6 percent clergy, and 1.5 percent other, per estimates by Donald Greer, *Incidence of the Terror during the French Revolution* (Cambridge, MA: Harvard University Press, 1935), 97. Note that these estimates do not take account of the many more victims who were lynched without trial.

83 **accused of treason:** Schama, *Citizens*, 1477.

83 **"devours its children":** Jacques Mallet du Pan, *Considérations sur la nature de la Révolution de France, et sur les causes qui en prolongent la durée* (1793), 63.

84   **"he has to be God":** William Doyle, *The Oxford History of the French Revolution*, 2nd ed. (Oxford: Oxford University Press, 1990), 278.

86   **mass popular enthusiasm:** David Bell, *Men on Horseback: The Power of Charisma in the Age of Revolution* (New York: Farrar, Straus and Giroux, 2020), argues that, after the divine right of kings was shattered, the Napoleonic model showed a path to power by posing as a "man of the people," fusing democratic and militarist impulses in the "cult of the strongman."

86   **"the catalyst, of modernity":** Schama, *Citizens*, 184.

87   **naval engineering techniques:** Mansel, *King of the World*, 123.

87   **"Protestant capitalism":** Schama, *Citizens*, 189.

88   **grand historical irony:** Similarly, the term doux commerce, "gentle" or peaceful commerce, was espoused by French philosopher Montesquieu . . . but such a vision, of war for conquest being replaced by mutually beneficial trade, was a vision more implemented by the increasingly free-trading British of the nineteenth century, not by the Jacobins, nor Napoleon, nor successive French regimes. Baron de Montesquieu, *The Spirit of the Laws*, trans. Thomas Nugent, ed. Franz Neumann (New York: Hafner, 1949).

88   **"People of Bordeaux":** Quoted in Mansel, *King of the World*, 180.

88   **French fleet:** Mansel, *King of the World*, 357, 643.

88   **60 percent of the French:** Table from Stephen Broadberry and Leigh Gardner, "Africa's Growth Prospects in a European Mirror: A Historical Perspective," working paper series at the University of Warwick (2013): 18.

89   **provincial towns:** Blanning, *Pursuit of Glory,* 54–56.

89   **launched the field of aviation:** Schama describes the scene in *Citizens*: This was an era of "Charismatic physics . . . they were witnessing a liberating event—an augury of a free-floating future . . . exemplified the philosopher's vision of a festival of freedom: uplifting glimpses of the Sublime in which the experience, not the audience, was noble." Schama, *Citizens*, 131.

90   **achievements of 1688:** See Rachel Hammersley, "Parallel revolutions: seventeenth-century England and eighteenth-century France," in *The English Republican Tradition and Eighteenth-Century France: Between the Ancients and the Moderns* (Manchester: Manchester University Press, 2016).

90   **"Why should we be ashamed":** Monsieur Navier, "Address" (1789), in Richard Price, "A Discourse on the Love of Our Country" (1789), quoted in Steve Pincus, *1688: The First Modern Revolution* (New Haven, CT: Yale University Press, 2011), 11.

91   **liberalized agrarian laws:** See: Peter McPhee, "The French Revolution, Peasants, and Capitalism," *American Historical Review* 94, no. 5 (1989): 1265–80.

91   **free market:** The most famous proponent of this argument: Georges Lefebvre, *The Coming of the French Revolution*, trans. R. R. Palmer (Princeton, NJ: Princeton University Press, 2015).

91   **movement that had taken centuries:** We see in the Jacobin program of sudden, drastic land reform the glimmerings of later failed experiments like Stalin's high-speed and deadly collectivization, or Mao's Great Leap Forward.

91   **"silent bombardment":** Hobsbawm, *Age of Revolution*, 158–59.

92   **"Utopian attempt":** Margaret Thatcher, *The Downing Street Years* (New York: HarperCollins, 1993), 753.

92   **twelve months were renamed:** Ed Simon, "Why the French Revolution's 'Rational' Calendar Wasn't," *JSTOR Daily,* JSTOR, May 23, 2018.

92   **graffiti carved:** Fondation Napoléon / K.Huguenaud, GRAFFITIS À L'ENTRÉE DU TEMPLE D'ISIS À PHILAE, 1798, Egypt.

94   **"unity of the Republic":** "The Lévée en Masse" (August 23, 1793), Fordham Modern History Sourcebook.

95   **"militarized nationalism":** Schama, *Citizens*, 858.

95   **"Returning to his vomit":** William Wordsworth, "The Prelude," Book 11, Vol. 4 (1850).

95   **"ideas that underpin our modern world":** Roberts, *Napoleon: A Life*, 37.

96   **Napoleonic reforms:** Francis Fukuyama, *Political Order and Political Decay* (New York: Farrar, Straus, and Giroux, 2015), 17.

97   **labyrinth of licenses:** Not unlike the "License Raj" of post-independence India that hampered growth there for decades.

98   **Fewer than twenty-five thousand men survived:** Roberts, *Napoleon: a Life*, 936–37. Note that different historical estimates of the number of survivors from the Grande Armée vary, from 40,000 to as high as 120,000.

98   **"another chariot":** Alistair Horne, *Seven Ages of Paris* (New York: Knopf, 2002), 181–82.

98   **top of the arch:** Jean-Alexandre-Joseph Falguiere, La Triomphe de la Revolution, 1882, wax figure, 97 × 130 × 99 cm, Musee de Grenoble, Grenoble, France.

99   **numerous other crises:** Charles de Gaulle seized power in 1958 in what amounted to an extralegal coup, even if his rise was later "ratified" by an election.

100   **"Phantom Terror":** Drawn from the title of his illuminating history of the post-Napoleonic era: Adam Zamoyski, *Phantom Terror: The Threat of Revolution and the Repression of Liberty, 1789–1848* (United Kingdom: William Collins, 2014).

100   **"revolutionary novelties":** Zamoyski, *Phantom Terror*, 96.

100   **"forest of bayonets":** Count Franz Anton von Kolowrat, letter of June 1833, quoted in Zamoyski, *Phantom Terror*, 342.

101   **"volcano":** The full quote: "This, gentlemen, is my profound conviction: I believe that we are at this moment sleeping on a sleeping volcano. I am profoundly convinced of it . . . I was saying just now that this evil would, sooner or later, I know not how nor whence it will come, bring with it a most serious revolution: be assured that that is so." Alexis de Tocqueville, *Recollections of Alexis de Tocqueville* (New York: 1893).

101   **exploded:** For a recent narrative account of 1848, see Christopher Clark, "The Revolutionary Waves of 1848," in *Revolutionary World*, ed. David Motadel (Cambridge: Cambridge University Press, 2021).

104   **"things will have to change":** Giuseppe Tomasi di Lampedusa, *Il Gattopardo*, trans. Archibald Colquhoun (New York: Pantheon, 1960), 22.

105   **"many were guillotined":** Leon Trotsky, "Two Speeches at the Central Control Commission, 1927," trans. John G. Wright, *The Stalin School of Falsification* (New York: 1972).

105   **plummeted from 20 percent to 10 percent:** Guillaume Daudin, Kevin O'Rourke, and Leandro Prados de la Esosura, "Trade and Empire, 1700–1870," OFCE, 23.

105   **France's level:** Alfred Cobban, *A History of Modern France, Vol. 2* (Penguin, 1963), 49–52, quoted in Andrew Roberts, *Napoleon: A Life* (New York: Penguin, 2015), 571.

106   **"capitalist part of the French economy":** Hobsbawm, *Age of Revolution*, 177–78.

106   **planting the seeds of later economic growth:** Daron Acemoglu et al., "The Consequences of Radical Reform: The French Revolution" (Cambridge, MA: National Bureau of Economic Research, April 2009), https://doi.org/10.3386/w14831.

106   **"swallowed the (French) political revolution":** Eric Hobsbawm, *The Age of Capital, 1848–1875* (New York: Vintage, 1996), 15.

CHAPTER FOUR: THE MOTHER OF ALL REVOLUTIONS

107 **"most important event":** Hobsbawm, *Age of Revolution*, 29.

109 **inventors flourished:** The economic historian Joel Mokyr draws a distinction between "savants" (theoretical scientific thinkers) and "fabricants" (industrial workmen who got their hands dirty) in his 1992 book *The Gifts of Athena*. Joel Mokyr, *The Gifts of Athena* (Princeton, NJ: Princeton University Press, 2002).

109 **low on wood:** William M. Cavert, *The Smoke of London: Energy and Environment in the Early Modern City, Cambridge Studies in Early Modern British History* (Cambridge: Cambridge University Press, 2016), 21.

110 **1,300 horses:** Vaclav Smil, *Energy and Civilization: A History* (Cambridge, MA: MIT Press, 2018), 12, 301.

110 **patent protections:** Alessandro Nuvolari and Christine Macleod "Patents and Industrialisation: An Historical Overview of the British Case, 1624–1907," *SSRN (Social Science Research Network)* (2010), 6.

110 **Thomas Lombe's patent:** Robert Burrell and Catherine Kelly, "Parliamentary Rewards and the Evolution of the Patent System," *Cambridge Law Journal* 74, no. 3 (2015): 423–49.

110 **destroyed the machinery:** S. R. Epstein, "Craft Guilds, Apprenticeship, and Technological Change in Preindustrial Europe," *Journal of Economic History* 58, no. 3 (1998): 684–713.

111 **dizzying factor of 150:** Blanning, *Pursuit of Glory*, 243–44.

111 **"Victorious Century":** David Cannadine, *Victorious Century: The United Kingdom, 1800–1906* (New York: Viking, 2018).

111 **50 percent:** Robert C. Allen, "Engels' Pause: Technical Change, Capital Accumulation, and Inequality in the British Industrial Revolution," *Explorations in Economic History* 46, no. 4 (2009): 418–35, see Fig. 1 and Table 1.

111 **five thousand calories:** J. Braford DeLong, *Slouching Towards Utopia: An Economic History of the Twentieth Century* (New York: Basic, 2022), 18.

111 **3.5 years:** The data is noisy but shows life expectancy hovering around 37.5 years at the beginning of this period and 41 toward the end. See "Life Expectancy, 1743 to 1875," Our World in Data.

112 **topping thirty million:** Britain's population soared, despite mass migration to North America and Oceania. (Note: This figure excludes Ireland, which saw population decline amid the Potato Famine). See "Population of England over history, Our World in Data, "https://ourworldindata.org/grapher/population-of-england-millennium.

112 **majority-urban society:** "Impact of the Industrial Revolution," in *Britannica.com*.

112 **by 1900:** Tim Hitchcock, "London, 1780–1900," Digital Panopticon.

112 **one hour and 45 minutes:** "Railways in Early Nineteenth Century Britain," UK Parliament.

112 **twenty thousand miles of rail:** "British Railways," *Britannica.com*.

113 **huge rewards:** Daniel Boorstin, *The Discoverers* (New York: Vintage, 1983), 71–73.

113 **the clock:** Boorstin, *Discoverers*, 89.

114 **"weekend":** Oxford English Directory Online, s.v. "week-end."

115 **Sports:** Ian Buruma, *Anglomania: A European Love Affair* (New York: Vintage, 200), 138.

115 **"moral revolution":** Buruma, *Anglomania*, 150.

115 **"armed battle":** Buruma, *Anglomania*, 156.

115 **"base football player":** *King Lear*, ed. Barbara A. Mowat and Paul Werstine (New York: Simon & Schuster, 2015), 1.4.

116   **"40% of the population":** Bret Devereaux, "Collections: Clothing, How Did They Make It? Part III: Spin Me Right Round . . . ," A Collection of Unmitigated Pedantry, March 19, 2021, citing E. W. Barber, *Women's Work: The First 20,000 Years: Women, Cloth, and Society in Early Times* (New York: W. W. Norton, 1996).

116   **seven hours a day:** Devereaux's estimate cites work by John S. Lee, *The Medieval Clothier*, Working in the Middle Ages Vol. 1 (Woodbridge: Boydell, 2018); Eve Fisher, "The $3500 Shirt—A History Lesson in Economics," SleuthSayers, June 6, 2013; Gregory S. Aldrete, Scott Bartell, and Alicia Aldrete, *Reconstructing Ancient Linen Body Armor: Unraveling the Linothorax Mystery* (Baltimore: Johns Hopkins University Press, 2013). Note that his estimate is an average of ancient and medieval figures to generate a pre-modern composite, and emphasizes that the late medieval spinning wheel was the biggest boost to efficiency prior to the industrial era.

117   **"mind of metal and wheels":** J. R. R. Tolkien, *The Two Towers* (Boston and New York: Houghton Mifflin, 1954, reprint 1994), Book Three, Chapter 4, "Treebeard," in 462.

117   **idyllic pre-Industrial Shire:** J. R. R. Tolkien, *The Return of the King* (Boston and New York: Houghton Mifflin, 1955, reprint 1994), Book 11, Chapter 8, "The Scouring of the Shire," 981.

118   **"the world until yesterday":** Diamond uses the term to refer not to the pre-industrial world of settled agricultural societies but to the nomadic hunter-gathering that preceded both industrialization and farming.

118   **"age of great expectation":** Frederic Harrison, "Words on the Nineteenth Century," quoted in Walter E. Houghton, *The Victorian Frame of Mind, 1830–1870* (New Haven, CT: Yale University Press, 1963), 42.

118   **"humble happiness":** Oliver Goldsmith, "The Deserted Village," Poetry Foundation.

119   **"Engels' Pause":** Robert C. Allen, "Engels' Pause: Technical Change, Capital Accumulation, and Inequality in the British Industrial Revolution," *Explorations in Economic History* 46, no. 4 (2009): 418–35.

119   **boosted workers' bargaining power:** For this explanation, I am relying on: W. Arthur Lewis, "Economic Development with Unlimited Supplies of Labour," *Manchester School* 22, no. 2 (1954): 139–91, as cited in Allen, "Engels' pause"; as well as Carl Benedikt Frey, *The Technology Trap: Capital, Labor, and Power in the Age of Automation* (Princeton, NJ: Princeton University Press, 2019), 131–37.

121   **poor working conditions:** See: Richard Conniff, "What the Luddites Really Fought Against," *Smithsonian Magazine*, March 2011.

121   **less than 2 percent of Britons:** Neil Johnston, "The History of the Parliamentary Franchise," House of Commons Library, Research Paper 13/14, March 1, 2013. The author estimates 516,000 eligible voters before the 1832 Reform Act, in a country of some twenty-four million inhabitants.

121   **75 percent:** E. A. Wasson, "The Penetration of New Wealth into the English Governing Class from the Middle Ages to the First World War," *Economic History Review* 51, no. 1 (1998): 28, fig. 1.

122   **"pocket" or "rotten" boroughs:** Hillary Burlock, "Rotten Boroughs," Eighteenth-Century Political Participation and Electoral Culture Project, UK Arts and Humanities Research Council, Newcastle University and Liverpool University, 2020–23.

122   **illiterate onlookers:** Richard D. Altick, *The English Common Reader: A Social History of the Mass Reading Public, 1800–1900, 2nd ed.* (Columbus: Ohio State University Press, 1998), 324–26.

122   **"dissenting churches":** Emma Griffin, *Liberty's Dawn: A People's History of the Industrial Revolution* (New Haven, CT: Yale University Press, 2014), 220.

124   **"natural growth of society":** Thomas Babington Macaulay, "Ministerial Plan

of Parliamentary Reform—Adjourned Debate" (speech, London, March 2, 1831), accessed via House of Commons Hansard.

125 **roughly 20 percent of England's adult male population:** There were 650,000 voters after 1832 out of an adult male population of 13 million in England and Wales. See: John A. Phillips and Charles Wetherell, "The Great Reform Act of 1832 and the Political Modernization of England," *American Historical Review* 100, no. 2 (1995): 414.

125 **their demands to be fully met:** The only Chartist goal still left unfulfilled is annual parliamentary elections. Given the frenzy of near-constant political battle in the United States, with its biennial congressional elections, there is perhaps good reason for not adopting this reform.

126 **An aghast duchess:** Adam Zamoyski, "Scandals," in *Phantom Terror: Political Paranoia and the Creation of the Modern State* (New York: Basic, 2015), 368.

126 **most accurate clock:** "Constructing the most accurate clock in the world," UK Parliament.

127 **"full stomache":** Adam Zamoyski, "Order," in *Phantom Terror: Political Paranoia and the Creation of the Modern State* (New York: Basic, 2015), 94.

127 **three hundred thousand people:** Walter Scheidel, Escape from Rome: The Failure of Empire and the Road to Prosperity (Princeton, NJ: Princeton University Press, 2019), 383.

128 **"vain and foolish project":** George Julian Harney to Friedrich Engels, March 30, 1846, in *The Harney Papers*, ed. Frank Gees Black and Renée Métivier Black (Assen: Van Gorcum, 1969), 240, quoted in Henry Weisser, "Chartism in 1848: Reflections on a Non-Revolution," *Albion* 13, no. 1 (1981): 14.

128 **low-priced commodities:** Miles Taylor, "The 1848 Revolutions and the British Empire," *Past & Present* 166, no. 1 (2000): 146–80.

128 **150,000 special constables:** "What Was Chartism?," National Archives (UK).

128 **anti-government activism:** Henry Weisser, "Chartism in 1848: Reflections on a Non-Revolution," *Albion*, 13, no. 1 (1981): 16.

129 **grinding rural poverty:** Avner Greif and Murat Iyigun, "Social Institutions, Violence, and Innovations: Did the Old Poor Law Matter?," December 25, 2012; and Marjorie Keniston McIntosh, "The Poor Laws of 1598 and 1601," in *Poor Relief in England, 1350–1600* (Cambridge: Cambridge University Press, 2011), 273–93.

129 **Elizabethan economic system:** Griffin, *Liberty's Dawn*, 27–28.

129 **"the root of all evil":** Timothy 6:10, King James Version.

130 **"immeasurable Steam-engine":** Thomas Carlyle, "The Everlasting No," in *Sartor Resartus* (1833), 164–65, quoted in Walter E. Houghton, *The Victorian Frame of Mind, 1830–1870* (New Haven, CT: Yale University Press, 1963), 73–74.

130 **"mechanization" of labor:** John Ruskin, *The Stones of Venice* (London, Smith, Elder, 1853).

130 **"little piece of intelligence":** Ruskin, *Stones of Venice*, 162–63.

131 **repeal of the Corn Law:** Douglas A. Irwin and Maksym G. Chepeliev, "The Economic Consequences of Sir Robert Peel: A Quantitative Assessment of the Repeal of the Corn Laws," *Economic Journal* 131, no. 640 (2021): 3322–37.

132 **a third of millionaires:** W. D. Rubinstein, "Wealth, Elites and the Class Structure of Modern Britain," *Past & Present*, no. 76 (1977): table 1, "Occupations of Wealth-Holders: Concise Ranking," 102.

132 **rural ruffians:** George Eliot, *Middlemarch* (United Kingdom: Wordsworth, 1998), 458–59.

134 **ancient Greek at age three:** Alexander C.R. Hammond, "Heroes of Progress, Pt. 41: John Stuart Mill," *Human Progress* blog, Cato Institute.

138 **"Self-satisfaction":** Charles R. Morris, *The Dawn of Innovation: The First American Industrial Revolution* (New York: PublicAffairs, 2012), 70.

139 **military spending:** Kennedy, *Rise and Fall of the Great Powers,* 153.

139 **some two hundred *times* cheaper:** John Darwin, *The Empire Project: The Rise and Fall of the British World-System, 1830–1970* (Cambridge: Cambridge University Press, 2009), 37.

139 **exploitation of non-European peoples:** Joel Mokyr, review of *How the World Became Rich: The Historical Origins of Economic Growth* by Mark Koyama and Jared Rubin, EH.net, July 2022.

140 **"a plate of strawberries and cream":** George Orwell, *The Road to Wigan Pier* (London: Penguin Classics, 1937; reprint 2007), 229; cited in Alex Tabarrok, "Orwell's Falsified Prediction on Empire," Marginal Revolution, May 30, 2023.

140 **"*faster* than before":** Tabarrok, "Orwell's Falsified Prediction," Marginal Revolution, May 30, 2023, relying on data from Maddison Project Database 2020.

140 **possible breakup of China:** Kennedy, *Rise and Fall of the Great Powers,* 227.

CHAPTER FIVE: THE REAL AMERICAN REVOLUTION

143 **greater income equality:** Chrystia Freeland, "America, Land of the Equals," *New York Times,* May 3, 2012.

143 **"born equal":** Alexis De Tocqueville, "Individualism Stronger," in *Democracy in America,* vol. 2, *Influence Of Democracy On Progress Of Opinion.* Later historians agree: see Daniel Walker Howe, *What Hath God Wrought: the Transformation of America, 1815–1848* (Oxford: Oxford University Press, 2009), 490.

143 **"Tudor polity":** Samuel Huntington, "Tudor Polity and Modernizing Societies," in *Political Order in Changing Societies* (New Haven, CT: Yale University Press, 1968), 134–35.

143 **"a corrupt constitution":** Bernard Bailyn, *The Ideological Origins of the American Revolution* (Cambridge, MA: Belknap, 1992), 283.

144 **"most important acts":** Quoted in Howe, *What Hath God Wrought,* 562–63.

145 **export of ideas:** Charles R. Morris, *The Dawn of Innovation: The First American Industrial Revolution* (New York: PublicAffairs, 2012), 89.

145 **pirated copies:** Edward G. Hudon, "Literary Piracy, Charles Dickens and the American Copyright Law," *American Bar Association Journal* 50, no. 12 (1964): 1157–60.

145 **first modern cotton mills:** Paul Wiseman, "In trade wars of 200 years ago, the pirates were Americans," Associated Press, March 28, 2019.

145 **"What hath God wrought":** This Biblical phrase, at once awestruck and ominous, lent its title to historian Daniel Walker Howe's history of America in the age of the telegraph and railroad: *What Hath God Wrought: The Transformation of America, 1815–1848.*

145 **Erie Canal:** Abraham Lincoln, writing to Joshua Speed, quoted in Richard Cawardine, *Lincoln: A Life of Purpose and Power* (London: Vintage, 2003), 12, cited in Howe, *What Hath God Wrought,* 596.

146 **twenty-eight times higher:** Chester W. Wright, *Economic History of the United States* (New York: McGraw Hill, 1941), 707.

146 **overtook British GDP:** Adam Tooze, *The Deluge: The Great War, America and the Remaking of the Global Order, 1916–1931* (New York: Penguin, 2015).

146 **astonishing 3.9 percent:** Morris, *Dawn of Innovation,* 82.

146 **clocks:** Morris, *Dawn of Innovation,* 89.

147 **"invented invention":** Bradford J. DeLong, *Slouching Towards Utopia: an Economic History of the Twentieth Century* (New York: Basic, 2022), 62.

147 **surged from 25 percent:** Robert Gordon, *The Rise and Fall of American Growth:*

The U.S. Standard of Living since the Civil War (Princeton, NJ: Princeton University Press, 2017), 6.

147   **more Americans lived in cities:** Jonathan Rees, *Industrialization and the Transformation of American Life* (Armonk, NY: M. E. Sharpe, 2013), 44.

147   **"Burn high your fires":** Walt Whitman, "Crossing Brooklyn Ferry," Poetry Foundation, https://www.poetryfoundation.org/poems/45470/crossing-brooklyn -ferry.

148   **"upon all oppression and shame":** Walt Whitman, "I Sit and Look Out," The Walt Whitman Archive.

148   **optimistic and skeptical:** Frances Dickey and Jimmie Killingsworth, "Love of Comrades: The Urbanization of Community in Walt Whitman's Poetry and Pragmatist Philosophy," *Walt Whitman Quarterly Review* 21, no. 1 (2003): 1–24.

148   **Old-World cultural identities:** David Kennedy, *Freedom from Fear: The American People in Depression and War, 1929–1945* (Oxford: Oxford University Press, 2001), 14.

148   **Leland Stanford:** Gordon, *Rise and Fall of American Growth*, 30.

148   **industrial meat processing:** Sam Bass Warner Jr., *The Urban Wilderness: A History of the American City* (New York: Harper and Row, 1972), 93.

149   **Foreign-born people:** Gordon, *Rise and Fall of American Growth*, 36.

149   **"do nothing":** Quoted in Michael Lind, *Land of Promise: An Economic History of the United States* (New York: HarperCollins, 2013), 223.

151   **factory strikes and boycotts:** Seymour Martin Lipset and Gary Wolfe Marks, *It Didn't Happen Here: Why Socialism Failed in the United States* (New York: W. W. Norton, 2001), 263.

151   **white elites:** David Roediger, *The Wages of Whiteness: Race and the Making of the American Working Class* (Brooklyn: Verso, 1991).

153   **"stupendous industrial revolution":** Theodore Roosevelt, quoted in Frank Ninkovich, *Modernity and Power: A History of the Domino Theory in the Twentieth Century* (Chicago: University of Chicago Press, 1994), 4.

154   **one of the two mainstream political parties:** The parallel here might be with Ross Perot's campaign in 1992, an early augur of populism, which failed but foreshadowed a major political party, the Republicans, being captured by populism in 2016.

154   **"William Jacobin Bryan":** Thomas Frank, *The People, No: A Brief History of Anti-Populism* (New York: Metropolitan, 2020), 69.

155   **1964 essay:** Henry M. Littlefield, "The Wizard of Oz: Parable on Populism," *American Quarterly* 16, no. 1 (1964): 47–58.

157   **"he'll empty his pockets":** Bill D. Moyers, "What a Real President Was Like," *Washington Post*, November 13, 1988.

158   **"believe in a square deal":** David M. Kennedy and Elizabeth Cohen, "Progressivism and the Republican Roosevelt," *The American Pageant* (New York: Houghton Mifflin, 2001).

159   **"wealthy criminal class":** Theodore Roosevelt, *The Works of Theodore Roosevelt, National Edition* (New York: Charles Scribner's Sons, 1926), 16–84.

159   **"vulgar imitators":** Kathleen M. Dalton, "Theodore Roosevelt, Knickerbocker Aristocrat," *New York History* 67, no. 1 (1986): 40.

159   **moral responsibility:** Dalton, "Theodore Roosevelt, Knickerbocker Aristocrat," 41.

161   **"Mr. Coolidge's genius for inactivity":** Walter Lippmann, "Puritanism De Luxe in the Coolidge Era," *Vanity Fair*, May 1926.

161   **"least government was the best government":** Peter Clements, "Silent Cal," *History Today*, September 2003.

162   **$100 million bond:** Terry Golway, "The making of the New Deal Democrats," *Politico*, October 3, 2014.

162   **Smith's ideological heir:** Bernard Bellush, *Franklin D. Roosevelt as Governor of New York* (New York: Columbia University Press, 1955), 282.

163   **"mastery, not drift":** Kennedy, *Freedom from Fear*, 11–13.

163   **"too damn greedy":** Kennedy, *Freedom from Fear*, 43.

163   **"historical role of Mr. Hoover":** Kennedy, *Freedom from Fear*, 55.

164   **"definite goal":** Franklin D. Roosevelt, "Annual Message to Congress," The American Presidency Project, January 4, 1935.

164   **"sustain balance and equity":** Kennedy, *Freedom from Fear*, 247.

165   **early 1900s:** Sheri Berman, *The Primacy of Politics: Social Democracy and the Making of Europe's Twentieth Century* (Cambridge: Cambridge University Press, 2006).

Chapter Six: Globalization in Overdrive

170   **more than two-thirds:** Ivan T. Berend, *Decades of Crisis: Central and Eastern Europe before World War II* (Berkeley: University of California Press, 2001), 14.

170   **dropped nearly 60 percent:** Jeffry A. Frieden, *Global Capitalism: Its Fall and Rise in the Twentieth Century* (New York: W. W. Norton, 2007), 8.

171   **ground to a halt:** Nicolas Barreyre, "The Politics of Economic Crises: The Panic of 1873, the End of Reconstruction, and the Realignment of American Politics," *Journal of the Gilded Age and Progressive Era* 10, no. 4 (2011): 403–23.

172   **searched for new lands, people, and markets:** Johan Norberg, *Open: The Story of Human Progress* (New York: Atlantic, 2020), 21–22.

172   **industrialization of the nineteenth century:** Even though the term "globalization" did not come into widespread use until the 1990s, its fundamental dynamics have been at play since the early 1800s.

172   **displace local trade:** Kevin H. O'Rourke and Jeffrey G. Williamson, "When Did Globalisation Begin?" *European Review of Economic History* 6, no. 1 (2002): 23–50.

172   **"markets, not monarchs":** Frieden, *Global Capitalism*, 5.

172   **increased eightfold:** Frieden, *Global Capitalism*, 4.

172   **improved the material living conditions:** Recall history's "hockey stick" graph showing flat income for millennia, until an exponential take-off in living standards around the turn of the nineteenth century. In 1800, 90 percent of the global population lived on the equivalent of less than $1 per day; today, no more than 10 percent of the global population lives in this state of extreme poverty. As the economist Deirdre McCloskey has demonstrated, average access to goods and services has increased 3,000 percent since 1800, and literacy rates have increased by roughly 80 percent. Norberg, *Open: Story of Human Progress*, 167–68.

173   **just one carcass spoiled:** Colin Williscroft, *A Lasting Legacy: A 125 Year History of New Zealand Farming since the First Frozen Meat Shipment* (NZ Rural Press, 2007).

173   **more than four-fifths:** Frieden, *Global Capitalism*, 5; Nayan Chanda, *Bound Together: How Traders, Preachers, Adventurers, and Warriors Shaped Globalization* (New Haven, CT: Yale University Press, 2008), 56.

174   **beacon of peace and harmony:** *The telegraphic messages of Queen Victoria and Pres. Buchanan*, August 16, 1858, photograph, https://www.loc.gov/item/2005694829/.

174   **transmitting eight words per minute:** Chanda, *Bound Together*, 66–67, 207.

174   **growing 260 percent:** Hobsbawm, *Age of Capital,* 34.

174   **"one in fourteen humans":** DeLong, *Slouching Towards Utopia*, 38, citing W. Arthur Lewis, *The Evolution of the International Economic Order* (Princeton, NJ: Princeton University Press, 1978), 14.

174 **"became world history":** Hobsbawm, *Age of Capital*, 47.

174 **"interconnected whole":** Mark Mazower, *Governing the World: The History of an Idea, 1815 to the Present* (New York: Penguin, 2013), 26.

174 **internationalism:** Mazower, *Governing the World*, 19–20.

175 **"love of freedom":** Fareed Zakaria, *Ten Lessons for a Post Pandemic World* (New York: W. W. Norton, 2020), 219, citing William E. Gladstone, "Third Midlothian Speech, West Calder, 27 November 1879," English Historical Documents, 1874–1914, edited by W. D. Hancock and David Charles Douglas, citing Political Speeches in Scotland (1880), 1:115–17.

176 **its waters full of fish and whales:** See Oona A. Hathaway and Scott J. Shapiro, *The Internationalists: How a Radical Plan to Outlaw War Remade the World* (New York: Simon and Schuster, 2017), 188.

176 **galvanized political outsiders:** Peter Alexis Gourevitch, "International Trade, Domestic Coalitions, and Liberty: Comparative Responses to the Crisis of 1873–1896," *Journal of Interdisciplinary History* 8, no. 2 (1977): 281–313.

176 **terrorism:** Richard Jensen, "Daggers, Rifles and Dynamite: Anarchist Terrorism in Nineteenth Century Europe," *Terrorism and Political Violence* 16, no. 1 (2004): 116–53.

176 **Decade of Regicide:** Jensen, "Daggers, Rifles and Dynamite," 134; Mary S. Barton, "The Global War on Anarchism," *Diplomatic History* 39, no. 2 (2015): 303–30.

177 **"exhausted volcanoes":** Quoted in David Harris, "European Liberalism in the Nineteenth Century." *American Historical Review* 60, no. 3 (1955): 514.

177 **conservative nationalists:** Gourevitch, "International Trade, Domestic Coalitions, and Liberty: Comparative Responses to the Crisis of 1873–1896," 281–313.

177 **"chessboard":** Quoted in David S. Mason, *A Concise History of Modern Europe: Liberty, Equality, Solidarity* (New York: Penguin, 2013), 95.

177 **held 84 percent:** Mason, *A Concise History of Modern Europe: Liberty, Equality, Solidarity*, 100.

178 **labor-intensive plantation crops:** Frieden, "Failures of Development."

180 **jacked up tariffs:** Mario J. Crucini and James Kahn, "Tariffs and the Great Depression Revisited," Staff Reports, Federal Reserve Bank of New York, 2003, 5.

180 **living space:** Adam Tooze, *The Wages of Destruction: The Making and Breaking of the Nazi Economy* (New York: Viking, 2007), 8–12.

181 **dominant model:** Berman, *Primacy of Politics*.

181 **"fully reversed":** DeLong, *Slouching Towards Utopia*, 190.

181 **pre-1914 levels:** Maurice Obstfeld, "Globalization and Nationalism: Retrospect and Prospect," Italian Economic Association Annual Meeting, October 24, 2019.

182 **"The American Century":** Henry R. Luce, "The American Century," *Diplomatic History* 23, no. 2 (1999): 159–71.

183 **rise by 75 percent by 1973:** Frieden, *Global Capitalism*, 278–81.

183 **more than 200 percent:** "World GDP Over the Last Two Millennia," Our World in Data, citing Max Roser, "World GDP Over the Last Two Millennia."

183 **Malcolm McLean:** Marc Levinson, "The Trucker," in *The Box: How the Shipping Container Made the World Smaller and the World Economy Bigger*, 2nd ed. (Princeton, NJ: Princeton University Press, 2016), Chapter 3.

184 **cheaper to ship goods:** Chanda, *Bound Together*, 57; Ben Thompson, "The History of the Shipping Container created in 1956," IncoDocs (blog), August 31, 2018.

184 **trade accounted for two or even three times:** Frieden, *Global Capitalism*, 289.

184 **Jet Age:** Don Harris, *Pan Am: A History of the Airline that Defined an Age* (Anaheim: Golgotha, 2011), 35.

184 **nearly five times:** Our World in Data, 2023, citing Bastian Herre, Veronika Samborska, and Max Roser, "Tourism—International arrivals by world region"; Harris, *Pan Am: A History of the Airline that Defined an Age*, 60.

184   **jumbo jets:** Harris, *Pan Am*, 41.

184   **upwards of one billion tourist arrivals:** "Our World in Data, 2023, citing Bastian Herre, Veronika Samborska, and Max Roser, "Tourism—International arrivals by world region."

185   **below the 8 percent average:** Frieden, *Global Capitalism*, 297–99.

185   **exceeded 70 percent:** "Top marginal income tax rate, 1971 to 2017," Our World in Data.

186   **cut taxes but increased spending:** Adam Tooze, *Crashed: How a Decade of Financial Crises Changed the World* (New York: Viking, 2018), 30.

187   **Bank of England:** Aled Davies, *The City of London and Social Democracy* (Oxford: Oxford University Press, 2017), 80.

187   **2008 financial crisis:** Rana Foroohar, *Makers and Takers: The Rise of Finance and the Fall of American Business* (New York: Crown, 2016), 16.

187   **decade of steady GDP growth:** Daniel Chudnovsky and Andrés López, "Foreign Investment and Sustainable Development in Argentina" (discussion paper, Working Group on Development and Environment in the Americas, 2008), 6.

188   **grew by 62 percent:** Chanda, *Bound Together*, 254.

188   **world's ten largest private banks:** Tooze, *Crashed*, 54.

188   **increased to around 40 percent:** Jordan Weissman, "How Wall Street Devoured Corporate America," *Atlantic*, March 5, 2013.

188   **Western European corporations:** Tooze, *Crashed*, 123.

189   **sending 82 percent of these abroad:** Luca Ciferri, "New flagship model will complete Skoda rebirth," *Automotive News Europe*, July 2, 2001.

189   **seemingly limitless growth:** Tooze, *Crashed*, 120.

189   **country's largest GDP increase:** Filipe Larrain B., Luis F. Lopez-Calva, and Andres Rodriguez-Clare, "Intel: A Case Study of Foreign Direct Investment in Central America," CID Working Paper No. 58, *Center for International Development at Harvard University*, December 2000, 13.

189   **hyper-globalization:** Brian Reinbold and Yi Wen, "How Industrialization Shaped America's Trade Balance," Federal Reserve Bank of St. Louis, February 6, 2020.

189   **hyper-globalization:** Jeffrey D. Sachs, *Ages of Globalization* (New York: Columbia University Press, 2020), 179.

189   **more than tripled by 2015:** "World GDP over the Last Two Millennia," Our World in Data, citing Roser, "Economic Growth—The World Economy over the Last Two Millennia."

189   **increased by 133 percent:** Fareed Zakaria, *The Post-American World* (New York: W. W. Norton, 2008), 7, 21.

190   **norm in every region but North and Sub-Saharan Africa, Central Asia, and the Middle East:** Our World in Data, July 19, 2022, citing Bastian Herre, "People around the world have gained democratic rights, but some have many more rights than others."

190   **almost 112 states:** Zakaria, *Post-American World*, 44.

190   **"the end of history":** Francis Fukuyama, *The End of History and the Last Man* (New York: Free Press, 2006).

191   **development of free-market liberal democracy:** For a fuller picture of just how long and arduous the road to liberal democracy in the West was, see Sheri Berman, *Democracy and Dictatorship in Europe: From the Ancien Régime to the Present Day* (New York: Oxford University Press, 2019).

191   **independent rule:** Stephen Kotkin, *Uncivil Society: 1989 and the Implosion of the Communist Establishment* (New York: Modern Library, 2010).

191   **handful of extremely wealthy oligarchs:** Mark Beissinger and Stephen Kotkin, "The Historical Legacies of Communism: An Empirical Agenda," in *Historical*

Legacies of Communism in Russia and Eastern Europe, ed. Mark Beissinger and Stephen Kotkin (Cambridge: Cambridge University Press, 2014).

191 **life expectancy fell:** Tamara Men, et al, "Russian Mortality Trends for 1991–2001: Analysis by Cause and Region," *BMJ* 327, no. 7421 (October 25, 2003): 964.

192 **"beautiful structures and beautiful titles":** Quoted in Timothy J. Colton, *Russia: What Everyone Needs to Know* (New York: Oxford University Press, 2016), 104.

192 **fell by double-digit or near double-digit percentages:** Joseph Stiglitz, *Globalization and Its Discontents Revisited: Anti-Globalization in the Era of Trump* (New York: W. W. Norton, 2018), 191.

193 **fastest and most sustained rate:** Zakaria, *Post-American World*, 102.

194 **close to one third:** Nicholas R. Lardy, "Issues in China's WTO Accession," *Brookings Institution*, May 9, 2001, https://www.brookings.edu/testimonies/issues-in-chinas-wto-accession/.

194 **skyrocketed to $475 billion:** Lardy, "Issues in China's WTO Accession."

194 **definitive leader in global exports:** Alessandro Nicita and Carlos Razo, "China: The Rise of a Trade Titan," UNCTAD, April 27, 2021.

194 **latter two stages:** Raymond Vernon, "International Investment and International Trade in the Product Cycle," *Quarterly Journal of Economics* 80, no. 2 (1966): 190–207.

195 **assembled in China:** David Barboza, "An iPhone's Journey, From the Factory Floor to the Retail Store," *New York Times*, December 29, 2016.

195 **lion's share of global manufacturing:** "Why Did the China Shock Hurt so Much?," *The Economist*, March 7, 2019.

195 **backlash from globalization:** Thomas Friedman, *The World Is Flat: A Brief History of the Twenty-First Century* (New York: Picador, 2007), 563.

196 **relative deprivation:** As cited in Fukuyama, *End of History and the Last Man*, 175.

196 **size of the average American home:** Mark J. Perry, "New US Homes Today Are 1,000 Square Feet Larger Than in 1973 and Living Space per Person Has Nearly Doubled," American Enterprise Institute, June 5, 2016.

196 **only 8 percent remain without:**"Percentage of Households by Number of Vehicles, 1960–2020," The Geography of Transport Systems.

196 **costing about half:** Mark J. Perry, "Even with Baggage Fees, the 'Miracle of Flight' Remains a Real Bargain; Average 2011 Airfare Was 40% Below 1980 Average," American Enterprise Institute, October 6, 2012; "Domestic Round-Trip Fares and Fees," Airlines for America, June 1, 2023.

196 **half as much of the average household's income:** Eliza Barclay, "Your Grandparents Spent More of Their Money on Food than You Do," NPR, March 2, 2015.

196 **little over 3 percent:** Peter Liquori, "The History of American-Made Clothing," Goodwear, August 30, 2017.

196 **38 percent:** United States Census Bureau, "1960 Census: Population, Supplementary Reports: Educational Attainment of the Population of the United States"; United States Census Bureau, "Census Bureau Releases New Educational Attainment Data."

196 **10 percent today:** Christopher J. Conover, "How Private Health Insurance Slashed the Uninsured Rate for Americans: Health Fact of the Week," American Enterprise Institute, September 16, 2011; Jennifer Tolbert, Patrick Drake, and Anthony Damico, "Key Facts about the Uninsured Population," KFF, December 19, 2022.

196 **Ultrasound:** Michelle Millar Fisher and Amber Winick, "A Brief History of the Sonogram," *Smithsonian Magazine*, September 22, 2021; "CT scan and MRI introduced," PBS, *People and Discoveries* databank.

196 **kills less than one-third of patients:** Rebecca L. Siegel et al., "Cancer statistics, 2023," *CA: A Cancer Journal for Clinicians* 73, no. 1 (2023): Table 6.

197 **median white income:** "Historical Income Tables: People," United States Census Bureau, table P-4.

197 **antiglobalization movements:** Harold James, *The Creation and Destruction of Value: The Globalization Cycle* (Cambridge, MA: Harvard University Press, 2012); Stiglitz, *Globalization and Its Discontents Revisited: Anti-Globalization in the Era of Trump.*

197 **profoundly undemocratic fashion:** Quinn Slobodian, *Globalists: The End of Empire and the Birth of Neoliberalism* (Cambridge, MA: Harvard University Press, 2018).

198 **"democratic excess":** Helen Thompson and David Runciman, "Helen Thompson/Disorder," February 24, 2022 in *Talking Politics*, podcast, MP3 audio, 48:26.

198 **never be fully insulated:** Karl Polanyi, *The Great Transformation* (1944).

198 **nearly 100 percent:** "Household debt, loans and debt securities," International Monetary Fund.

200 **absorbed the Tea Party's ideas:** Geoffrey Kabaservice, "The Forever Grievance," *Washington Post*, December 4, 2020; Jeremy W. Peters, "The Tea Party Didn't Get What It Wanted, but It Did Unleash the Politics of Anger," *New York Times*, August 28, 2019.

202 **American workers:** "Remarks by National Security Advisor Jake Sullivan on Renewing American Economic Leadership at the Brookings Institution," The White House, April 27, 2023.

202 **"greater economic inequality and political extremism":** Adam S. Posen, "The Price of Nostalgia," *Foreign Affairs*, May 2021.

CHAPTER SEVEN: INFORMATION UNBOUND

205 **"low-hanging fruit":** Tyler Cowen, *The Great Stagnation: How America Ate All the Low-Hanging Fruit of Modern History, Got Sick, and Will (Eventually) Feel Better* (New York: Dutton, 2011).

205 **Silicon Valley:** Francis J. Gavin, "How 1970s California created the modern world," Engelsberg Ideas, Axel and Margaret Ax:son Johnson Foundation, April 3, 2023.

206 **92 percent of Americans:** Pew Research Center, "Internet/Broadband Fact Sheet," April 7, 2021.

206 **a third of people:** "What Share of People Are Online?," Our World in Data.

206 **over three hundred billion emails:** The Radicati Group, "Email Statistics Report, 2022–2026," Statista, November 2022.

207 **just two months:** Shradha Aneja, "ChatGPT hits 100 million users in two months—here's how long Instagram and TikTok took," *Business Insider India*, February 6, 2023.

208 **the digital revolution:** Erik Brynjolfsson and Avinash Collis, "How Should We Measure the Digital Economy?," *Harvard Business Review*, November 2019.

208 **$7 billion:** Erik Brynjolfsson and Andrew McAfee, *The Second Machine Age: Work, Progress, and Prosperity in a Time of Brilliant Technologies* (New York: W. W. Norton, 2016), 109, relying on data from Daniel Weld, "Internet Enabled Human Computation," July 22, 2013, Slide 48.

208 **increased nearly tenfold:** International Federation of the Phonographic Industry, "IFPI:05 Digital Music Report," 6; International Federation of the Phonographic Industry, "Digital Music Report 2009," 6.

208 **around one hundred times as much information:** Wikipedia: Size

comparisons, "Comparison of encyclopedias," comparing Wikipedia circa 2023 to the last printed *Britannica* of 2013.

208   **117,000 copies:** "Britannica for Sale," *Christian Science Monitor*, 1995.

208   **1.5 billion unique visitors:** "Unique devices," Wikimedia Statistics.

209   **ten times as many person-hours:** Brynjolfsson and McAfee, *Second Machine Age*, 116.

209   **"beyond the compass":** John Maynard Keynes, *The Economic Consequences of Peace* (1999), 11.

209   **over 70 percent of book sales:** "Book Sales Statistics," WordsRated, June 13, 2023; April Berthene, "Ecommerce is 46.0% of All Apparel Sales," Digital Commerce 360, June 28, 2021; "What Is the Share of E-Commerce in Overall Retail Sales?," CBRE, May 16, 2022.

210   **"I alone can fix it":** Yoni Applebaum, "'I Alone Can Fix It'," *The Atlantic*, July 21, 2016.

210   **"position of Louis Pasteur":** Marshall McLuhan and Lewis H. Lapham, *Understanding Media: The Extensions of Man* (Cambridge, MA: MIT Press, 1994), 18.

211   **backbone of American society:** In data gathered by scholar Tanner Greer, the number of American associations with more than one million members nationally has broadly declined since the early twentieth century: Tanner Greer, "A School of Strength and Character," *Palladium*, March 30, 2023.

211   **deterioration of their communal ties:** Joshua Hochberg and Eitan Hersh, "Public Perceptions of Local Influence," *SageJournals*, January 14, 2023.

212   **3 to 15 percent:** Daniel A. Cox, "Men's Social Circles Are Shrinking," Survey Center on American Life, AEI, June 29, 2021.

212   **fifteen cigarettes a day:** "Our Epidemic of Loneliness and Isolation," US Department of Health and Human Services, 4, citing research by psychologists like Julianne Holt-Lunstad, among others.

212   **significantly worse:** Zach Rausch and Jon Haidt, "The Teen Mental Illness Epidemic Is International, Part 1: The Anglospher," After Babel, Substack, March 29, 2023.

212   **"incel" support group:** Olivia Solon, "'Incel': Reddit Bans Misogynist Men's Group Blaming Women for Their Celibacy," *Guardian*, November 8, 2017.

213   **"an everyday experience":** Hannah Arendt, *Origins of Totalitarianism* (New York: Harcourt, 1968), 478.

215   **"Anywheres":** David Goodhart, *The Road to Somewhere: The Populist Revolt and the Future of Politics* (London: Hurst, 2017).

215   **"flyover country":** "Josh Hawley: Coastal Elitist and Ticking Missouri Time Bomb," *St. Louis American*, March 22, 2018.

215   **"toxic" message:** David Skolnck, "Vance flips on people leaving hometowns," *Vindicator*, August 13, 2022.

216   **glittering (and unaffordable) superstar cities:** Alan Ehrenhalt discusses this in his 1996 book: Alan Erenhalt, *The Lost City: Discovering the Forgotten Virtues of Community in the Chicago of the 1950s* (New York: Basic, 1996).

216   **one month later:** Judy Bachrach, "WIKIHISTORY: Did the Leaks Inspire the Arab Spring?" *World Affairs* 174, no. 2 (2011): 35–44.

216   **"flaunting her designer wardrobe":** Claudia Rosett, "The Age of the Celebrity Tyrant," *Forbes*, August 27, 2009.

216   **"The First Lady of Hell":** Roy Greenslade, "How Syria's 'Desert Rose' became 'the First Lady of Hell,'" *Guardian*, August 1, 2012.

217   **"extraordinary rate":** Brynjolfsson and McAfee, *Second Machine Age*, 11.

217   **top 20 percent of earners:** "A Guide to Economic Inequality," *American Compass*, April 27, 2021.

218 **"democratizing expression":** Ada Palmer, "We Are an Information Revolution Species," Microsoft.

219 **"nail Jello to the wall":** "Full Text of Clinton's Speech on China Trade Bill," *New York Times*, March 9, 2000.

220 **"Social ostracism":** Noah Smith, "It's Not Cancel Culture, It's Cancel Technology," Noahpinion, Substack, February 16, 2021.

221 **appropriating others' lived experiences:** Alexandra Alter, "She Pulled Her Debut Book When Critics Found It Racist. Now She Plans to Publish," *New York Times*, April 28, 2019.

222 **around two-thirds of Republicans:** Philip Bump, "Six in 10 Republicans still Think 2020 Was Illegitimate," *Washington Post*, May 24, 2023.

223 **invaded Russia:** Maroosha Muzaffar, "Deepfake Putin Declares Martial Law and Cries: 'Russia Is under Attack,'" *Independent*, June 7, 2023.

223 **his party's corruption:** Nilesh Christopher, "An Indian Politician Says Scandalous Audio Clips Are AI deepfakes. We Had Them Tested," *Rest of World*, July 5, 2023.

224 **rise of self-checkout:** "Employed Full Time: Wage and Salary Workers: Cashiers Occupations: 16 Years and Over," FRED Economic Data, St. Louis Fed.

224 **lost over 1,100 automatic car washes:** "Hand Car Washes," UK Parliament, November 6, 2018.

224 **suffered from a labor shortage:** "Will the US Go into Recession?," Goldman Sachs, April 19, 2022.

224 **so short-staffed:** Jane Black, "How to Make an Unloved Job More Attractive? Restaurants Tinker With Wages," *New York Times*, September 20, 2021; Jeanna Smialek and Sydney Ember, "Companies Hoarding Workers Could Be Good News for the Economy," *New York Times*, October 12, 2022.

224 **"the end of work":** Derek Thompson, "A World Without Work," *Atlantic*, July 2015.

224 **created:** "The Future of Jobs Report 2020," World Economic Forum, October 20, 2020.

225 **"eating the world":** This section is adapted from a segment that aired on my CNN show on April 30, 2023, and can be viewed at Fareed Zakaria (@FareedZakaria), "Today's last look: ChatGPT is going to help software 'eat the world'," X, April 30, 2023, https://twitter.com/FareedZakaria/status/1652837826323439618. It was inspired by Kedrosky and Norlin's blog post: "Society's Technical Debt and Software's Gutenberg Moment," *Irregular Ideas with Paul Kedrosky & Eric Norlin of SKV*, SKV, March 21, 2023.

225 **answer all kinds of questions:** Alexandra Garfinkle and Dylan Croll, "How Business Is already Using ChatGPT and other AI Tech," Yahoo, February 14, 2023; Andrew Perlman, "The Implications of ChatGPT for Legal Services and Society," Center on the Legal Profession, Harvard Law School, March 2023.

225 **less formal if needed:** Techzine, "Salesforce Einstein GPT for Sales," YouTube, March 7, 2023, video, https://www.youtube.com/watch?v=UH4lIIcAZdY; Salesforce Artificial Intelligence," Salesforce.

225 **launched a ChatGPT feature:** J. J. Zhuang, "Introducing the Instacart Plugin for ChatGPT," Instacart, March 23, 2023.

225 **build their own software:** "Society's Technical Debt and Software's Gutenberg Moment," Irregular Ideas with Paul Kedrosky and Eric Norlin of SKV, SKV, March 21, 2023.

226 **"hottest new programming language":** Andrej Karpathy (@karpathy), "The hottest new programming language is English," Twitter, January 24, 2023, https://twitter.com/karpathy/status/1617979122625712128.

226 **ban driverless trucks:** Ben Shapiro, "Should We Limit Technology to Protect

Jobs? | With Tucker Carlson," Youtube, video, https://www.youtube.com/watch?v=awM0nrlOZxk.

226 **a net loss of jobs:** Lisa Baertlein, "Focus: Jobs at Stake as California Port Terminal Upgrades to Green Technology," Reuters, June 8, 2023.

226 **"trying to build a canal":** Stephen Moore, "Missing Milton: Who Will Speak For Free Markets?," *Wall Street Journal*, May 27, 2009.

227 **"the end of work":** Thompson, "World without Work."

227 **only fifteen hours a week:** David Kestenbaum, "Keynes Predicted We Would Be Working 15-Hour Weeks. Why Was He So Wrong?," NPR, August 13, 2015.

227 **faith in AI:** Henry A. Kissinger, Eric Schmidt, and Daniel Huttenlocher, *The Age of AI and Our Human Future*, 16–18. Disclosure: I serve as a senior advisor to Schmidt Futures and received support for the writing of this book.

227 **our own place:** Ken Goldberg, "Let's Give AI a Chance," *Boston Globe*, May 30, 2023.

228 **untold number of breakthroughs:** Robert F. Service, "'The Game Has Changed.' AI Triumphs at Protein Folding," *Science* 6521, no. 370, December 4, 2020.

228 **"ability to edit not only the DNA":** Jennifer A. Doudna and Samuel H. Sternberg, *A Crack in Creation: Gene Editing and the Unthinkable Power to Control Evolution* (New York: Mariner, 2018), xvi.

228 **"God created life":** Bill Clinton, "Announcing the Completion of the First Survey of the Entire Human Genome" (speech, Washington, DC, June 26, 2000), The White House at Work.

228 **under $1,000:** "DNA Sequencing Costs: Data," National Human Genome Research Institute.

228 **2 a.m. on Sunday:** Gregory Zuckerman, *A Shot to Save the World: The Inside Story of the Life-or-Death Race for a COVID-19 Vaccine* (New York: Penguin, 2021), 231.

229 **based on messenger RNA:** Zuckerman, *A Shot to Save the World*, 157.

229 **just over half as much money:** Zuckerman, *A Shot to Save the World*, 220.

229 **"achieve the impossible":** Stuart A. Thompson, "How Long Will a Vaccine Really Take?," *New York Times*, April 30, 2020.

229 **taketh away:** Fareed Zakaria, "Some Republicans Are Pushing People to Get Vaccinated. It May Be Too Late," *Washington Post*, July 22, 2021.

229 **"naked authoritarianism":** Jill Colvin, "Biden's Vaccine Rules Ignite Instant, Hot GOP Opposition," AP News, September 10, 2021.

230 **"a blizzard of useless":** Tom Nichols, "How America Lost Faith in Expertise," *Foreign Affairs*, February 13, 2017.

230 **farmland the size of Africa and South America combined:** Susan Hockfield, *The Age of Living Machines: How Biology Will Build the Next Technology Revolution* (New York: W. W. Norton, 2020), 135.

230 **80 percent of Hawaiian papaya:** Pamela Ronald, "The Case for Engineering Our Food," filmed in March 2015 in Vancouver BC, Canada, TED video; A. S. Bawa and K. R. Anilakumar, "Genetically Modified Foods: Safety, Risks and Public Concerns—A Review," *Journal of Food Science and Technology* 50, December 19, 2012.

231 **half a million blind:** Ed Regis, "The True Story of the Genetically Modified Superfood That Almost Saved Millions," *Foreign Policy*, October 17, 2019.

231 **multinational corporations:** Mark Lynas, "The True Story about Who Destroyed a Genetically Modified Rice Crop," *Slate*, August 26, 2013.

231 **resistant to HIV:** Helen Regan, Rebecca Wright, and Alexandra Field, "The Scientist, the Twins and the Experiment That Geneticists Say Went Too Far," CNN Health, CNN, December 1, 2018.

232 ***Homo deus:*** Zakaria, *Ten Lessons for a Post-Pandemic World*, 119, citing Yuval Noah Harari, *Homo Deus: A Brief History of Tomorrow* (New York: HarperCollins, 2018).

232   **more optimistic possibilities:** Natasha Singer, "New A.I. Chatbot Tutors Could Upend Student Learning," *New York Times*, June 8, 2023.

233   **insoluble problems:** Zakaria, *Ten Lessons for a Post-Pandemic World*, 120.

233   **"masters would not need slaves":** Aristotle, *Politics*, trans. CDC Reeve (New York: Hackett, 1998) Book 1, Chapter 4, lines 33–38.

CHAPTER EIGHT: REVENGE OF THE TRIBES

235   **country's long postwar boom:** Mark Kurlansky, *1968: The Year That Rocked the World* (New York: Random House, 2004), 5.

235   **"forbidden to forbid":** "Les Murs Parlent," *Le Monde*, May 3, 1973.

236   **penetrated Humphrey's:** Joel Achenbach, "'A Party That Had Lost Its Mind': In 1968, Democrats Held One of History's Most Disastrous Conventions," *Washington Post*, August 24, 2018.

236   **"The whole world is watching!":** Kurlansky, *1968: Year that Rocked the World*, 282–83.

236   **In Rome:** Sylvia Poggioli, "Valle Giulia Has Taken on Mythological Stature," NPR, June 23, 2008.

236   **"golden age of patriotism":** David Frum, *How We Got Here: The 70's: The Decade That Brought You Modern Life* (New York: Basic, 2001), 349.

238   **abstract values:** Ronald Inglehart, "The Nature of Value Change," in *The Silent Revolution* (Princeton, NJ: Princeton University Press, 1977).

238   **swiftest and most radical:** This is not to discount the work of the suffragettes in the US and UK, but theirs was a reformist movement aimed mostly at extending voting rights to women, not at revolutionizing society.

238   **as Mark Lilla notes:** Mark Lilia, "Still Living with '68," *New York Times Magazine*, August 16, 1998, 34.

238   **rarely politicized:** The recent near-total ban in conservative Poland is an exception.

239   **"cultural war":** Patrick Joseph Buchanan, "Culture War Speech: Address to the Republican National Convention," Transcript of speech delivered on August 17, 1992, Voices of Democracy: The U.S. Oratory Project.

239   **"history of class struggles":** Karl Marx and Frederick Engels, *Communist Manifesto*, trans. Samuel Moore, 14, Marxists Internet Archive.

240   **above 90 percent:** Lewis L. Gould, *The Republicans: A History of the Grand Old Party* (Oxford: Oxford University Press, 2014), 238; Emmanuel Saez and Gabriel Zucman, "The Rise of Income and Wealth Inequality in America: Evidence from Distributional Macroeconomic Accounts," *Journal of Economic Perspectives* 34 no. 4 (2020): 21.

240   **"heyday of American social democracy":** Dorothy Sue Cobble, *For the Many: American Feminists and the Global Fight for Democratic Equality* (Princeton, NJ: Princeton University Press, 2021), 4.

240   **only 4 percent of Black Americans:** Ira Katznelson, *Fear Itself* (New York: W. W. Norton, 2013), 15.

240   **subjugation of Black Americans:** Katznelson, *Fear Itself*, 95.

240   **largely Black:** Katznelson, *Fear Itself*, 260.

240   **97 percent of the vote:** Katznelson, *Fear Itself*, 165.

241   *more* **polarization:** "Summary of Conclusions and Proposals," *The American Political Science Review* 44, no. 3 (1950): 1–14.

241   **"beyond your command":** Bob Dylan, "The Times They Are A-Changin'," *Bob Dylan Newsletter*.

242   **concept of marriage:** Richard Zacks, "Easy Come, Easy Go," in *Rolling Stones: The Seventies*, ed. Ashley Kahn, Holly George-Warren, and Shawn Dahl (Little, Brown, 1998), 54.

242   **only 5 percent of Americans:** Frum, *How We Got Here*, xxi.

242   **51 percent:** Jon B. Gettman, "Crimes of Indiscretion: Marijuana Arrests in the United States," NORML, 2005, 28.

242   **shrank from 75 percent:** Frum, *How We Got Here*, 149.

242   **71 percent of Americans trusted:** Frum, *How We Got Here*, 4.

242   **29 percent:** "Public Trust in Government: 1958–2022," Pew Research Center, June 6, 2022.

243   **"postmaterialism":** Inglehart, *The Silent Revolution*, 104.

243   **those who prioritized "postmaterialist" values:** Ronald Inglehart, "The Silent Revolution in Europe: Intergenerational Change in Post-Industrial Societies," *American Political Science Review* 65, no. 4 (1971): 996. Though this is based on correlation and not controlled for age, Inglehart's findings still show a striking disconnect between generations.

243   **affiliated with the Nazi regime:** Kurlansky, 1968: The Year That Rocked the World, 145.

243   **"Auschwitz generation":** Robert Gerald Livingston, "Violence Is the Only Way," *New York Times*, January 3, 1988.

243   **number of annual divorces in West Germany:** "Marriages, divorces (time series)," Statistisches Bundesamt.

243   **Catholics attending weekly mass fell by half:** Hugh McLeod, "The Religious Crisis of the 1960s," *Journal of Modern European History / Zeitschrift Für Moderne Europäische Geschichte / Revue d'histoire Européenne Contemporaine* 3, no. 2 (2005): 205.

244   **76 percent of American Christians:** "Being Christian in Western Europe," Pew Research Center, May 29, 2018.

244   **petition signed by 343 women:** Tony Judt, *Postwar*, 488.

244   **removed penalties for abortion:** While West Germany first technically legalized abortion in 1974, that law was struck down by the Constitutional Court in 1975. A revised law was then passed in 1976, which has remained in force with slight alterations until today. See here: Deborah L. Goldberg, "Developments in German Abortion Law: A U.S. Perspective," *UCLA Women's Law Journal*, 1995.

245   **4 points more Republican:** Everett Carll Ladd, "The Shifting Party Coalitions—from the 1930s to the 1970s," in *Party Coalitions in the 1980s*, ed. Seymour Martin Lipset (San Francisco: Institute of Contemporary Studies, 1981).

245   **"I am invisible":** Ralph Ellison, *Invisible Man* (New York: Random House, 1952), 3.

245   **nearly 75 percent of Americans:** James C. Cobb, "When Martin Luther King Jr. Was Killed, He Was Less Popular than Donald Trump is Today," *USA Today*, April 4, 2018.

245   **a third thought he was to blame:** Harry Enten, "Americans see Martin Luther King Jr. as a Hero Now, but that Wasn't the Case during His Lifetime," CNN, January 16, 2023.

246   **war long remained popular:** "CBS News Poll: U.S. Involvement in Vietnam," January 28, 2018.

246   **"the great silent majority":** Richard Nixon, "Address Accepting the Presidential Nomination at the Republican National Convention in Miami Beach, Florida" (speech, August 8, 1968), The American Presidency Project.

246   **provoked the carnage:** Rick Hampton, "1970 Kent State Shootings Are an Enduring History Lesson," *USA Today*, May 3, 2010.

246   **"white flight":** Steven Pinker, "Decivilization in the 1960s," in *The Better Angels of Our Nature: Why Violence Has Declined* (New York: Penguin, 2012).

247   **"an asinine concept":** Astead W. Herndon and Sheryl Gay Stolberg, "How Joe Biden Became the Democrats' Anti-Busing Crusader," *New York Times*, July 15, 2019.

247   **opposed busing:** Frum, *How We Got Here*, 262.

247   **strikingly segregated:** Alana Semuels, "Where the White People Live," *The Atlantic*, April 10, 2015.

247   **"simple emotion and very unpleasant to him":** Kurlansky, *1968: Year That Rocked the World*, 43.

247   **"Republican party is the ship":** Lewis Gould, *The Republicans: A History of the Grand Old Party* (New York: Oxford University Press, 2014), 52.

247   **two-to-one:** Katznelson, *Fear Itself*, 175.

247   **just 6 percent of the Black vote:** Rick Perlstein, *Reaganland: America's Right Turn 1976–1980* (New York: Simon & Schuster, 2020), 19.

247   **"we may have lost the South":** Charles Kaiser, " 'We May Have Lost the South': What LBJ Really Said about Democrats in 1964," *Guardian*, January 23, 2023.

247   **fell to 13 percent:** Perlstein, *Reaganland: America's Right Turn 1976–1980*, 19.

250   **quarter of whom were using the pill:** "Trends in Contraceptive Practice: United States, 1965–76," CDC, 2023.

250   **selling nearly three million copies:** "Betty Freidan and *The Feminine Mystique*," *The First Measured Century*, FMC Program Segments 1960–2000, PBS.

250   **around thirty women:** Dorothy Sue Cobble, *For the Many*, 374.

251   **only about one marriage in twenty:** Frum, *How We Got Here*, xxi.

251   **88 percent of college women:** Barbara A. DeBuono et al., "Sexual Behavior of College Women in 1975, 1986, and 1989," *New England Journal of Medicine*, March 22, 1990.

251   **more than doubled:** "Number and rate of divorces and number and percent of children under 18 involved annually in divorces: 1950 to 1993," National Center for Education Statistics

251   **find a suitable husband:** Betty Friedan, *The Feminine Mystique* (New York: W. W. Norton).

251   **more than halved:** "Stay-at-home mothers through the years," U.S. Bureau of Labor Statistics, September 2014.

251   **25 percent:** "The Data on Women Leaders," Pew Research Center, September 13, 2018.

251   **"lavender scare":** "Homosexuals in the Federal Government and Personnel Security," Eisenhower Library.

252   **five points higher:** Tom W. Smith, "Public Attitudes toward Homosexuality," NORC/University of Chicago, September 2011.

252   **52 percent:** Albert L. Winseman, "Religion "Very Important" to Most Americans," Gallup, December 20, 2005.

253   **about 20,000:** Perlstein, *Reaganland: America's Right Turn 1976–1980*, 348.

253   **widened to 11 percent:** Liliana Mason, *Uncivil Agreement: How Politics Became Our Identity* (Chicago: University of Chicago Press, 2018), 36–39.

253   **abortion was not a wedge issue:** Ezra Klein, *Why We're Polarized* (New York: Simon and Schuster, 2020), 59.

253   **support a constitutional ban:** "Reagan Gets Backing of Right to Life Group for Stand on Abortion," *New York Times*, June 28, 1980.

253   **their Democratic counterparts:** Christina Wolbrecht, *The Politics of Women's Rights: Parties, Positions, and Change* (Princeton: Princeton University Press, 2000), 88.

254   **"irritates the women's libbers":** Hanna Kozlowska, "Phyllis Schlafly, Arch-Enemy of American Feminists, Died at 92," *Quartz*, September 6, 2016.

254   **"Bring God Back":** Perlstein, *Reaganland: America's Right Turn 1976–1980*, 724.

254 **"another Sodom and Gomorrah":** Perlstein, *Reaganland: America's Right Turn 1976–1980*, 626.

254 **turned out in force:** Perlstein, *Reaganland: America's Right Turn 1976–1980*, 911.

254 **more likely to support the GOP:** E. J. Dionne Jr., "There Is No 'Catholic Vote.' And Yet, It Matters," Brookings Institute, June 18, 2000.

255 **71 percent of white churchgoers:** Justin Nortey, "Most White Americans who regularly attend worship services voted for Trump in 2020," Pew Research Center, August 30, 2021.

255 **converted to Republicanism:** Jacob Weisberg, "The Road to Reagandom," *Slate*, January 8, 2016.

256 **first time in forty years:** Gary Gerstle, *The Rise and Fall of the Neoliberal Order: America and the World in the Free Market Era* (New York: Oxford University Press, 2022), 156.

256 **Glass-Steagall Act:** "The Clinton Presidency: Historic Economic Growth," The Clinton-Gore Administration: A Record of Progress; Gerstle, *The Rise and Fall of the Neoliberal Order: America and the World in the Free Market Era*, 157.

256 **the best Republican president":** " 'Meet the Press' transcript for Sept. 30, 2007," NBC News, September 30, 2007.

256 **Margaret Thatcher:** Halimah Abdullah, "Reagan and Thatcher: 'Political soulmates,'" CNN, April 9, 2013.

257 **"Tony Blair":** "The lasting legacy of Mrs Thatcher," *Financial Times*, April 8, 2013.

257 **around 10 percent of Germany's active labor force:** Peter Gatrell, *The Unsettling of Europe: How Migration Reshaped a Continent* (New York: Basic, 2019), 144.

258 **Enoch Powell groused:** Ian Aitken, "Enoch Powell dismissed for 'racialist' speech," *Guardian*, April 21, 1968.

258 **61 percent of Britons:** Marcus Collins, "Immigration and opinion polls in postwar Britain," *Modern History Review* 18 no. 4 (2016): 8–13.

258 **10 percent to 70 percent:** Gatrell, *Unsettling of Europe*, 290.

258 **only 52 percent:** Liesbet Hooghe, "Europe Divided? Elites vs. Public Opinion on European Integration," IHS Political Science Series, April 2003, 2.

259 **use cannons:** "Italian Minister Calls on Navy to Open Fire on Illegal Immigrants," *Sydney Morning Herald*, June 17, 2003.

259 **most of the country's manual laborers:** Alexandra Grass, "Stammwählerschaft ist auf knapp 50 Prozent geschrumpft," *Wiener Zeitung*, July 4, 2000.

259 **less than 60 percent:** Jasmin Luypaert, "Decline of Mainstream Parties: Party Responses After Electoral Loss in Flanders," presented at the Belgian State of the Federation on December 2019, 3.

259 **a million irregular migrants:** "Infographic—Irregular Arrivals to the EU (2008–2023)," European Council, June 2023.

260 **2.14 million migrants:** Cynthia Kroet, "Germany Set Immigration Record in 2015," *Politico*, July 14, 2016.

260 **led the Sweden Democrats:** Danielle Lee Thompson, "The Rise of Sweden Democrats: Islam, Populism and the End of Swedish Exceptionalism," Brookings Institute, March 5, 2020.

260 **winning over 17 percent:** Thompson, "The Rise of Sweden Democrats."

260 **"Islam is fighting against":** Mark Gevisser, "How Globalisation Has Transformed the Fight for LGBTQ+ Rights," *Guardian*, June 16, 2020.

261 **outlaw the construction of minarets:** Ian Traynor, "Swiss vote to ban construction of minarets on mosques," *Guardian,* November 25, 2009; Marco Muller, "Which countries Have a 'Burqa Ban'?," Deutsche Welle (DW), August 1, 2019; Dustin Jones, "Switzerland Approves 'Burqa Ban' to Prohibit Some Face Coverings In Public," NPR, March 7, 2021.

261   **"betray, bizarre, decay":** Mason, *Uncivil Agreement*, 132.

262   **triggered two government shutdowns:** See, for example, Steven Levitsky and Daniel Ziblatt, "The Unraveling," in *How Democracies Die* (New York: Penguin Random House, 2019).

262   **highest final approval rating:** Lydia Saad, "Bush Presidency Closes With 34% Approval, 61% Disapproval," Gallup, January 14, 2009.

262   **"compassionate conservatism":** Peter Baker, "Mourning 'Compassionate Conservatism' Along With Its Author," *New York Times*, February 10, 2023.

262   **some 44 percent of the Latino vote:** Roberto Suro, Richard Fry, and Jeffrey S. Passel, "IV. How Latinos Voted in 2004," Pew Research Center, June 27, 2005.

262   **"a Chicago Tea Party in July":** "CNBC's Rick Santelli's Chicago Tea Party," The Heritage Foundation, February 19, 2009, 2:55 to 4:36, https://www.youtube.com/watch?v=zp-Jw-5Kx8k&t=145s&ab_channel=TheHeritageFoundation.

263   **"hands off my Medicare":** Bob Cesca, "Keep Your Goddamn Government Hands Off My Medicare!," *HuffPost*, September 5, 2009.

263   **was born abroad:** Lymari Morales, "Obama's Birth Certificate Convinces Some, but Not All, Skeptics," Gallup, May 13, 2011; Stephanie Condon, "One in Four Americans Think Obama Was not Born in U.S.," CBS News, April 21, 2011.

263   **convinced that Obama was a secret Muslim:** Jennifer Agiesta, "Misperceptions Persist about Obama's Faith, but Aren't so Widespread," CNN, September 14, 2015.

263   **nuclear disarmament negotiations:** Fox Butterfield, "Trump Urged to Head Gala of Democrats," *New York Times*, November 18, 1987.

263   **unusual obsession:** Ilan Ben-Meir, "That Time Trump Spent Nearly $100,000 On an Ad Criticizing U.S. Foreign Policy In 1987," Buzzfeed News, July 10, 2015.

263   **supported universal healthcare:** Hunter Schwarz, "The Many Ways in which Donald Trump Was once a Liberal's Liberal," *Washington Post*, July 9, 2015.

265   **17 points wider:** Fareed Zakaria, "The Abortion Battle May Be the Precursor to Even Larger Struggles," *Washington Post*, May 5, 2022.

265   **overwhelmingly opted for Trump:** Klein, *Why We're Polarized*, xiii.

265   **never fell below 77 percent:** "Presidential Approval Ratings—Donald Trump," Gallup.

265   **solid majority of Republicans:** Lane Cuthbert and Alexander Theodoridis, "Do Republicans Believe Trump Won the 2020 Election? Our research Suggests They Do," *Washington Post*, January 7, 2022.

265   **more disappointed:** Maxine Najle and Robert P. Jones, "American Democracy in Crisis: The Fate of Pluralism in a Divided Nation," PRRI, February 19, 2019.

265   **an existential threat:** Pippa Norris and Ronald Inglehart, *Cultural Backlash: Trump, Brexit, and Authoritarian Populism* (Cambridge: Cambridge University Press, 2019), 15–16.

266   **nearly tripled to over 13 percent:** "U.S. Foreign-Born Population Trends," Pew Research Center, September 28, 2015.

266   **made up only 74 percent of voters:** "Voting and Registration in the Election of November 1970," Bureau of the Census, figure 2; "Voter Turnout Demographics," United States Elections Project.

266   **strangers in their own countries:** Daniel Cox, Rachel Lienesch, and Robert P. Jones, "Beyond Economics: Fears of Cultural Displacement Pushed the White Working Class to Trump," PRRI, May 9, 2017.

266   **radical departure:** Norris and Inglehart, *Cultural Backlash*, 353.

266   **immigration:** Fareed Zakaria, "The Democrats should rethink their immigration absolutism," *Washington Post*, August 3, 2017.

267   **to 23 percent:** Derek Thompson, "Three Decades Ago, America Lost Its Religion. Why?," *Atlantic*, September 26, 2019.

267   **biggest drop in religiosity:** Ronald F. Inglehart, *Religion's Sudden Decline: What's Causing It, and What Comes Next?* (Oxford: Oxford University Press, 2021), 14.

267   **only 23 percent:** Inglehart, *Religion's Sudden Decline,* 15.

267   **became more Republican:** Michelle Margolis, "When Politicians Determine Your Religious Beliefs," *New York Times,* July 11, 2018.

268   **23 percentage point gap:** Zakaria, "The Abortion Battle May Be the Precursor to Even Larger Struggles."

268   **four times as likely:** Ronald Brownstein, "How religion widens the partisan divide," CNN, October 22, 2019.

268   **skyrocketed to 84 percent:** Klein, *Why We're Polarized,* 12.

268   **approval for interracial marriage:** Milan Singh, "The rise of the liberal Democrat," Slow Boring, August 5, 2023.

268   **"Great Awokening":** Klein, *Why We're Polarized,* 130.

269   **half of American youths:** Lydia Saad, "Socialism as Popular as Capitalism among Young Adults in U.S.," Gallup, November 25, 2019.

269   **34 percent:** "Students Show Mixed Support for Police and Movement to Defund," Generation Lab, July 6, 2020.

270   **Two weeks after:** Peter Smith, "Moscow Patriarch Stokes Orthodox Tensions with War Remarks," AP News, March 8, 2022.

270   **author J. K. Rowling:** Pjotr Sauer, "Putin says West Treating Russian Culture Like 'Cancelled' JK Rowling," *Guardian,* March 25, 2022.

CHAPTER NINE: THE DUAL REVOLUTIONS

272   **"rise of Athens":** Graham T. Allison, *Destined for War: Can America and China Escape Thucydides's Trap?* (Boston: Houghton Mifflin Harcourt, 2017), vii.

272   **"Thucydides Trap":** Allison, *Destined for War.* (Note that Allison himself calls the dilemma "Thucydides' trap.")

273   **twelve ended in war:** Allison, *Destined for War.*

273   **most powerful nation:** This paragraph draws on my 2008 book *The Post-American World.*

275   **about 30 percent in 1913:** "Globalization over 5 Centuries," Our World in Data. Data from Mariko J. Klasing and P. Milionis, "Quantifying the Evolution of World Trade, 1870–1949," *Journal of International Economics* 92, no. 1 (2014): 185–97; A. Estevadeordal, B. Frantz, and A. Taylor, "The Rise and Fall of World Trade, 1870–1939," *Quarterly Journal of Economics* 118, no. 2 (2003): 359–407; World Bank—World Development Indicators; Robert C. Feenstra, Robert Inklaar, and Marcel P. Timmer, "The Next Generation of the Penn World Table," *American Economic Review* 105, no. 10 (2015): 3150–82.

275   **1.5 billion international trips:** "International Tourism Growth Continues to Outpace the Global Economy," United Nations World Tourism Organization, January 20, 2020; "International Tourism Swiftly Overcoming Pandemic Downturn" United Nations World Tourism Organization, September, 19, 2023.

275   **the Long Peace:** John Lewis Gaddis, *The Long Peace: Inquiries Into the History of the Cold War* (Oxford: Oxford University Press, 1989).

276   **"what war did":** Fareed Zakaria, "A Conversation with Lee Kuan Yew," *Foreign Affairs,* March 1, 1994.

276   **"illiberal democracy":** Fareed Zakaria, "The Rise of Illiberal Democracy," *Foreign Affairs,* November 1, 1997; and Fareed Zakaria, *The Future of Freedom: Illiberal Democracy at Home and Abroad* (New York: W. W. Norton, 2007).

278 **based on natural rights and reason:** Hugo Grotius, *The Rights of War and Peace* (2005 ed.) vol. 1 (Book 1) (Indianapolis: Liberty Fund, 1625).

278 **"Toward Perpetual Peace":** Immanuel Kant, "Toward Perpetual Peace," in *Kant: Political Writings* (Cambridge: Cambridge University Press, 1991).

278 **seized some 1,600 slave ships:** "Chasing Freedom: The Royal Navy and the suppression of the transatlantic slave trade," *1807 Commemorated*, Institute for the Public Understanding of the Past and the Institute of Historical Research, 2007.

279 **an accommodation with Germany:** Niall Ferguson, *The Pity of War* (New York: Basic, 1999).

279 **"rights of the savage":** William Ewart Gladstone, "Remember the Rights of the Savage" (speech, Dalkieth, UK, November 26, 1879), *Journal of Liberal History*, Liberal History Democrat Group.

281 **large stretches of the globe:** This paragraph, and the following three, draw from my 2019 *Foreign Affairs* piece, "The Self-Destruction of American Power" (July–August 2019). Reprinted by permission of *Foreign Affairs*, copyright 2019 by the Council on Foreign Relations.

281 **the dollar, the yen, and the deutsche mark:** R. W. Apple Jr., "The Houston Summit; A New Balance of Power," *New York Times*, July 12, 1990.

281 **"Japan and Germany won":** "Tsongas Campaign Rally," video, C-SPAN, March 16, 1992.

281 **"The Unipolar Moment":** Charles Krauthammer, "The Unipolar Moment," *Foreign Affairs* 70, no. 1 (1990): 23–33.

281 **"will be brief":** Charles Krauthammer, "The Unipolar moment," *Washington Post*, July 20, 1990.

282 **"the Yugoslav problem":** Mark Wintz, "Origins of the Crisis: The Breakup of Yugoslavia," in *Transatlantic Diplomacy and the Use of Military Force in the Post-Cold War Era* (New York: Palgrave Macmillan, 2010).

282 **"The Committee to Save the World":** "Rubin, Greenspan & Summers," *Time*, February 15, 1999.

282 **best practices for nations:** Even the People's Republic of China holds (heavily stage-managed) elections of a sort, and many dictatorships cloak themselves as "democratic."

283 **unambiguously upward:** Zakaria, *Post-American World*.

283 **close to half:** Based on nominal GDP figures supplied by the IMF for the years 1990 and estimates for 2023.

284 **put together:** "The top 10 largest economies in the world in 2023," *Forbes India*, October 16, 2023.

284 **recovered faster and stronger:** "GDP (current US$)," World Bank.

284 **spending more on defense:** "U.S. Defense Spending Compared to Other Countries," Peter G. Peterson Foundation, April 24, 2023.

284 **750 percent larger than China's:** "GDP (current US$)—China, United States," World Bank.

284 **grow faster than the US economy:** "GDP (current US$)–India, United States, China, Brazil, Turkey, Saudi Arabia," World Bank.

285 **dozens of other non-Americans:** Devon Pendleton, "These Are the World's Richest Families," Bloomberg, October 28, 2022.

285 **five tallest skyscrapers in the world:** Rosie Lesso, "What Are the 5 Tallest Buildings in the World?," The Collector, February 16, 2023.

287 **second-largest funder of the UN:** Andrew Hyde, "China's Emerging Financial Influence at the UN Poses a Challenge to the U.S.," Stimson Center, April 4, 2022.

287 **covets leadership positions:** Bonnie S. Glaser and Courtney Fung, "China's Role in the United Nations," German Marshall Fund of the United States, December 1, 2022.

287 **contributes more peacekeeping troops:** Fareed Zakaria, "The New China Scare," *Foreign Affairs*, December 6, 2019.

287 **"risen as never before":** Xi Jinping, "Secure a Decisive Victory in Building a Moderately Prosperous Society in All Respects and Strive for the Great Success of Socialism with Chinese Characteristics for a New Era," Delivered at the 19th National Congress of the Communist Party of China, Xinhua, October 18, 2017.

287 **new guarantor of the global trading system:** Fareed Zakaria, "The Decline of U.S. influence Is the Great Global Story of Our Times," *Washington Post*, December 28, 2017.

288 **"China is a big country":** Joshua Kurlantzick, "The Belligerents," *New Republic*, January 27, 2011.

288 **rallying the underdeveloped Third World:** See: Julia Lovell, *Maoism: A Global History* (New York: Alfred A. Knopf, 2019).

288 **plateaued, not plummeted:** "2023: Trade in Goods with China," United States Census Bureau.

288 **China needs American consumers:** Parts of this paragraph and the following paragraph are drawn from Fareed Zakaria, "U.S. and China are in a Cold Peace," *Washington Post*, August 5, 2021.

289 **caused Russia's GDP to almost double:** "GDP (Constant 2015 US$, Russian Federation)," World Bank.

290 **hundreds of billions of dollars in Russian assets:** "Confiscate Russian Assets? The West Should Resist," The Editorial Board, Bloomberg, July 18, 2023.

290 **food prices skyrocketed:** "Russia's Invasion of Ukraine Exacerbates Hunger in Middle East, North Africa," Human Rights Watch, Human Rights Watch, March 21, 2022.

290 **same life expectancy:** Fareed Zakaria, "Russia's biggest problem isn't the war. It's losing the 21st century," *Washington Post*, June 30, 2023, citing Nicholas Eberstadt, "Russian Power in Decline: A Demographic and Human Resource Perspective," American Enterprise Institute, AEI Foreign & Defense Policy Working Paper 2022–01, August 2022.

291 **other European countries:** "School Enrollment, Tertiary (% gross)—Russian Federation, European Union," World Bank; "Literacy Rate, Adult Total (% of people ages 15 and above)—Russian Federation," World Bank.

291 **enraging Russia:** Fareed Zakaria, "Russia *Is* the last Multinational Empire, Fighting to Keep Its Colonies," *Washington Post*, March 31, 2022.

292 **"the greatest geopolitical catastrophe of the century":** "Putin: Soviet Collapse a 'Genuine Tragedy,'" NBC News, April 25, 2005.

292 **returning Ukraine to the motherland:** Zakaria, "Russia Is the Last Multinational Empire."

293 **sold arms to Taiwan:** This section draws on Zakaria, *Ten Lessons for a Post-Pandemic World*, 197–98 and Zakaria, "The New China Scare." Reprinted by permission of FOREIGN AFFAIRS, January/February 2020. Copyright 2020 by the Council on Foreign Relations, Inc. www.ForeignAffairs.com.

294 **"Made in China":** Translation: Notice of the State Council on the Publication of 'Made in China 2025,'" Georgetown Center for Security and Emerging Technology, March 10, 2022; see also James McBride and Andrew Chatzky, "Is 'Made in China 2025' a Threat to Global Trade?," Council on Foreign Relations Backgrounder.

295 **rapid industrialization:** Fareed Zakaria, "What the West is still getting wrong about the rise of Xi Jingping," *Washington Post*, October 6, 2022.

295 **dropped to 6.2 percent:** "GDP Growth (annual %)–China," World Bank.

295 **"Japanification":** Tracy Alloway, Joe Weisenthal, and Isabel Webb Carey, "Richard Koo on China's Risk of a Japan-Style Balance Sheet Recession," Bloomberg, July 10, 2023.

296 **"Four D's" crippling Chinese growth:** Zongyuan Zoe Liu, interviewed by Tracy Alloway and Joe Weisenthal, "The Odd Lots," Bloomberg, August 21, 2023.

296 **society dominated by capitalism:** Zakaria, "What the West Is Still Getting Wrong about the Rise of Xi Jingping."

296 **tracking dissidents:** Tiffany May, "He Fled China's Repression. But China's Long Arm Got Him in Another Country," *New York Times*, August 26, 2023.

296 **term limits:** Zakaria, "It Takes Two to Tango. But Does China Want to Dance?," *Washington Post*, July 27, 2023.

297 **"third revolution":** Elizabeth Economy, *The Third Revolution: Xi Jinping and the New Chinese State* (New York: Oxford University Press, 2018).

297 **Partnership and Cooperation Agreement:** Angela Stent, *Putin's World: Russia against the West and with the Rest* (New York: Twelve, 2019), 51.

297 **superior to the cosmopolitan rootlessness:** Stent, *Putin's World*, 27.

297 **"orthodoxy, autocracy, and nationality":** Political scientist Angela Stent, among others, has highlighted this echo. See: Stent, *Putin's World*, 27.

298 **Night Wolves:** Peter Pomerantsev, *Nothing Is True and Everything Is Possible: the Surreal Heart of the New Russia* (PublicAffairs; Reprint edition, 2015), 186.

298 **giant black Labrador:** Tim Hume, "Vladimir Putin: I didn't mean to scare Angela Merkel with my dog," CNN, January 12, 2016.

298 **"mother and father":** "'There will be dad and mum': Putin rules out Russia legalizing gay marriage," Reuters, February 13, 2020, another translation: "Extracts from Putin's speech at annexation ceremony," Reuters, September 30, 2022.

298 **representation of LGBTQ relationships:** Emma Bubola, "Putin Signs Law Banning Expressions of L.G.B.T.Q. Identity in Russia," *New York Times*, December 5, 2022.

298 **gender transitions:** Neil MacFarquhar, "Putin signs a harsh new law targeting transgender people in Russia," *New York Times*, July 24, 2023.

299 **killed their teachers:** Youqin Wang, "Student Attacks against Teachers: The Revolution of 1966," *Issues & Studies* 37, no. 2 (March/April 2001).

299 **use of English:** Li Yuan, 'Reversing Gears': China Increasingly Rejects English, and the World, *New York Times*, September 9, 2021.

300 **"cooling-off law":** Helen Davidson, "China Divorces Drop 70% after Controversial 'Cooling Off' Law," *Guardian*, May 18, 2021.

300 **prohibited from freezing their eggs:** Carina Cheng, Oliver Hu and Larissa Gao, "Barred from Freezing Their Eggs at Home, Single Chinese Women Are Traveling Elsewhere," NBC News, September 4, 2023.

300 **"sissy men":** Robert Burton-Bradley, "Has China's push to ban 'effeminate' and 'sissy' men claimed its first victim? The tragic case of Zhou Peng," *South China Morning Post*, January 4, 2022.

300 **Politburo:** Throughout this section, I am relying on the excellent analysis by pseudonymous China watcher and commentator N. S. Lyons: see N. S. Lyons, "The Triumph and Terror of Wang Huning," *Palladium*, October 11, 2021.

300 **"Chinese Alexis de Tocqueville":** Lyons, "Triumph and Terror of Wang Huning."

301 **neither liberal, nor international, nor orderly:** Niall Ferguson, "The Myth of the Liberal International Order," Harvard Belfer Center, January 11, 2018.

301 **"the jungle":** Robert Kagan, *The Jungle Grows Back: America and Our Imperiled World*, First Vintage Books edition (New York: Vintage, 2019).

304 **largest external trading partner:** For sub-Saharan Africa, see: "Trade Summary for SSD for Sub-Saharan Africa 2021," World Integrated Trade Solutions, World Bank; for South America, see: "China Regional Snapshot: South America," Foreign Affairs Committee.

305 **"high fence" around a "small yard":** Fareed Zakaria, "Biden's Course Correction on China Is Smart and Important," *Washington Post*, April 21, 2023.

305 **fifth-largest economy:** "GDP (current US $)—India, China, United States, Germany, Japan," 1960–2022, World Bank.

306 **infuse their day-to-day decisions:** This paragraph draws on "The one hopeful sign coming out of Davos this year" by Fareed Zakaria, first published by the *Washington Post* on May 26, 2022.

307 **"illiberal democracy":** This paragraph draws on "The narrow path to liberal democracy" by Fareed Zakaria, first published by the *Washington Post* on July 29, 2021.

307 **morphed into dictatorships:** Fareed Zakaria, "The Narrow Path to Liberal Victory," *Washington Post*, July 29, 2021.

307 **"democratic recession":** Larry Diamond, "All Democracy Is Global," *Foreign Affairs*, September 6, 2022.

307 **"the last Englishman":** " 'It Was India's Good Fortune to Be a British Colony'," *Outlook*, February 5, 2022.

CONCLUSION: THE INFINITE ABYSS

309 **"dissolution of their ancestral ways":** Walter Lippmann, *A Preface to Morals*, Social Science Classics Series (New Brunswick, NJ: Transaction, 1929, reprint 1982), 21.

309 **"Whirl is King":** Aristophanes, *Clouds*, trans. Lippmann, *A Preface to Morals*, epigraph.

309 **"acids of modernity":** Lippman, *Preface*, 19–20.

310 **lifespan on average would be half:** Max Roser, Esteban Ortiz-Ospina and Hannah Ritchie, "Life Expectancy," Our World in Data, first published 2013; last revised October 2019.

311 **"To be human is to be free":** Desmond M. Tutu, "The First Word: To Be Human Is to Be Free," *Journal of Law and Religion* 30, no. 3 (October 2015): 386–90.

311 **"infinite abyss":** Blaise Pascal, *Pensées,* trans. W. F. Trotter, 113.

311 **"dizziness of freedom":** Søren Kierkegaard, *The Concept of Anxiety: A Simple Psychologically Oriented Deliberation in View of the Dogmatic Problem of Hereditary Sin,* trans. Alastair Hannay (New York: Liveright, 2015), 188.

312 **"last man":** Friedrich Nietzsche, *Thus Spoke Zarathustra*, Prologue.

312 **"The frightened individual":** Erich Fromm, *Escape from Freedom* (New York: H. Holt, 1994), 150–51.

312 **"family, nation, God":** Interview with Viktor Orbán by Tucker Carlson, August 29, 2023, About Hungary (blog), https://abouthungary.hu/speeches-and-remarks/interview-with-viktor-orban-by-tucker-carlson.

313 **loyalty, authority, sanctity:** Jesse Graham, Jonathan Haidt, and Brian A. Nosek, "Liberals and Conservatives Rely on Different Sets of Moral Foundations," *Journal of Personality and Social Psychology* 96, no. 5 (May 2009): 1029–46.

313 **much cruelty and oppression:** Fukuyama later developed the idea of Thymos, as both necessary and counterproductive force in human society, into his book: Francis Fukuyama, *Identity: The Demand for Dignity and the Politics of Resentment* (New York: Farrar, Straus and Giroux, 2018).

314 **tight-knit web of communities:** Alan Ehrenhalt, *The Lost City: The Forgotten Virtues of Community in America*, 2nd ed. (New York: Basic, 1996).

314 **life of stoops:** Ehrenhalt, *Lost City*, 95.

314 **"conquered but unconvinced":** Lippmann, *Preface*, 10.

316 **below-average college graduation rates:** "The Inflation Reduction Act and US Business Investment," US Department of Treasury, August 16, 2023.

316 **fifty-three largest American metro areas:** Fareed Zakaria, "National Service Can Bring Us Together as a Nation," *Washington Post*, May 19, 2019, citing data provided by Mark Muro of the Brookings Institution.

316 **captained a PT boat:** Mickey Kaus, *The End of Equality*, A New Republic Book (New York: Basic, 1996), 50.

316 **heal America's intense polarization:** Fareed Zakaria, "National Service Can Bring Us Together as a Nation," *Washington Post*, May 9, 2009.

316 **2.4 million unauthorized crossings:** "Southwest Land Border Encounters FY22," US Customs and Border Prediction.

317 **"the job liberals refuse to do":** David Frum, "If Liberals Won't Enforce Borders, Fascists Will," *The Atlantic*, April 2019.

317 **"left the past behind":** Fareed Zakaria, "A Conversation with Lee Kuan Yew," *Foreign Affairs*, March 1, 1994.

319 **"stranger in my own country":** Daniel Cox, Rachel Lienesch, and Robert P. Jones, "Beyond Economics: Fears of Cultural Displacement Pushed the White Working Class to Trump" Public Religion Research Institute/*The Atlantic* Report, May 9, 2017.

321 **"throne-and-altar":** George F. Will, *The Conservative Sensibility* (New York: Hachette, 2019), xxviii.

322 **2,500 bombings on American soil:** Eric Alterman, "Remembering the Left-Wing Terrorism of the 1970s," *Nation*, April 4, 2015.

323 **"just go on breaking eggs":** Isiah Berlin, "A Message to the Twentieth Century," Commencement Address at University of Toronto, November 25, 1994, *New York Review of Books*.

324 **"Reform, that you may preserve":** Thomas Babington Macaulay, *Speeches, Parliamentary and Miscellaneous* (London: H. Vizetelly, 1853), vol. 1, pp. 11–14, 20–21, 25–26.

324 **"moral capital of the Victorians":** Gertrude Himmelfarb, *On Liberty and Liberalism: The Case of John Stuart Mill* (San Francisco, CA: ICS Press, 1990).

325 **"big bright blue flags":** Von Bono, "Europe is a thought that needs to become a feeling," *Frankfurter Allgemeine Zeitung*, August 27, 2018

CREDITS

TEXT CREDITS

The epigraph is taken from Karl Marx and Frederick Engels, *Manifesto of the Communist Party*, "Chapter I: Bourgeois and Proletarians," translated by Samuel Moore in cooperation with Frederick Engels, 1888, and corrected against 1888 English Edition by Andy Blunden 2004; published on the Marx/Engels Internet Archive (marxists.org) 1987, 2000, originally sourced from *Marx/Engels Selected Works,* Vol. One, Progress Publishers, 1969. Permission is granted to copy and/or distribute this document under the terms of the Creative Commons Attribution-ShareAlike License.

The discussion of ChatGPT in Chapter Seven, "Information Unbound," is adapted from a segment that aired on the author's CNN show on April 30, 2023, and can be viewed at Fareed Zakaria (@FareedZakaria), "Today's last look: ChatGPT is going to help software 'eat the world'," X, April 30, 2023, https://twitter.com/FareedZakaria/status/1652837826323439618. It was inspired by Kedrosky and Norlin's blog post: "Society's Technical Debt and Software's Gutenberg Moment," *Irregular Ideas with Paul Kedrosky & Eric Norlin of SKV*, SKV, March 21, 2023.

Portions of Chapter Nine, "The Dual Revolutions," draw on "The Self-Destruction of American Power." Reprinted by permission of FOREIGN AFFAIRS, July/August 2019. Copyright 2019 by the Council on Foreign Relations, Inc. www.ForeignAffairs.com; and "The New China Scare." Reprinted by permission of FOREIGN AFFAIRS, January/February 2020. Copyright 2020 by the Council on Foreign Relations, Inc. www.ForeignAffairs.com.

This book draws on the author's previously published work, notably his columns in the *Washington Post*, all of which are available at https://www.washingtonpost.com/people/fareed-zakaria/, and his 2008 and 2020 books, *The Post-American World* and *Ten Lessons for a Post-Pandemic World*, both originally published by W. W. Norton & Company.

ILLUSTRATION CREDITS

33   Kat Cantner, *Map of the Netherlands from 1300 to the present.* Copyright © 2019 American Geosciences Institute and used with their permission.

72   *Louis XVI has put on the red cap, he has cried "Long Live the Nation"* . . . Library of Congress, 1792.

72   *The Populace Compelling Louis XVI. to Adopt the "Red Cap,"* in *Cassell's Illustrated History of England, Volume 5,* 1865.

82   *An engraving of Robespierre guillotining the executioner after having guillotined everyone else in France,* taken from *La Guillotine en 1793* by H. Fleischmann, 1908, 269.

108   "World GDP over the last two millennia," Our World in Data, Global Change Data Lab, 2017, accessed June 29, 2023. Note from Our World in Data: "The data presented here from 1990 onwards is from the World Bank. It is total global GDP in 2011 international-$ as published here: http://data.worldbank.org/indicator/NY .GDP.MKTP.PP.KD (accessed on April 16, 2017). Data earlier than 1990 is backwards extended from the World Bank, observation for 1990 based on the growth rates implied by Maddison data. The Maddison data is published here: http://www. ggdc.net/maddison/oriindex.htm."

127   James Gillray, "French Liberty, British Slavery," December 21, 1792, London. The Metropolitan Museum of Art.

136   *The Interior of the Crystal Palace (Fountain, Seen from the Front), The Illustrated Exhibitor,* 1851.

136   Adam Simpson, artwork for Tom Shone, "Surveillance State," *New York Times* book review of Jenni Fagan, *The Panopticon,* July 18, 2013.

158   *Union and Confederate veterans shaking hands at reunion to commemorate the 50th anniversary of the battle of Gettysburg,* Library of Congress, 1913.

207   *The computer ENIAC (Electronic Numerical Integrator and Computer) developed at the University of Pennsylvania in 1946: 1st electronic computer,* January 1, 1946, Apic / Hulton Archive via Getty Images.

221   Norman Rockwell, *Freedom of Speech,* 1943. Printed by permission of the Norman Rockwell Family Agency, Copyright © 1943 the Norman Rockwell Family Entities.

247   Stanley Forman, *The Soiling of Old Glory,* in *Boston Herald American,* April 5, 1976.

277   Bastian Herre, Esteban Ortiz-Ospina, and Max Roser, "Democracy," Our World in Data, Global Change Data Lab, 2013 (updated 2023).

INDEX